Eleanor Roosevelt
on Screen

Eleanor Roosevelt on Screen

The First Lady's Appearances in Film and Television, 1932–1962

ANGELA S. BEAUCHAMP

McFarland & Company, Inc., Publishers

Jefferson, North Carolina

Library of Congress Cataloguing-in-Publication Data

Names: Beauchamp, Angela S., author.
Title: Eleanor Roosevelt on screen : the First Lady's appearances
in film and television, 1932-1962 / Angela S. Beauchamp.
Description: Jefferson, North Carolina : McFarland & Company Inc., Publishers, 2024 |
Includes bibliographical references and index.
Identifiers: LCCN 2023048509 | ISBN 9781476693026 (paperback : acid free paper) |
ISBN 9781476651071 (ebook) ∞
Subjects: LCSH: Roosevelt, Eleanor, 1884-1962—In motion pictures. | Roosevelt, Eleanor, 1884-1962—
On television. | Presidents' spouses—United States—Biography. | United States—Politics
and government—20th century. | BISAC: PERFORMING ARTS / Film /
History & Criticism | SOCIAL SCIENCE / Women's Studies
Classification: LCC E807.1.R48 B424 2023 | DDC 917.917092 [B]—dc23/eng/20231106
LC record available at https://lccn.loc.gov/2023048509

British Library cataloguing data are available

ISBN (print) 978-1-4766-9302-6
ISBN (ebook) 978-1-4766-5107-1

Front cover image: Moderator Ned Brooks, producer Lawrence Spivak, and
Eleanor Roosevelt on the set of NBC's *Meet the Press* at the RCA Exhibition Hall in
New York City, September 16, 1956. Courtesy of Franklin D. Roosevelt Presidential
Library and Museum; *background* © Fer Gregory/Shutterstock

Printed in the United States of America

*McFarland & Company, Inc., Publishers
Box 611, Jefferson, North Carolina 28640
www.mcfarlandpub.com*

Acknowledgments

Thank you to my colleagues in the Film and Digital Arts department at the University of New Mexico, especially James Stone, Susan Dever, Nina Fonoroff, and Deborah Fort, and to the UNM Feminist Research Institute for financial support. Research was conducted with the assistance of Jane Klain at the Paley Center for Media, Kevin Thomas and Patrick Fahy at the Franklin D. Roosevelt Presidential Library and Museum, Emily Noffke at the Wisconsin Historical Society, Rebecca Reynolds at Colorlab for the National Archives and Records Administration, Mirit Lerner Naaman at the United States Holocaust Memorial Museum, Phil Gries at Archival Television Audio, Elizabeth Youle at the Margaret Herrick Library at the Academy of Motion Picture Arts and Sciences, Laurie Austin and Jim Armistead at the Harry S. Truman Presidential Library and Museum, Abigail Malangone at the John F. Kennedy Presidential Library and Museum, Kris Ford at the Robert W. Woodruff Library at Atlanta University Center, Mazie Bowen at the University of Georgia Special Collections Libraries, Julianna Jenkins at the UCLA Film and Television Archive, Chloe Gerson at Brandeis University Robert D. Farber University Archives, and the staff of the University of New Mexico Libraries.

For your forever support, thank you to my parents, Sue and Walter Rysz and Jack and the late Carolyn Beauchamp, and my sister, Beth Lichty. Gracias to our Galisteo gang for their encouragement—Ed Epping, Peggy Diggs, Lucy Lippard, Jim Faris, and especially Laura Yeats for offering her Orcas Island retreat. I could not have managed this project without the most brilliant person I know, my spouse Caroline Hinkley, who has done so much to foster a creative, supportive space and accompanied me on sojourns to Hyde Park. She also did wonders scanning many of the photographs for this book.

Finally, thank you to Eleanor Roosevelt, who has remained a North Star during life's journeys.

Table of Contents

Preface

When Eleanor Roosevelt's public affairs television show *Today with Mrs. Roosevelt* announced Paul Robeson as an upcoming guest, conservatives swiftly put pressure on the network. NBC officials announced the following day that the Black civil rights leader and entertainer with Soviet ties would not be appearing with Mrs. Roosevelt after all, and she was forced to accept interference in the March 1950 program schedule. However, although Eleanor often differed with Robeson's more radical tactics, she voiced concerns about the threats of censorship in her "My Day" syndicated newspaper column:

> I think I will always have confidence in the common sense and clear judgment of the American people as a whole if they hear all sides of any question. Above everything else, we must guard our freedoms, and that means that all must have a right to be heard. When we begin to discriminate we can never tell where the discrimination may end [21 Mar. 1950].

ER, as she signed her letters, was an early adopter of the television medium as an educational tool to reach a mass audience, but although volumes have been written about her life as a lecturer, a writer, a radio host, an activist, and a humanist, none have thoroughly explored her work connected to the film and television industries. Paul Robeson was barred from appearing, but this was only one small defeat in a long history of educating and inspiring the public—and giving voice to others who were not always allowed the opportunity to be heard. The first words she spoke to open the premiere of her 1950 series were "I believe the people of this country, and of all the world, are entitled to hear various points of view on the national and international decisions which are going to affect our lives in the future." Eleanor Roosevelt's career was dedicated to those principles.

This work centers who many consider *the* most important American woman of the 20th century and her relationship to movies and television in the three decades from the presidential campaign of 1932 until her death in 1962. ER saw enormous potential in these two interrelated entertainment mediums in the same way that she was a master of print and radio communications and part of a savvy Roosevelt political team that used mass media to shape the opinions of the public in the United States and abroad. President Franklin Roosevelt's fireside chats intimately connected Americans to government in a new way, and the couple both staged unprecedented photo and newsreel opportunities for the press. In addition to writing 8,000 newspaper columns, 500 articles, and 27 books in her lifetime, Eleanor started her own radio program in 1932, even speaking to the nation following the 1941 attack on Pearl

Harbor before FDR addressed the nation. For 30 years, polls consistently placed her at the top of the public's picks for the most popular woman in the country.

While she wrote about the power of visual media, ER created her own archival legacy. However, early television broadcasts were sparingly preserved, and there has been little scholarship on Eleanor Roosevelt's moving image record. The following archival collections were consulted for this book: the Paley Center for Media, the Franklin D. Roosevelt Presidential Library and Museum, the Eleanor Roosevelt Papers Project at George Washington University, National Educational Television and the Dore Schary papers at the Wisconsin Historical Society, the National Archives and Records Administration, the Media History Digital Library, the American Archive of Public Broadcasting, Chronicling America at the Library of Congress, American Radio History, Archival Television Audio, the Margaret Herrick Library at the Academy of Motion Picture Arts and Sciences, the *Variety* Archives, the Internet Archive, Newspapers.com, the Harry S. Truman Presidential Library and Museum, the John F. Kennedy Presidential Library and Museum, the Elizabeth McDuffie papers at the Robert W. Woodruff Library at Atlanta University Center, the University of Georgia Special Collections Libraries, the United States Holocaust Memorial Museum, and the UCLA Film and Television Archive. Drawn from the fragments that exist of more than two hundred appearances on film and television, as well as a rich chronicle of newspaper and entertainment industry criticism, letters, and program notes from many archival collections, ER's daily columns and articles for fan magazines, and the memoirs of entertainers written after the fact, what follows is the record of a complex political powerhouse, social reformer, civil rights activist, human rights pioneer, and feminist. From newsreels, interaction with the classic Hollywood studio system and its movie stars, three different series of her own, and many guest appearances in television's nascent 1950s and early 1960s, a picture emerges of a shrewd media performer light years ahead of her time. Just as she practiced as our initial U.S. representative to the United Nations, ER used persuasion and diplomacy on TV to help move opponents to see her points of view, maintaining and giving respect to all involved. However, the primary goal—to promote her beliefs and understandings of any issue—always played a significant role in these appearances.

ER's son Elliott wrote an article for *TV Screen* in 1951 addressing his mother's television viewers. He leads by quoting her specific intentions around much of the work she did in the media:

> The world situation is such that a tremendous amount depends upon the ability of the United States to provide wise and intelligent leadership. This cannot be accomplished if the American people themselves are not fully aware of their own and other people's problems. They must be able to formulate intelligent opinions, to give moral and personal support to their leaders. If I can present their problems in a palatable form, so that they will think for themselves, I will be helping in my small way to be of service ["My Mother" 17].

"Service" at that time included working as a U.S. delegate to the United Nations and chair of the UN Commission on Human Rights, writing a daily syndicated newspaper column and monthly feature in *McCall's Magazine*, presenting a radio show on weekdays and a television program on Sunday afternoons, and serving on the board of the NAACP (National Association for the Advancement of Colored People), among the other lectures, articles, political campaigns, and boards she somehow fit into her schedule.

This book is organized into two parts dealing with the film and television worlds. After introducing Eleanor's presence in these two interconnected industries, I address how the Roosevelt team portrayed ER's work in gendered terms, allowing her to enter the public world of men as a less threatening wife and mother do-gooder, rather than the skilled political force we now know her to be. The first part on the movies is divided into 10 chapters. It begins with a brief examination of her presence in the newsreels, as that could be a book-length topic on its own, although it does detail specific newsreel coverage. Although quite comfortable by then on radio, she was initially reluctant to speak on camera. However, ER was extremely interested in how the movies could be used to educate the public on national and international issues. The following chapters address her public views on film industry censorship. Son James Roosevelt begins a position assisting producer Samuel Goldwyn and enlists Eleanor to appear in a prologue for the 1940 anti–Nazi film *Pastor Hall*. They draw the ire of isolationists in the Senate Subcommittee on Propaganda in Motion Pictures and Radio, but she also disappoints activists when she chooses to cross a picket line protesting segregated cinemas in Washington, D.C. When the House Un-American Activities Committee (HUAC) targets a motion picture music composer for whom she requested special consideration for a visa in 1939, she is taken to task for supporting supposed communists. Eleanor is appalled by the McCarthy-era investigations of the public and Hollywood. She takes an excited tour of the studios in 1938, and child star Shirley Temple visits Hyde Park, doing something to the First Lady that made Shirley's mother deliver a swat on the bottom that night. The part ends with the movie recommendations she made over the years, usually in her daily "My Day" newspaper column.

Eleanor appears in the movie short *Hobby Lobby* (1940) and begins to be referenced or impersonated in films like *Babes in Arms* (1939) and *Mr. Smith Goes to Washington* (1939). In the war years, she encourages the participation of women. ER and her travels become staple jokes in wartime Hollywood comedies, and the British film *Great Day* (1945) centers on her visit to inspect women's activities in the U.K. The postwar period continues connections and promotion of films like Jean Renoir's *The River* (1951) when she visits India or *The Defiant Ones* (1958), which earned Sidney Poitier an Oscar nomination. She negotiates representations of FDR after his death in films like *The Beginning or the End* (1947) and *The Roosevelt Story* (1947). ER participates in the production of *Sunrise at Campobello* (1960), which earned Greer Garson accolades for her portrayal of Eleanor as a loving wife and mother.

Part II transitions to the world of television. Positive reviews of guest spots on *Meet the Press* and *Author Meets the Critics* prepare her for *Today with Mrs. Roosevelt*, the 1950 NBC weekly public affairs panel discussion show. After she takes a break to work in Europe with the United Nations, the name and format change to *Mrs. Roosevelt Meets the Public* in 1950–51. She would not have another regularly scheduled television show until 1959 but was able to express views on political candidates and focus more on her own issues with appearances on popular shows throughout the decade. Her speeches for the 1952, 1956, and 1960 Democratic Party conventions were televised, and she made a notable national political impact on both *Meet the Press* and *Face the Nation* in 1956 promoting Adlai Stevenson. ER used a television interview to call John F. Kennedy out for his failure to oppose Senator Joseph McCarthy, and it would take quite some time for her to become an active Kennedy supporter. Fighting anti-communist crusades often dominated the 1950s. In 1957, she journeyed to the Soviet Union to interview Nikita Khrushchev, and the Soviet premier's visit to Hyde Park in 1959 was televised.

Chapter 19 tells the full story of Paul Robeson's planned appearance on *Today with Mrs. Roosevelt* and follows up on her other attempts to address issues of race on television. Next is a focus on her work with the United Nations and the tactics she honed as chair of the Human Rights Commission and as a television moderator. As she got older, ER continued to inspire others with a liberal message of always moving forward, illustrated by prime-time appearances with stars like Bob Hope and Frank Sinatra, while she herself was feted on TV for her 75th and 76th birthdays. From 1959 to shortly before her death in 1962, Eleanor hosted *Prospects of Mankind*, a monthly public affairs television show with some of the most important political and cultural figures of the time as guests. Although she remained active until the end, Eleanor Roosevelt finally succumbed to illness. Just weeks before she passed away, she was writing to Martin Luther King, Jr., with an invitation to join her on a new television program, *The American Experience*. This ends with her death in November 1962, a momentous loss to many across the world.

During the mid–1970s heyday of the television miniseries, *Eleanor and Franklin* appeared on ABC in January 1976. Telling the story of the Roosevelts, it would go on to win 11 Primetime Emmys and spawn a sequel the following year, *Eleanor and Franklin: The White House Years*. At the time, I was an 11-year-old girl watching from my living room in Indiana and actively searching for role models outside my small town. The mass-market paperback of the biography by Joseph Lash, on which the miniseries was based, is the oldest book I still own, tattered cover barely attached. My memories of reading it on the school bus and reaching up to put it onto the top shelf of my locker each day are still vivid. I latched on to the forward-thinking activist Eleanor Roosevelt and never let go. Feminist historian Blanche Wiesen Cook's towering three-volume ER biography, which illuminates her as a passionate woman and powerful political figure, served to reinvigorate that interest, and I remember writing Cook a fan letter describing my memories of the Lash book in my hands, knowing that other young women and girls would feel the same with her first volume, only more so. My appreciation for Allida Black's efforts at making so many of ER's written works available to the public is immense. Years later, while writing about portrayals of women in biographical films and docudramas, I found myself in the Paley Center for Media television archive watching not only representations but actual footage of Eleanor on TV. After realizing that no one had done significant research on her moving image history, I dove in.

Introduction

Eleanor Roosevelt entered the Los Angeles Memorial Sports Arena and slowly made her way to an assigned seat at the 1960 Democratic Party Convention. When the older woman wearing a floral dress and hat was noticed by the crowd of thousands, riotous applause and a standing ovation interrupted Florida governor LeRoy Collins as he spoke about purposeful leadership, even prompting the band to begin playing. Cameras from the three television networks swung from the platform to watch as she unassumingly waved to rock-star adulation from passionate, devoted fans of the "First Lady of the World" who traveled as an informal ambassador promoting human rights across the globe. A symbol of former president Franklin Roosevelt and the New Deal, she remained a persistent influence within the Democratic Party, at times suggested as a candidate for senator from New York, ambassador to France, vice president, and even president of the United States. Convention chair Collins had to plead with the partisan gathering to be seated so that they could get to the important business of selecting a presidential candidate. However, "Mrs. Roosevelt" was television news in the midst of what was just another convention speech.

The following day, plainclothes officers encircled Eleanor as she walked through the arena to ascend the rostrum and second the nomination of Adlai Stevenson. The men firmly held her elbows as they maneuvered, prompting ER to comment in her autobiography about being older and female: "This happens to be one of the few things which indicate to me that I am supposed to be unable to navigate in the ordinary manner at my age and I resent it very much. Consequently, I kept trying to get away from and shake off their helpful hands. Presumably this showed up on television, because I received a number of letters from people who wrote to assure me that I had behaved in a most rude and disagreeable manner" (426–27). She was surprised at what multiple cameras picked up at a distance, but by 1960 she was no stranger to utilizing TV appearances to further political interests and agendas. Eleanor Roosevelt recognized the power of film and television early on, especially as an educational tool to reach young people, and hosted three different political talk shows in the 1950s and early 1960s, frequently making herself available for interviews and guest spots. She began cultivating a long-term relationship with the film industry as early as the 1930s.

In 1932 Hollywood fan magazine *Screenland* ran an interview with the wife of the then–president-elect titled "Mrs. Franklin D. Roosevelt Talks About the Movies" in anticipation of her position as First Lady, while *Modern Screen* printed her article "What Are the Movies Doing to Us?" (1932), which was the first of many anti-censorship messages. During her tenure in the White House, ER would write two articles for *Photoplay* on "Why We Roosevelts Are Movie Fans" (1938) and "Film Folk I Have Known" (1939) in addition to a profile in *Movie Mirror* on "Movies in the White House" (1935). Later she would pen two pieces for *Variety*, "Eleanor Roosevelt Sees Films as Force for Culture" (1939) and "How the Movies Can Help Keep Us Out of War" (1940), followed by "Democracy on the Screen" (1947) for *Modern Screen*. Her daily newspaper column "My Day" reveals that the Roosevelts viewed films regularly, and she offered movie recommendations to readers. These are especially prevalent from the 1930s and early 1940s when the White House had a special screening room, and movies were a major form of relaxation for the commander in chief and guests including British prime minister Winston Churchill. However, Eleanor's involvement would expand to lending her name to advertising for films like *Stella Dallas* (1937) and *Our Very Own* (1950) and her voice and script-writing talents to civilian defense efforts like *Women in Defense* (1941) and *Training Women for War Production* (1942).

Starting in the late 1930s, sons James and Elliott and daughter Anna all became involved in the entertainment industry, which catapulted ER into both film and television in ways that used her celebrity to further their careers. Jimmy worked as a producer for Samuel Goldwyn before starting his own production company and enlisting her in projects such as recording the prologue for *Pastor Hall* (1940). John Boettiger, Anna's second husband, parlayed Roosevelt connections to work for Will Hays as an assistant in the Motion Picture Production Code office. Big Hollywood stars visited the White House annually to raise money for the March of Dimes to combat infantile paralysis (polio) and later to promote war bonds. ER visited the studios when in Los Angeles, and Shirley Temple even came for a picnic at Hyde Park with Fox cameras in tow.

The president's wife appeared on the platform when FDR inaugurated the 1939 World's Fair on NBC to an initial one to two hundred receivers. The television industry would not take off until after World War II, but Eleanor made her TV interview debut on the afternoon following VE Day (Victory in Europe Day) in May 1945 on NBC. Elliott launched his mother's first television series on NBC, and *Today with Mrs. Roosevelt* (1950) and *Mrs. Roosevelt Meets the Public* (1950–51) attracted guests like Albert Einstein and J. Robert Oppenheimer, while Anna co-hosted with her on radio, benefiting financially from the TV ventures. Eleanor understood that by the 1950s, she could reach millions of viewers, many of whom no longer got their news from newspapers and increasingly less from radio. It was only natural that she would become a regular fixture in the new medium of television.

A history of CBS notes what a boon it was for the fledgling, experimental television news industry that Mrs. Roosevelt lived in New York City and made herself available for interviews on local telecasts as early as 1946 (Slater 123). Appearances across the U.S. networks, often on public affairs programs like *Face the Nation* or *Meet the Press*, talk shows like *The Sarah Churchill Show* or *Person to Person*, and even the game show *What's My Line?* served to promote her postwar interest in the United Nations and international affairs as well as to promote favored Democratic candidates at election time. Eleanor and Republican senator Margaret Chase Smith conducted a televised debate on behalf of presidential candidates Adlai Stevenson and Dwight Eisenhower in 1956, modeling the famous Kennedy-Nixon debates to come. This was after hosting a New York City mayoral candidate showdown on her own program in 1950, which may have been the first televised political debate. In 1959, her third regular television program began airing under the guidance of producer Henry Morgenthau III, son of good friend Elinor and FDR's secretary of the treasury Henry Morgenthau, Jr. *Prospects of Mankind* ran on NET (National Educational Television), the precursor of PBS, until just months before Eleanor's death in 1962. Once again, she attracted some of the most important political and cultural figures of the era, including Ralph Bunche, John F. Kennedy (as both senator and president), Henry Kissinger, Luis Muñoz Marín, Edward R. Murrow, Julius Nyerere, Bertrand Russell, Adlai Stevenson, and Paul Tillich.

Eleanor Roosevelt spoke with authority yet had a kind, grandmotherly appearance and mode of delivery as she aged. Television commentators and guests often behaved deferentially to her personage, resisting the trivialization or sexualization that plagued most women at the time. Although she had consistent off-screen detractors, very few confronted ER directly on TV, so the medium regularly provided an effective platform for her liberal voice during the Republican Eisenhower administration and beyond. Because of her status as a larger-than-life figure, both loved and hated by segments of the public, filmmakers largely avoided documentary and biographical film coverage of both Eleanor and Franklin Roosevelt until after her death. In 1960, Dore Schary produced the notable exception *Sunrise at Campobello*, a hagiographic dramatization of Franklin's struggle and comeback from polio with the loving support of his wife. ER commented that the production was "about as much like the Roosevelt family as some people from Mars," although she cooperated so that the children profited from the successful Broadway play and resulting feature (Bellamy 247).

What did Eleanor think about her own on-screen appearances? In reference to the 1940 film *Pastor Hall*, she noted, "I can't say that I like myself on the screen" ("My Day" 23 Sept. 1940). Still relatively new to television in 1949, she envied the performance of then–daughter-in-law Faye Emerson, who was married to Elliott at the time and hosted the late-night CBS talk show *The Faye Emerson Show*. Instead, ER said of herself, "Needless to say, I never am happy when I am in a television show. In the first place, I cannot remember that I am being photographed every minute and I do such stupid things as lick my lips when they get dry, which makes you look exactly as though you were sticking your tongue out at someone. Perhaps with greater experience I will do a little better.… The lights are hot and, on the whole, I think the results are none too happy for me" ("My Day" 27 June 1949).

She did, of course, persevere and got better at it. ER learned to read cue cards rather than notes from her lap. What began as a foreign experience in the makeup chair became routine. By 1959, she wrote Anna excitedly, "I went on Frank Sinatra's show in Hollywood (the pay for 5 minutes was fantastic & my part rather nice) but I'm not very good at 'entertainment.' I have never had so many compliments however & I found watching the mechanics amusing!" (Asbell 330). She would make

In June 1960, the cast and crew of *Sunrise at Campobello* (1960, Warner Brothers) shoot on location from the Roosevelt home in Hyde Park, New York. Foreground, from left: Ralph Bellamy as FDR, the real Eleanor Roosevelt, and Greer Garson playing a younger Eleanor from the 1920s (Franklin D. Roosevelt Presidential Library & Museum).

many more television appearances, although she generally did not watch TV herself. She did not have the time. For several years, Eleanor was a judge for the Sherwood Awards sponsored by the Fund for the Republic and helped choose the best shows on the theme of civil rights and liberties. Since she was never home to watch programs when they aired, ER visited their offices in New York each year to screen the entries. She also noted staying up late to watch former president Hoover speak at the 1952 Republican National Convention and not getting enough sleep after watching the 1954 election returns come in. *Meet the Press* was one of the few programs she tried to see regularly, calling it informative, instructive, and stimulating (NBC-New York "Noted").

"I watch television only when I want to see certain special programs. And if I possibly can, I watch when the President of the United States appears; or when any other public official speaks on a subject on which I think citizens should be informed. I have no favorite program, since I have no time to listen or watch just for pleasure," she responded in an August 1959 *McCall's Magazine* "If You Ask Me" column. ER did reveal a fondness for Edward R. Murrow and his news programs, but she really did not like shows dealing with murder or violence. This was because of the medium's influence on young people, and "television must bear the responsibility of forming taste" (Torre "Best"). In a 1959 article published in *TV Guide*, "Television's Contribution to the Senior Citizen," she also advocated for the potential of television to keep older people connected to the world and developing new interests.

Eleanor recorded audio commentary in the summer of 1962 for the 26-part ABC documentary mini-series *F.D.R.* that aired in 1965. It includes interviews with many who worked in the Roosevelt administration, notably Lorena Hickok, the former Associated Press journalist and intimate friend who reported to Harry Hopkins on Depression-ravaged areas across the country. There had been caricatures of ER's voice and spoofs of her traveling schedule in the movies during the 1930s and 1940s, for example, in the film *Babes in Arms* (1939) and the reverent *Great Day* (1945) as a British village plans for her visit. However, after Eleanor's death in November 1962, the path was open for filmmakers and documentarians to put her life and that of Franklin on film and television screens. *The Eleanor Roosevelt Story* (1965) won the Oscar for Best Documentary, and as the 1970s dawned, she became the subject of Emmy Award–winning television dramas such as *Eleanor and Franklin* in 1976. She has been a major or supporting character in more than 50 different narrative films or television shows, including Showtime's *The First Lady* series in 2022, and a major topic of at least 25 documentaries.

She was also an early advocate of visual literacy. Specifically referring to the newsreels, ER wrote in 1938, "I contend that seeing things is almost a necessity in this visual-minded period of our development." She recognized that the movies were primarily enjoyed as entertainment but also identified them as "something which may be used to shape public opinion" and act as "a powerful imaginative stimulus" ("Why We" 17). By 1951, ER hosted an episode of *Mrs. Roosevelt Meets the Public* to discuss the topic of television itself, sensing that it would eventually reach a far greater number of people than any other medium, impressed by its potential as an educational resource but already concerned with how "convincing in selling you the products of various sponsors" it was proving to be. Interpreting, evaluating, experiencing, and exploiting these visual mediums was part of her skill set from the explosion of the film industry in the early sound era through the time in which television became a dominant cultural force.

1

Manipulating
Gender Expectations

On inaugural eve 1933, Eleanor Roosevelt and Lorena Hickok convened in a bathroom on the train from New York to Washington, the only place where they could find enough privacy to conduct an exclusive interview introducing the new First Lady to the nation. The next day, Americans read about Eleanor's role as President Franklin Roosevelt's "eyes and ears," explaining her wide range of activities in light of a husband with limited mobility. Thus, the media-wise Roosevelt political team, of which "Hick" was a crucial member, preempted some of the criticism of an activist Eleanor by couching everything she did in terms of being an extension of FDR, merely a wife and helpmate, not a woman with ambitions of her own. The country now marvels that the ordinary person did not know that polio-stricken Franklin could not walk, but this was not the only illusion engineered by the Roosevelts. Eleanor, a woman whose marriage was a complicated façade, intentionally characterized herself in heteronormative terms, allowing her to participate in what was largely a man's world of public policy with a persona that was generally not interrogated. She actively gendered her actions to make them more acceptable.

For decades, ER's contributions as an activist, a humanitarian, and a politician stood out as bold and unexpected for a woman. Her detractors, and there were many, also called attention to Eleanor's intrusion into the world of men with cartoons and editorials. The "first lady of liberalism"—an advocate for civil rights, workers' rights, and women's rights; a champion of the poor; a peace activist; and a primary author of the United Nations Universal Declaration of Human Rights—was a new model for what women could be across the nation from the 1930s through her death in 1962, before which she chaired the first Presidential Commission on the Status of Women. Only 24 percent of American women earned wages in 1930, most in the lowest paid, lowest status positions, and cultural attitudes that looked disdainfully on White women employed outside the home intensified during the Depression years, when the number of women elected to public office also declined from 1920s levels (Ware 21–23, 95). It was in this atmosphere that confined women largely to their homes that Eleanor Roosevelt entered with daily newspaper columns, political radio shows, and appearances in the newsreels that ran before films in theaters. When most women in the public eye were entertainers, she took part in a man's world, seeking and receiving unprecedented press coverage for women of the time.

Eleanor wrote 27 books and more than 8,500 columns and articles, held regular press conferences in the White House for women reporters only, hosted a regular radio show, and in later years moderated three political panel television shows. She was prolific, to say the least, and it would be accurate to say that ER used her position as wife of the president of the United States to advance the causes and issues in which she believed, both directly by influencing the president and his staff and by addressing the issues herself and garnering press coverage. This gave her a national and significantly international platform, but how she positioned herself shows additional political prowess.

In a very quick review of her oft-repeated life story, Eleanor Roosevelt was born in 1884 into a patrician New York family, the niece of President Theodore Roosevelt. Her father was an alcoholic; her mother, the beautiful Anna Hall Roosevelt, was disappointed that Eleanor was an ordinary-looking child, and as an adult, Eleanor often noted that Anna thought her ugly. Her mother died of diphtheria when ER was eight, and her father Elliott Roosevelt drank himself to death when she was nine. The orphan went to live with her strict Grandmother Hall. Overall, she led a very lonely existence as a girl. The life-changing move was to send Eleanor to school at Allenswood in England at age 14, where she studied with French Madame Souvestre and was the recipient of a worldly, liberal education. Grandmother Hall insisted that Eleanor return home at age 18 to come out in society, rather than continue her education. ER then volunteered in a New York City tenement house, which opened her eyes in new ways to poverty, immigration, and child labor issues. She began seeing her distant cousin FDR at age 19, and against the wishes of Franklin's controlling mother Sara Delano Roosevelt, the two were soon married and produced six children, one of whom died in infancy. Childbirth and motherhood took up much of her life as a young woman. The couple moved to Washington, D.C., when the Wilson administration appointed Franklin assistant secretary of the navy, and it was during World War I that he had an affair with ER's social secretary, Lucy Mercer. Eleanor offered him a divorce, but they agreed to stay married for political and financial reasons, never again sharing intimacies. The family moved back to New York, where Franklin worked as a lawyer and Eleanor began writing and political activities. He unsuccessfully ran as a Democratic vice presidential candidate with James Cox and then contracted polio in 1921. After several years of recovery, he became governor of New York in 1929 and won his first presidential election in 1932.

The staple story, that Eleanor was FDR's "eyes and legs" or "eyes and ears" as a service to the nation when he could not easily travel, was repeated by the Roosevelt camp and served as an explanation for her busy schedule in a variety of locales. This justification allowed many of ER's activities to go without heavy criticism, since she was seen as merely serving as an extension of FDR. Clues found within her own writing reveal that it was not this simple, but it was one way to avoid some of the scathing ridicule that other women, single or married, endured. For example, in the 1920s the story went that Eleanor became active with the Democratic Women of New York as a means to keep the Roosevelt name alive while Franklin recovered from polio. FDR's right-hand man Louis Howe taught her public speaking skills, and even though she was terrified in the beginning, she became a well-known speaker in New York as a handmaiden to FDR's political ambitions. However, ER's autobiography notes that she began working with Esther Lape, Elizabeth Read, and the League of Women Voters *before* Franklin's polio (112). Later in the same volume, she tells us, "When the last child went to boarding school, I began to want to do things on my own, to use my own mind and abilities for my own aims" (279). This period coincides with FDR's years privately convalescing but reveals different interests and motivations behind the façade of devoted public servant who would have been at home had her husband not required her assistance. She edited the *Women's Democratic News* and worked for 17 different organizations, including serving on the boards of the Women's Trade Union League, International Ladies Garment Workers Union, and National Consumers Union. This was full-time work, not a simple PR campaign in FDR's name. The woman who did the bidding of a husband with limited mobility was likely a public relations invention in a time when women with ambition and drive of their own were not well accepted in the public sphere. Life partners Lape and Read were crucial to ER's political development in the early 1920s, as were partners Nancy Cook and Marion Dickerman in the late 1920s and Lorena Hickok in the early 1930s. These were women-identified women, close friends and mentors who shaped ER's social life and reformist political agenda, influences she would carry with her from New York to Washington, D.C.; however, Eleanor's friends were also part of the larger Roosevelt team that used the image of a conventional married woman to bring issues to a larger public in ways that her "single" friends could not (A. Beauchamp).

Although she was making money with her articles, columns, appearances, and radio shows, and her writing reveals that economic self-sufficiency was of paramount importance to ER, she pitched these efforts as a wife who was reluctant to burden her husband by asking for money for presents and charitable giving. Eleanor's activities carefully avoided "career" implications, couching it all in the traditional role of helpmate and do-gooder—even though she also presented a new model of a very independent woman, one who brought in more money than her husband did during the first year of his presidency (Cook Vol. II 3). Actor Billie Burke, best known as Glinda the Good Witch of the North in *The Wizard of Oz*, identified ER's strategy in a 1938 *Modern Screen* interview. Discussing the range of scatterbrained and smart women she was asked to play, Burke pointed out, "It takes a doubly clever woman to hide her cleverness. Look at Eleanor Roosevelt, for example. She is a brilliant woman who manages to conceal the fact that she is so clever" (Albert 39).

Eleanor Roosevelt does not mention FDR's World War I–era affair with Lucy Mercer in any of her own writing. Her life, so different from most married women of her time, has since often been rationalized by biographers and filmmakers as a reaction to her husband's philandering, defining her as jilted wife who must find fulfillment outside the home. Other interpretations include her assumed frigidity as a "Victorian woman," thus excusing FDR's transgressions, allowing her to move into a saintly, chaste position in society. The release of the loving and sometimes erotic correspondence with Hickok and the three-volume biography by Blanche Wiesen Cook give Eleanor more agency as a woman with ambitions and desires of her own, not defined by her marriage or any aspect of her marital state. Those critical friendships in the 1920s with other women, for example, show ER as a person who built a life quite separate from her husband and children, a socially radical move. Yet it was FDR who paid to build Val-Kill cottage for Eleanor and her friends, the home in which ER would live until her death in 1962, not in the "big house" with the rest of her family. Her public life would never acknowledge the arrangements that were far beyond the norm and a marriage that son James calls "an armed truce that endured to the day [FDR] died" (101). Jimmy also refers to "their long and successful marital partnership," an indication that both participated in and received the benefits of marriage in the public eye, regardless of how it privately looked little like the American heteropatriarchal ideal (63).

There is no doubt that some in the press called her unflattering names, caricatured her buck teeth, and were very "ugly" themselves in what they said about Eleanor. In her autobiography, ER herself tells a story of her mother being "troubled by my lack of beauty" as a young girl (6). She promotes the idea that she had been ugly all her life, despite some very conventionally beautiful photographs as a young woman and bride and elegant inaugural ball photos featuring her sparkling eyes as an older woman. The press and politicians took her more seriously because of this "ugliness," as it placed her somewhat outside the category of conventional woman, seen and not heard. Because she resisted sexualization and being made an object of men's sexual desire, this allowed her to move into a more liminal category of the matron who commanded a level of respect, while at the same time marriage and later widowhood provided a non-threatening cover for her activities. Thus, Eleanor was categorized outside of the normative wife and mother role, because she did not fit in with standard constructions of beauty and male desire, chaste because of her husband's assumed infirmities while still enjoying the privilege of heterosexual marriage. In her autobiography, she confesses to a lack of skill and interest in mothering and leaving much of it to nurses and her mother-in-law, which also moves her outside of the ideals of the nuclear family and a woman's place within it. It is her "ugly" otherness, long before knowledge of the loving letters to Hick, that played a critical role in "queering" Eleanor Roosevelt and thus lending her a distinctive place in public discourse. However, it is also Hick, defined as a lesbian by historians, who helped to construct ER's image in the early 1930s. The top female reporter for the Associated Press, Lorena Hickok received an assignment to cover Eleanor during the first presidential campaign, and the two became remarkably close—so close that Hick began clearing her stories with the Roosevelt camp before publication. Journalism historian Maureen Beasley credits Hickok with a critical role in crafting what the public was to know about their new First Lady and explains, "She was able to translate Mrs. Roosevelt's complex personal aspirations into an acceptable public image during the pivotal preinaugural period" (36). Hickok planned ER's White House press conferences for female reporters only at a time when the administration did not allow women in FDR's press conferences and when newspapers largely consigned women to writing society columns. The resulting new jobs for female reporters in Washington gave Eleanor steady support from this group of newspaperwomen even after the White House years, and May Craig often questioned ER as a *Meet the Press* panelist. An April 1950 *Today with Mrs. Roosevelt* episode, "Mrs. Roosevelt Cross-Examines the Press," featured four panelists from those Washington, D.C., days—Emma Bugbee, Doris Fleeson, Genevieve Herrick, and Craig. No longer able to feign impartiality, Hick resigned from her job with the AP in 1933 and began working in the New Deal under Harry Hopkins, traveling the country and reporting on Depression conditions. She would live in the White House for several years in the bedroom across the hall from Eleanor's and remained a lifelong friend.

Eleanor was part of a team of political image-makers that dominated American public life, and it did not go unrecognized that her column, lectures, and radio broadcasts might have actively done more to sell the New Deal philosophy than did the president himself. She led all the rest as "the best public relations woman the New Deal ever had," wrote a columnist in 1957 (Rowan). After her years as First Lady, she continued on an international stage, including appointment as a founding delegate to the United Nations. She found ways to exploit the public's understanding of the proper role of a married woman at a time when the media did not contradict this with behind-the-scenes information. The gendered public face that everything she did was to help others belies the power gathered to wield such profound influence on a variety of men, institutions, organizations, political parties, and governments. In the post–White House years, she sought out television opportunities because she knew that she could reach the largest audience. Political endorsements, the United Nations, international relations, issues of race, the nuclear threat, dangers of anti-communist hysteria, interests of labor, the Soviet Union, and more were subjects she tackled on the air. Especially in Eisenhower's conservative America of the 1950s, she was a consistent voice of liberal politics. No longer wife and mother, Eleanor Roosevelt was now the commentator who looked and sounded like a grandmother but skewered Senator Joseph McCarthy's anti-communist hysteria, for example, and set herself up as the moral compass for human rights at home and abroad. Along the way, she invited prime ministers, presidents, scientists, government officials, and members of the public to join her on television to work on solving international and local problems. She believed these discussions could make a difference and inspire education and global cooperation.

Behind the motherly, and later grandmotherly, persona was an experienced political force with a practiced demeanor that led men in power to underestimate her intentions and impact. At the 1956 Democratic Convention, for example, ER was given a platform in which she spoke about looking forward to young leadership, not back to the New Deal, in a way that dismissed former president Truman's endorsements without ever mentioning his name. Arthur Schlesinger, Jr., reacted in his journal at the time by writing, "Mrs. Roosevelt came to town and proceeded, in the kindest possible way, to destroy Mr. Truman" (180). In the context of the United Nations, a *New Yorker* columnist observed that ER often went out of her way not to appear opinionated or directly contradictory. Instead, she got others to say "yes" or "maybe" by working around the issue. "A State Department career man, after watching her artfully maneuver her way through a delicate discussion, once murmured, 'Never have I seen naïveté and cunning so gracefully blended'" (Kahn, Jr.).

Although her own NBC series *Mrs. Roosevelt Meets the Public* was the lead-in to *Meet the Press* in 1950–51, Eleanor was perhaps at her most influential on television in a 1956 appearance on the more dominant long-running program. In what has been called a "turning point for TV news," ER is said to have played a significant role in the 1956 presidential campaign with her direct condemnation of Richard Nixon's campaign tactics (Gomery 118). Then on *Face the Nation*, four years before the televised Kennedy-Nixon presidential debates, she and Republican senator Margaret Chase Smith went head to head on the merits of Adlai Stevenson versus Dwight Eisenhower. Thus, she was part of the first television debate about presidential candidates, warranting blow-by-blow coverage in *The New York Times*. The day that John F. Kennedy announced his candidacy for the presidency in 1960, he flew to make an appearance on ER's *Prospects of Mankind* television show that afternoon, feeling that her endorsement was that important. The story of Eleanor Roosevelt in film and television is one of consistently using her political and cultural voice, creating platforms to bring out the best in her panel guests and educating the public on the prominent issues of her time.

PART I

In the Movies

2

Reluctance to Speak

On the 20th anniversary of U.S. entry into World War I, popular Arctic and Antarctic explorer Admiral Richard Byrd joined ER in the Diplomatic Reception Room of the White House. At the First Lady's invitation, the two spoke over the radio in April 1937 to launch a "No Foreign War" campaign seeking international action to promote peace and avoid another great war in Europe. They then transitioned to Movietone coverage, speaking for the Fox newsreel cameras on the same subject. The next day in her "My Day" column, readers got an uncharacteristic glimpse of Eleanor's assessment of the limitations of her performance skills. She admitted, "I have never been successful in talking naturally for the newsreels so for some time I have insisted that I should be seen and not heard. They made such a point however, of my welcoming Admiral Byrd into this phase of peace work that I finally spoke one little sentence and I only pray that I shall not regret this lapse from my usual procedure. It would not matter so much only I think it hurts any cause to have someone take part in any part of it and do it extremely badly" (8 Apr. 1937).

Eleanor Roosevelt was very much a regular on theater screens by 1937, but newsreels often featured silent clips with narration, or she was recorded while giving a planned speech, rather than extemporaneous remarks. The "My Day" comment reveals that she had apparently designed it this way. Early on, her radio and newsreel voice had been criticized as too high and shrill, but lessons in 1938 with speech coach Elizabeth von Hesse allowed her to maintain more control, lowering her voice by four major notes and eradicating the high butterfly effect. Eleanor credited von Hesse with teaching her how to place her voice and end the squeak when she became nervous (Wamboldt 182–83). However, ER's old friends insisted that it was an increase in confidence that brought about the improvement in voice control (R. Black 123). Eleanor's precise articulation became more casual after a 1946 automobile accident broke off her two front teeth, replaced by new, less protruding porcelain ones. Doctoral student Helen Wamboldt observed from newsreels that "on such sounds as 's,' 'th,' 'f,' and other fricatives she seems to have difficulty adjusting her tongue to the new oral contours that these false teeth have given her" (292–93). One suspects that the normal alterations in the voice with age may have also been a factor.

Before the days of television news, beginning in the silent 1910s until fading out in the 1950s and early 1960s when they were replaced by TV, short reports of five to 10 minutes were shown before or after feature films in theaters. In major cities, special theaters ran newsreels all day long. ER's speeches, public appearances, and participation in events were often filmed and included as clips. She also delivered public service messages, like promoting the National Recovery Administration, encouraging women to join the paid workforce during the war, or calling for contributions to the March of Dimes, which worked to cure polio. Annually in January on FDR's birthday, theaters took part by passing donation jars throughout the audience while ER's fundraising appeal ran on the screen. Industry publications printed the contents of the newsreels on a weekly basis. For example, in the last week of January 1944, the Roosevelts were both welcoming General Isaías Medina Angarita of Venezuela to the White House, and ER and Mary Pickford opened the fundraising drive against infantile paralysis ("In the Newsreels").

Eleanor appeared on a regular basis over the years, but one particularly contentious newsreel incident was connected to her travels in the South Pacific to visit troops during World War II. When she told the president's favorite joke, with an anti–Republican punch line, on camera to a group of GIs in October 1943, some Republicans were livid. Missouri representative Walter C. Ploeser asked for a congressional investigation into alleged misuse of the motion picture industry for

Eleanor Roosevelt and Madame Chiang Kai-Shek (Soong Mei-ling) of China pose for newsreel and still photographers on the White House lawn, February 24, 1943. Madame Chiang was in the U.S. to gather support for China during the war (Harry S. Truman Library & Museum).

Democratic Party propaganda purposes. Michigan senator Clare E. Hoffman went to the press to charge that it was a misuse of government funds for personnel to be tasked with reviewing footage of her war zone tour ("Newsreel Clip," "Man"). *The March of Time* also produced short documentary news journals, longer than traditional newsreels and shown in theaters from 1936 to 1967, sponsored by the publishers of *Time Magazine*. They produced the 10-minute short *My Trip Abroad*, released on December 31, 1950, in which Eleanor reports on rebuilding efforts in countries that received funds from the Marshall Plan after World War II. She narrates over footage of visits to Denmark, England, Finland, France, Holland, Norway, and Sweden on behalf of the Economic Cooperation Administration.

Overall, ER appreciated the newsreels and their power to educate the public, especially since such a substantial proportion of Americans went to the movies weekly before television led to a drastic decline in those numbers. In the 1932 article "What Are the Movies Doing to Us?" she asked: "Have the news reels any value in making better citizens? I think their power is very great for they bring the greatest education in current events to young and old alike. They force upon the attention of many people who do not even read the papers any new and important discovery or any new and important event in the political world." She felt that people absorbed valuable information without even recognizing it, exposing them to issues and enabling greater participation in political discussions (27). ER had titled the rough draft of this piece for *Modern Screen* "Educational Value of the Movies," which better explains her mission.

She often focused on the benefits of the movies instead of fear of the negative impact of violent or sexual content. In the October 30, 1939, edition of *Daily Variety*, she contributed a short column, "Eleanor Roosevelt Sees Films as Force for Culture." Accompanied by a half-page photo of her visit with Jimmy at Samuel Goldwyn Studios, it begins quite humbly: "I have been asked to write these few words on the motion picture industry, and anyone less gifted to write on this subject could hardly be found. I see movies occasionally, but I realize that I am not a really good critic. However, I have one great interest in the movies, namely, how can the movies become a force in education." She recognizes that most people watch for recreation and to escape, but ER's interest was in the potential to help develop interests in literature, arts, and history and to teach ideals, values, and standards. Even when she did not stay for the feature film in the White House screening room, she watched the news that brought the entire world to viewers, including events that happened hundreds of miles away. However, she also understood that for most, "the newsreels, interesting as they are however, are only the appetizer for the real film" ("Why We" 17).

3

Film Industry Censorship

Little Sistie and Buzzie Dall, along with 60 of their friends, took over the East Room of the White House and romped through the corridors in a party their grandparents threw just for children. Even *The New York Times* reported that President Roosevelt joined in the fun the day after Christmas in 1933 ("Roosevelts"). At the time, most Americans would have recognized "Sistie" and "Buzzie" as the names of the young Roosevelt grandchildren who had moved into the executive mansion with their mother Anna in September. Over the years, the five Roosevelt children entered into 19 marriages among them, and daughter Anna was separated from first husband Curtis Dall, a stockbroker. She had fallen in love with reporter John Boettiger on the campaign trail the previous year, an affair supported by Eleanor, who was fond of the journalist (Cook Vol. II 31).

In July 1934, the future son-in-law quit his job with the conservative *Chicago Tribune* and began working for Will Hays and the Motion Picture Producers and Distributors of America (MPPDA). A *Saturday Evening Post* article claimed that FDR's assistant Louis Howe asked Hays to give Boettiger the position to resolve the uncomfortable issue of the reporter's obligation to write anti–Roosevelt pieces (Neuberger). Son John Boettiger, Jr., later wrote that Joseph Kennedy, father of the future president, important Roosevelt supporter, and a Hollywood investor, obtained Boettiger's new post. In a business deal, Jimmy Roosevelt had played a significant role in securing Kennedy's permits to begin importing alcohol for "medicinal" purposes and setting up contacts with whiskey producers in Britain, timed so that the liquor imports were at the ready when Prohibition was lifted (C. Beauchamp 327). John organized MPPDA public relations staffs in both New York and Hollywood and met with newspaper publishers and writers and civic and religious groups all over the country. He and Anna were married in January 1935, and although they briefly considered moving to Hollywood to continue meetings with the likes of Louis B. Mayer at MGM, Boettiger called in another Roosevelt favor from media magnate William Randolph Hearst, leaving the MPPDA New York office to run the Hearst *Seattle Post-Intelligencer* newspaper in November 1936. Anna edited the women's pages of the paper (Boettiger, Jr. 191–92).

At the time Boettiger joined in July 1934, Hays and the MPPDA were beginning to enforce the Motion Picture Production Code censorship rules. Under its auspices, the Production Code Administration led by Joseph Breen issued seals of approval for all Hollywood films and demanded revisions of scripts and finished products to meet restrictions that cut out sex, violence, and anything that did not support religious and governmental institutions. The three general principles, with many more detailed specific rules, demanded:

1. No picture shall be produced that will lower the moral standards of those who see it. Hence the sympathy of the audience should never be thrown to the side of crime, wrongdoing, evil or sin.

2. Correct standards of life, subject only to the requirements of drama and entertainment, shall be presented.

3. Law, natural or human, shall not be ridiculed, nor shall sympathy be created for its violation.

ER lauded these measures in a radio broadcast, supporting both the Roosevelt administration and the film industry, instead of a more progressive stance on the regulations that we might expect. However, at this time, public pressure required a response such as the voluntary Code in the face of calls for more extreme boycotts and censorship measures. She announced:

> The matter of moving pictures is very important to the whole country. I am extremely happy the film industry has appointed a censor within its own ranks. Mr. Joseph Breen, assistant to Will H. Hays, will act as censor in their ranks. It has long been a question of great interest to women's organizations, particularly, of course, because of the fact that moving pictures are so popular with children.
>
> Lately it has been felt that the tendency to glorify the racketeer and criminal, or at least to make him appear a sympathetic character was having something of a bad effect upon the children of the country. Consequently, this new announcement should do much to make these organizations feel the film industry as a whole desires to cooperate and use its tremendous power for the improvement of the country ["Mrs. Roosevelt Lauds Film"].

Her remarks were praised as "a dignified beacon in the bewildered sea of cinema hysteria" amid religious and women's organizations threatening to boycott movie theaters if the studios did not institute a censorship program (Alicoate). ER recognized the power of the industry and the advantage of self-censorship, rather than religious or government control, and took a middle-of-the-road approach that satisfied church groups and kept the industry from even more draconian content lockdowns that would have been imposed from outside.

Several Hays office personnel were intimately tied to politics. In 1941, ER recommended that Charles Pettijohn receive special recognition from the Academy of Motion Picture Arts and Sciences ("Suggests Oscar"). He had been instrumental in forming the MPPDA and served as its general counsel while overseeing relationships with newsreel distributors and exhibitors to Roosevelt advantage. Pettijohn traveled on the same train with FDR's campaign manager James Farley and fundraiser Joseph Kennedy during 1932 presidential election efforts, making an indirect donation not only to the ticket, but ongoing newsreel exposure of the Roosevelts across the country. During the 1936 campaign, Pettijohn and Boettiger rode together on the train while they both worked for the MPPDA and charted audience reactions to Roosevelt and Republican opponent Alf Landon coverage in the newsreels (Muscio 51–52). Pettijohn was an honored guest at the 1938 White House Birthday Ball festivities with Hollywood stars ("East Meets," "Roosevelt Calls"). ER's promotion of a special award for Pettijohn's work against additional censorship measures appeared in "My Day":

> They might recognize the fact that, for a quarter of a century, Mr. Pettijohn has been preaching all over this country freedom of expression and, therefore, freedom of production for the stage and screen. He has, however, emphasized as well, that all freedom brings responsibility. That if the stage and screen are not to be censored, then they must not abuse the privilege and must use their mediums for better education and for a general raising of standards as to artistic and moral values [6 Dec. 1941].

The Code officially ruled until 1967, replaced by the ratings system, but lost its teeth in the late 1950s as American culture changed with the times.

She would speak out on other occasions over the years to combat censorship on the local level. In a visit to the Philadelphia Motion Picture Preview Study Group luncheon in April 1940, she saw no actual harm in *The Lone Ranger* or "blood-and-thunder" radio programs and movies: "If you emphasize the things they should not see or like, it only drives them to it. You should emphasize the things they should see. But don't say 'ought' or 'should.' Say you find something interesting and tell them why it is so, and you will find they will take to it. Therefore, it is not a question of censorship but intelligence" ("Thrillers Upheld"). She had given a similar message in a speech to the Civil Liberties League in Chicago the previous month and told the audience she preferred that "picture selection should be left to the intelligence of the people" rather than censors ("First Lady Opposes").

Variety reported that she did not "want censorship of pix" from comments in her September 1941 *Ladies' Home Journal* column responding to a question about directives that restricted export of Hollywood films to South America that might show the United States in a poor light ("Literati"). This was part of prewar efforts to combat Nazi propaganda and secure Latin American allies by only showing the best of the United States in its movie exports. Eleanor replied, "I have a great objection to censorship. I would far rather see us doing a constructive job of producing movies which tell the truth about this country and really give the South American people some idea of what our problems are and what we are trying to do to meet them." She argued that this was the only way for people of other countries to understand American difficulties, drawing us closer together ("If You Ask Me" Sept. 1941).

The month that the "If You Ask Me" column was published, ER became involved in another censorship issue. Written by John Steinbeck and narrated by Burgess Meredith, the short documentary *The Forgotten Village* depicts life in a remote Mexican village and the young boy who will go away to be trained and bring back knowledge to help his people combat parasites in the water. Director Herbert Kline received a nomination for the Golden Lion award at the Venice Film Festival for what was considered a commentary on religious and government institutions that help keep people in poverty. Today we would recognize this work more as ethnofiction, rather than documentary. New York's Motion Picture Division banned the film from being shown on the grounds that scenes showing a birth and a nursing mother were "indecent" and "inhuman" ("Press vs Censors"). Producer Pan-American Films countered with an appeal stating that childbirth was quite human and "if the screen is ever to become a mighty vehicle for the spread of ideas, it must present the truth without evasion and hypocrisy" ("Regents"). ER, the Women's City Club, the American Civil Liberties Union (ACLU), and many clergy, physicians, writers, and social workers endorsed the film's exhibition, finally leading to an overturn of the ban ("Steinbeck"). ER described it as a "very beautiful movie" and was especially interested in what it might teach the United States about improving rural medical services in this country ("My Day" 4 Sept. 1941).

Even before the White House years, Eleanor had been credited with intervening when New York banned exhibition of the 1931 German film *Mädchen in Uniform* directed by Leontine Sagan. Focusing on the attraction of a girl for her female teacher in a Prussian boarding school, it is now considered the first feature film with a lesbian theme. The Home Vision Cinema VHS release of the movie in the United States reads on the box, "With Eleanor Roosevelt's help, the U.S. ban was lifted." After substantial edits removing implications of a lesbian relationship, the film played in New York City in September 1932 while ER was First Lady of New York ("What Shocked"). John Krimsky, the distributor who brought *Mädchen* to the U.S., claimed in interviews in the 1970s that he arranged a private screening in the Albany statehouse, prompting ER to intervene and personally call the New York censors to champion the film. Krimsky affirmed that Eleanor said, "It was one of the finest films she had ever seen" (Whitbeck, McGilligan).

She would publicly get into the thick of controversy over restrictions on anti–Nazi pictures prior to U.S. entry into World War II and the postwar HUAC hearings that resulted in the blacklist of those in Hollywood accused of association with communists. As Eleanor worked in the United Nations in 1947 on what would become the Universal Declaration of Human Rights, *Film Daily* inquired if the statements on a free press and freedom of information also included "freedom of the screen." Her response made clear that the U.S. delegation was committed to the freedom of "press, radio, motion pictures and other media for the dissemination of information" ("Pix in UN").

4

Isolationism and *Pastor Hall*

The most famous photo of Montana Democratic senator Burton Wheeler shows his arm raised in what appears to be a Nazi salute at an America First Committee rally in 1941. He stands next to aviation hero Charles Lindbergh, who accepted the Order of the German Eagle from Hitler in 1938 and is also extending his arm in a Sieg Heil gesture. The two supported American isolationism at all costs, covertly anti-Semitic and more visibly pro–German (Seaton). As Nazi tanks rolled across Europe and FDR prepared an officially neutral nation for war, Hollywood began releasing anti–Nazi and pro–British films, especially after the president's "Arsenal of Democracy" fireside chat in December 1940, in which he laid out the arguments for American aid to Britain. Lindbergh, Wheeler, and the America First crowd increased their racist rhetoric.

Wheeler, who had obviously broken from FDR, launched a Senate Subcommittee on War Propaganda, which became the Subcommittee on Propaganda in Motion Pictures and Radio. North Dakota Republican senator Gerald Nye, another America Firster, led Senate efforts to investigate "alleged war propaganda efforts on the part of the movie industry" and what they saw as Hollywood's undue ability to reach the American people, specifically calling out what he saw as the problematic Jewish movie studio heads "born abroad" and their concerns with war in Europe. Democratic Idaho senator Worth Clark charged that the European immigrant movie moguls held an ideological monopoly on the public, and the Senate group investigated 48 different American and foreign films they suspected of being "anti–American" ("Demand War Pix"). MGM's Louis B. Mayer had emigrated from the Russian Empire, Universal's Carl Laemmle from what is now Germany, Samuel Goldwyn and the Warner family from Poland, William Fox and Paramount's Adolph Zukor from Hungary—all of them Jewish.

Page one of *Motion Picture Daily* described ER's comments when she "took up the cudgels on behalf of the motion picture industry" on her weekly radio show in October 1941:

> The motion picture industry has been under investigation by a Congressional committee. The question seems to be whether the producers have a right to present their views through the plays they produce. I think it is permissible for Senator Nye, Senator Wheeler and Mr. Lindbergh to present their views to the world, but I think it is equally permissible for all others. Why is one propaganda any different from any other? Freedom of speech should be accorded to all. The real test is whether a citizen has a right to say "no," and that right we have had for 150 years and is still ours today ["Eleanor Roosevelt Scores"].

The studios were represented by Wendell Willkie, who had run against FDR as the Republican challenger in the 1940 election but was more allied with an interventionist philosophy. He was applauded by the industry for not being afraid to step into the middle of a hot argument ("*Movie-Radio*"). However, Roosevelt loyalist Pettijohn was forced to resign from the MPPDA when some Hollywood executives were not satisfied with his reaction to the Senate committee (Muscio 53). ER's call for his Oscar came after he left and officially offered his services to the administration.

Son Jimmy's initial foray into Hollywood came as a vice president at Samuel Goldwyn Productions in 1938, a job he realized was not offered to the average outsider. Goldwyn was a loyal political supporter of FDR and liked to brag that the president's son worked for him. Traveling more than 87,000 miles that first year to meet with theater managers, film distributors, and critics in 11 countries, Jimmy left Goldwyn and created his own production company, Globe Productions, Inc., in December 1939 (*My Parents* 252). ER began receiving hundreds of screenplays in her White House mail from people asking her to try to sell scripts or send them on to her son. This was a service she did not provide (R. Black 119).

Jimmy negotiated a releasing contract with United Artists and arranged for his mother to record an uncompensated prologue to the British anti–Nazi film *Pastor Hall* for a summer 1940 release in the United States. The biographical drama is the first film to graphically deal with the issue of concentration camps as it follows the real story of German Lutheran minister Martin Niemöller, sent to Dachau for criticizing the Nazis. His words are still remembered today: "First they came for the socialists, and I did not speak out—because I was not a socialist. Then they came for the trade unionists, and I did not speak out—because I was not a trade unionist. Then they came for the Jews, and I did not speak out—because I was not a Jew. Then they came for me—and there was no one left to speak for me." The Grand National Pictures fictionalized story originated as a 1939 play written by Ernst Toller, a German Jewish emigrant to the U.S. who committed suicide after the fascists took Spain.

When the United States was still officially neutral and with vocal anti-interventionist factions across the country, *Variety* opined that this voicing of Roosevelt anti–Nazi sentiments was a risky move, supplying political ammunition against FDR's campaign for a third term (Walt). Goldwyn initially wanted to distribute the film, but was opposed by Production Code Administration officials Joseph Breen and Geoffrey Shurlock over what Breen called "avowedly British propaganda" and concerns over setting precedents for the industry. Goldwyn insisted that if he were not given the blessing to go ahead, then Will Hays should block all the other major studios from buying the film. Enter the president's son and his independent company, which was quietly issued a seal of approval after the most violent scenes were removed (Koppes 32–33). ER considered the decision to distribute the film a tribute to Toller's call to action (Cook Vol. III 317). In "My Day," she noted that the movie would reach more Americans than the play and make them more familiar with the issues—exactly what the Senate subcommittee feared (30 July 1940). They required submissions of advertising and press materials from *Pastor Hall*, prompting a *New York Daily News* columnist to ask Senator Nye why he was so concerned with a motion picture when the real story had already been reported across the country. "Do you believe, honestly, Senator Nye, that a picture like…. *Pastor Hall* was as effective as the Page One reports of the bravery of Niemoeller? Come, come, Senator, act your age!" (*"News* Pulls"). Later, director Roy Boulting and his twin brother John would be put under investigation by HUAC as "British agents and Communists" whose film was said to be designed to drag the United States into war with Germany ("Statue of Liberty").

ER recorded the prologue in Fox Movietone's Manhattan studio on July 17, 1940, and Betty Shannon describes the scene in *Screenland*: "Robert E. Sherwood, the Pulitzer Prize playwright, was in a lather, pounding out changes in Mrs. Roosevelt's script on a portable typewriter on a dressing-table." A throng of crew, producers, reporters, and photographers filled the set, the floor covered in cables and cords, while ER had a comfortable chair in front of the camera. "Eleanor Roosevelt had just entered, radiant, charming as always, and with a certain 'smoothness' which had just been pointed out to her by her eldest son [Jimmy] when he had seen her emerge from behind the bibs of the make-up man." She wore blush, suntan powder, mascara, and lipstick, with her hair done in a broad, flat wave: "It was the movies giving the First Lady 'the works'" ("First Lady" 97–98). One headline read, "Eleanor Roosevelt Becomes Glamor Girl for Sake of Movies." Friend Joe Lash recalls her coming back from the session with uncharacteristic makeup around her eyes, bringing out their blueness, as she worried that she would face intense criticism over taking this unprecedented step into the movies (Lash *Eleanor Roosevelt* 131). The shoot took place in the middle of the Democratic National Convention during which FDR would be nominated for a third term, and ER would quickly be enlisted to fly to Chicago to deliver her "no ordinary time" speech uniting the party. Photographs from the convention show her new coiffure.

Versions of *Pastor Hall* currently available do not retain ER's introduction, which was written by Sherwood, a speechwriter for FDR and winner of the Pulitzer Prize for *Abe Lincoln in Illinois* and two other plays. He became director of the Office of War Information from 1943 to 1945 and would win another Pulitzer

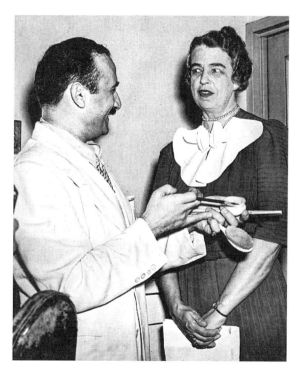

Ed Senz finishes applying Eleanor Roosevelt's makeup in the Fox Movietone Manhattan studio, July 17, 1940. She is preparing to film the prologue to the anti–Nazi movie *Pastor Hall* (1940, United Artists) (United States Holocaust Memorial Museum Collection, Gift of Ken Sutak and Sherri Venokur).

for his book *Roosevelt and Hopkins: An Intimate History* and a Best Screenplay Academy Award for *The Best Years of Our Lives*. The United States Holocaust Memorial Museum collection includes the press book for the film, including the text of the prologue:

> I am glad to introduce this motion picture because I believe it tells a story of the most vital importance to all of us. It is a story that is true—tragically true—a story of the insidious growth of the spirit of hatred, intolerance and suppression of liberty which is now sweeping over the face of this earth.
>
> The leading character in this picture is a simple man of God, a man whose life is devoted to the fundamental Christian principles of faith, hope and charity. He is the same kind of minister that you and I have known and loved—in Vermont, in Tennessee, in Oregon—in every community, large or small, where men and women are free to worship God in their own way.
>
> To me this picture carries a message of inspiring truth. It is deeply encouraging. For the story of Pastor Hall—of his undying faith, his unconquerable courage—is the story of all men who love freedom and justice so deeply that they are prepared to live eternally for their convictions. In such men is the hope of common humanity, the greatest hope for ourselves and our children.

The film is dedicated "to the day when it may be shown in Germany."

Reviews were split along political lines, often remarking on the shocking nature of the concentration camp depictions. *The Hollywood Reporter* called it "the most dramatic screenplay this reviewer has ever seen" ("*Pastor Hall* Is"). Even Nazi Minister of Propaganda Joseph Goebbels screened the film, recording in his diary, "Rabble rousing American film, *Pastor Hall*. The supposed fate of Niemöller. A moronic piece of rubbish" (Taylor 133). Conservative William Randolph Hearst editorialized that the film was inflammatory and communist, specifically objecting to ER's prologue ("*Pastor Hall* Philly"). Other conservative papers followed suit and slammed both mother and son for their lack of neutrality.

Some commented on the prologue itself. *Motion Picture Reviews* said, "Mrs. Roosevelt has done a courageous thing in appearing in the prologue of this film, because *Pastor Hall* is the strongest and most serious indictment of the Nazi philosophy ever released in America" ("*Pastor Hall*"). The *Hollywood* review pointed out that "the warmth of her personality is seen to telling advantage," while a *Box Office* column lamented that Sherwood's prepared script meant that observers were not able to hear her own opinions on the movie or the issues (Miller, Spear). Jimmy sent radio personality Walter Winchell a copy of the prologue, mentioning that Sherwood "edited" the text, but all other indications are that he was the primary author (J. Roosevelt to Winchell). The *Newsweek* critic was moved to tears but viewed her introduction as unnecessary due to the power of the film itself: "Much as I love Mrs. Franklin D. Roosevelt, I think her foreword to the picture is unfortunate. At the beginning Mrs. Roosevelt speaks some good words of Robert E. Sherwood's that warn you are in for an experience. I am of the opinion that the words are wasted" (O'Hara). From isolationists, there were snide comments like a recommendation "for those so fascinated in watching Mrs. Roosevelt in her movie make-up that they find it difficult to keep their minds on the lines she is obviously reading from a blackboard just out of camera range" (Martin "British"). Letters to the editor in various newspapers were less genteel, calling ER's words "blather" or charging that she was "made up like a chorus girl" (Jedlicka Jr., Eastman). On the other hand, mother-in-law Sara Delano Roosevelt was reported to have "applauded vigorously" at the prologue when she attended a screening with friends ("President's Mother").

The August 22 U.S. premiere in Philadelphia encountered a slight controversy when the local AFL Musicians Union was picketing Warner theaters at the time and asked ER not to attend. She responded that she had not been planning to, but the union withdrew pickets that evening anyway. Thousands jammed the streets for the premiere, which sold out in 20 minutes for the 1,300-seat house, and an unscheduled midnight show was added ("*Pastor Hall* Smash"). The crowded house applauded ER's prologue, and "God Bless America" played at the end of the picture ("*Pastor Hall* Philly"). Proceeds from opening night at the Esquire Theater in Los Angeles were donated to the British Relief Fund, and in New York, release of the film sparked an anti–Nazi protest in Times Square ("*Pastor* Benefits"). ER attended this NYC premiere along with Jimmy and Franklin Jr. in addition to Edward G. Robinson, Eddie Cantor, Lillian Hellman, Chicago mayor Ed Kelly, and Ralph Bellamy, who would play FDR in *Sunrise at Campobello* in 1960. In "My Day," she revealed not yet being accustomed to performing for cameras in this way: "It seemed strange to see my son's name blinking at me from the front of a Broadway theatre and it seemed even stranger to see myself announced at the beginning of a feature picture. I can't say that I like myself on the screen, but I do hope people will go to see the picture and remember the lesson it carries." She wrote that it was important to see what a system could do to bring out the worst in human beings (23 Sept. 1940).

In Chicago, the Police Censorship Board banned the film because it would "wield undesirable influence" with subject matter that "creates tension between races." The censors had previously prohibited several other anti–Nazi movies, while approving pro–Nazi works like *Blitzkrieg in Poland* ("Papers Denounce"). Local German anti–Nazi activists charged that Chicago German organizations were led by those with pro–Nazi sentiments, including members of the German-American Alliance, the Bund, and the Patriotic Research Bureau ("Would Curb"). Only after protests from local newspapers, the ACLU, American Jewish Congress, women's groups, and Mayor Kelly was the film allowed to be shown, and the result of the flap was that the city council dissolved the police board, replacing it with a group appointed by the mayor ("Strong Letter").

The controversy helped sell tickets across the country with ads that promoted "uncut" and "uncensored," although it had already been edited to gain the MPPDA seal of approval. *Box Office Digest* even suggested that the ban in Chicago was all a publicity stunt, with Kelly in on the plan to gain national attention for the film ("Let's See"). Others viewed the incident as proof of the power of Nazi propagandists in the United States. The Catholic Legion of Decency censorship group approved the film for viewing by adults. The countries of Argentina, Chile, Brazil, and the Philippines forbade showing the movie, although the ban was later lifted in all but Argentina ("Argentines"). In Mexico City, the Cine Chino Palacio received bomb threats to prevent screenings, and tear gas and stink bombs were set off inside the theater, with pro–Nazi demonstrations outside. A heavy police guard protected the theater, but it was forced to stop screenings. German and Italian studios were making inroads in Latin American cinemas at this time, and cities such as Rio de Janeiro and Buenos Aires screened Nazi newsreels. Understanding that the Axis might win the war, exhibitors were susceptible to censorship requests, and *Pastor Hall* was not easily distributed in these markets (Welky 221).

In December 1940, Jimmy wrote U.S. theaters that had not booked the film, offering a visit from a United Artists representative, since "it means a great deal to me to have you as one of those who is playing my first contribution to the motion picture screen." He could not make an appointment personally because he had been assigned to active duty in the Marine Corps in San Diego (J. Roosevelt Photostat). At the end of the year, *Box Office Barometer* credited Boulting and Toller with one of 1940s biggest successes, and the production received honorable mention in the *Film Daily* annual critics poll for the year's 10 best pictures ("Guiding Hands," Bahn). By July 1941, ER was attending the New York premiere of Warner's *Sergeant York*, which depicted the true story of a man transforming from pacifist to World War I hero. The inspiration to fight for democracy was analogous to intervention, but supported as patriotic and thus not opposed in the same way (Koppes 37–39). The Senate Subcommittee on Propaganda in Motion Pictures and Radio was disbanded shortly after the December 1941 attack on Pearl Harbor, but these efforts at censorship set the stage for the HUAC hearings to come. In a strange twist of events, ER opposed consideration of Niemöller as part of the first postwar German government. The pastor, who emerged alive from Dachau, turned out to be too much of an authoritarian himself ("My Day" 7 Aug. 1945). Watching the film today, its message is still powerful. However, the real evils of the concentration camps revealed at the end of the war overshadow the disturbing images here.

Although she was not forced to deal with the moral dilemma of crossing a picket for *Pastor Hall*, ER did cross the line to see RKO biopic *Abe Lincoln in Illinois*, following up in her column to educate the public on issues of racial segregation. Eleanor's involvement in the national premiere made news as she signed on to a January 22, 1940, Women's Press Club fundraising event benefiting the Children's Hospital Fund, heading an audience of "ambassadors and congressional bigwigs" who saw the movie penned by Robert Sherwood ("*Abe Lincoln*"). The evening before, the White House had screened the film after dinner with the group involved in its production, and she reflected, "Lincoln's words made a deep impression on me. Perhaps, more of us today should begin to stand for the things which we believe, even if it seems almost impossible that these beliefs would be accepted at the present time. Some one must lead crusades just as Lincoln did in order to start new trends of thought in the nation" ("My Day" 23 Jan. 1940). Raymond Massey, who played Lincoln, would be nominated for an Oscar for Best Actor, while James Wong Howe received a nomination for Best Cinematography.

The picture covers Lincoln's life up until he was elected president of the United States, which in 1940 was an inspiring message of honesty, hard work, and standing up for what one believes, including opposition to the "complacent policy of indifference to evil" and the "monstrous injustice of slavery itself." Today, the overwrought drama might read as simplistic for modern audiences, but Lincoln's own words against the institution of slavery remain moving and relevant. However, those lessons about the slave-owning South were all too familiar to Jim Crow Washington, D.C., in 1940. District of Columbia cinemas were segregated, and Black audiences were not allowed inside for the film screening at the RKO Theater. ER chose to attend the fundraiser, crossing a picket line organized by the Washington Civil Rights Committee led by Eugene Davidson. Photos show her passing protesters with signs reading, "Negroes Are Barred from Theatres in the Nation's Capital" and "German Theatres Bar Jews. Washington Theatres Bar Negroes." One report said that police locked hands to form a corridor for Eleanor to enter (Washington, Judkis). After the movie, she told the press, "I think it is particularly tragic that the people whom Lincoln freed should not be allowed to see the show about him" ("Negroes Picket"). The following day, she wrote:

> This occurrence in the nation's capital was but a symbol of the fact that Lincoln's plea for equality of citizenship and for freedom has never been quite accepted in our nation. May we not, if we limit the freedoms of people because of race, or religion or color, someday find that our own freedom is limited too? Not in the way that the Constitution limits it for us all, but in other arbitrary and sinister ways? There are basic rights, it seems to me, which belong to every citizen of the United States and my conception of them is not a rule in the nation's capital which bars people freed from slavery from seeing in a public place one of the greatest dramatic presentations of that story ["My Day" 24 Jan. 1940].

However, what seems like an uncharacteristic decision to ignore the protesters on the night of the event must have been quite a disappointment to activists nationwide. This was less than a year after her resignation from the Daughters of the American Revolution (DAR) when, based on her race, the DAR refused Marian Anderson's request to sing in their venue. A group from Brooklyn telegrammed the White House expressing regret at her lack of leadership in the decision to cross the picket line, suggesting that the "situation must be met by courageous action, not mere words" ("Protest").

In December 1946, British film *Men of Two Worlds* was not distributed in the United States after a screening committee consisting of ER and members of the NAACP advised, after much debate, that it might be objectionable to Black Americans. It depicts a London-educated African man returning to Tanzania to help his people but "lapsing into voodooism." Perhaps more telling, *Daily Variety* notes that the film "would have been objectionable in the South since it depicts a Negro as a crusader for his people." Based on this assessment, Universal decided not to distribute the film in the U.S. for fear that it might hurt ticket sales for other British movies ("2 Pix"). Today it reads as a colonial adventure deep in the White savior trope. The television age in the 1950s and 1960s would later invite more opportunity for Eleanor to engage with issues of race.

5

"Eleanor Roosevelt
is a bad security risk"

In September 1947, industry papers reported on HUAC as they called Austrian motion picture music composer Hanns Eisler to testify, charging him with being a communist. Eisler was most well known for collaborating with Bertolt Brecht in Germany, and the Nazis had banned his music. He was admitted to the U.S. from Germany as a political refugee and wrote music for films including *Hangmen Also Die!* and *None but the Lonely Heart*, with both scores nominated for Oscars. Eisler said that he had applied for membership in the German Communist Party in 1926 but had not been politically active in the United States, denying that he was currently a communist. Both of his siblings had been German communist leaders in the 1920s.

The memo ER wrote to Under Secretary of State Sumner Welles in 1939 on behalf of the songwriter and his wife to request special consideration for visas made headline news. Welles testified that he routed the letter on to a subordinate and did not give it much attention. Eleanor had written in the letter that the couple's friend appealing to her was "perfectly sure the Eislers are not Communists," but by 1947, she had no recollection of the memo and did not know Eisler ("Note"). ER explained that she received hundreds of such requests each month, some of which she passed along to the appropriate government department, and this one was "strictly routine" ("Strictly Routine"). To some, this was evidence that Mrs. Roosevelt was the target of questionable appeals because she had been "vulnerably sympathetic" (Flannery). To Roosevelt haters like Westbrook Pegler, the whole affair was "further evidence that Eleanor Roosevelt is a bad security risk," arguing that if she was "too stupid to be dangerous," then she was "too stupid to be trusted." Those were just a few of his choice words as he once again dedicated an entire column to denigrating ER (Pegler "Eleanor"). The HUAC sessions on "alleged infiltration of Commies into pictures" would begin in earnest the following month ("Note"). Eleanor was an outspoken opponent of these McCarthy-era hearings that ruined lives and created a longstanding Hollywood blacklist of anyone suggested to be connected to communism. Eisler returned to Europe after being blacklisted, eventually going to East Berlin, and would write the national anthem of the German Democratic Republic. Brecht was also called by HUAC and made his way back to East Berlin as well.

Soon HUAC got to work in earnest with harassing and haranguing those in Hollywood whose politics did not coincide with the committee's limited understanding of proper American loyalties. While working in the United Nations, ER found herself defending U.S. freedom of the press against Soviet attacks, bringing her to a conclusion: "Just this angle, too, is one of the things which worries me a little about the Congressional investigation into the Hollywood movie world. When you begin to let this and that person testify against this or that actor or writer, you take a step toward Nazi and Communist totalitarian attitudes toward the individual. It is so easy to depart from the path of democracy and succumb to the attraction of totalitarian edicts!" ("My Day" 27 Oct. 1947). Page one of *Film Daily* put ER's conclusions front and center: "In our country we must trust the people to hear and see both the good and the bad and to choose the good. The Un-American Activities Committee seems to me to be better for a police state than for the USA" ("As the Press"). She continued in "My Day":

> One thing is sure—none of the arts flourishes on censorship and repression. And by this time it should be evident that the American public is capable of doing its own censoring…. The film industry is a great industry, with infinite possibilities for good and bad. Its primary purpose is to entertain people. On the side, it can do many other things. It can popularize certain ideals, it can make education palatable. But in the long run, the judge who decides whether what it does is good or bad is the man or woman who attends the movies. In a democratic country I do not think the public will tolerate a removal of its right to decide what it thinks of the ideas and performances of those who make the movie industry work [29 Oct. 1947].

HUAC indicted 10 writers and directors, the "Hollywood Ten," for refusing to testify before Congress, handing down jail sentences and fines. Scores more were unable to work in the film and television industries after the studios instituted loyalty oaths and agreed not to employ anyone suspected of communist connections or associations of any kind. ER's name was often associated with those on the blacklist, which was finally broken in the early 1960s, but her position kept her from being required to testify.

Film Bulletin's August 1956 full-page coverage of controversial marketing campaigns for *Storm Center* includes mention of Eleanor urging viewers to see the film as "powerful dramatic entertainment and a revelation of the real principles of democracy" ("Controversy"). Bette Davis stars as a small-town librarian who refuses to ban a controversial book on communism from the shelves, so is branded a communist herself, fired, and shunned by locals. The first Hollywood movie to directly take on issues of McCarthyism and free speech, it also implies that anti-communist hysteria goes hand in hand with anti-intellectualism. ER endorsed the film in "My Day," writing, "I hope this picture will be widely seen. Something similar could so easily happen in almost any American community—the misunderstandings, the exaggerated fears, the lack of real belief in the principles that underlie our democracy all come out in this story" (11 June 1956). *Storm Center* was recognized at Cannes, where it was judged "this year's film which best helps freedom of expression and tolerance," winning the Prix de Chevalier da la Barre.

One of those attacked early on was actor Myrna Loy in 1946. Mentioned in *The Hollywood Reporter* with other Hollywood liberals as "part of the Communist fifth column in America," she sued for libel and forced a retraction. Loy found the suggestion that the few actual communists in Hollywood might be able to make subversive movies under both the studio system and the Production Code "insane." From her point of view, "if you were a staunch Democrat, politically involved, and a friend of Eleanor Roosevelt, if you advocated peace and the United Nations, you were ripe for the pickin'" by the right wing (205–06).

HUAC was still on ER's mind in January 1962 when she devoted an entire column to promoting the short documentary *Wasn't That a Time?* in which brothers Michael and Philip Burton tell the story of lives ruined in the anti-communist witch hunts. Her account eloquently illustrated the damage done to people like William Sherwood, destroyed by HUAC because he fought for the Spanish loyalists; Carl Braden, who worked for integration in the South and was thus branded a communist; and folk singer Pete Seeger, accused of performing for communist groups ("My Day" 15 Jan. 1962).

6

Movies and the White House

Child star Shirley Temple did not often fear a spanking from her mother, but the evening of July 9, 1938, found her receiving a quick swat on the behind in their New York hotel room. Earlier that day at Hyde Park, Shirley had been irritated at the First Lady and took out her frustrations by employing the slingshot she carried in her little white lace purse. A well-aimed pebble hit ER in the backside while she was leaning over the grill cooking their picnic lunch.

The saga had begun when Eleanor stopped by the set of *Little Miss Broadway* a few months earlier in March. In "My Day," she wrote:

> Our first visit was to Shirley Temple, whom I have had the pleasure of meeting before and who is, without exception, one of the most charming children I know. She is simple and unaffected and accepts the inevitable photographers and her as naturally as if this was the way every little girl lived her life.
>
> She asked at once about "Sistie" and "Buzzie" and I went back to her auto-trailer to receive some police badges for them. Then she showed me where she took her lessons. I marvel at her mother's achievement in keeping her well and unspoiled. Shirley told me she was coming to Washington to see the President soon and I hope she will not delay her visit too long [19 Mar. 1938].

Shirley later contradicted the column, saying that the First Lady was mistaken, and they had not met before. However, her mother sent a piece of birthday cake to the White House from a Los Angeles celebration of FDR's birthday, so perhaps that was what Eleanor had in mind. The former child star describes ER's entrance to the set in the middle of a scene with wind machines blowing ceremonial flags, when "looking rather gray and bedraggled" with a "smashed down" hat, she shook the hands of cast and crew and then lightheartedly danced with Jimmy Durante. She asked to see the nine-year-old's backlot schoolroom, where they talked about school, books, and dancing, and ER signed an autograph book. The little girl deputized Eleanor as a member of her police department, but when asked for badges for Sistie and Buzzie, Shirley hesitated. She did not normally hand them out as souvenirs but decided to do so with the First Lady. This was to have consequences later. Saying goodbye, ER "kissed me lightly on the forehead. Lots of visitors said goodbye like that" (214–15).

Shirley and her parents visited the White House to see FDR and then vacationed in New York City with a day trip to Hyde Park. Fox Films captured footage of the occasion in which ER cooks hamburgers and lamb chops on the grill in a sun dress. The voiceover says:

> When the First Lady of the films is entertained by the First Lady of the land. "Now, what would you really like, Shirley? A picnic?" So on the grounds of the Roosevelt estate at Hyde Park, a feast. They're great on picnics at the President's home, the healthy open air, and a good appetite. It's great fun for the queen of the films who is just a little girl.

Eleanor's version of the visit is detailed in "My Day," including mention that the grandchildren had left their badges at home.

> I was amused when we walked out together for the first picture to have her tell me just what to do. "We should walk," she said, "from far back and wave at the camera as we come out." When I did not realize that the camera was following us, she said, "They are still taking us," and we turned for a final wave together. After that was over, there was no more preoccupation with pictures [11 July 1938].

The New York Times, kept at the estate entrance by state troopers, reported that Sistie and Buzzie were the true hosts of the party, helped by their grandmother. ER went swimming, but little Shirley did not "because of my hair." The Shirley Temple look with ringlets in her hair could not be ruined with a swim as the cameras whirled. As she and her parents left, the child star told reporters that she had "a swell time," not revealing what she would write years later ("Shirley").

The adult Shirley Temple Black remembers the visit differently, including a humorous child's response to an apparent slight. She describes Eleanor's home at Val-Kill with an adjacent store selling pewter mugs and reproductions of Early American furniture. Because she could not go swimming with the other children, Shirley chose to go with the First Lady on an errand to the cottage, and her description fits what Val-Kill looks like today. They talked about experiences that had not come to fruition on the vacation in New York City, and ER advised that "whenever opportunity for broader experience arose, it should be grasped. Eternal contentment and stifled curiosity were, to her mind, fatal errors in living." Returning to the cameras, Eleanor "seemed giggly and self-conscious," so the professional actor decided how they should approach, wave, and end the walk back to the pool area. However, as ER lit the charcoal for the grill, little did she know that Shirley was stewing over the fact that Sistie and Buzzie were not carrying their badges. The kids laughed and jumped back in the pool when asked to pay a fine, ignoring their obligations. "Here was a serious problem. My force was no joke and the badges no everyday souvenir. It was a mistake to have deputized anybody else to explain obligations and penalties of membership. Confronted by hilarity while exercising proper authority of leadership left me privately annoyed and thwarted. Mrs. Roosevelt had gotten me in a fine pickle."

As the host leaned over the grill turning lamb chops, the charming child took out the slingshot she carried and hit the First Lady in the backside with a pebble. "Mrs. Roosevelt straightened up with a jerk, holding her long-handled barbecue fork thrust upward like the Statue of Liberty. With the other hand she reached around the back and smoothed her dress over the target area." No one else had seen Shirley do it.... except her mother. Back in the hotel in the city, Shirley got a swat on the bottom "right where I had hit Mrs. Roosevelt." But she had no regrets, feeling it necessary "to rebut a challenge to my authority" and the rules of her police organization. "The whole incident was tactfully ignored by Mrs. Roosevelt" (235–38).

To Mrs. Roosevelt
Love,
Shirley Temple.

Eleanor Roosevelt visits child star Shirley Temple on the Twentieth Century–Fox lot during the March 1938 production of *Little Miss Broadway* (1938) (Franklin D. Roosevelt Presidential Library & Museum).

Temple Black would go on to become a U.S. delegate to the United Nations, ambassador to Ghana and Czechoslovakia, and chief of protocol for President Jimmy Carter. ER, whom she considered a friend, served as a shining example, admired for hard work and an interest in the field of human rights. "I've tried to emulate her in both of those areas, and I'll always be grateful for her for providing me with such an impressive role model," said Shirley in the 1970s (Temple Black and Bell 139).

Eleanor portrayed FDR and the rest of the family as ordinary movie fans, just like any other Americans, in ways that were much like the equalizing tactic the president used when addressing the nation as "my friends" during fireside chats on the radio. She often downplayed her own interest in films, but excitedly wrote about a 1938 visit to the studios in the movie magazine *Photoplay*. Her "Why We Roosevelts Are Movie Fans" article began as a more serious draft called "Movies We Roosevelts Enjoy." Studio tour details were inserted before publication and made the piece more relatable, while other segments, like opinions on Shakespeare adaptations or the fact that in Albany they watched movies to relieve the tension of a pending execution, were omitted from the final article, for which she made $300. Editor Ernest Heyn asked her to update references to more marketable stars and recent pictures, rather than mentioning actors like George Arliss as a Roosevelt favorite in the initial draft (Heyn).

Eleanor wrote, "I think a little trip to Hollywood would make every movie-goer more appreciative of the films which he sees. I spent one morning seeing three of the big movie studios. My time was so limited that I could only get an impression of each one but it was a breath-taking experience." At Warner Brothers, she was carried away by the backlots with streets from Paris and New York and fascinated by the research department's library of books. At MGM, she realized that movie making was not only acting and writing, but involved engineering and painting to create illusions. Shirley Temple took up her time at Fox. "With this visit as background and the very pleasant acquaintanceships made at the time of the Birthday Balls each year when I have a chance to meet and talk with some of the movie stars, my interest is growing greater. I must see whatever films my acquaintances are in and I understand a little better all that goes into giving us this entertainment" (17). Her familiarity with specific actors meant that ER would often choose to watch Temple or Ginger Rogers films when they were screened at the White House.

On this trip, she did not have time for an interview with Hedda Hopper, prompting the conservative gossip columnist to note the slight and add a negative comment about FDR's defense preparations in her article that week ("Hedda"). ER was invited to a Motion Picture Arts Committee tea hosted by Bette Davis, with Joan Bennett, Dashiell Hammett, and producer Walter Wanger attending, but was unable to make it (Arthur). She did tour the Twentieth Century–Fox lot with President Joseph Schenck; visit the sets of *Yellow Jack*, *The Toy Wife*, and *Three Comrades* at MGM, meeting with Luise Rainer and Robert Taylor; and look in on the Warner lot with Harry Warner. ER stopped at the sets of *Boy Meets Girl* and *The Amazing Dr. Clitterhouse*, as well as the research department at Warner, and met with James Cagney, Pat O'Brien, and Edward G. Robinson, lunching with Davis (Lonergan, Skolsky). Photos also show her with Louis B. Mayer at MGM that day.

In the July 1935 issue of *Movie Mirror*, ER shared President Roosevelt's love of the movies with the public in an article titled "Movies in the White House." A close-up of actor Janet Gaynor filled the cover, and the article title was announced across the white lace of her blouse: "Public Citizen No. 1 establishes a new record by becoming the country's leading movie fan and severest critic." Writer Sheila Worth also includes a short paragraph about ER's screening habits:

> Mrs. Roosevelt is a far tougher audience than the President, for while she's a movie fan too, she doesn't react quite so enthusiastically. She doesn't see as many films as the President does because during movie time at the White House, she busies herself with her voluminous correspondence, which is more than any former mistress of the White House has ever had. But don't get the idea that she doesn't like pictures. She does, and whenever she has any free time, she attends the White House showings. *Little Women* was one of the pictures she saw and enjoyed [84].

Both Roosevelts met with Hollywood stars and producers in the White House, and numerous inaugural activities and the president's annual Birthday Balls to benefit the National Foundation for Infantile Paralysis, better known as the March of Dimes, provided publicity and newsreel coverage for all involved.

Will Rogers headlined the first Birthday Ball in January 1934. Even though a Republican, Ginger Rogers attended the 1936 Balls and, after dancing for the president, twice ran into ER that night as they each said a few words at different hotel ballrooms across Washington, D.C. (Rogers 138–41). Jean Harlow and Robert Taylor topped the 1937 festivities, meeting the president, enjoying lunch with Eleanor, and then hitting the balls that evening. Harlow joined ER on stage for press photos cutting a huge cake and had such a wonderful time that she told reporters that the Washington visit was "the highlight of my whole life" (Schroeder 12). Janet Gaynor and Eleanor Powell led the celebrations in 1938, and Errol Flynn in 1939 (Darnton, "East Meets"). By the 1940 Ball, Eleanor and Franklin were hosting a luncheon for 18 in the State Dining Room, including Gene Autry, Olivia de Havilland, James Cagney, Dorothy Lamour, Tyrone Power, Edward G. Robinson, Mickey Rooney, and Red Skelton, followed by a tour of the White House and then six ballrooms across the city. At the Mayflower Hotel, ER cut the red, white, and blue birthday cake, five feet high and three feet across, while Rooney looked on (Rooney 285–88). Lamour wore a dress of "Eleanor Blue" as a subtle compliment to the First Lady's favorite color, but as they all walked through the White House rooms, she describes Tyrone Power whispering things into her ear. Power looked innocent, she kept laughing, and "Mrs. Roosevelt must have thought I was a little daft" (Lamour 91–92).

In 1941, Lana Turner, Glenn Ford, and George Raft led the group, while in 1942, Douglas Fairbanks, Jr., Robert Montgomery, and Jimmy Stewart attended in uniform, along with Ava Gardner, Betty Grable, Dorothy Lamour, and Mickey Rooney. Al Jolson, Abbott and Costello, Edgar Bergen and Charlie McCarthy, James Cagney, Dean Murphy, Roy Rogers, and Loretta Young performed in 1943, although FDR was away (Kelley, "Celebs"). Joan Crawford, Pat O'Brien, Rosalind Russell, and Jimmy Stewart appeared in 1944, causing Russell to remark on the unexpected charm of both FDR and ER: "After three minutes you stopped thinking about her funny teeth; you were convinced she was beautiful" (Russell 138). The First Lady also interviewed Mary Pickford on the radio from the White House in January 1944 as part of the March of Dimes appeal.

The last Roosevelt Birthday Ball in 1945 featured Joe E. Brown, Danny Kaye, Gene Kelly, Alan Ladd, Veronica Lake, Myrna Loy, Margaret O'Brien, and Jane Wyman, along with Vice President Harry Truman and his daughter Margaret, who wanted to meet the stars ("Foundation," Schroeder 13–15). Loy was so excited to finally meet the president that she had a special dress and hat made, only to be disappointed that he was not available, gone for what turned out to be the secret conference in Yalta with Churchill and Stalin. When ER met her at the reception desk and said that FDR would be so distressed that he had not been there to meet the actor, Myrna thought, "Well, you're something!" She later wrote about Eleanor, "I fell in love with her then and there. What a terrific thing for her to say." The group had a tour of the White House, then three days and nights of events including shows at military hospitals, luncheons, dinners, radio spots, and midnight appearances at local theaters to raise hundreds of thousands of dollars for the March of Dimes. "I followed Mrs. Roosevelt around, and I want to tell you, she was something to follow around. That lady could cover more ground, and trying to keep up with her was no joke," remembered Loy. The two stayed together through six Birthday Balls at Washington hotels, plus the Lincoln Colonnade, capped off by the Stage Door Canteen.

Loy wrote, "The G.I.s spotted her and gave a rousing ovation, cheering and clapping and stamping their feet. They thought she was just terrific. So did I. Here was a shy, private woman whose vital participation changed for all time the concept of the First Lady as simply a glorified housewife" (Loy 188–89). Sitting at a small table with ER and the Trumans, Lake also enjoyed herself at the luncheon. She wrote, "Mrs. Roosevelt seemed terribly interested in Hollywood and my career to date … and I ended our conversation with, 'You know what I'd love, Mrs. Roosevelt?'" When asked what that was, Veronica said, "A spoon. A spoon from the White House," whereupon Eleanor discreetly handed her one from the table to take home. Little eight-year-old Margaret O'Brien captivated everyone, and Lake observed, "I think Mrs. Roosevelt wanted to adopt her" (Lake 113–14).

Several months after her first article in *Photoplay*, ER was back in the January 1939 issue with "Film Folk I Have Known." Inside, "America's most distinguished lady brings you an intimate glimpse of the picture people she has met." She regaled readers with more tantalizing news of visits to Hollywood and celebrities in the White House. In a draft for the piece, Eleanor revealed a lack of self-confidence during that first Birthday Ball luncheon with Taylor and Harlow. "They all came to lunch with me having first been taken to greet my husband in his study. I confess I asked them with some trepidation if they would like to see the White House, thinking that a middle-aged woman like myself could have very little interest to offer them." The last version was edited so that she wonders if they might have "historic interests" in a tour, rather than questioning her own appeal ("Film Folk" drafts).

Celebrities were deliberately engaged in campaign activities, and a 1936 *Hollywood Reporter* poll found readers six to one for Roosevelt over Alf Landon (Rosten 160). By 1940, an estimated 85 percent of the industry supported Roosevelt, although the studio moguls were still largely Republicans. Melvyn Douglas headed the Hollywood for Roosevelt organization, with other members like Joan Bennett, Douglas Fairbanks, Jr., Henry Fonda, Edward G. Robinson, and Rosalind Russell. Lucille Ball, Humphrey Bogart, and Groucho Marx joined in radio broadcasts sponsored by the Democratic Party for the 1940 election (Muscio 44). ER would get in hot water from congressional critics for appointing Melvyn Douglas, who later called her "a most unusual individual, earnest, intelligent and fearless," as director of the Office of Civilian Defense Arts Council in 1942 (M. Douglas 112, "Eleanor Gets"). Fairbanks stayed at the White House during the 1941 inaugural celebrations and was called upon to broadcast the opening speech of the Constitution Hall ball when Robert Sherwood took suddenly ill. Charlie Chaplin and Mickey Rooney were photographed with ER at the festivities (Fairbanks Jr., 377–78). Hollywood support was even greater for the president in 1944, and Charles Boyer, Helen Gahagan Douglas, and Eleanor all spoke at a luncheon rally of the Theatrical and Motion Picture Industry Committee for Roosevelt, with Frank Sinatra singing the national anthem. Others on the committee included Irving Berlin, Eddie Cantor, George Cukor, Bette Davis, Paul Muni, Warner Brothers producer Jesse Lasky, Albert Warner, and Harry Warner. Orson Welles, Bob Hope, and Edward G. Robinson attended 1945 inaugural dinners and luncheons (Daly "Along," "Theatrical," "Theatre"). Throughout these years, ER continued to play a critical role in the Roosevelt team's relationships with

Hollywood. Many actors became lifelong friends, for example Robinson, who visited Hyde Park for lunch before giving the May 1957 Memorial Day address in the rose garden (Robinson).

Of course, the industry was intimately involved in the war effort. Eleanor often praised "what the people of the entertainment world have done" and appeared with celebrities and producers to promote the purchase of war bonds ("Eleanor Roosevelt Commends"). Even after FDR's death, she headlined a December 1945 Victory Bond Show in New York that raised over $8 million with a variety of musical and comedic acts, including Joe E. Brown and Duke Ellington ("Mrs. FDR Tops"). Myrna Loy connected with her to help generate more aid for Greek War Relief, describing the First Lady as charming, helpful, and as hospitable as when they first met in the White House. Ten thousand movie theaters were to participate in the 1941 drive for the Greek War Relief Association, and ER's communication with Paramount's Adolph Zukor was reported in industry dailies ("Theatres"). Shortly after this, Loy was scheduled to perform in a sketch put on for Queen Wilhelmina of the Netherlands in Hyde Park, but canceled at the last minute. ER ended up taking her lines in the act as a last resort, learning later that Myrna's husband had given her a black eye (Loy 179–80). The Victory Caravan war relief tour made its way across the country to Washington raising money in April 1942, and Eleanor hosted tea for Desi Arnaz, Joan Bennett, Joan Blondell, Charles Boyer, James Cagney, Claudette Colbert, Bing Crosby, Olivia de Havilland, Cary Grant, Bob Hope, Laurel and Hardy, and Groucho Marx ("H'wood"). In a June 1946 speech to the Independent Theater Owners Association of New York, she praised the industry for its war efforts and observed that it also faced a great responsibility to play its part to help keep up the public interest in preserving postwar peace—a reference to the United Nations ("ITOA").

Although producers were eager to screen their films for FDR, Press Secretary Stephen Early strictly ruled out any publicity associated with White House viewings, with exceptions for patriotic productions during the war. Studios and filmmakers did not have access to promotion or endorsements from the president (Muscio 28–29). However, those rules did not apply to Eleanor.

Before Jimmy went to work for Sam Goldwyn, the moviemaker and ER already had a business relationship. In July 1937, she was "considerably vexed" by news stories announcing that she had been hired to write advertising copy for the Samuel Goldwyn Company film *Stella Dallas*, distributed by United Artists ("Mrs. Roosevelt to Write"). Directed by King Vidor, the title character is a working-class young woman (Barbara Stanwyck) who targets an upper-class man (John Boles) for marriage and family. When daughter Laurel (Anne Shirley) is a teenager, Stella realizes that what is best for her daughter is a life with her father, since the town disapproves of Stella's unsophisticated ways. She sees that Laurel is often embarrassed about her mother and hides her from friends. Stanwyck won an Oscar nomination for Best Actress and Shirley a nomination for Best Supporting Actress.

Eleanor was asked to write a "treatise on motherhood" that accompanied full-page ads for the film in *Variety*, *Ladies' Home Journal*, *True Story*, *Woman's Home Companion*, and other publications. Goldwyn and the press were required to release apologies about the misinterpretation, including information that her fee for writing the two-hundred-word editorial went to charity. There was to be no suggestion that she would write advertising copy for motion pictures ("Mrs. Roosevelt Wrote"). These "erroneous reports" seem to have been fueled by anti-administration papers, especially gossip columnist Harriet Parsons, substituting when her mother Louella Parsons vacationed in Europe. Harriet reported that she had "seen the proofs of the first ad with my own eyes" as part of a whole series of copy Eleanor was writing (H. Parsons). *The Hollywood Reporter* countered, "We've seen Mrs. Roosevelt's copy … and it's in no way an endorsement of the film" (Hoffman "Tales" 1937). The anti–Roosevelt press "yelled to high Republican heaven" in editorials, and the controversy created great publicity for the film (C.V.L.). The industry applauded Goldwyn as a "crafty showman," proving to other producers that there were still new sales angles possible (Wilkinson).

The top half of the single-page advertisement featured a photo of "Barbara Stanwyck in her greatest role as Stella Dallas in Samuel Goldwyn's new production." The text of ER's paid editorial, accompanied by a thumbnail-sized byline photo, filled the bottom half of the page under the title, "*Stella Dallas* Inspires a Discussion of a Mother's Vital Problem by Mrs. Franklin D. Roosevelt." She gave her opinions on how much a mother should sacrifice for her children and warned that women must not give up everything, since they must be able to live their own lives after children are grown. "When they are old enough to get out and stand their own experiences, she will let them go, hoping they will return to her when they need companionship and sustenance and that she has given them strength and courage enough to meet the world on their own" ("*Stella Dallas*"). Her words did not specifically address the film, although ER's name associated with its release certainly served as an advertisement. Stanwyck's performance is outstanding, but the film's theme about a mother's sacrifice in the face of snobbishness does not hold up well for today's audiences.

In publicity that must have escaped Early, or perhaps because the work directly supported New Deal philosophies, it was *Film Daily* news when Monroe Greenthal from United Artists flew to Washington, D.C., to arrange a special screening of *Our Daily Bread* in the White House for FDR and ER in October 1934 ("Show"). The King Vidor production depicts a couple who are hit hard by the Great Depression and flee the city to an abandoned farm. Arduous work and sharing with others make their "back to the land" effort succeed enough to keep them all going in a cooperative community. Now in the public domain, the film is often included in Depression-era collections and was chosen for preservation by the National Film Registry.

Decades later, television star Dick Van Patten told the story of what brought him to success in what would be an extensive career in Hollywood, starting as a child. In 1935, Loew's Theaters in New York sponsored a contest with the grand prize of a trip to Hollywood and a contract with MGM. ER and Mayor Fiorello La Guardia were the judges who selected Dick as the winner (E. Ball). Van Patten was especially well known for his work in television and has a star on the Hollywood Walk of Fame.

In January 1938, newspapers announced that White House staff member Elizabeth "Lizzie" McDuffie had scored the role of the slave "Mammy" in the much-anticipated film adaptation of Margaret Mitchell's Civil War plantation story, *Gone with the Wind*. ER arranged for a "prominent movie executive" to see a play put on by the Black kitchen staff with McDuffie in the cast, leading the visitor to wire producer David O. Selznick, "I have found Mammy!" The Roosevelts paid for McDuffie's travel to New York five times for screen and voice tests and meetings that "clinched her contract," and Eleanor wrote a letter of recommendation ("Movies Find," Gwin). *Time Magazine* called the casting decision "publicity-wise," but in the end, the role went to more experienced actor Hattie McDaniel, who won a ground-breaking Oscar ("Congress"). Understandably, Lizzie was disappointed after all the attention, including a casting bulletin from Walter Winchell and a pronounce-ment from Louella Parsons that McDuffie was "as good as signed" for the part. Even Mitchell herself visited McDuffie, the daughter of former slaves who had appeared on stage throughout high school and now worked in the White House (McDuffie "Back Door," Letter). The film won the Academy Award for Best Picture—without Lizzie.

While on the west coast for lectures, ER visited all the departments on the United Artists lot and was invited as both honored guest and working member of the press to the March 24, 1939, press preview of *Wuthering Heights*, a compelling film adaptation of Emily Bronte's novel (Durant, "Mrs. Roosevelt Preview"). She and Jimmy, who was then working for Goldwyn, dined at the home of Sam and Fran-ces Goldwyn with Irving and Ellen Berlin, Norma Shearer, and Merle Oberon, the star of the film. Afterward, they arrived at the premiere, walking down the red car-pet with Eleanor on one of Sam's arms and Oberon on the other, flashbulbs popping. Her presence added something new and newsworthy to the event, and a photo of Oberon, ER, and Jimmy appeared in *The New York Times* ("Headliners").

The event attracted a "top Hollywood crowd," including Marlene Dietrich, Wil-liam Paley, Tyrone Power, Frank Capra, Douglas Fairbanks, Jr., David O. Selznick, and Paulette Goddard ("Rambling Reporter"). Hedda Hopper wrote about the film in glowing terms as an almost perfect picture and shared a curious observation related to the theme of loves lost and the intense passions of youth: "It was fitting that the First Lady of the Land, Mrs. Roosevelt, should attend the preview. I watched the play of emotions on her face. And when her eyes dimmed I knew she, too, was going back in her memory book of a great love." Hopper followed up by saying that she did not think any of ER's children would ever "reach her pinnacle" ("Studios").

In "My Day," ER revealed that she had not actually stayed through the whole screening, which certainly calls Hopper's observation into question. Jimmy and his mother had a *Wuthering Heights* private viewing in the afternoon, followed by din-ner with the Goldwyns, so she only appeared for the opening of the film premiere before leaving for another engagement (27 Mar. 1939). Goldwyn used Eleanor's quote in promotional advertisements: "It will be hard for anyone seeing this picture not to lose themselves in the story." Directed by William Wyler, and also starring Laurence Olivier and David Niven, the movie was tremendously influential on many other adaptations of the book that followed, as was Gregg Toland's cinematography with a focus on the moors. Jimmy traveled to London to host the premiere and screened the film for the King and Queen at Windsor Palace, as arranged by Ambassador Joseph Kennedy. Once there, as the son of the U.S. president, he also discussed the invita-tion for the royals to visit the United States (Berg 331–33).

Industry publications pictured Goldwyn and ER appearing together for the July 1939 New York premiere of *They Shall Have Music*. The Archie Mayo–directed film about a poor runaway boy who is taken in at a music school for children features expert violinist Jascha Heifetz, with ER's name confirmed first on the list of celebrities appearing for the fundraiser ("First Lady Hears," "Some Industry"). The premiere benefited both the Greenwich House Music School and the High School of Music and Art in New York City; others invited included Edward G. Robinson, Fannie Hurst, Irving Berlin, and Lillian Hellman ("Goldwyn on Duals"). The film is dedicated to music schools throughout the world that encourage the development of musical talent among poor children, and Heifetz performances throughout highlight the show.

The June 1950 trade advertisement for Goldwyn's *Our Very Own* featured a thumbnail picture of ER along with her endorsement: "Eleanor Roosevelt says: *Our Very Own* is about something very important—and delightfully entertaining, too." The movie is the story of Gail Macaulay (Ann Blyth), a privileged teenager who learns that she is adopted and goes in search of her birth mother, finding the woman living on the other side of the tracks. Farley Granger plays very understanding boyfriend Chuck in the teenage romance subplot. David Miller directs what is a routine 1950s melodrama, except for an impressive performance by Blyth, best known for her Best Supporting Actress nomination for *Mildred Pierce*. The full-page ad also included quotes from Joe DiMaggio, Hedda Hopper, Louella Parsons, Quentin Reynolds, Ted Williams, Walter Winchell, and others, but it was Eleanor's photo and endorsement that led the advertisement. It went on to say, "From every source of expert opinion—from every walk of life—from every divergence of opinion-maker—comes a genuine wave of acclaim that Samuel Goldwyn—with his unfailing instinct for putting the *essence of universal appeal* in his films—has done it again." Some magazines like *Cosmopolitan* and *Redbook* and select newspapers published ads that only featured ER's words and photo, without the other celebrities. In another version, both ER and archconservative, name-calling columnist Westbrook Pegler supplied endorsements for the promotion. Although Eleanor still appeared at the top of the ad, this combination in itself became news enough to make it into the syndicated gossip columns (Lyons). "Probably the only thing this pair EVER agreed on!" noted *The Hollywood Reporter* (H. Stein). This might have also been said of competitors Parsons and Hopper, and Williams and DiMaggio, all featured in advertising. Quentin Reynolds, part of the larger ad, had sued Pegler for libel and won.

The world premiere of romantic musical comedy *Pot o' Gold*, the only film Jimmy Roosevelt produced himself from start to finish, screened in Mexico City on April 12, 1941, and associated events confirm his position beyond that of the usual movie executive. The Mexican government turned the United Artists release into a full-fledged film festival and sent out invitations to prominent Americans. *Variety* noted, "Mrs. Eleanor Roosevelt is reported preparing to lead a party of senators, congressmen, diplomats and newspaper writers from Washington" ("Makes It Official"). However, "My Day" reveals that ER was busy with other events around that time, never mentioning the film or the trip. Later press coverage reflects the scaled-down version in which Eleanor did not fly to Mexico, although a contingent from each of the Hollywood studios and several U.S. government offices did make the trip ("All Studios"). George Marshall directed the film, which starred James Stewart and Paulette Goddard. Originally a successful radio game show, this hokey romantic musical comedy tells a fictional story of the people who originated the *Pot o' Gold* show. The war interrupted Jimmy's producing career, and he would not return to it after enlisting.

7

"First Lady in Movie Debut!"

"Eleanor Roosevelt's first experience as a player on a real movie set, not in a newsreel, presents a new and gracious picture of the versatile First Lady." Betty Shannon's cover story in the November 1940 issue of *Screenland* announces, "First Lady in Movie Debut!" The article goes on to describe her May 2, 1940, experience in the Fox Movietone New York studio on the set of the first in a series of three film shorts called *Hobby Lobby*, directed by Arthur Leonard for Columbia. The one-reeler was based on Dave Elman's popular radio show featuring people with unusual hobbies, and ER had both appeared as a guest and substituted for him as host for three evenings while he was in the hospital in 1939 ("My Day" 25 Aug. 1939). Others in the 11-and-a-half-minute program include a young woman who teaches children to sing opera, a mechanic who has developed an extremely sensitive microphone, a man who trains dogs to play musical instruments, and a newspaper vendor who models in clay. In her movie debut, ER talks briefly at the end of the film about the hobbies of members of the Roosevelt family. She reveals that FDR's main hobby is his naval collection, Jimmy collects historical books, Elliott works his ranch, Johnny rides, Franklin Jr. likes to argue, and Anna's hobby is her women's page in the *Seattle Post-Intelligencer* newspaper. Considering the president's fishing, birding, stamp, and nautical collections, she adds, "As for myself, well, I don't think I have many hobbies. When you live in a house with someone who has a good many, you can't afford to have many yourself. The house gets cluttered up. And so we'll say that mine is writing and meeting people" ("Movie Debut," "Hobbies").

Eleanor told host Elman, "This is new to me and I love every minute of it." She impressed the crew with her graciousness, talking and listening to each person on set. However, she gave the director a laugh when she showed up in a plain blue dress and a small hat. They had written her to ask that she wear a flowered dress and big hat, but she had not been home to get the mail (Shannon). As was the practice when reporting about women at the time, *The New York Times* noted her attire: "Mrs. Roosevelt wore an ensemble consisting of a powder blue silk dress and a navy blue Spring coat lined with the same material as the dress, a navy blue straw hat with light blue flowers, blue gloves and a blue alligator bag, tan stockings and brown shoes. She also wore three strands of pearls and a diamond clip" ("Movie Debut"). ER went through the makeup process and several retakes under the hot lights, enjoying the adventure and laughing later about how it took two days to remove all the cosmetics (R. Black 117–18).

She also wrote about the experience in "My Day": "I know now what 'make-up' for the movies is like! … I was enormously interested in the mechanics of taking a few short scenes which we did together. They were very patient with me for, of course, being a novice, I must have been trying. The way it was all done was fascinating to watch" (4 May 1940). A full-page ad for *Hobby Lobby* included a review calling hers a "scoop presentation," and one advance report said that she was "remarkably photogenic" (Walker). In an odd piece of publicity, ER was also described as "the nation's foremost exponent of spare time activities" ("Roosevelt Releases"). Betty Shannon predicted, "Now that it has been found that Eleanor Roosevelt has a charming screen individuality there are probably many things she will be called upon to do. Her voice is of as excellent quality as any male commentator." However, it would take the age of television before Americans were to see Eleanor on-screen on a regular basis outside of the newsreels. She had been offered a "tremendous sum" to appear in 10 movie shorts in which she would stand and lecture, but she chose not to take part (R. Black 117).

Director Leonard and producer Dick Hyland met Jimmy on the *Hobby Lobby* set and signed on with him for a project to produce movie slot machines for hotel lobbies and bars. Short musical numbers were featured in the "jukebox films" ("Emphasis"). The effort was reported in the film industry papers for several years but ran into trouble producing the machines during the war. The idea became obsolete with the coming of television.

Before the war, ER's only other on-screen performance was in *Pastor Hall*, but the movies did increasingly refer to her. In April 1933, Universal Pictures released the adoring FDR biographical documentary *The Fighting President*. He had just been inaugurated less than a month prior to this release, and it is a message of hope before the accomplishments for which we know him today. Eleanor is merely the dutiful helpmate at this point. After the rundown of FDR's Harvard career, narrator Edwin C. Hill briefly mentions ER: "Out of college, he turned to the law for a career and headed to school at Columbia University, and while absorbing black stone within these walls, he married Eleanor Roosevelt, his distant cousin and a niece of President Theodore Roosevelt." When British prime minister Ramsay MacDonald visits the Roosevelt White House, Hill says, "An agreeable, almost startling surprise awaits Premier MacDonald at the White House, the American presidential residence. Instead of stiffness and formality, the president and his charming wife are out on the front steps to great with warmth and true American hospitality their guests from overseas." The biopic moves back and forth in time, and after learning about campaigning in his run for vice president in 1920, the narrator says, "But his thoughts were back home in beautiful Hyde Park with Mrs. Roosevelt and their four children, and very little folks they were in those days, and with his favorite dog. His thoughts went back to the wife who'd been his boyhood sweetheart and always his loyal helpmate." ER, the dog, and the four oldest children are shown in archival footage, which might explain why there is the assumption of four children, rather than five. After the loss in the vice presidential campaign, "then came an interval of political quiet spent with Mrs. Roosevelt and with their four youngsters." The hour-long film does not have anything substantial to say about ER.

In 1934, Alan Crosland directed *Massacre*, an unusual pre-code Warner Brothers and First National Pictures drama about the victimization and exploitation of Native Americans. Boarding school-educated Joe Thunderhorse, played by White actor Richard Barthelmess, has been off working in a Wild West show and comes home to the reservation to find his father dying and his people cheated and suffering. The film was clearly produced prior to enforcement of the Motion Picture Production Code, as evidenced by its focus on race, a White man raping an Indigenous woman, the harm done by government and Christian religious institutions, and miscegenation. Joe's girlfriend Norma (Claire Dodd) in Chicago is White. None of these subjects were allowed by the Code by July 1934, but *Massacre* had been released in January.

After being railroaded by corrupt government officials on the reservation, Joe travels to Washington, D.C., to get justice. The commissioner of Indian affairs (Henry O'Neill) promises to help but lets him know that powerful interests are behind many of the problems—water, power, oil rights, cattle ranges, and timber. They get as far as a special Senate investigation. In his book on pre-Code Hollywood, Thomas Doherty asserts that the group of supportive New Dealers at the Senate hearings include "an Eleanor Roosevelt stand-in wearing the First Lady's trademark fur-lined wrap" (266). The actor looks to be a "type" rather than direct inference; however, one might assume that ER would be present if it helped the cause of Native Americans.

The most common references were parodies and jokes about Eleanor's penchant for travel or what was widely known as the unpalatable food served in the White House. Busby Berkeley directed the 1939 MGM musical *Babes in Arms* starring Judy Garland and Mickey Rooney based on the hit Broadway musical of the same name. Mickey Moran (Rooney) and Patsy Barton (Garland) are a young couple who put on a show to raise money for their parents, vaudevillians struggling to compete with sound motion pictures. Rooney received an Oscar nomination for Best Actor in a Leading Role, and Roger Edens and George Stoll were nominated for Best Musical Score. During the finale, the two leads caricature Franklin and Eleanor, and after driving up in an open car, Rooney spoofs FDR's fireside chats and then passes the microphone to Garland. She sits and knits, as ER often did, while singing in a high voice:

> My day, my day
> Has been a lovely day.
> I breakfasted in Idaho
> Then lunched in Indiana.
> I opened up a Turkish bath
> In Helena, Montana.
> I launched a lovely Ferris wheel
> And then dined in Louisiana.
> My day has been a lovely day.

After those references to the "My Day" column and Eleanor's travel schedule, the two then sing, "It's been a lovely day here in the USA" followed by a final chorus of the patriotic number, "God's Country."

The New York Times reviewer noted that Garland "does a beautiful imitation of Mrs. Roosevelt's broadcasting manner," and their scene as the First Couple was pictured in the Sunday *Times* two days later (Nugent). A *Chicago Daily Tribune* columnist reported the impersonations as one of the highlights of the movie, even scoring points with family members: "Jimmy Roosevelt, who saw it, tells me that it is hilarious mimicry" (Sullivan). *Modern Screen* said, "Judy gets one off on Mrs. Roosevelt which the lady, herself, will thoroughly enjoy." Permissions from the White House were required for MGM to include the impersonations (Svensrud). After FDR's death this segment was edited from the film, and the footage was reported to have been lost for decades. Garland took part in World War II fundraising with Eleanor, and years later attended Democratic fundraisers, seated with her.

The Frank Capra–directed Columbia political dramatic comedy *Mr. Smith Goes to Washington* (1939) has become a classic after enormous success at the box office, 11 Oscar nominations, and selection for preservation by the United States National Film Registry. Yet it was quite controversial, with some concerned that it showed the Senate in the wrong light. James Stewart plays Jefferson Smith, a new arrival in the U.S. Senate, who finds himself fighting the corruption of fellow politicians. Esteemed senior senator Joseph Paine (Claude Rains) is a potential candidate for president, and Smith begins to fall for his daughter, vapid socialite Susan Paine (Astrid Allwyn), who does her father's bidding to distract the younger man. Smith's assistant Clarissa Saunders (Jean Arthur) sees right through Susan and responds to the suggestion that the Paine family might make it into the White House: "Imagine reading 'My Day' by Susan Paine-in-the-neck." Her impression of Susan and her supposed "glamor" is meant to contrast with ER's substance-over-style approach and the real "My Day" column. In the end, the woman who is not taken seriously in Washington (Saunders) and the greenhorn with principles (Smith) win the day with Eleanor Roosevelt–like values versus those of the Paines. Presumably, the subtle reference to ER slipped by the censors.

An example of a comment that was challenged by the Production Code Administration appears in archival correspondence about low-budget Republic musical western *Melody Ranch* (1940). Cowboy crooner Gene Autry, comedian Jimmy Durante as his business sidekick, and love interest Ann Miller star. Joseph Santley directs with a story about Autry, playing himself, coming back to his Arizona hometown to be honorary sheriff during the Frontier Days Celebration and running local gangsters out of town. Autry also had a radio show called *Melody Ranch*, and ER appeared with Autry when he broadcast live from the president's Birthday Ball in January 1940. Joseph Breen wrote producer M.J. Siegel in September 1940 informing him that the movie dialogue referencing President and Mrs. Roosevelt could not be approved without specific permissions from the White House. When Autry stays and runs for town sheriff, Veronica Whipple's (Barbara Jo Allen) line in the final product was adjusted to read: "The elections get noisier every year. I haven't seen so much excitement since I voted for Roosevelt…. I mean Theodore, of course." The five-page Breen memo objects to a range of issues, leading with the body count. Since this was a modern western, it was not given the same latitude as a western based in the past, and killings had to be curtailed to two or three (Breen). The film

Mickey Rooney and Judy Garland imitate Franklin and Eleanor Roosevelt in *Babes in Arms* (1939, MGM). Judy is singing about "My Day" while she knits (author's collection).

was chosen for preservation by the National Film Registry as part of the Gene Autry singing cowboy heritage.

Comedian Milton Berle, who wrote a column for *Variety*, also joked about ER's travel schedule. In July 1941, he wrote, "Just got word that Paramount is thinking of starring Eleanor Roosevelt in a new picture called *Oh! For the Open Road!*" This is just one in a lengthy list of one-liners.

8

Women in Defense

Eleanor contributed "How the Movies Can Help Keep Us Out of War" to the February 1940 issue of *Photoplay* with a sub-headline that reads, "Our First Lady courageously faces the most vital problem of our time—and offers a provocative solution." ER's message is about the positive, educational power of the film industry and the message of peace that is a constant in her philosophy. She notes that men are never satisfied, which is the basis of war, and when she is asked repeatedly about how the U.S. can stay out of the European war, she thinks on a large scale about the whole of humanity and how we might change measures of success: "We have acquired in the course of the past few years, tools for mass education which we never had before. Among these tools are the moving-pictures, and so when I am asked by them what can be done to help keep us out of war, I can only answer that the best way to keep us out of war is to keep all nations out of war, and the best way to do that is to educate human beings to live together with good will in the world." She knew that some would say that this suggestion was "absurd" but felt that interdependence and a necessity for cooperation had to be communicated worldwide somehow. She listed movies like *The Story of Louis Pasteur* as an example of a film that demonstrated a story of selfless service, rather than a focus on material possessions; documentaries such as *The River* and *The City* that helped U.S. viewers learn about their own country; and fictional stories like *The Good Earth*, *Man of Aran*, and *Goodbye, Mr. Chips*, which contributed to our knowledge of other countries. *All Quiet on the Western Front* and *The Grand Illusion* demonstrated the futility of war itself:

> But this is only the beginning. The movies, by showing us through these pictures what they can do, must now exert themselves further along educational lines to the end that not only may we keep out of this war, but that all men everywhere may keep out of all war.
> Here and now, however, it seems to me there are some concrete things which the movies can do to serve this particular time and to direct, through all the methods at their disposal, the people's attention to the fact that sometime soon we must be at peace again in the world.

It put Hollywood and American movies into a global context, just as she believed the country needed to open its eyes to the world and not turn inward. "Because we either go up together or we go down together" ("How the Movies").

On the doorstep of U.S. entry into World War II, Eleanor stepped up her activism in defense preparation films and became a staple for reference in wartime, patriotic movies. The 10-minute short *Women in Defense* made by the Film Unit of the Office for Emergency Management was released on December 21, 1941, and speaks to American women about participating and making a significant impact in the national defense effort. The varied factory footage is fascinating, from parachutes to munitions. ER wrote the commentary, which was spoken by Katharine Hepburn, but neither appear on camera. Hollywood director John Ford directed and produced, and it was nominated for an Academy Award for Best Documentary Short (Brady "Forecast"). The film was offered free to exhibitors as part of the administration's efforts to educate and instruct the public during the wartime crisis, and by February 1942, three-quarters of the theaters in the U.S. had pledged to show government productions like this one ("Broad Changes").

ER wrote about it briefly in "My Day":

> A picture about to be released on women in defense is a good and informative film. I liked it much better when I saw it yesterday than I did in the preparatory period. I feel that six months from now we shall be able to make a more varied film than this one. Women will find so many openings in which to serve their communities, that their activities someday will give us a pattern for good community organization, and the film of these activities will be of great value to the nation [2 Dec. 1941].

The Hollywood Reporter recommended that every theater book it right away due to its timeliness and importance, beautiful photography, and "stirring informative commentary" penned by Eleanor and "dramatically and effectively" spoken by Hepburn ("*Women in Defense* Timely"). Even *Women's Wear Daily* carried coverage of the design and drape of the defense workers' uniforms in the film ("Film Dramatizes"). "More smug than effective" at describing wartime activities of American women, the "didactic commentary" written by ER and "stridently delivered" by Hepburn was not well received by columnist Mildred Martin, who showed her usual anti–Roosevelt sentiments ("*Pacific*"). *New York Times Magazine* gave the film two full pages of coverage on December 7, 1941, the day of the attack on Pearl Harbor. The article began with the opening from the script: "Yesterday the pioneer woman helped to win a continent. Today, with the same spirit of determination, American women are working to save this way of life, working to save the nation from the impact of total war, working to build a sure defense." Screenshots from the 11 areas of laboratory, cloth testing, women of science, nutrition class, industrial costume, parachute worker, ball bearings, electrical switches, volunteer services, Red Cross, and blood bank are accompanied by captions from the script ("*Women in Defense*"). The film was selected for preservation by the Academy Film Archive in its Academy War Film Collection.

The eight-and-a-half-minute *Training Women for War Production* was produced by the National Youth Administration (NYA) in 1942, and ER introduces and narrates the effort to encourage young women to join in domestic production during World War II. She sits on a couch with a colorful blue vase with pink flowers nearby. The use of Technicolor for her introduction, much more expensive than black and white film, may have been designed to reach a young, female audience. She says:

> At the present time, it is of paramount importance that the women and girls of our country be given training so that they may do their share in the war emergency. How this training is given and who does it is of great interest to us all. To some of us, the National Youth Administration stands out as the agency which is doing the best job along these lines at present.

Therefore, I congratulate Mr. Aubry Williams on having inaugurated this training, and I congratulate the young people and having this administration with which to work.

Her voiceover continues over scenes of young women working, with an emphasis on the NYA and opportunities for training and work in a broad range of industries.

The Warner Brothers 1943 short film *Women at War* was nominated for an Oscar for "Best Short Subject, Two-reel" and stars Faye Emerson, who would marry Elliott Roosevelt the following year, as one of four young women who join the newly formed Women's Army Corps (WAC). Designed to educate the public about the value of women's contributions to the war effort, the 21-minute Technicolor film was inspired by ER's discussions about the roles of women during wartime ("Film on"). The actors are embedded into real WAC units and training exercises, with White women only. However, the movie's opening shot of WACs marching shows an integrated group.

In the weeks after the December 1941 attack on Pearl Harbor, the film industry trade publications openly discussed how they could best support the war effort and recognized that helping to take the public's minds off the fighting was of value. Page one of *Film Daily* quoted Eleanor's point of view: "For heaven's sake, keep them laughing" ("Films Must"). References to ER in Hollywood films increased just prior to and during the war, most often in a comedic context that made her the butt of a light joke. *Louisiana Purchase* (December 1941) stars Bob Hope as naive Senator Jim Taylor, caught as the scapegoat in a web of corruption located in a fictional Louisiana. The Paramount musical comedy directed by Irving Cummings is based on a hit Broadway musical with music and lyrics by Irving Berlin. The plot involves setting up the squeaky-clean federal investigator Senator Oliver P. Loganberry (Victor Moore) to appear to be engaged in a romance with Marina Von Minden (Vera Zorina) to blackmail him. Loosely based on former Louisiana governor Huey Long's administration, the whole production is forgettable. It was Hope's first Technicolor film and satirizes the New Deal as well as *Mr. Smith Goes to Washington*. As Taylor tries to get Loganberry to sweep the crimes of his friends under the rug, but his colleague refuses to compromise his honor, Taylor says, "OK, but if you're still in Washington a year from now, you'll see less of the White House than Eleanor." This is an empty threat. In the end, Taylor is recognized as a victim as well. *Louisiana Purchase* was Oscar nominated for both color cinematography and color art direction-interior, and illustrates Eleanor's frequent traveling as a common popular culture reference. ER enjoyed the play, mentioning seeing it on stage both in New York and Washington, D.C., but did not write about ever viewing the film.

A *Film Bulletin* reviewer shared the observation that Arthur Lake's female impersonation in 1941 Columbia release *Blondie Goes Latin* "faintly resembles" Eleanor Roosevelt (Nonamaker). Lake plays Dagwood in the eighth film adaptation of the classic comic, disguising himself as a woman playing drums in a band so that his boss Mr. Dithers (Jonathan Hale) is unable to recognize him on a cruise to South America. As one might expect, the reference to ER is a stretch, but Lake is quite tall with a wig not unlike Eleanor's hairstyle of the time. The musical comedy reads today like a television sitcom that has not aged very well.

Bette Davis, Ann Sheridan, and Monty Woolley star in the January 1942 War-ner Brothers comedy *The Man Who Came to Dinner*, based on the hit Broadway show of the same name, supported by Jimmy Durante and Billie Burke and directed by William Keighley. Obnoxious celebrity author and radio personality Sheridan Whiteside (Woolley) slips on the ice, breaks his hip, and then stays at the home he had been visiting to recuperate. Soon he is faking a prolonged recovery. On the day he arrives, dialogue helps to establish Whiteside's national reputation. He asks his secretary Maggie Cutler (Davis), "Did you put through that call to Mrs. Roosevelt?" Cutler responds, "Yes, I called her in Portland, but she'd already left for San Diego." He follows up: "Well, try her tomorrow in Phoenix." Finally, when he is ready to leave, Whiteside walks down the steps as Daisy Stanley (Burke) answers the phone. "Hello. Mrs. Roosevelt? Eleanor Roosevelt! Oh, just a moment, please. Mr. White-side? Oh, Mrs. Roosevelt, I want you to know my husband didn't vote for your hus-band, but I did. Oh, you're welcome, I'm sure. And I'd love to vote for your husband again some time." Putting down the phone, she murmurs, "Oh…. Mrs. Roosevelt!" Then she calls, "Oh, Mr. Whiteside, Mrs. Roosevelt's on the phone." He is excited, "What, Eleanor?!" and falls running up the icy steps. He has injured himself again! Everyone springs into action, leaving the phone unanswered. A high Eleanor-like voice calls, "Hello, hello, hello. Oh dear, something must have happened to Sherry. Operator, operator!" The end. The Whiteside character was based on *New Yorker* critic Alexander Woollcott, who in real life was a long-term, sometimes unwelcome guest at the White House. Both Franklin and Eleanor attended a performance of the play *The Man Who Came to Dinner* in 1941, when Woollcott played the Whiteside character himself ("Roosevelt Attends"). Later television versions, like *Best of Broad-way* in 1954 on CBS and NBC's *Hallmark Hall of Fame* in 1972, omit these Roosevelt references, no longer as culturally relevant.

Albert S. Rogell directs the 1942 Paramount musical *Priorities on Parade* about swing band members who leave the road and work in an aircraft factory during World War II. Ann Miller, Johnny Johnston, and Jerry Colonna wield blowtorches and rivet in an aircraft factory as well as entertaining their fellow workers at mid-night dances. Of course, there is the requisite 1940s style conflict of the sexes in the plant with women welders threatening male pride, but in the end, they always fall in love. Luigi Luraschi, head of Paramount's Domestic and Foreign Censorship Depart-ment, wrote to producer Sol C. Siegel summarizing potential policy violations in the original script. This included a note about dialogue considered inadvisable because of the criticism to which Mrs. Roosevelt's actions had been subjected (Luraschi). In response, the final version of the movie, which had been known as *Priorities of 1942*, does not reference ER or her civil defense actions at all. The three-page memo out-lined other domestic, foreign, and Motion Picture Production Code issues that var-ied from the realism of the response of workers to an air raid siren to objections of the use of words like "nuts" and "lousy."

The MGM 1942 romantic comedy *Woman of the Year*, directed by George Ste-vens, features driven international affairs reporter Tess Harding (Katharine Hep-burn), who works at the same newspaper as sportswriter Sam Craig (Spencer Tracy). What is initially consternation with one another turns to love. The problem is that she is devoted to her job, too much so for the times, and one review described her as "leading an Eleanor Roosevelt sort of existence" (*Woman of the Year*). As the movie opens, Craig listens to the radio with other bar patrons, and Harding is on the air taking part in a quiz show in which she knows even the most obscure answers. The bartender says, "Federman says she's the number two dame in the country, right next to Mrs. Roosevelt." ER mentioned watching the movie at an Office of Civilian Defense party, observing that "Katharine Hepburn plays a most amusing and delightful role" ("My Day" 23 Feb. 1942). The film won the Oscar for Best Original Screenplay, earning Hepburn a Best Actress Nomination, and was chosen for preservation by the National Film Registry.

James Cagney is song and dance man George M. Cohan in the May 1942 patriotic Warner Brothers musical biography *Yankee Doodle Dandy*, directed by Michael Curtiz. Cohan (Cagney) plays a singing and dancing President Roosevelt on Broadway in *I'd Rather Be Right* and receives the Congressional Medal of Honor from FDR, in an over-the-shoulder shot acted by Captain Jack Young and voiced by Art Gilmore. He tells his life story to the president, and the film plays out in flashback. The movie was a huge hit, winning three Oscars—Cagney for Best Actor in a Leading Role, Nathan Levinson for Sound Recording, and Ray Heindorf and Heinz Roemheld for best score. It was also nominated for Best Picture, Director, Actor in a Supporting Role (Walter Huston), Writing Original Story, and Editing, and was chosen for preservation in the National Film Registry.

Cohan as FDR sings:

> When I was courting Eleanor, I told her Uncle Teddy
> I wouldn't run for President unless the job was steady.
> Don't print it, strictly off the record.
> We entertained the royalty, but we were never flustered.
> We gave them Yankee hot dogs with Coleman's English mustard.
> Don't print it, strictly off the record.
> It's pleasant at the White House, but I'll tell you how I feel.
> The food is simply terrible, just sauerkraut and veal.
> If Mrs. R would stay at home, I'd get a decent meal.

He launches into a dance number before continuing the song and the FDR tribute. It includes commentary on ER's travel habit, as well as the poor food at the White House and the instance in which the Roosevelts served hot dogs to the King and Queen of England.

During World War II, well-known director Commander John Ford ran the photographic unit for the Office of Strategic Services. Sent to remote Midway Island in the Pacific in 1942, he filmed the Battle of Midway for the U.S. Navy and was wounded in the arm by shrapnel. Ford brought the 16mm Technicolor footage back to the U.S. to be edited, using actors such as Henry Fonda for narration. However, there was dissension among each of the armed services claiming credit for the U.S. victory, and Ford feared that the *Battle of Midway* film would not be released to the public. On the day in August 1942 that he was to screen the short in the White House for President Roosevelt, the director had editor Robert Parrish splice in a close-up of Major James Roosevelt saluting the Midway funeral services after the action was over. FDR and ER watched with Chief of Staff Admiral William Leahy, Press Secretary Stephen Early, and members of the Joint Chiefs of Staff. Parrish later recalled that the president talked throughout the screening until he fell silent when Jimmy appeared on-screen. "When the lights came up, Mrs. Roosevelt was crying. The president turned to Admiral Leahy and said, 'I want every mother in America to see this picture'" (Parrish *Growing Up* 150–51).

American Cinematographer rated the film a must-see, a "fine piece of camera reporting," and a "magnificent piece of film craftmanship" ("Photography"). "The thrills are unsurpassed" in *Film Daily*, and it was "eighteen minutes of cinema dynamite" in trade publication *The Exhibitor* (Daly "Make," Emanuel). *The New York Times* reviewer concurred that it was "eighteen tingling and harshly realistic minutes" ("Film of *Midway*"). In 1942, footage of the real Japanese attack with the camera thrown around on impact and the sounds and views of planes diving, bombs, fire, anti-aircraft guns, and the naval and air counterattack must have been more like being in the battle than anything the public had ever seen before. The 18-minute film won an Oscar for Best Documentary and was selected for preservation by the Academy Film Archive in its Academy War Film Collection. In 1943, Ford approached Jimmy about working with him when they were back in civilian life. Instead, the Roosevelt son put Hollywood behind him and went into politics.

Editor Parrish also mentions being shown a 1942 German propaganda film as a lesson in what real propaganda was versus the patriotic films that Ford believed he and his U.S. compatriots were creating. The print brought in from Portugal opens with the title *America the Beautiful* on-screen while Bing Crosby sings the title song. Footage of vicious police attacks on Black people during the 1930s in Detroit is paired with close-ups of FDR laughing. Scenes of women wrestling in mud and with dead fish are intercut with footage of ER dressed for the opera, smiling and applauding politely. The final scene consists of newsreel footage of the Roosevelts at Hyde Park for Thanksgiving, and as FDR begins carving the turkey, the knife dissolves to a scene of the president cutting off Scandinavian countries from a map of Europe and handing the plate to British prime minister Winston Churchill. Then he slices off Italy, giving that plate to France's Charles de Gaulle. FDR smiles happily. "*That's a propaganda picture*," said Ford (Parrish *Hollywood* 27–28).

Vice President Henry Wallace narrates the 14-minute short film *The Price of Victory*, produced by Paramount and the Motion Picture Bureau of the Office of War Information. Based on a May 1942 speech delivered to the Free World Association in New York, the message was designed to inspire Americans in the fight against the Axis powers ("Vice President"). Wallace sits at his desk and performs the speech, at times cutting to newsreel and Hollywood stock footage. He outlines four duties of the people: the duty to produce to the limit, the duty to transport as quickly as possible to field of battle, the duty to fight with all that is in us, and the duty to build a peace, just and enduring. The film, directed by William H. Pine, was released to the public on December 3, 1942, and received an Oscar nomination for Best Documentary. ER made an appearance at a special December screening for the First World Conference and Dinner of the World Confederation of International Groupments, an organization dedicated to international cooperation. Pictured with her at the

Hotel Astor in New York were deputy prime minister of New Zealand Walter Nash, Chinese ambassador to the United States Wei Tao Ming, James Waterman Wise, who had written about the Nazi threat as early as 1933, president of the World Confederation Li YuYing, author Ralph Bates, and Paramount's Adolph Zukor with wife Lottie Zukor. Representatives from 31 other countries also attended ("At Screening").

The Stage Door Canteen served as an entertainment venue in Manhattan during World War II, offering music, shows, dancing, and free food to American and Allied service members. ER visited at midnight there one evening and helped set up a Washington, D.C., wing of the popular canteens that inspired the 1943 Frank Borzage–directed *Stage Door Canteen* film from United Artists (Lytell). The plot involves three soldiers on leave who visit the Canteen nightly and fall in love before they are abruptly shipped off. A cavalcade of famous movie and music celebrities stop by for cameos, serving the men or supplying entertainment and wartime songs, including Judith Anderson, Tallulah Bankhead, Count Basie, Ralph Bellamy, Edgar Bergen and Charlie McCarthy, Ray Bolger, Xavier Cugat, Arlene Francis, Benny Goodman, Helen Hayes, Katharine Hepburn, Peggy Lee, Guy Lombardo, Harpo Marx, Ethel Merman, George Raft, Ethel Waters, and Johnny Weissmuller. When the movie was in production, Hollywood industry sources leaked, "Don't be surprised at an announcement that Eleanor Roosevelt will do a scene for *Stage Door Canteen*" to be filmed on the East Coast (Gwynn). That never came to be, but with her involvement with the actual project and appearance in a *Stage Door Canteen* radio show, it seems quite plausible that she might have done a guest spot in the film ("American Theatre").

Bob Hope plays incompetent reporter Robert Kittredge, sent home from Moscow when he does not notice that Germany invades Russia, in the March 1943 release, *They Got Me Covered*. He then tries to prove himself by cracking a Nazi spy ring in Washington, D.C. Dorothy Lamour is Christina Hill, Kittredge's love interest, and Otto Preminger plays Nazi leader Fauscheim in this Samuel Goldwyn musical comedy directed by David Butler. In the first five minutes of the film, Kittredge is on the plane back to the U.S. when his seatmate asks, "Are you going anywhere special?" He gets a laugh with the reply: "No, I'm just keeping the seat warm for Mrs. Roosevelt."

Lucille Ball and Dick Powell star in the MGM musical *Meet the People*, released in June 1944. Shipyard worker Bill "Swanee" Swanson (Powell) writes a patriotic play supporting war industries, and when he meets Broadway star Julie Hampton (Ball), they put on a show together. Directed by Charles Reisner, it was based on the Broadway musical of the same name. The Commander (Bert Lahr) asks Julie to launch his boat with a champagne bottle. When she is not sure how it should be done, he replies, "There's a definite technique. Now, take Mrs. Roosevelt. With one motion, she makes the pitch, ducks neatly, smiles into the camera, and hops a plane for Seattle." Both serve as examples of ER's well-known travel schedule during the war.

The Washington, D.C., housing shortage during the war is the target of the March 1943 Columbia Pictures comedy *The More the Merrier*, directed by George Stevens. Benjamin Dingle (Charles Coburn), Connie Milligan (Jean Arthur), and Joe Carter (Joel McCrea) all share an apartment, and it is a screwball affair. Coburn won the Oscar for Best Supporting Actor, while the production received five other nominations for Best Picture, Best Actress in a Leading Role (Arthur), Best Director (Stevens), Best Writing Original Story, and Best Writing Screenplay. There is an obscure reference to ER when they discuss Mr. Pendergast (Richard Gaines). Benjamin wonders why Connie does not call her fiancé by his first name. She responds by telling him, "You don't realize that Mr. Pendergast is the type of man who has twice been to the White House to dinner." Benjamin replies, "Worst food in Washington" before Joe chimes in: "I'll bet the president's wife calls him by his first name sometimes." In real life, ER made wartime housing a political issue. The White House food was also known for being unpalatable, served up by housekeeper Henrietta Nesbitt.

Warner Brothers comedy *The Doughgirls* (1944), directed by James V. Kern, is also about the D.C. housing shortage with reference to ER's travel schedule. Three newlywed couples must share the same honeymoon suite in this film based on a stage play. The arrangement causes problems for all, and the women are unhappy that their men are working so hard and rarely around. Edna (Ann Sheridan) says, "You're beefing? I've seen so little of my husband they're starting to call me Eleanor." Vivian (Jane Wyman) replies, "Well, Eleanor, I mean Edna, you've got to go," as they work out the hours that they will each be able to inhabit an apartment. In addition, two characters receive an invitation to lunch at the White House with the Roosevelts.

Michael Curtiz directs the musical comedy *This Is the Army*, in which Kate Smith sings Irving Berlin's "God Bless America" and boxer Joe Louis makes an appearance. The ensemble cast includes Ronald Reagan, as well as U.S. Army soldiers who were performers in civilian life. The film revolves around an all-soldier show on Broadway that eventually plays in Washington, D.C., for President Roosevelt, played by Jack Young. ER, financier and Roosevelt adviser Bernard Baruch, and other national military and civilian leaders headed the "First Nighters" Committee for the August 1943 premiere in the capital. The movie was "assured of as distinguished a send-off as any motion picture has ever had," with Eleanor's support mentioned in a *Daily Variety* headline ("Mrs. Roosevelt One"). The film is patriotism as only served up in World War II–era comedic musicals from Hollywood.

Ruth Clifton, age 18, "the nation's number one teen-age authority on war-time youth problems," met with ER and then testified before a Senate subcommittee concerned with juvenile delinquency. Clifton was a technical adviser to producer Val Lewton on the RKO film *Youth Runs Wild* (previously known as *Are These Our Children?*) and toured the country in conjunction with key city premieres after the Washington, D.C., visit in March 1944 ("*Are These*"). The Mark Robson–directed film addresses the issue of teenagers getting in trouble while both parents are either away in the military or working in factories.

Based on the Broadway show *Very Warm for May*, the thinly plotted MGM Technicolor "let's put on a show" backstage musical revue *Broadway Rhythm* (1944) features songs composed by George and Ira Gershwin, Oscar Hammerstein, and Jerome Kern, with direction by Roy Del Ruth. As part of the studio's *Broadway Melody* series of films, George Murphy and Ginny Simms star here, but Lena Horne steals the show with two musical numbers. Tommy Dorsey and his orchestra and the contortionist Ross Sisters also contribute to the April 1944 release. (Songs like "Solid Potato Salad" and "I Love Corny Music" are some of the less sophisticated offerings.) Successful Broadway producer Jonnie Demming (Murphy) offers the lead in his new show to Helen Hoyt (Simms), but instead she joins a barnyard production organized by Jonnie's retired vaudevillian father Sam (Charles Winninger) and singing sister Patsy (Gloria DeHaven). Jonnie, who is falling in love with Helen, is upset, but does not recognize the talents of his family members.

The film refers to both ER and FDR. Trixie (Nancy Walker) stumbles across the hired man, comedian Dean Murphy, in a haystack outside the rehearsal barn, and he performs several impersonations of well-known figures at the time, including Charlie McCarthy and Jimmy Stewart. After she recommends that he stay on the farm, rather than pursue an acting career, he launches into a jaunty Franklin with chin aloft. Trixie jokes, "It's the best Churchill I've ever heard." As she hops into a car to escape the farm and says, "Boy, have I had a day," the farm hand impersonates Eleanor in a high voice with teeth protruding, "My day hasn't been so hot either." The "My Day" column allusion is one many American viewers would have easily recognized in 1944.

Murphy often did impersonations of FDR, and after the president's mother Sara Delano Roosevelt saw a live performance, Murphy was invited to the White House. Becoming friendly with the Roosevelts, he also came to Hyde Park when the King and Queen of England visited ("Beverly"). Murphy was still impersonating ER on the February 13, 1951, *Texaco Star Theater* television program hosted by Milton Berle on NBC. A *Boston Globe* reviewer called the episode "practically perfect, and might have hit 100 percent if Dean Murphy, in his impression of Mrs. Roosevelt, hadn't cheapened it with the play on Elliott's name" (McPartlin). Following impressions of Ronald Colman, Bette Davis, Clark Gable, and Jimmy Stewart, he ended the segment with a high-pitched ER voice, hands flailing, referencing her NBC television show *Mrs. Roosevelt Meets the Public*, which was currently on the air and produced by son Elliott. "Thank you again tonight. It's such a pleasure at any time to send greetings to all of you. I do it rather regularly through NBC. This morning I picked up my telephone to talk with my son Idiot. I mean Elliott! I said to my son, much as I say to you, I don't want to be too slow. I'd like to turn over the show to Mr. Berle and Texaco. Thank you. Good night!" It is hard to imagine that ER continued to feel the same about Murphy after the televised slight on her son.

William Berke directs September 1944's *That's My Baby!*, an unusual Republic Pictures mix of comedy, musical numbers, and animation. Betty Moody (Ellen Drew) and boyfriend Tim Jones (Richard Arlen) try to cheer up Betty's father R.P. (Minor Watson) by hiring dancers, singers, comedians, and odd acts who attempt to make him smile until they finally realize that R.P. always wanted to be a cartoonist. Jones and his colleagues create a short animated film based on a baby R.P. drew 20 years earlier, and that finally makes the older man laugh. The animated baby is holding a newspaper and reads, "What do you know? Eleanor's back," another reference to her travels. The film as comedy and entertainment is a bit of a painful viewing experience today.

In an entirely animated short, Warner Brothers released the seven-minute

Merrie Melodies cartoon *Booby Hatched* in October 1944. A mama duck hatches a brood of chicks and names them Franklin, Eleanor, and Winston. Their sibling, poor little Robespierre, gets stuck in his shell and lost. Paramount Technicolor musical comedy *Bring on the Girls* was released in March 1945 and starred Veronica Lake. In the Spike Jones "Chloe" song, he reportedly incorporated a joking reference to "Eleanor," but the sequence was edited out after the theatrical run and FDR's death. Existing versions of the movie and the song do not contain the segment with the Eleanor wisecrack.

The highlight of wartime era films with references to ER is 1945 British drama *Great Day*, about women's industries to support the troops in a small English village. It was inspired by Eleanor's real visit to England, when she made a surprise stop to inspect the women's local war effort in Kent (Hobson). Directed by Lance Comfort and distributed by RKO in the U.S., the family drama is bookended by preparations for a visit from Eleanor Roosevelt, a great honor for locals. The character of Eleanor finally appears at the very end of the film, with only her back, portrayed by an uncredited actor, visible to the audience. Lady Mott (Isabel Jeans) organizes the Women's Institute and tells the assembled group, "She's not coming as the First Lady of America, but as one of yourselves, a woman with a husband and a family and a home of her own. Just give her an idea of your war effort and of life in a wartime village." This statement launches the film's plot, which was written by female screenwriter Lesley Storm and concentrates on themes of women's solidarity. We do not actually see Eleanor until the final scene, when the proud village women receive her to display woolen boots, bandages, jams, and other supplies for the troops that they have made. Filmmakers shoot her only from the back, keeping the focus on this group of women and their accomplishments. This is a noticeable use of ER as being just like other women in the context of marriage and family. However, the film celebrates their work, which is sometimes hindered by the men in their lives. The portrayal models women taking control of their own lives and situations, just like Eleanor Roosevelt, and it is a contemporary illustration of her worldwide influence as "a woman with a husband and family and home of her own." The messages about women and their abilities are complex, showing inspirational independence, yet making sure to define this behavior in the context of marriage. The one negative portrayal of a female character is a woman who has chosen a single life and suffers for it. By extension, the portrayal of ER is also ambivalent in its insistence on leadership only in the context of proper marriage and family roles (A. Beauchamp). After a good deal of romantic drama and family problems, the "great day" finally comes. A band plays and the entire village gathers at the hall. ER's car appears, and the crowd goes wild. A little girl brings Eleanor, only seen from the back, her flowers: "Mrs. Roosevelt, Denley greets you. We offer these English flowers to the First Lady of America in token of our friendship for our great ally in the common struggle." Despite the struggles of the past two days, family, friends, and village residents are all supremely proud.

Reviews were mixed. The *Motion Picture Herald* noted, "The film will warm the hearts of neighborhood audiences hereabouts" in the U.K. and had a similar appeal in the U.S. (Burnup). But *Variety* said, "British made yarn about Eleanor Roosevelt's visit to England looks thin for the U.S." ("Miniature"). Another *Variety* reviewer disparagingly called it "good matinee fare for the housewife and the unsophisticated" (Clem). In contrast, the U.K. fan magazine *Picturegoer* published a full page of eight stills from the film. Its full review of the film was entirely positive, which illustrates the difference between U.K. and U.S. reception (*"Great Day,"* L. Collier).

9

Postwar on Film

After President Roosevelt's death, ER's departure from the White House, and the end of World War II, she became less of a popular culture presence in the movies and was mentioned much less often. Her interests turned more to the United Nations and international relations, with a growing attraction to television, rather than film. However, *Modern Screen* published her September 1947 article "Democracy on the Screen" in which she called on the American movie-going public to educate themselves on what democracy really means. She drove home that discrimination should not exist in the United States, so perhaps the movies could help educate the populace. "If the screen could show the inception and growth of our government processes and the obligations that now lie upon us when our nation is at the peak of its power, the people would learn their lesson." As a leader among nations, she was worried that the rest of the world and burgeoning democracies were getting the wrong idea about the U.S.: "Certain types of movies have been shown in other countries which show us as a nation of bronco-busters, gangsters, movie stars and luxurious ladies and gentlemen of leisure. The democracy of the farm, the mill, the industries, the thousands and thousands of people who are the backbone of this country, are little known to the millions who build up their countries in much the same way." She wished that the movies could help to make democracy more of a living thing in our daily lives and then translate that example to the world.

Some connections to the film industry persisted. *The African Queen* (1951) is remembered for brilliant performances from both of its leads: Humphrey Bogart, who won the Oscar for Best Actor, and Katharine Hepburn, who was nominated for Best Actress. The story about a mismatched couple traveling together in German-controlled colonial Africa and falling in love under dire circumstances has become a beloved classic, but both Hepburn and director John Huston discussed struggling with development of the character Rose Sayer, a prim and proper minister's sister. ER's smiling demeanor during her trip to the Pacific visiting numerous military hospital wards during World War II became the model for the character, as Hepburn describes in her memoir:

He [Huston] was an amazing character. He had flashes. And those flashes were brilliant—when he told me to base my character of Rosie on Eleanor Roosevelt when she visited the hospitals of the wounded soldiers, always with a smile on her face. He had felt that I was playing Rosie too seriously, and that since my mouth turned down anyway, it was making the scenes heavy. Since I (as Rosie) was the sister of a minister, my approach to everyone and everything had to be full of hope. A smile. It was indeed a FLASH of brilliance. In short, he had told me exactly how to play the part [226].

Huston also talks about working with Hepburn on the role:

I went to her one night before we were about to begin the important scenes of the picture. I asked her just to listen to me, and finally I said, "I think she is more of a lady." Katy said, "A lady?" And she has every reason to believe that she is a lady of the first order. She said, "What lady?" I thought for a moment and then said, "Eleanor Roosevelt." I saw Katy's mind go to work, and the next day, her performance had entirely changed ["*John Huston*"].

Hepburn was a Roosevelt supporter and friend who had been invited to the White House.

Carson McCullers adapted her novel *The Member of the Wedding* for the screen in 1952. The story about Frankie Addams, a White Southern tomboy who does not fit in, and her Black caretaker Berenice Sadie Brown, was directed by Fred Zinnemann in the 1952 feature film. Julie Harris was nominated for an Academy Award in her role as Frankie, while Ethel Waters played Berenice, with lines to help place the action in the Roosevelt era:

Katharine Hepburn as Rose Sayer in *The African Queen* (1951, United Artists). She and director John Huston modeled the character on Eleanor Roosevelt's demeanor during her trip to the Pacific during World War II, that of a lady who always has a smile on her face even when visiting the wounded in military hospitals (author's collection).

> **FRANKIE:** Why is it against the law to change your name?
> **BERENICE:** What's that on your neck? Thought that was a head you carried on that neck.
>   Just think. Suppose I ups and calls myself Mrs. Eleanor Roosevelt?

The 1982 and 1997 television adaptations also include this dialogue to help set the time frame. The 1958 *Dupont Show of the Month* version on CBS drops the line, since the play's length was shortened for television broadcast.

The Elia Kazan Fox historical drama *Wild River* (1960) details the story of the Tennessee Valley Authority (TVA), the damming of the Tennessee River for electric power by the New Deal in the 1930s, and the reluctance of some families to move off the land. Starring Montgomery Clift, Lee Remick, and Jo Van Fleet, the National Film Registry selected the film for preservation in 2002. TVA officer Chuck Glover (Clift) works up the ire of local White residents by hiring Black men to clear land at the same wage as White residents. A group tries to bully Glover and scare him back home to Washington, D.C. One in the crowd asks, "When are you goin' home? How's Eleanor up there?" Another says, "Who's Eleanor?" and in case there is doubt in the audience, he is answered with, "Eleanor Roosevelt." The reference casts the outsiders with both Roosevelts, especially ER and her concern for civil rights.

Frank Capra directs the 1961 Technicolor feel-good *Pocketful of Miracles*. In the 1930s, New York gangster Dave (Glenn Ford) and girlfriend Queenie (Hope Lange) transform alcoholic street peddler Apple Annie (Bette Davis) into a society lady. Annie has been stealing stationery from a high-end hotel to write to her daughter Louise (Ann-Margret) in Spain, pretending to live there. When Louise visits the U.S., Dave reluctantly puts Annie up in a friend's penthouse suite to complete the ruse and complains, "You at the Marbury Hotel! Why didn't you swipe some stationery from the White House? You could have said you were Eleanor Roosevelt!"

Eleanor's involvement with moviemaking throughout the late 1940s and 1950s was eclectic and often tied to political goals, especially the United Nations and issues of world peace. In contrast to her earlier reluctance to speak for the cameras, she can be observed readying for a regular presence on television. In 1947, documentary filmmaker Julian Roffman, who also directed *FDR at Hyde Park* in 1952, made the 25-minute short *A Greater Tomorrow* for the African Academy of Arts and Research as part of its program to promote cultural and economic understanding between Africa and the United States. ER appears in the film, as do singer Marian Anderson, boxer Joe Louis, and baseball great Jackie Robinson. The documentary was specifically produced for screening in Nigeria, Liberia, and Ghana, and Kinsley Mbadiwe, president of the academy, traveled to West Africa with the film for an extensive lecture tour in December 1947 ("First Documentary").

The 1949 10-minute British film *His Fighting Chance*, directed by Geoffrey Innes and produced by the Crown Film Unit for the Central Office of Information, is a documentary about polio rehabilitation techniques. The opening credits say, "Commentary Spoken by Mrs. Eleanor Roosevelt and Michael Redgrave as a contribution to the Fight for Johnny." Johnny Green is two years old with polio. Archival footage is shown from ER's 1948 visit to London and the unveiling of the FDR memorial in Grosvenor Square. King George VI says, "It is with both pleasure and sadness that I welcome Mrs. Roosevelt here today. I am shortly going to invite her to unveil the monument to her husband, the late president of the United States of America." With Queen Elizabeth at her side, Eleanor pulls the covering down to reveal the statue of Franklin Roosevelt, standing with a cane. Inscribed in the platform are FDR's Four Freedoms: "Freedom from want. Freedom from fear. Freedom of speech. Freedom to worship." Commentary from ER follows over footage of patients receiving polio therapy, as her narration focuses on advances in treatments and outcomes.

Eleanor, New York mayor Robert Wagner, and AFL-CIO president George Meany were just some of the guests at the 25th anniversary celebration of David Dubinsky's presidency of the International Ladies Garment Workers Union (ILGWU). Seventeen thousand union members were expected to attend at Madison Square Garden on June 13, 1957, with another 10,000–15,000 gathered outside ("Pay-Hurray"). A 30-minute film was made on the history of the ILGWU, including footage from the event in which Eleanor spoke ("Anniversary").

As the 1957 film *The Joker Is Wild* opens, Joe E. Lewis (Frank Sinatra) sings in a 1930s Prohibition speakeasy. When he tries to leave and move on to another legitimate gig, mobsters cut his vocal cords, and after falling into alcoholism and gambling, Lewis eventually transitions to work as a comedian. The story is based on the real life of Joe E. Lewis, and Mitzi Gaynor, Jeanne Crain, and Eddie Albert also star. Charles Vidor directs this Paramount musical drama and biopic, which won the Oscar for Best Music Original Song for "All the Way," sung by Sinatra. The song made it to number two on the *Billboard* charts. To mark the passage of time and recovery, newspaper headlines move across the screen, including "Roosevelt Elected." Archival footage is shown of FDR and ER on Inauguration Day. Then "Prohibition Repealed" appears, followed by "F.D.R. Wins Second Term!" before the action picks up again, the audience realizing that years have passed.

Oftentimes, ER promoted films or attended premieres to encourage support or donations to causes in which she believed. On the February 18, 1949, episode of *The Eleanor and Anna Roosevelt Program*, the ABC radio show ER hosted with her daughter Anna, their guest was Ida Lupino, the only female director working in Hollywood at the time, who was known for social problem films. Lupino talked about her new movie *Not Wanted*, about an unmarried woman with an unwanted pregnancy. It was quite controversial, with a struggle to get the film past the MPPDA, and documents show that the "most important item of all" from the censors was that "the sin is shown to be wrong." Attacks from the public and press were virulent, and Eleanor was taking a stand by booking Lupino to talk about her first film as a producer and director.

A letter from John Chapple, managing editor of the *Ashland* (Wisconsin) *Daily Press*, exemplified extreme conservative objections: "The Hollywood attack upon normal family life has been and is deadly, and the criminals consciously carrying it on as a money-making proposition are criminals against our society, and if I had my way would be eliminated from circulation as traitors by electrocution." On the radio show, ER speaks first from New York on expanding markets overseas, and then after Anna makes clear that "both Mother and I have always felt that there is no such thing as an illegitimate child," Anna goes on to interview Lupino about the issues surrounding the film. Eleanor did not herself speak to Lupino, who was in

Hollywood with Anna, but progressive attention was brought to a taboo issue with the attachment of the Roosevelt name ("Eleanor and Anna").

Variety discussed the film's grosses with the accepted misogyny of the era: "Lack of box-office names, despite it being a sex picture, probably hurt" ("Bob Hope"). *The New York Times* felt that in the desire "to avoid cheap sensationalism, the producers have come up with a picture that is dramatically limp when it is not downright dull" ("The Screen"). But the public flocked to see the movie, which grossed an astonishing $1 million. The film begins with heartfelt text on the screen: "This is a story told one hundred thousand times each year. We wish to express our deep appreciation to the many hospitals and institutions of mercy the country over, without whose gracious help this picture could never have been made." Unfortunately, lead Sally Forrest as Sally Kelton is a B movie actor in a B movie. She is a young woman led astray by an older smooth-talking piano player and the promise of a more exciting life, but he is a man who really cares nothing for her. At least the Production Code Office allowed her to live in the end, after being punished for her "crime."

News item, Hollywood, November 10, 1954: "Mrs. Eleanor Roosevelt narrowly escaped injury when a large spotlight exploded while she was visiting the set of *The Desperate Hours* on the Paramount lot. Luckily she had her back turned to the light. Humphrey Bogart, star of the picture, and three members of the crew were cut by flying glass and treated at the studio hospital" ("Chatter"). According to another report, the "1000-watt light exploded with a roar" three feet away from ER, just after she walked onto the Paramount set and was speaking with Bogart. "I ducked," she explained ("FDR's Widow"). In the 1955 Paramount release, directed by William Wyler, a group of escaped convicts led by Bogart invades a home in Indianapolis and takes the family hostage. Fredric March and Arthur Kennedy also star, but Bogart's performance dominates in a surprisingly gripping story. ER plays down the production incident in "My Day":

> I went to one of the film lots, and while there I paid a visit to the studio where Humphrey Bogart and Frederic [*sic*] March were rehearsing. As we stood there, one of the big light bulbs burst. No one was badly hurt. Mr. Bogart had a slight scratch on his forehead from which blood trickled down. But I saw no other casualty and was not even startled by the explosion which, though a little louder than that from an ordinary bulb, was not very unusual.
>
> Little did I realize that the newspapers would seize on this mild excitement to give us some very hectic hours answering the telephone because of the reports that there had been some real danger present. This was all nonsense, but just showed me again how easy it is to create an excitement out of nothing [8 Nov. 1954].

Bogart was a Roosevelt supporter and a member of the Hollywood Victory Caravan during the war. ER had also seen him on previous visits to Los Angeles ("My Day" 18 Jan. 1950).

With all the hullabaloo about the incident on *The Desperate Hours* set, gossip columnist Hedda Hopper also reported that ER was on the Paramount lot to screen singer and comedian Danny Kaye's film *Assignment Children*, just stopping by to see Bogart. Photographers followed Kaye on a trip to Asia for the United Nations Children's Fund, bringing medicine, inoculations, and food to impoverished children. Stops included India, Japan, Korea, Myanmar, and Thailand, with powdered milk, tuberculosis and polio vaccines, penicillin to combat yaws, and DDT to wipe out malarial mosquitoes. The short film was shown in U.S. movie theaters, and patrons were encouraged to donate to UNICEF. However, Hopper made sure to note that ER was there to see the film Kaye "made with taxpayers' money for the United Nations" ("Looking" 1954). In fact, his trip was for the UN, but the picture itself was produced by Paramount, which holds the copyright. Eleanor wrote, "The concept abroad of a Hollywood actor and of Hollywood films is usually something very different from this present film. It will be a help for Europeans to realize that a very successful Hollywood actor cares enough about the children of the world to give so much of his time and of his money to help a U.N. organization" ("My Day" 20 Oct. 1955).

In March 1956, ER took part in a broadcast in which the foreign language newspapers of New York gave their annual awards for the three best films of the year, one to a British film, one European, and one American. *The Prisoner* was chosen as the British film, *Umberto D* as the Italian film, and *Marty* from the United States. She shared that *Marty* had been successful in New York City, but she was unsure about the rest of the nation ("My Day" 14 Mar. 1956). The U.S. winner, about a middle-aged woman and man who meet and fall in love after they both think the time has passed for such things, was certainly popular across the country. It won the Oscar for Best Picture, as well as Best Actor for Ernest Borgnine, director for Delbert Mann, and screenwriter for Paddy Chayefsky. ER appeared in press coverage of the Foreign Language Press event with United Artists advertising director Roger H. Lewis and Foreign Press members Sigmund Gottlober and Dr. Nathan Swerdlin ("They Made").

Winning the Oscar for both screenwriting and cinematography, director and producer Stanley Kramer was also nominated for both Best Picture and Best Director, and Tony Curtis and Sidney Poitier were both nominated for Best Actor Oscar for 1958's *The Defiant Ones*. Poitier was the first Black actor nominated in this category, and he would also win the BAFTA. The film is about two convicts in the South, one Black and one White chained together, who must cooperate to escape and avoid capture. ER presented Poitier with the Silver Bear from the 1958 Berlin International Film Festival in her New York apartment ("To Present"). She wrote about his magnificent performance and potential impact of the movie:

> The story itself is dramatically done. Although I did not find it always completely convincing, the story does show that two human beings can come to look upon each other as fellow men, not as a Negro or a white man. In the present circumstances, I wonder if this film will reach the South. That is where it ought to be played; but I suppose even the superb acting of Tony Curtis and Mr. Poitier will not induce Southern moviegoers to see something which forces them to recognize a reality. But it will do us good in the North, too, so I am glad to hear that it will be shown in many cities all over the country ["My Day" 26 Aug. 1958].

It must have felt quite revolutionary for the time, although Eleanor's comment about unconvincing scenarios is on the mark.

In April 1961, the Republican National Committee released a mock list of Oscar nominations targeting the Democrats. Lyndon Johnson, Robert Kennedy, Adlai Stevenson, and others in the Kennedy administration made up most of the list, while Eleanor Roosevelt received the tongue-in-cheek nomination for Best Actress for *On the Beach* ("GOP"). Directed by Stanley Kramer and starring Gregory Peck, Ava

Gardner, Fred Astaire, and Anthony Perkins, the movie was nominated for two real Oscars and was one of the first post–nuclear apocalypse films to appear on-screen. The implication was that ER and other Democrats were on the way to causing a nuclear war.

Advertisements for the Italian film *Anna's Sin* featured a Black man and a White woman in an embrace under the text, "Only our shadows are equal." Around this: "It sears the screen!" "It scalds the screen!" "Some called it sin…. Some called it shame! But none dared call it by its real name." The film is now not available to the public, so potential viewers can only assume its real name is interracial love. A Black American actor goes to Italy and falls in love with a White woman. In "My Day," Eleanor wrote about the diversity of the Americans who fell fighting for their country in World War II, which led her into a provocative comment about *Anna's Sin*:

> I could not help thinking of this while I watched a preview of a movie the other night, called *Anna's Sin*, which deals with one phase of the color problem here in our country. An arresting story, it is delicately handled and is interesting from beginning to end. If and when it is commercially produced, I am sure it will be of interest to many people. Though the theme may be deduced from the title, *Anna's Sin*, it makes one wonder exactly whose sin it is [5 Apr. 1961].

An advertisement in *Box Office* magazine featured ER's words about the picture: "An arresting story from beginning to end … delicately handled" ("*Anna's Sin*").

Other premiere events made the news. United Artists released *The Time of Your Life*, based on the existential Pulitzer Prize–winning play by William Saroyan. H.C. Potter directed, James and his sister Jeanne Cagney costarred, and brother William Cagney produced. A group of regulars hang around a bar in San Francisco, talk, dance, play the piano, and tell stories. The sign outside says "Come and be yourself." The New York benefit premiere of the 1948 film aided the Wiltwyck School for Boys, a residential school for troubled adolescents in upstate New York and one of ER's favorite charities. She often invited the boys to Hyde Park in the summer. For the New York premiere, she hosted a fundraising dinner party before the opening, with additional hosts including Ruth Field, Alfred Gwynne Vanderbilt, Jr., and friend Trude Lash ("Wiltwyck"). Identified as a member of Wiltwyck's executive board, Eleanor addressed the audience from the stage and appears with Jimmy Cagney in press photos. "James Cagney is especially sympathetic to underprivileged youths and their problems since he himself was born in the district known to N.Y. police as 'guerrilla jungle,'" she said ("The Times"). Cagney campaigned for FDR and described himself as a "strong Roosevelt liberal" (Cagney 120). He gives his usual commanding performance, but sister Jeanne does not act on the same level. It is not a film easily enjoyed today, although the banality is part of the point.

In September 1948, French company Pathé Cinema opened Paris, a new foreign-language theater in New York City. Proceeds from the opening night film *La symphonie pastorale* (*Pastoral Symphony*), directed by Jean Delannoy, went to five French charities, and Eleanor served as one of the sponsors of the event. The site of the 16-story building of which the new theater was a part once held the mansion of Charles B. Alexander, a next door neighbor of the Vanderbilts and an uncle of a different Eleanor Roosevelt, married to Theodore Roosevelt, Jr. Marlene Dietrich cut the ribbon during the opening ceremony for the Paris (Waldman). ER also attended the August 1951 New York premiere of the Twentieth Century–Fox biblical drama *David and Bathsheba* starring Gregory Peck, Susan Hayward, and Raymond Massey. Other noted guests included Aubrey S. Eban, Israeli ambassador to the U.S., along with Milton Berle and Dietrich ("Broadway").

In September 1951, ER went to see *The River*, directed by Jean Renoir, now known as the greatest of all French directors, and produced by American Kenneth McEldowney. British writer Rumer Godden grew up in India and is best known for *Black Narcissus* (1947). *The River* focuses on three young women in India recently returned home after being educated in the U.K., all in love with the same American man. Renoir uses Technicolor for the first time as these lives are contrasted with the Ganges River along which they live in Bengal. Eleanor wrote: "As far as the story goes, of course, it is laid in the background of Indian tradition and religion, but the human emotions of the people, whether Indians or Britishers or any other nationality, are about the same. Perhaps the real message of this feast for eye and ear on the human side is that we remember that the basic qualities of all people seem the same" ("My Day" 20 Sept. 1951).

Although she had not yet been to India, ER visited in March 1952, when she and American ambassador Chester Bowles attended the film's premiere in Delhi along with Indian dignitaries. Eleanor delivered a welcome speech from the stage in a fundraiser for the Indian National Children's Fund, along with McEldowney. *The New York Times* reported that the event was more significant than just a film: "The extraordinary Indian premiere of *The River*, prize winning film made in Bengal by a United States producer dovetailed spectacularly tonight into a stream of enthusiasm for United States that has been swelling in this country since the $190,000,000 wheat loan and the $54,000,000 in the technical assistance program were delivered" ("India-U.S."). Director Martin Scorsese speaks about seeing this film at age nine, believing it to be one of the greatest Technicolor films ever made (FilmStruck). In the coming-of-age story, the river always keeps flowing, regardless of individual lives or deaths along its banks. Today there is a documentary-like quality to viewing India in Technicolor from 1950, despite the overly dramatic British actors who make it uncomfortable to watch. The colonialist nature of the story is extremely dated, and a British mother states to her daughter that "having children for the man you love is a precious, sanctified work. It's the meaning of a woman."

In September 1952, a delegation of top-ranking actors, producers, directors, and cinematographers from the Indian film industry arrived in the United States for a four-week tour. Stops included a visit with President Truman in Washington, D.C., a luncheon at the United Nations Secretariat, and a tour of Hollywood. Also on the schedule for the group was tea with ER in Hyde Park ("Indian").

She was expected to turn out for the January 1953 New York premiere of *The Jazz Singer*, a remake of the 1927 sound sensation, minus Al Jolson's blackface. This Warner Brothers Technicolor version was directed by Michael Curtiz, starring Danny Thomas and Peggy Lee in the story of the cantor who really wants to be a singer on Broadway. Proceeds of the event went to the National Foundation for Infantile Paralysis, with ER mentioned first in the list of notables attending, including the film's leads, plus Milton Berle, Sid Caesar, Salvador Dalí, Marlene Dietrich, Zsa Zsa

Gabor, Jackie Gleason, New York mayor Vincent Impellitteri, Rosalind Russell, and Robert Taylor ("Notables," "*Jazz*").

The June 1954 full-page *New York Times* advertisement for the New York "Gala World Premiere" of *The Unconquered*, a documentary about Helen Keller's life, featured ER along with other celebrity endorsements from Judith Anderson, Henry Fonda, Lillian Gish, Helen Hayes, and Mary Martin. The text of Eleanor's endorsement read, "*The Unconquered* is a most moving and dramatic picture!" Struck both deaf and blind by illness, Keller learned to communicate and worked as a disability rights advocate, author, and lecturer. ER became a friend and would later write the 1961 reprint introduction to Helen's autobiography *The Story of My Life*. She is said to have also helped raise money for the movie's production, which won director and producer Nancy Hamilton an Oscar for Best Documentary Feature (Sweeney). The film is alternatively known as *Helen Keller in Her Story* and has been selected for preservation by the Academy Film Archive.

The American Association for the United Nations (AAUN), with ER as chair of the board of governors, sponsored the March 1959 Twentieth Century–Fox premiere of *The Diary of Anne Frank* at the RKO Palace Theatre in New York. Eleanor was dedicated to carrying the message of the UN across the country and the world, and this special benefit was an AAUN fundraiser. Douglas Fairbanks, Jr., organized a special invitation-only screening, followed by the world premiere for which ER purchased the first tickets ("*Anne*," "News Capsules"). *The Diary* is the true story of Jewish teenager Anne Frank, who hid for two years with her family in an attic in Nazi-occupied Amsterdam before being captured and dying in the Bergen-Belsen concentration camp. It is a story of resilience, hope, and appreciation of life. Eleanor had written an introduction to the U.S. edition of the book in 1952. Directed by George Stevens, this was the first film adaptation, winning three Academy Awards for Best Black and White Cinematography, Black and White Art Direction, and Shelley Winters as Best Supporting Actress.

ER was guest of honor at a special New York screening of Allied Artists' German import *The Bridge* (*Die Brücke*) in February 1961 ("New York Sound Track"). The film depicts a time at the end of World War II when Germany is being overrun, its military fleeing, but young teenage boys are pressed into action to fight for Nazi honor. A sympathetic officer keeps a group of 16-year-old recruits from going to the front where they would be slaughtered, assigning them to defend a bridge that has no consequence in the outcome of the war. The production won the Golden Globe for Best Foreign Language Film and was nominated for an Oscar in the same category. It was rare for ER to criticize a film in "My Day," as she routinely mentioned only those she recommended. However, Eleanor devoted an entire column to the movie and the profound issues it brought up for her and the young people with whom she watched. She was not ready to accept a story that could be read to glorify the German cause, even though it does so while commenting on the innocence of the young men who were brainwashed into believing the Nazi lie. Their deaths meant nothing. She wrote:

> Apart from propaganda purposes I can see little real value in it. The film, however, does show the horrors of war, and apparently the young people with me had been invited on the theory

that the young should know what war is like. Now, it may be granted that the young should know. But isn't a film like this just a little deceiving? We are never again going to fight as we did in World War II. A nuclear war will be one in which people will be destroyed in a matter of seconds…. Above everything, we must insist that we learn to live together in the future and that the primary aim of a nation is no longer to learn to die for one's country. It is more difficult, but far more necessary, to learn to live for one's country [27 Feb. 1961].

Learning to live, rather than die, for one's country may be one of the most important statements ever made in an Eleanor Roosevelt film review.

10

Negotiating FDR
on the Big Screen

MGM gave Eleanor the "final okay" on the actor chosen to play President Franklin Roosevelt in *The Beginning or the End* (1947), a docudrama about the development of the Manhattan Project and deployment of the atomic bomb. The production was already in progress only a year after the actual event. ER rejected Lionel Barrymore because of disparaging remarks made while the actor campaigned for Republican opponent Thomas E. Dewey in the 1944 election (East 1946). Jimmy lodged a complaint with the studio, and Barrymore wrote a letter of explanation that was hand-delivered to ER in New York by Nicholas Schenk, president of MGM's parent company Loew's. However, she did not withdraw the objection (Brady "Metro's"). "Barrymore denied the inference that he had ever cast any slurs upon the great President," but MGM chose to respect her wishes ("Studio Size-Ups"). The well-known actor told his side of the story a few years later, admitting that he may have "purpled up my prose a bit":

> After the President's death, it was proposed at Metro-Goldwyn-Mayer that I portray Mr. Roosevelt in a picture, *The Beginning of* [*sic*] *the End*. I made a test and it was considered all right. I was not permitted to do this, however, because when Mrs. Roosevelt heard about the casting she said firmly that she would withhold permission if the terrible Barrymore played her husband. This, of course, is all over the dam now, so I think I will not be misunderstood if I say that, although I was naturally disappointed by her rejection of me, I had then and I have now nothing but admiration for Eleanor Roosevelt for her attitude.
>
> I did not say the things about her husband which I was supposed to have said, but these alleged sayings were reported to her and she had every reason to believe them. Therefore, good for her! [172].

Eleanor preferred Raymond Massey for the part of Franklin, but he believed that it was particularly important to capture FDR's voice and did not feel qualified to deliver on that aspect of the performance (Harris).

By February 1947, the finished product directed by Norman Taurog was privately screened for ER, and she expressed "sentimental objections" to the five or six minutes in which Barrymore's replacement Godfrey Tearle portrayed FDR. She did not demand that the scenes be eliminated but felt that the public should be left with the real images of the president in their minds, rather than an actor, so soon after FDR's death ("Metro"). However, a week later on page one, *Variety* announced that the film had "so disturbed the late President's widow that she had consulted attorneys on the possibility of obtaining injunctions." The objection was centered around the expectation of over-the-shoulder views like those used in *Yankee Doodle Dandy*, rather than full-face shots of the actor ("Advise"). The film was released without more edits concerning the presentation of Franklin Roosevelt, while the White House objected to scenes involving President Truman—retakes were shot with a different actor, over the shoulder in shadow ("Pres. Truman"). FDR gets much more screen time than the then-current president. Truman's scene is an exposition, and not a particularly good one, detailing all the reasons for the decision to drop the bomb, something he had requested as an addition to the script ("Redo"). *Variety*'s review called Tearle's performance an "extraordinary personation" of Roosevelt, pointing out that the full-frontal view was in keeping with established tradition around representing past presidents, while living presidents like Truman were only shown in silhouette (Green). *Parents' Magazine* admired Tearle's "remarkable portrayal" of President Roosevelt, "which alone makes the film worth seeing" (C. Edwards). However, Hedda Hopper protested, "I don't blame Eleanor Roosevelt for objecting to the impersonation of her husband in the film. Godfrey Tearle was good in the role, but lacked F.D.R.'s vigor, personality and charm" ("Hollywood"). *Newsweek* called the scenes with both FDR and Truman artificial and stilted, and *The Hollywood Reporter* joked that someone had heard Sam Goldwyn say that "if President Roosevelt were alive, he'd turn over in his grave!" ("Hollywood's Atomic," Hoffman "Tales" 1947).

In March 1947, Hopper reported that J. Richard Kennedy had a two-and-a-half-hour conference with ER about his outline for a film about FDR, receiving her approval. The movie was to be titled *There's Nothing to Fear but Fear Itself*, focusing on Franklin's battle with paralysis and other experiences that led to his political philosophies. Kennedy had a six-year agreement with Jimmy on the project, expecting this film to debut in 1948. He did not know who might play FDR, but Hopper wrote, "I'd like to bet it won't be Godfrey Tearle" ("Looking" 1947). By May, the title of the film had evolved to *Freedom from Fear*, and Jimmy would share in the profits from the movie, which would be a treatment of FDR's victory over his handicap (Brady "Hollywood Briefs"). Jimmy told the press:

> Both my mother and I are in agreement that we must face the practical realities which have already become facts. Metro-Goldwyn-Mayer has already shown that regardless of the family position my father will be impersonated in motion pictures and there is a strong possibility that he may also be impersonated on stage. Therefore, we are in agreement that it is better to give full assistance and cooperation to those in whose judgment, good taste and integrity we have full confidence rather than allow a multitude of inaccuracies and false impressions to be created [Brady "Hollywood Slack"].

Kennedy said that Eleanor's motivation for approving the film was to "re-emphasize for the world in these critical times a philosophy which will tend to bring to all the peoples of the world a measure of mental security." A series of movies on the life of FDR were expected, and "more than two dozen top Hollywood stars" had been screen tested for the role, with a movie budget of $2 million ("Freedom From"). The following year, a script had been developed to follow Louis Howe as a central character, with ER's tacit commitment ("$3,850,000"). Isolationists had plenty of negative things to say about the proposed work, suggesting collecting "facts" from the likes of Westbrook Pegler, rather than "following Eleanor Roosevelt's script," which would be a "bald and unconvincing narrative" (O'Donnell 1947). The film was never actually produced, but the motivation seemed in part to be to take charge of representations of FDR after the flap over *The Beginning or the End*.

Just two years after his death, United Artists released the 1947 feature-length documentary *The Roosevelt Story* as a tribute to FDR's early legacy, primarily constructed from newsreel footage. "Joe, an average, forgotten man," tells a tale of life during the Great Depression, until Roosevelt came along to lead the nation through the economic hardships creating the WPA, CCC, NRA, TVA, and other programs to help Americans who needed a hand. The experiences of young men working in New Deal programs is given credit for creating future soldiers who would follow the president to victory. There is also a voice of the opposition, calling FDR a "traitor to his class." Five different voices selected as typical Americans perform the narration ("Documentary"). Son Elliott served as a consultant on this production directed by Lawrence M. Klee, and ER officially gave her endorsement and approval on the script ("*Roosevelt Story*"). Watching a preview in February 1947 with United Nations Secretary General Trygve Lie, she termed it "magnificent." In her written feedback to Tola Productions, Eleanor stated, "I think this documentary film is an extraordinary editing job…. While I am aware of the fact that about every incident could make a picture in itself, as an overall review of a life, I think it is well done. I am very happy to have this film shown" ("Mrs. FDR Okays").

She lent her name to the film to help her children's finances, which was a recurring theme in later life. In a letter to friend Trude Lash, Eleanor wrote, "I am doing things, in endorsing this film and financing the place & farm & helping Elliott with a book of his Father's letters that may cause criticism. I'm letting Jimmy go ahead on a film & with his book & will help him by not interfering though I know all will cause criticism but I surmise Elliott has to be established & encouraged to become secure. Jimmy needs to make more money to give his wife the security she demands & if I can help without doing anything I think wrong, the criticism doesn't bother me" (Lash *Years Alone* 172–73). ER attended the August 1947 New York premiere with Elliott at a Globe Theatre benefit for the National Foundation for Infantile Paralysis, where she described the film as "something very real" (Allen, "F.D.R. Film"). Others in attendance included Lie, Bernard Baruch, Irving Berlin, head of the British delegation to the UN Sir Alexander Cadogan, Eddie Cantor, Henry Morgenthau, Jr., New York mayor William O'Dwyer, and Ambassador Extraordinary of the Philippines General Carlos Romulo, with three thousand people gathered outside the theater. In a short speech before the screening, she declared that the picture showed the culmination of her husband's hopes, "the spirit of world neighborliness through which the United Nations without which, if it fails, nothing we do will matter very much" ("Many Celebrities").

The film was judged most likely to contribute to world peace at the 1947 Brussels International Film Festival ("Our Respects"), and ER wrote about it in "My Day" both before and after the New York screening. "We have come to New York to see *The Roosevelt Story* tonight—the documentary film which won an international prize in Brussels as the film which would do the most for peace this year. With all my heart I hope that this is so, and if it is so, let us hope that every person in the United States will see the film" (22 Aug. 1947). "It is going to remind each one of us of that which meant something to us in the years from 1933 to 1945. And perhaps we need that reminder to keep accepting the responsibilities which are ours today" (23 Aug. 1947). In the film, Eleanor only merits a mention of FDR's marriage to her during his younger years. Later, she appears in the background of campaign and inaugural footage. Finally, when Franklin wins the second election in a landslide, the narrator says, "When congratulations were in order, Mrs. Roosevelt was there as usual, happy because she was proud and because he was happy. Yes, there's no doubt about it. The First Lady in the White House was also first with FDR, and more than anyone else, FDR knew her value to him and to the country." Soon the focus turns to trouble in Europe and the royal visit to the United States. "The King and Queen of England got a warm welcome from FDR and Mrs. Roosevelt. There were hot dogs with mustard right on the President's lawn. They got a taste of real American hospitality." FDR wins a third election and leads the nation as we prepare for war and begin the fight. Average Joe is serving in North Africa now. We see the final years during World War II and the fourth election before Franklin's death in 1945. His legacy lives on in the lives of everyday Americans and in the dream of the United Nations. "To the old folks he left security and comfort. To the young folks he left hope and the chance to live and look ahead like human beings. And to the kids he left peace."

The Roosevelt Story was packaged as a double bill for theaters along with *Fame Is the Spur*, a political drama about the career of former British prime minister Ramsay MacDonald ("Political Dualer"). *Variety* marked its release as the "first gun" fired in the perception that films could be a powerful force of persuasion in presidential campaigns, with U.S. politicians "realizing the potency of such fare if harnessed into a vote-getting apparatus" ("CIO"). Plans were to dub it in 14 different languages for worldwide distribution ("Documentary"). *Newsweek* called it a top-notch and exciting documentary dramatization that took 16 months to produce by reviewing and editing two million feet of newsreel and family footage at a total cost of $250,000. Although FDR's "virtues perhaps are not overdone," they noted that the president's "vices go virtually unmentioned." The total effect was "one of emotionalized eulogy" but nevertheless a successful representation covering a 40-year span in the public and private life of FDR ("Forty Years"). NAACP leader Walter White, who had not always agreed with Franklin Roosevelt, urged his readers to see the film, feeling as if FDR's "moving words about freedom and opportunity for the working man" would reveal how far to the right the country had moved since his death ("People"). Earl Robinson, who composed the film's music as well as folk songs such as "Joe Hill," was later targeted in "Red Channels: The Report of Communist Influence in Radio and Television." Published in 1950, the pamphlet listed Robinson with *The Roosevelt Story* as one of the pieces of "evidence" of his contribution to communist manipulation in the entertainment industry. Perhaps *The Hollywood Reporter* review supplied the best summation: "Those who loved FDR will love *The Roosevelt Story*. Those who hated him and his loved ones will hate it" (Hoffman "*Roosevelt*").

British Pathé newsreel program *People in Camera* included footage of ER

Franklin, Eleanor, and Sara Delano Roosevelt in a photograph from 1931 used to promote the 1947 documentary *The Roosevelt Story*, distributed by United Artists (Franklin D. Roosevelt Presidential Library & Museum).

in London for the premiere of *The Roosevelt Story* in 1948. Other topics in the three-minute newsreel include a program for young men building new houses in Wales, a feather factory in Poland, and the All-American Girls Professional Baseball League in the United States. The narrator says:

> Coincidental with the unveiling of Britain's memorial to Franklin Roosevelt comes the screen presentation of his life. The occasion is unique, for the crowds milling in Leicester Square come to pay tribute not to the usual film stars, but to the wife of a great man, Mrs. Eleanor Roosevelt. Meeting a number of Britain's leading film personalities attending the premiere, Mrs. Roosevelt receives a bouquet from child star Margaret O'Brien, whose part is to recall the late President's call to youth of all ages.

ER would watch the film again with Her Majesty Queen Mother Elizabeth in April 1947 and in November 1948 for a French preview in Paris ("My Day" 20 Apr. 1948, 24 Nov. 1948). Princess Elizabeth, the future Queen Elizabeth II, also accepted a print of the film as a wedding gift from producers Martin Levine and Oliver Unger ("*FDR Story*").

A 1951 page-one headline in *Motion Picture Daily* trumpeted, "Stanley Kramer to Film Life of F.D. Roosevelt." The producer and director had been granted rights to film the life story of FDR in collaboration with Eleanor for a Columbia Pictures release. He estimated that the project would take three years to research and put on the screen. "I am happy that Mr. Kramer will be the one to make this picture," ER said. "I am familiar with his work and have great confidence in his honesty and integrity as well as his ability" ("Stanley"). ER had interviewed Kramer previously on her radio show ("Eleanor Roosevelt Program"). *Time Magazine* predicted that Pulitzer Prize–winning FDR speechwriter Robert Sherwood was the most likely scriptwriter, with ER serving as adviser ("Cinema"). This same year, HUAC was targeting Kramer's partner Carl Foreman as part of its anti-communist crusade, and Foreman became a victim of the Hollywood blacklist. Kramer produced a series of controversial films such as *The Defiant Ones* (a Black and White prisoner escape chained together), *On the Beach* (nuclear apocalypse), *Inherit the Wind* (on trial for teaching evolution), *Judgment at Nuremberg* (war crimes of German civilians), *High Noon* (parable of the Hollywood blacklist), and *Guess Who's Coming to Dinner* (an interracial couple visits her White parents) and defined himself as a "Roosevelt liberal" (Kramer 8). As late as 1990, he was working on adapting the book *Eleanor Roosevelt's Niggers* into a film about the 761st Black tank battalion in World War II, but it was never produced (Broeske).

In ER's February 1952 "If You Ask Me" column, there was further discussion of the biopic about FDR when she was asked, "You said in *McCall's* recently that you didn't want the movies to make a picture of your husband's life. Is it true that you've changed your mind, and why have you?" She replied:

> It is true I have been averse to having a picture made as long as my husband's actual looks and personality were still fresh in people's minds. Mr. Stanley Kramer, however, recently pointed out to me that if no one were allowed to do research while the people who knew my husband were still alive it would be difficult to produce a picture which would give the true sense of a living person. Mr. Kramer also pointed out that the research and preparation for such a picture as he wished to make would take a few years. I saw his point and have agreed to let him go ahead.

Kramer's widow revealed much later that a history with Eleanor Roosevelt was fundamental to Stanley Kramer the man and his legacy as a controversial filmmaker. In a 2018 interview, Karen Sharpe Kramer noted that Stanley read about the Marian Anderson incident in which the DAR refused to let her sing at Constitution Hall because of her race. ER resigned from the organization and prompted a concert at the Lincoln Memorial instead when the filmmaker was 13 years old. "That impressed a young Stanley Kramer and he wrote her a letter and told her how proud he was of her," said Karen. "She wrote him back, and that began a long relationship and she became his mentor at a very young age. I think she informed a lot of his opinions and his ideals" (Ballesteros).

However, Kramer lost his deal with Columbia Pictures and with it the option to film the FDR biopic. In December 1954, *Variety* reported on page one that the William Morris Agency represented the family to offer the rights to someone else ("Heirs"). A few months later, "Mrs. Eleanor Roosevelt had some execs in the picture business puzzled this week with her comments on whether there's to be, or not to be, a film based on the life of Franklin D. Roosevelt" ("If FDR"). They refer to a testy reply in her April 1955 "If You Ask Me" column. She was asked a question about the details of a movie about FDR and responded:

> I am not surprised that you have only found fragmentary reports, because no "deal" has been made. I doubt very much that I will ever give you all the details, since I don't think it is anybody's business except the members of the family and those who made the agreement with us.
>
> It would be impossible for me to give you any information now, because I have only said I would be willing to consider a proposition if it should be made. The choice as to who will play the parts will be in the hands of the people more accustomed to casting than I am.

Daily Variety found the reaction amusing, considering the controversy over who played FDR in *The Beginning or the End*. "Switch from a Celeb: Well, remake the press—stop the front page—tear out the editor—here's news: Mrs. Eleanor Roosevelt, in March *McCall's* mag, says she doesn't know who's going to play her in the FDR pic—and she doesn't care!" (Swisher).

The first completed FDR biopic and major portrayal of Eleanor for audiences came with *Sunrise at Campobello*, a Tony-winning Broadway play and 1960 film centering on FDR's comeback from polio. The film's tagline reveals other themes: "Ralph Bellamy as the man who never forgot how to smile…. Greer Garson as the woman who never forgot how to love." The big, happy Roosevelt family is challenged by Franklin's disease and recovery, but all come together to prepare him for the speech nominating Al Smith as presidential candidate, marking FDR's ascendency on the national stage. Eleanor is the loving wife and nursemaid who cries with him, shares embraces and intimate conversations about his loneliness, and sacrifices herself on his behalf. Her motivation is her love and appreciation, with lines like "When I was an orphan adolescent, I felt unloved, unwanted. With you, I've always felt needed, wanted. That's a blessing."

Greer Garson won the Golden Globe and an Oscar nomination for the role as Eleanor, whose total devotion is credited in large part for her husband's success. FDR (Ralph Bellamy) overcomes physical adversity and, in the process, begins to better understand the struggles of the common person. ER served as a consultant on the film, and writer Dore Schary, who had replaced the iconic Louis B. Mayer as head of production at MGM, only to be forced out himself in 1956, was in the business of making both Roosevelts larger-than-life individuals. For movie-version Eleanor, this means becoming super-wife and mother without an identity outside of her family.

FDR's portrayal is quite different from that of most men in biographical films, as it is unusual for a man to be as centrally concerned with love and marriage as part of his life story. Franklin Roosevelt could be said to be feminized here, in need of love and care, but this portrayal is considered the result of his infirmities, as in the end, he is shown leaving the domestic sphere, going out into the political world of men again when he is able to achieve the appearance of walking again in public. The film closely ties ER's activities to FDR's condition and includes political mastermind Louis Howe (Hume Cronyn) coaxing her to begin political speaking engagements. "Eleanor, this work has to be done. You are for a time Franklin's eyes, ears, and legs. You must go places he can't go." This despite protestations from Franklin's mother Sara (Ann Shoemaker): "Is it true that Eleanor is out making another speech? You know my feelings about politics generally. It's a tawdry business for a man and I believe shocking for a woman." Both Louis and FDR overrule Sara in favor of Eleanor's "eyes, ears, and legs" keeping the Roosevelt name active, but there is no discussion of the kind of issues with which she is concerned or the people and groups she meets outside of the household. Unlike the wartime visit in *Great Day*, for example, ER does not primarily connect with other women, only her family. *Sunrise at Campobello* supports 1950s American familial ideals by presenting ER as the perfect wife and mother who only leaves her home to support her husband and always comes back to her large, happy family.

What did Eleanor think of *Sunrise at Campobello*? She did not comment on it extensively, but noted, "It was a play, so far as I personally was concerned, about someone else" (*Autobiography* 411). Mary Fickett's stage portrayal was "sweet," but "I am afraid I was never really like Mr. Schary's picture of myself" ("My Day" 4 Feb. 1958). Son Jimmy merely said, "Life is not always as the movies would have it" (*My Parents* 55). ER's character is too perfect, too devoted, too much of a saint, concerned only for her husband's recovery and political success. One reviewer at the time pointed out its "particular brand of wholesomeness and sentimentality," a view

more prevalent for those watching today in more cynical times ("*Sunrise*"). It was not until after Eleanor's death that Jonathan Daniels wrote about FDR's affair with Lucy Mercer in *The Time Between the Wars*, published in 1966. Later that same year, Jimmy addressed the affair in a collection of FDR's personal letters, and Joseph Lash's 1971 book *Eleanor and Franklin* extensively examined its impact on ER. Later, both sons Elliott (1973) and Jimmy (1976) had more to say in books about their famous family. However, in the period before public knowledge of the affair, although there were whispers and an obnoxious 1949 Westbrook Pegler column about Lucy's presence in Warm Springs

Ralph Bellamy and Greer Garson star as Franklin and Eleanor Roosevelt in *Sunrise at Campobello* (1960, Warner Brothers). The film focuses on FDR's recovery from polio and ER's unwavering support as his wife (author's collection).

when Franklin died, coverage of Eleanor was likely to focus on her role as wonderful wife (Pegler "Why Is").

Friend Edna Gurewitsch mentioned that the "motivation for cooperating with the project became clear when she explained to David [Gurewitsch] that her five children, seemingly always in need of money, would share in the royalties" (119). Tax documents show that Schary paid Franklin Jr. $98,092.24 in 1958 to be divided among the five siblings equally, for approximately $18,000 each after legal fees to reimburse them for invasion of their rights of privacy ("Tax Court"). *Variety* reported that Schary and "members of the Roosevelt family" were to share in the film's profits ("Guild"). The night that the Broadway show premiered, Gurewitsch remembers ER saying, "The play had nothing to do with me.... I did not recognize myself at all" (120). FDR biographer Geoffrey Ward notes that ER told her friends that the play had as much to do with her and her family "as the man in the moon" (Ward 621). Bellamy recalled her comments on the New York opening night as "a good play, but about as much like the Roosevelt family as some people from Mars." But there is more to the story. Bellamy attended a dinner afterward and describes Jimmy rushing up to Eleanor when she arrived. "Mother! What's this I hear you said about the play? … That it's about as much like the Roosevelt family as some people from Mars. You didn't say that, did you?" "Yes, I did," she replied. "You didn't really mean it, did you?" Bellamy says, "She was visibly moved, and with quivering lips and downcast eyes she said, 'No, I didn't.' Then she wrapped herself up again for the cold January night and left." Bellamy declines to offer further commentary but notes that "the manuscript had been approved by each of the family and much of the dialogue was verbatim" (247). Jimmy wrote later, "She thought it inaccurate and overly dramatic, but most of us thought it all right. Most of its inaccuracies were unimportant and provided dramatic effect…. The play was a good piece of fictionalized fact and at the least a tribute to the spirit of our parents" (313).

Eleanor mentioned the project for the first time in a 1957 "My Day" column. Of note is the fact that both the movie and play were planned from the beginning:

> I went to Hyde Park late Thursday afternoon with Dore Schary, who has just announced that he will write a play and produce a movie on a short period of my husband's life. He wished to visit the library there and talk over some of his plans. I hope that he will be successful, for the period he has chosen to write about was a dramatic one where the qualities of a man of character can be universally shown to apply to many situations in life [13 Apr. 1957].

Schary worked as chair of the Hollywood for Roosevelt committee when FDR ran for a third term and explains, "I met Mrs. Roosevelt for the first time when she visited Los Angeles and, of course, fell in love with her" (106). They had seen one another many times over the years, and when he had the idea for *Sunrise at Campobello* as a play, he and wife Miriam stopped in for lunch at Val-Kill with the sketch of the basic story. ER asked for a more detailed outline and suggested that he contact Franklin Jr. for further discussions.

After finishing the writing, he describes his trepidation at what ER might think:

> At eight o'clock promptly I stood alone in front of Mrs. R's town house in the east seventies, adjusted my tie, took a deep breath, and pushed the bell button. Typically, Mrs. R. herself opened the door, welcomed me, and moved me into the living room, where were gathered

Lady Reading, a cherished friend of Mrs. R., Henry Morgenthau, Jr., Jimmy and Franklin Roosevelt, Jr., Trudi Lash, and Mrs. R., which made an audience of six. Mrs. R. seated herself facing me only three feet away to accommodate her bad hearing…. When I finished reading there was a pause. No one said anything. I surmised they were waiting for Mrs. R. to have the first word. I saw that she had wiped her eyes—then she gently raised her head. Her eyes were red. She said, "It sounds exactly like Franklin" [Schary 317].

Now the others joined in and discussed some issues like the harsh treatment of Sara Delano Roosevelt, the fact that there was no electricity at Campobello then, and whether FDR was using canes or crutches in 1928. ER's feedback included "that I was too kind to her. I said I truly didn't think so." Eleanor told him, "Dore, you've written a beautiful play—even though you've been much too generous to me." Schary reveals, "What I didn't know at the time, nor did most people, was the truth of the story of FDR and his affair with Lucy Mercer and the biting hurt it had brought to Eleanor. But what pleased her, Franklin, Jr., told me later, was that I had handled the illness and her valiant response to FDR's travail with truth and compassion." As he left, Schary kissed her cheek (342–45).

The play's audience on opening night in New York included ER, all five Roosevelt children, Adlai Stevenson, President Truman's daughter Margaret Truman Daniel and husband Clifton Daniel, and Senator John F. Kennedy. "Mrs. R chose to sit in the second row from the back on opening night. She said, 'I want them to look at the play and not at me.'" If he heard it, Schary does not mention ER's statement that night about her portrayal (356, 366). He wrote her a letter expressing "eternal admiration" and hoping that she had been "comforted and satisfied" by reactions to the play (Schary to ER). She responded saying that she was indeed delighted by its reception, and Schary was asked to give the May 1958 Memorial Day address at Hyde Park (ER to Schary, Schary "Address"). In a June 1960 "My Day" column, she casually mentioned working on the movie: "I went up to Hyde Park Tuesday morning with Nannine Joseph and Miss Corr, and we arrived at the library to find the filming for Dore Schary's movie, *Sunrise at Campobello*, in full swing…. We returned to my cottage for lunch and soon the whole movie cast came over to do some filming there" (9 June 1960).

Few of the films that feature Eleanor have been seriously analyzed by scholars, except *Sunrise* as a major FDR biopic. In his book on politicians in American movies, Harry Keyishian recognizes that this film was made when ER was still alive and "fiercely protective of her husband's legacy—which was, in large measure, her own as well—so the film projects the pair simply as a devoted, loving couple." However, by critiquing that "the actual state of their marriage" was not dramatized, he does not consider the timeframe here—before general knowledge of FDR's affairs or Eleanor's other loves (*Screening* 151). Another book by Bruce E. Altschuler on interpreting politics in American film makes the same point about *Sunrise*: "Overlooked, for example, are Franklin's infidelities" (28). Schary would have broached insider information or followed what were considered rumors in 1958 to make the weighty decision to include such material in a film of this period. The Motion Picture Production Code was still being enforced, albeit weakly; the old Hollywood reverence for the presidential historical film template had yet to be challenged; the presidency

In a promotional photograph for *Sunrise at Campobello* (1960, Warner Brothers), the real Eleanor Roosevelt pours tea for Greer Garson, who played Eleanor in the film, June 1960 (author's collection).

was still largely revered; and the towering figure of FDR had died only 15 years prior. Hagiography was no surprise. In another article, Keyishian pushed the point that Schary wrote *Sunrise* in part to support ER in her role representing FDR's legacy "in her continuing work for a better world" and longstanding commitment to the United Nations. He also called Garson's "a justly admired performance" for her turn as Eleanor ("Confidence" 119–20, *Screening* 150).

At the time, many reviewers recognized that they were looking at too loving a portrait of the former president. *The New Yorker* noted, "something more than mere Technicolor causes the screen to go soft, to run at the edges and sometimes at the center." Yet the same piece also praised Bellamy and Garson "for their often uncanny success in taking off F.D.R. and Eleanor Roosevelt" (Gill). The *Chicago Tribune* applauded Bellamy's performance, and "Greer Garson is excellent as his wife. She has done a remarkable job of capturing the inflections of Eleanor Roosevelt's careful diction and the high timber of her voice" (Tinee). The *Saturday Review* summed up ER's role as a "model of fortitude" and singled out Garson's performance: "Miss Garson does something more, it seems to me: she has utilized make-up tricks (even to false, protruding teeth) to achieve a physical likeness to the Mrs. Roosevelt of more than thirty-five years ago; she has mimicked the famous voice with extraordinary exactitude, and she has then played her part with feeling and sympathy. It's the kind of personal triumph that sometimes leads to Academy Awards, when the collective judgment involved in Hollywood's honors system operates with reasonableness and sound taste" (Alpert). For *Photoplay*, "Greer Garson is a stunning surprise" ("*Sunrise*"). The *Christian Science Monitor* review addressed what her portrayal brought to the story with FDR at the center: "With Greer Garson giving a performance full of strengths and insights, Eleanor Roosevelt shares more fully in the meaning of FDR's ordeal. Her husband's testing time is paralleled by Mrs. Roosevelt's transformation from uncertainty and awkwardness into a woman whose political and domestic education proceed in good part simultaneously" (Beaufort).

The *Variety* review was overwhelmingly positive, calling the film a grand slam feat and "a brilliant new showcase" for Garson, whose characterization "commands respect and affection" (Pryor). Jack Entin said, "Eleanor Roosevelt is portrayed in magnificent fashion by Greer Garson. Her make-up, her facial expressions, and her inflections are those of the great lady's…. The most amazing accomplishment was Greer Garson's in an exacting role" (Entin). Although *The New Republic* gave a less than glowing review overall, Garson, "who is made to pay Mrs. Roosevelt the dubious compliment of dental imitation, gives a warm, substantial portrayal" (Kauffmann).

No one talked about what ER might have thought about the use of protruding teeth as part of the costume. *Film Quarterly* disagreed with others, not about the performance, but about the prosthetics: "Greer Garson, triumphing over a grotesque job of make-up, brings dignity and warmth to the role of Eleanor Roosevelt" (Gerckhen). Prolific *New York Times* critic Bosley Crowther was also troubled: "Greer Garson's studied make-up with buck teeth seems almost a deliberate endeavor to caricature Eleanor Roosevelt" (Crowther). ER never wrote about her overbite and the many cruel caricatures she endured, but her two front teeth were broken in a car accident in 1946 and replaced. "Now I shall have two lovely porcelain ones, which will look far better than the rather protruding large teeth which most of the Roosevelts have," she wrote ("My Day" 16 Aug. 1946). The British publication *Monthly Film Bulletin* shared a negative review of the movie's lack of interest to British audiences and pointed out Garson's "outlandish vocal mimicry" for its artificiality, and a few U.S. reviewers did the same, feeling that the voice and accent used by Garson contributed to a sense of caricature for ER, rather than an homage (Dyer). Yet another British reviewer who quite liked the film blamed part of the "frighteningly high standard of elocution" on Garson, "an actress who has long confused acting with public speaking" (Croce). However, *Time*'s staff writer judged the acting magnificent: "As Eleanor, Greer Garson offers a first-rate physical caricature, but she offers a good deal more besides: a touching picture of a harried wife and mother making the best she can of a bad business, the heroine who makes the hero possible" ("New Picture").

Garson relished the role and considered portraying Eleanor Roosevelt a great privilege, with "projecting Mrs. Roosevelt's love, dignity, wisdom and compassion" foremost in her mind (Troyan 286–87). MGM dentist Scott Christensen, who coincidentally had once been ER's dentist, constructed the custom mouthpiece. Garson studied her subject's speech patterns, observing them to be more British than American. When the cast and crew shot at Hyde Park, Eleanor gave Garson, Bellamy, and director Vincent Donehue a full tour (Archerd June 1960). The actor was pleased when a tourist noted how much she sounded like ER, and afterward, Greer wrote to a friend, "It has been for me personally, a great inspiration to study her life and character. I do admire her so much" (Troyan 291). She also wrote Schary anticipating Mrs. Roosevelt's response: "I am holding my breath, hoping so much she will like our efforts and the portrait of Eleanor will not displease her in any way" (Garson to Schary). Schary responded by thanking Greer "for the fabulous Eleanor you put on the screen" (Schary to Garson). Garson was the only one in the cast to receive an Oscar nomination and won the Golden Globe for Best Actress in a Drama, as well as Best Actress from the National Board of Review of Motion Pictures ("*Sons*"). At the Academy Awards celebration, host Bob Hope joked, "She played the part of Eleanor Roosevelt so convincingly that Westbrook Pegler now hates *her*" ("33D"). Coincidentally, Greer had been chosen to sell the first Roosevelt Victory Bond to ER in New York, and the two posed for press photos. The $200 bond was issued in the fall of 1945 in memory of FDR ("Mrs. FDR Will").

There is no record of Eleanor's response to the performance, but beforehand in "If You Ask Me," she wrote a disconnected answer to a question about her thoughts on the casting of Garson: "No, I have no feeling. You do not remember what you yourself were like in different stages of your existence, and therefore, when you see someone act as you were supposed to have acted, you accept it as you would any other performance. I am quite sure the performance will be interesting and enjoyable, whatever Miss Garson makes of the part" (Sept. 1960). In what we can assume was meant to be funny among friends, director William Wellman sent a telegram to Hedda Hopper congratulating her on being cast to play Eleanor in *Sunrise at Campobello*. Conservative Hopper, once an aspiring actor, regularly jabbed both ER and Schary in her column (Wellman).

The year before *Sunrise* hit movie theaters, NBC's *Kaleidoscope* magazine show aired "Blueprint for Biography: The Story of *Sunrise at Campobello*" on April 5, 1959. This was television's first profile of a Broadway stage hit on the hour-long short-lived program, which ran in 1958–59. Jimmy, who was then a U.S. representative from California, appeared to talk about his family's reactions to the play, as well as their comments and suggestions during the preparation of the script. Schary discussed the process of developing the story and the production and served as executive producer of this episode. Bellamy playing FDR, Fickett as ER, Henry Jones as Louis Howe, Alan Bunce as Alfred E. Smith, and Michaele Myers as Missy LeHand presented scenes from the play. Others on the program were host Charles Van Doren; Lawrence Langner, administrator of the Theatre Guild; Dr. Herman Kahn, curator of the Franklin D. Roosevelt Library in Hyde Park; and historian Arthur Schlesinger, Jr. The Polaroid Corporation sponsored half of the broadcast (NBC-New York "Participants"). *The New York Times* gave the NBC show a positive review for its behind-the-scenes information on writing, casting, and production. Without knowledge of Schary's plans to adapt the play into a film, they praised the accessibility provided for viewers who would never have a chance to see the story on stage but were able to watch the performances on television (John Shanley). Timing of the *Sunrise* film was fortuitous, as in the final scene, FDR comes back into public life by nominating Al Smith for the presidency. Dialogue discusses prejudice against Smith for his Catholicism, and pundits were aware of the implicit messages about the ghost of FDR and his presumed support for Catholic candidate John F. Kennedy in the 1960 presidential election.

In a Joseph Lash journal entry from October 1958, he briefly mentioned that in the context of a conversation about *Sunrise*, "Mrs. R said the Philip Morris people wanted to do a film about her but she's reluctant. Turned it over to Frankie. Maybe an episode" (Lash *World of Love* 495). She referred the matter to son Franklin Jr., but since *Variety* reported her connection with the William Morris Agency over a possible FDR film, Lash may have misinterpreted the parties involved. Schary wrote about the possibility of a sequel covering later dramatic events in FDR's life, but that never came to be (Schary to ER).

11

Movie Recommendations

ER used her "My Day" newspaper column, as well as other opportunities in the press or by attending premieres, to promote films that she enjoyed or felt contributed positively on social and political issues. Some of her public endorsements over the years follow.

1936 *The Story of Louis Pasteur*—"a remarkable picture of a scientist's life ... points the way to a new standard of success—selfless service to man rather than the acquisition of material possessions"
1937 *Captains Courageous*—"really lovely and well worth seeing"
1937 *The Life of Emile Zola*—"One of the movies which I shall never forget ... very well acted by Paul Muni."
1937 *Snow White and the Seven Dwarfs*—"I have never seen anything as enchanting as the animals, the color is beautiful and so is the music.... Mr. Walt Disney certainly has an enchanting imagination and I hope he does many more such films."
1937 *Wee Willie Winkie*—"very charming and no one could help but like Private Winkie"
1938 *Magie africaine*—"You will find it unusual and enthralling if you are interested in strange people, strange places and strange animals."
1938 *Pygmalion*—"all of us found delightful"
1938 *The River*—"I wish every one who still questions the need of reforestation and soil conservation, could see this movie."
1939 *Bachelor Mother*—"The movie seems an impossible story, but it is amusing and charmingly done."
1939 *Boy Slaves*—"kept everyone breathless for over an hour"
1939 *Crisis*—"Perhaps the value of this picture for us is the mere realization of the difference which freedom backed by a sense of security gives in comparison with virtual dependency where security can no longer exist."
1939 *The Giant of Norway*—"impressed me very much"
1939 *Goodbye, Mr. Chips*—"Exquisitely done. 'Mr. Chips' is so well cast and acts the part to perfection."
1939 *Land of Liberty*—"very remarkable film"
1939 *The Wizard of Oz*—"one of the great movies for children"
1939 *Wuthering Heights*—"It will be hard for anyone seeing this picture not to lose themselves in the story."
1940 *Abe Lincoln in Illinois*—"I feel it is a very moving reminder of the principles which a great man, who did not want to fight, finally found he could only preserve by fighting."

1940 *Britannia Is a Woman*—"one of the most thrilling stories I have seen on the screen"

1940 *Pastor Hall*—"I think in many ways this movie will put the ideas which are in the play more clearly before the people of this country, and that they should become more familiar with them."

1940 *Rebecca*—"Excellent. It holds your interest all the time and Judith Anderson does a wonderful piece of character acting as Mrs. Danvers. The two principals are charming and convincing."

1940 *Wheels Across India*—"beautiful and most exciting"

1941 *The Corsican Brothers*—"I can recommend ... if you want to forget what is going on around you for a little while. Everyone listened and watched breathlessly until the very end."

1941 *The Forgotten Village*—"a very beautiful movie"

1941 *Kukan: The Battle Cry of China*—"very remarkable colored moving pictures"

1941 *Major Barbara*—"very human story and one I think many of us will enjoy ... well produced and is very effective as a movie"

1941 *They Died with Their Boots On*—"very thrilling Errol Flynn movie"

1941 *Women in Defense*—"a good and informative film"

1942 *In Which We Serve*—"a very fine film ... an extraordinary experience"

1942 *Native Land*—"beautiful piece of photography and most artistically produced"

1942 *Reap the Wild Wind*—"everyone found it absorbing"

1942 *To Be or Not to Be*—"an exciting spy story"

1942 *To the Shores of Tripoli*—"a good picture and very entertaining"

1942 *Woman of the Year*—"Katharine Hepburn plays a most amusing and delightful role."

1943 *Desert Victory*—"an extraordinary picture"

1943 *Gung Ho!: The Story of Carlson's Makin Island Raiders*—"A remarkable picture and I am sure that audiences all over this country will be interested."

1944 *Meet Me in St. Louis*—"charming and gave us all a pleasant evening"

1944 *The Negro Soldier*—"a very moving record of achievement"

1944 *A Report from Miss Greer Garson*—"one of the most striking pictures I have ever seen"

1944 *Thirty Seconds Over Tokyo*—"A very good film. I am afraid there were very few dry eyes in the audience when it came to an end."

1946 *The New France*—"a particularly valuable film"

1947 *The Roosevelt Story*—"Magnificent.... I think this documentary film is an extraordinary editing job.... I think it is well done. I am very happy to have this film shown."

1948 *The Quiet One*—"Profoundly moving ... a tremendously encouraging picture and gives one a lift.... You'll find it deeply interesting."

1949 *Crusade in Europe*—"They have given to all of us—the older generation, the young people of today, and our children tomorrow, a view of what millions endured during World War II."

1949 *Home of the Brave*—"I loved *Home of the Brave*. I thought it was wonderful."

1949 *Make Way for Youth*—"The motion picture seemed to me one of the best, for presentation in a dramatic way of the problems we have before us on every level."

1950 *Our Very Own*—"about something very important—and delightfully entertaining, too"

1951 *The River*—"Perhaps the real message of this feast for eye and ear on the human side is that we remember that the basic qualities of all people seem the same."

1953 *Anna's Sin*—"An arresting story, it is delicately handled and is interesting from beginning to end.... I am sure it will be of interest to many people."

1953 *Ugetsu*—"I hope many people will see it, first because of the beauty of the scenes, and then because it gives an insight into the past history of a people with whom we have been enemies, but with whom we are striving today to be friends."

1954 *Seven Samurai*—"I found the picture, like so many Japanese films, rather bloodthirsty, but it certainly held my interest. I feel sure it will have great success, because the photography is very beautiful."

1954 *The Unconquered*—"a most moving and dramatic picture"

1955 *Assignment Children*—"It will be a help for Europeans to realize that a very successful Hollywood actor cares enough about the children of the world to give so much of his time and of his money to help a U.N. organization."

1956 *The Pursuit of Happiness*—"a really remarkable film ... one of the most moving films I have seen"

1956 *Storm Center*—"Powerful dramatic entertainment and a revelation of the real principles of democracy.... I hope this picture will be widely seen."

1957 *See It Now*, "The Lady from Philadelphia: Through Asia with Marian Anderson"—"I hope that people in every part of this country will see it. First, it is beautifully done, and next I think it will introduce many people to one of our great Americans."

1957 *Segregation and the South*—"an excellent film documentary"

1957 *Time Limit*—"You will be tense and moved by this picture, from the first scene to the last. It is well acted and well written.... Not an evening of mere entertainment but one that had real value. I believe the movie will stir deeply its audiences."

1958 *The Defiant Ones*—Sidney Poitier "certainly is a superb performer and deserves *Newsweek*'s characterization of him as the country's finest Negro actor."

1958 *I Want to Live!*—"Holds one's attention every minute, and is skillfully acted by Susan Hayward and the supporting cast."

1959 *Come Back, Africa*—"It is well worth seeing and understanding these problems."

1961 *Hand in Hand*—"Young and old will profit by it. I hope it will be widely shown!"

1961 *The Sky Above, the Mud Below*—"beautiful and intensely interesting ... sure to hold spellbound those audiences that are interested in seeing the new and the unknown"

1962 *Judgment at Nuremberg*—"I hope many of my readers will see *Judgment at Nuremburg*. It will make you think much more clearly about the dangers of the past and of the present."

PART II

On Television

12

Early TV Appearances

It was an exciting time at the WNBT New York studio. Against a backdrop of United Nations flags, Eleanor Roosevelt highlighted NBC programming on May 8, 1945, the day following VE Day, Victory in Europe Day. The war was over in the European theater, and ER made her television debut on the oldest continuously operating commercial television station in the United States, now WNBC. Interviewed by well-known lecturer and documentarian Julien Bryan, she warned viewers against apathy and war weariness. Interspersed with a feed of the celebrating crowds in Times Square, other local prominent civic leaders, clergy, military personnel, and network commentators appeared throughout the day ("Television Covers").

Robert Slater's history of CBS notes that ER often made herself available in New York City during these early years of television news and networks, although little is documented about these appearances (123). On May 6, 1948, she was interviewed about her recent trip to London by reporter Douglas Edwards on the CBS evening news program, soon to be called *Douglas Edwards with the News*. It had just begun broadcasting three days earlier as the first regularly scheduled television news program in U.S. history, and she was questioned about her reactions to conditions in England and on British views of the United Nations and the Marshall Plan ("News of Radio"). This planned appearance after returning from unveiling the FDR statue in London was reported in *Variety* as a television guest spot ("Mrs. Eleanor Roosevelt Set").

Two days later, ER was among those honored on a May 8, 1948, CBS television special hosted by the Anti-Defamation League, although son Jimmy accepted the award in her stead for work at the United Nations. Others included Charles E. Wilson from General Electric for his civil activities, Darryl Zanuck as producer of *Gentleman's Agreement*, Barney Balaban for his Freedom Train work, and producer Dore Schary for the film *Crossfire*. Dramatic scenes from *Crossfire*, a mystery about an anti-Semitic murder, were incorporated with actors Edward G. Robinson, Robert Young, and Celeste Holm ("Anti-Defamation").

ABC was discussing the possibility of a dual radio and television broadcast of *The Eleanor and Anna Roosevelt Program*, set to begin October 4, 1948, but in the end, the 15-minute show only aired on radio. Anna transmitted from Hollywood, while ER recorded her segment from wherever she happened to be ("Roosevelt Series"). *Today with Mrs. Roosevelt* would finally hit the airwaves on NBC television and radio in February 1950.

Her first appearance on NBC public affairs series *Meet the Press* was timed to coordinate with the opening of the United Nations General Assembly in 1949 ("Radio and Television"). Journalist May Craig, who had covered ER's press conferences in the White House and was considered a friend, served as one of the interviewers on Friday evening, April 8 ("May Craig"). ER would appear on the show five times throughout the 1950s and warrants a special mention in a history of *Meet the Press*. Producers deliberately did not select reporters known to be hostile to guests, since participants might cancel the interview. One of the "notable hostilities" was between ER and Hearst columnist Westbrook Pegler (R. Ball 29). Pegler was contemptuous of the Roosevelts and defended those opposed to anti-lynching bills, for example. He even said that Giuseppe Zangara, who attempted the assassination of FDR, had "hit the wrong man" when Chicago mayor Anton Cermak died in the attack, and called ER "La Boca Grande"—the big mouth (Whitman). This did not stop some viewers from requesting "Westbrook Pegler asking the widow Roosevelt a few questions on *Meet the Press*. She's been treated with kid gloves a little too long" (W.S.).

Producer Lawrence Spivak wrote that there had been a wonderful reaction to ER's appearance in 1949, resulting in several more invitations (Lash *Years Alone* 183). But one editorial took her to task for saying that she had never been in politics, something that she would often repeat: "Although Mrs. Roosevelt has never been a candidate for an elective office, we can think of no one who would be a more formidable candidate if she were to file her candidacy" ("Never a Candidate"). The conversation must have been interesting, since columnist Walter Winchell reported that New Yorkers were talking about "Mrs. Roosevelt's adroit parrying and thrusting on the *Meet the Press* air duel" (Winchell).

Dorothy Doan hosted the CBS *Vanity Fair* "woman's magazine" daily talk show out of New York with a group of guests chatting in a living room setting. "Housewives" had become the daytime television target audience, and Doan represented the typical young, slim, White standard model of the female daytime host in this period (Arnold 217). However, she came from a background as a print reporter covering the United Nations for two years and said of her show, "Women who won't read international news in the papers become interested when they're spoon-fed on television by a person who has made or helped to make the news" (Adams "Self-Taught"). ER appeared on June 21, 1949, with other guests J. Marguerite Bowle and Indian activist Hansa Metha ("Programs"). Doan describes ER as the perfect guest, on and off camera: "Mrs. Roosevelt, an ideal guest, if there ever was one, was half an hour early the day she appeared on *Vanity Fair*. She didn't interrupt or demand special attention. Mrs. Roosevelt found each person she talked to stimulating and interesting. She asked questions and listened to the answers. Before the cameras, when broadcast time came, Mrs. Roosevelt was poised and assured. If each of us is to be a good hostess, I think we can learn from this example of a successful guest" (Doan). This gendered description of ER's appearance is unusual for television, since she did not often guest on programs targeted specifically to women. Most of the time, on her own show or that of others, the approach was more gender neutral with a focus on the issues at hand.

The Freedom House nonprofit promotes democracy and human rights with a focus on political rights and civil liberties worldwide. Still advocating today, it was established in 1941 with ER and Wendell Willkie, who ran as a Republican against FDR in the 1940 presidential election, as honorary cochairs. The annual Freedom House Award recognizes outstanding leaders in the cause of freedom and democracy, and the awards ceremony was televised on October 13, 1949, on CBS. Eleanor presented the award to David Lilienthal, then serving as chair of the Atomic Energy Commission. Secretary of Defense Louis Johnson also presented an award to General Lucius Clay, who administered occupied Germany after World War II and orchestrated the Berlin Airlift ("Programs").

In a new twist in ER's early television appearances, CBS televised the *Baking Contest Awards* from the Waldorf-Astoria Hotel in New York on December 13, 1949. Presenters were Philip and John S. Pillsbury, Philip Reed, Arthur Godfrey, and Art Linkletter, and Eleanor had the job of handing out $70,000 in cash prizes to the winners. Finalists were brought in from 39 states for the contest in which "Mrs. Ralph Smafield" of Detroit, Michigan, won $50,000 for her "Water-Rising Nut Twist" recipe. ER devoted an entire "My Day" column to describing the contest sponsored by Pillsbury and seemed to really enjoy the process. "It is a pleasant thing in itself to have the journey and the fun of a baking contest in the Waldorf, and every woman did her baking in a General Electric stove, which she will take home with her…. The really tense and moving moment came when Mr. Pillsbury and I went down to the little platform in front of the raised dais where we had lunch and the announcement of the prizes was begun" (15 Dec. 1949). The grand prize winner had tears in her eyes as Eleanor took a bite, describing the sample as delicious and handing over the big check. Mrs. Smafield, whose first name was never revealed, planned to buy a home with her prize ("Programs," "It's Corn").

From May through October 1949, ABC aired a 26-part documentary series *Crusade in Europe*, which was based on General Dwight D. Eisenhower's World War II memoirs of the same name. Produced by Twentieth Century–Fox as part of *The March of Time*, the series of half-hour episodes won one of the first Emmy Awards for Best Public Service, Cultural or Educational Program, as well as a Peabody Award. ER gave commentary for the June 16 episode "Rommel Routed," and her endorsement was used in advertising for the show during its second run in 1950. The copy read: "Mrs. Eleanor Roosevelt comments on *Crusade in Europe*…. They (the sponsors) have given to all of us—the older generation, the young people of today, and our children tomorrow, a view of what millions endured during World War II" ("Television Today," Gannon).

Eleanor's *This I Remember* memoir covering the years from 1924 to 1945 was serialized in *McCall's Magazine* starting in the June 1949 issue. Running for two weeks beginning at the end of May, television commercial spots promoting the publication were placed during programming on 22 stations in Boston, Chicago, Cleveland, Detroit, Minneapolis, New York, St. Louis, St. Paul, and Washington. Footage was shot with Eleanor in Hyde Park; this also marked the switch of her "If You Ask Me" column from *Ladies' Home Journal* to *McCall's*. Federal Advertising Agency of New York handled the television commercial campaign that "followed the basic psychological of soap operas ('What would you do if you were married to a man like the President of the United States whom you rarely saw?')." The results proved to *McCall's* that television commercials sell magazines, as the June issue completely sold out ("*McCall*," "Broadcasting Pulls").

Author Meets the Critics, an ABC talk show about books, followed a successful radio version of the series and featured two groups of critics debating a recently published book, one critical and one with praise. Then the author had a chance to respond. Associate producer Harriet Halsband recalled only one television episode in which that was not the case. When ER discussed *This I Remember* on February 9, 1950, they simply asked her questions (Haakenson 201). The "critics" in this case were FDR's secretary of the treasury Henry Morgenthau, Jr., son Elliott Roosevelt, and Judge Samuel I. Rosenman, who coined the term "New Deal" and served as White House counsel ("Tele Chatter"). Ironically, Elliott's then-wife Faye Emerson sometimes served as moderator on the program, although not for this episode.

Airing shortly before the premiere of *Today with Mrs. Roosevelt*, *Variety* remarked that ER's performance here indicated "that her gracious personality and

Philip Pillsbury and Eleanor Roosevelt award "Mrs. Ralph Smafield" $50,000 for her "Water-Rising Nut Twist" recipe in the Pillsbury-sponsored *Baking Contest Awards* from New York's Waldorf-Astoria Hotel on CBS, December 13, 1949 (author's collection).

manner of delivery will go well on TV" ("Tele Followups"). The *New York Herald Tribune* called it a very absorbing program, wishing that it ran longer. "It was all over too soon. I could have listened to a lot more" (Crosby "Sidelights"). The prime function of the other show participant, Virgilia Peterson, was seemingly "to infuriate the authors." She declared that the Eleanor had taken a tumultuous period of history and "ironed it out exceedingly flat" in the memoir. She added, "You have assembled the material and not written it. I can't find a less distinguished bit of writing." Recovering a bit, Peterson ended the comment by saying that ER emerged from the book "a very great lady" and a phoenix arising from her husband's ashes. Taken aback, Eleanor responded that she had not intended to write history, but "sidelights" of interest. "I wasn't interested in emerging as a personality." Although Eleanor disagreed with television guests and interviewers over the years, Peterson's jab was unique in that it went outside the bounds of polite discourse. Her *New York Times* obituary noted that the moderator was "renowned for sharp commentary" ("Virgilia").

The rest of the show featured a discussion between Morgenthau, Rosenman, and the two Roosevelts. The two older men revealed that they had not learned very much added information from the book, which surprised Elliott. He was introduced to his mother's point of view on quite a few events. Other topics of discussion included ER's disagreements with British prime minister Winston Churchill, the diverse group of people who influenced FDR before he made up his own mind, and the experiences that were the source of FDR's liberalism. Some of those Eleanor attributed to the people and issues she introduced to him in the pre–White House years, when "I always had a lot of queer friends" (Crosby "Sidelights"). Syndicated columnist Westbrook Pegler was so riled up about the show that he devoted an entire column to it. In his usual over-the-top name calling, he wrote, "The Empress Eleanor and the memory of her late consort and titular spouse were so nearly holy that the program would not follow its customary form." He went on to describe the conversation, referring to ER as "La Boca" and denigrating Peterson as "an overawed and faltering female" who attempted a swipe "but seemed to get scared at her own blasphemy" (Pegler "Empress Eleanor").

13

Today with Mrs. Roosevelt

"Not since Alice's celebrated tea party, a while back, has so remarkable a group been assembled at teatime as the one presided over by Eleanor Roosevelt a week ago Sunday on N.B.C. Mrs. Roosevelt, who was inaugurating a television series, plans to bring together at teatime every Sunday (4 p.m.) a collection of important guests to discuss pressing problems of the day. Her first program was something more than a high tea; it was an interstellar one" ("Mrs. Roosevelt's Tea Party," *The New Yorker*).

"On the television program *Today with Mrs. Roosevelt* (NBC-TV, Sunday, 4–4:30 p.m. EST) guests sip tea, served from a set specially brought from her former home, now the national museum at Hyde Park. The idea of the program, however, is to discuss 'the problems that face all of us in daily living.' Few people have such a limitless guest list on their phone tables as does the former First Lady. And few are as capable of running a modern salon as she" ("TV Tea Party," *Newsweek*).

"Mrs. Franklin D. Roosevelt's new weekly television program got off to a spectacular start last Sunday afternoon on NBC at 4 o'clock. Her list of guests, including Dr. Albert Einstein and many other authorities on atomic energy and the hydrogen bomb, probably was the most impressive panel yet assembled for a video discussion session, their opinions gaining a position of prominence on the front pages of most newspapers the following morning" (Jack Gould, *New York Times*).

Eleanor hosted her first Sunday afternoon television political talk show on NBC, with *Today with Mrs. Roosevelt* running weekly, February 12 through May 28, 1950, before she took a break to attend to United Nations business in Europe. They filmed 16 episodes, produced by Martin Jones, with part of the proceeds flowing directly to daughter Anna. Son Elliott packaged and sold the show by promising guests like British prime minister Winston Churchill, U.S. secretary of state Dean Acheson, and Soviet foreign minister Andrey Vyshinsky. However, Acheson would not appear until the next iteration of the show months later on *Mrs. Roosevelt Meets the Public*. ER personally telegrammed Churchill, asking him if he would be willing to be interviewed by the BBC and the film flown to the U.S. for broadcast, with a radio version simultaneously recorded. She also wrote to Dwight Eisenhower, who was then president of Columbia University, asking him to appear, followed by supper afterward with his wife Mamie (Schlup 140–41). Churchill, Eisenhower, and Vyshinsky all declined. Elliott handled most of the invitations, which went out with ER's signature. She was upset when one was sent to Bess Truman, wife of the president. "If I had known of this beforehand I would not have sent it because I know that she does not do anything of this kind and that I should not have asked her," she wrote Elliott's assistant Dee Tucker. Eleanor invited the Duke and Duchess of Windsor in a letter she wrote herself. "Elsa Maxwell is coming as a guest and I think we could have fun on this program if all four of us were there besides the solemn people who do the serious discussing" (Lash *Years Alone* 184–85).

Guests were invited for lunch at noon, followed by a briefing and rehearsal in the afternoon before the 4:00 p.m. show. Each episode opened with a printed invitation on the screen asking the viewer to join ER for tea, and the announcer began, "Mrs. Franklin D. Roosevelt cordially invites you to take tea with her again today in the Colonial Room of the Park Sheraton Hotel in New York City." The set, which was made to duplicate the Hyde Park sitting room and cost an estimated $5,000, aired from a large ballroom in the hotel with an area for guests to watch the show in progress (Wilson). The format was that of a tea party, with participants sitting on a couch and being served tea from the family's beautiful silver tea service brought down from Hyde Park, while political issues were discussed on a Sunday afternoon. Above the mantel behind them hung a portrait of FDR, a study done by Douglas Chandor for his painting, *The Big Three at Yalta*. The show opened with Eleanor talking individually with each guest, the number of which ranged from two to six (Johnston). Some episodes were live; others were recorded on Kinescope.

Variety loved the format and the host: "As a TV personality she has a graciousness and charm at the 'tea table' and a capacity to get right to the point and not permit the tea leaves to dampen the import of the topic under discussion. She has a way with her guests that that is irresistible" ("Tele Followups"). *Parade Magazine*'s writer felt that serving tea brought the discussion into viewers' living rooms, as if spending an afternoon with the family: "On a recent Sunday afternoon, with ten million other Americans, I had tea with Eleanor Roosevelt" (Gardner "Television").

ER moved into the Park Sheraton Hotel on West 56th Street near Central Park so that Elliott, unattached at the time, could live with her. She had the bedroom, her secretary "Tommy" Thompson in the room next door, and Elliott slept on a day bed in the sitting room. His company, Roosevelt Enterprises, occupied an office in the hotel as well, and he wrote about pitching and planning the show: "The format was easy to find. We would duplicate the scene I had witnessed on countless occasions at Val-Kill and invite world celebrities—Albert Einstein, for example—to come to the hotel on Sunday afternoons and converse with Mother on live television while she poured tea in front of cameras in the ballroom. The set would look like the corner of a paneled library—a silver teapot and fine china would be used as props" (*Mother R.* 154). A noticeable feature of shooting from the hotel is that traffic noise is sometimes heard from New York City streets. Initially, the plan had been to broadcast from Hyde Park "provided television relay facilities can be arranged," but this must have been too complicated technically ("TV Program May"). There was an early effort to produce a television and radio simulcast of the program, but the show was heard later in the evening on radio ("Inside Television").

One critic surmised that viewers tuned in to see Eleanor Roosevelt and who sat on the couch with her, rather than with an interest in the issues themselves. It was ER's name and personality that made the program successful (Haakenson 68). *Variety* noted, "In view of the universal respect in which she is held because of her honest fight to help mankind, Mrs. Roosevelt is in a position to bring to her tea table and the NBC-TV camera the cream of the crop—and name your own subject" (Rose). The New York Nielsen ratings in late February 1950 represented a 31.8 percent viewing audience share, followed by a 20.2 percent share in early March. Telepulse ratings for the March period showed a 21.7 percent audience share. It ran a close second in ratings to *Meet the Press* in public affairs programs, and in New York City, it rated a few tenths of a point higher than *Meet the Press* over the course of the show's run. However, oftentimes it was broadcast opposite feature films that garnered much higher ratings.

Even the clothes Eleanor wore on air made the news, much to her chagrin. Reports commented that she had been seen purchasing "quite a number" of new dresses to wear on television to replace those that had been too light on camera. "Everybody seems more concerned about the way I dress and the color of my clothes than they do about the subjects we're supposed to be discussing," she complained (Lohman 1950). At first, she also hated the makeup, but got used to the idea for television. Theatrical producer John Golden, who was a good friend, called to tell her that "she looked horrible on television and would she please put some make-up on." After that, NBC had no trouble convincing her to wear light cosmetics "to prevent the cameras from distorting her features" (Elliott Roosevelt "My Mother"). One review of the first episode included information that she was wearing a gray ensemble with light pancake makeup, and that she appeared nervous, hand trembling slightly as she read her notes ("Einstein Warns").

ER wrote about her hopes for the program in "My Day," noting that she had defended freedom of the press in the United Nations, but additionally felt that television had a responsibility to educate viewers:

> This is a great opportunity which NBC is offering the public and I only hope that my share may help to fulfill the purposes of the program. We feel very strongly that the American public is entitled to hear the people who carry responsibility for the decisions affecting the lives of our own people and sometimes the people of the world…. I believe in free speech, in free enterprise, in the right of everyone to have his say and in the right of everyone to be able to hear as many points of view as possible. Especially in times like these the public should discuss both national and international subjects and this program will be dedicated, as many others are, to providing the public with the material on which to base their own decisions [9 Feb. 1950].

She believed that these conversations really could contribute to solving the world's problems.

As the announcer opens the program, the camera pans over a group of people sitting on chairs and sofas, with Eleanor in the center chair and two men on either side of her. They all sit around a coffee table covered in a large pine needle display, no doubt there to disguise microphones, the tea set behind them. To watch the production now is to realize how early 1950 is in the development of the new conventions and protocols of television. As the voiceover finishes with an introduction of Mrs. Roosevelt, the camera dollies in, but she does not look into the lens. Instead, she looks off to camera right (as she must have been instructed), puts on eyeglasses, and reads from notes on her lap. Rather than engaging her television audience at home by directly looking at them, she remains distant. For viewers today, the effect is not what we would imagine someone inviting us into her living room might be. There is an unfamiliar 1950s formality. When she looks up for emphasis, ER is still oriented camera right, not into the camera. Her first words are: "I believe the people of this country, and of all the world, are entitled to hear various points of view on the national and international decisions which are going to affect our lives in the future." This was why the hydrogen bomb and the future of atomic energy had been chosen for the show's first topic. She adds, "My husband believed that the people of this country would always have the courage to face reality, and during the dark days seventeen years ago, he rallied behind a fundamental belief." Her expression changes to more relaxed with a smile as she moves from the subject of the bomb to that of FDR. Yet, she still does not talk to camera, but to her director on set.

A portrait of President Franklin Roosevelt appears on-screen, and we hear his voice from his first inaugural address, intoning, "The only thing we have to fear is fear itself." The camera moves to ER in a medium shot, and she looks as if she reacts to an off-camera cue. With notes clearly visible on her lap, she looks down and reads, "It is my belief today that we as citizens of the United States can be the leader in the search for a peaceful and more prosperous world." The camera zooms to a close-up as she continues reading and names her guests for the day. Now she removes her glasses and smiles generously. Each guest is given uninterrupted time to speak, all looking at Eleanor instead of the camera. She focuses her attention on the person speaking, listening intently, although occasionally looks off stage a bit nervously. In some camera angles, viewers can see a living room audience behind the speakers. It is an odd setup, since anyone sitting there is visible and gains attention when fidgeting. All remarks of the participants seem very rehearsed and not at all natural.

The New York Times noted the contributions of Dr. J. Robert Oppenheimer, then director of the Institute for Advanced Study at Princeton University and considered the father of the atomic bomb, as "television at its best" (Gould "Television"). Smoking a cigarette, he criticized the secrecy surrounding the hydrogen bomb and atomic energy, saying, "If we are guided by fear alone, we will fail in this time of crisis." Other guests included Connecticut senator Brien McMahon, chair of the Joint Congressional Committee on Atomic Energy, on a proposal to divert armament expenditures for the betterment of humankind; David Lilienthal, former chair of the Atomic Energy Commission, who held up a two-pound chunk of uranium; Dr. Detlev W. Bronk, president of Johns Hopkins University, speaking about nuclear medicine; Dr. Hans A. Bethe, Cornell University physicist, who urged that the U.S. promise never to use the hydrogen bomb unless an enemy used it first; Harry Winne, vice president of the General Electric Company, who predicted that atomic power central stations and shipboard plants might take 20–40 years to develop, discounting ideas of atomic cars in the foreseeable future; and Allan Kline, president of the American Farm Bureau Federation, who commented on the potential of atomic energy for agriculture. Albert Einstein joined the show remotely from his home in Princeton, New Jersey, for his first-ever television appearance, with a message focused on issues of mutual trust. Dr. Einstein almost never accepted interviews but took part because of his respect for Mrs. Roosevelt. With a thick German accent, he began his remarks by thanking her for the opportunity to express his convictions on this important political issue. *Newsweek* described the appearance: "The eminent scientist chose to read his speech with his nose—his spectacles delicately balanced on its end—buried in his script," and *The New York Times* noted his "sweater jacket and tieless, open-collared shirt" (Johnston, "TV Tea Party"). But his words were front-page news.

Eleanor does not share her opinions or ask interrogating questions of any of the guests. It is as if she serves as the conduit for these experts to speak to the public on prominent issues. After presenting Lilienthal with an engraved silver plate recognizing his years of public service, ER looks seriously into the camera: "I think that all of us have a keener sense of the importance of this subject and perhaps a keener sense of the responsibility that each individual citizen carries." She is finally speaking directly to the audience as she wraps up and thanks her guests, smiling. Eleanor closes the program: "May God grant us all the wisdom to find the true path to peace through cooperation with the other nations of the world."

Life Magazine covered the show with photographs, considering the panel "the most august that gathered anywhere to discuss the problem" ("Soul-Searchers"). Amid all the television equipment, newsreel cameras, and photographers gathered off stage that day stood a silver cup presented to "Senator Franklin D. Roosevelt" in 1911. By the end, it was filled with used flashbulbs (Johnston).

Einstein criticized the "close supervision of the loyalty" of United States citizens and the "indoctrination of the public," referring to the anti-communist hysteria of the era. FBI director J. Edgar Hoover was no friend of either Einstein or ER, and surveillance on the scientist was intensified after newspapers nationwide blasted front-page headlines like "Disarm or Die Says Einstein." His words warned of the possibility of the annihilation of humanity, with the hydrogen bomb as *the* most important political issue for the world. The notion that security could be achieved through armament was a "disastrous illusion," and the arms race between the U.S. and the Soviet Union had assumed an "hysterical character" (Johnston). Much of the show targeting the dangers of the atomic age contradicted President Truman's policies, although ER had cleared the idea of the program directly with him. The president watched the episode and told Lilienthal that he found the show interesting, recognizing that it was a good thing to talk about the issues publicly. Lilienthal admitted to Truman that he was a "pushover" for ER: "When she asks me to do anything, I do it, no matter what it is." The president said, "I feel the same way about her," and relayed the story about how she had recorded a radio message from Paris for his reelection effort. Truman never forgot that ER helped when he needed it badly, so he told her that it was fine to go ahead with the show (Lilienthal Vol. II 636). This public challenge to consensus on Truman's atomic policies would not likely have occurred on network television without Eleanor Roosevelt to prompt the discussion.

Calling the first episode "spectacular," one reviewer predicted that it "should prove to be the best current events show on television" (Vernon). *Newsweek* noted that on the following week's show, fewer panelists discussing a national health plan allowed ER "a better chance to display her gifts of charm and personality" ("TV Tea"). *The New Yorker* criticized the provocative information presented the first week without time for speakers to adequately address the issues, but also respected her for displaying the potential of television as a public forum ("Mrs. Roosevelt's Tea"). *The New York Times* also pointed out the "overcrowding" problem of the premiere, suggesting that ER take part more herself: "It is not often that television has such a gracious and well-informed hostess as Mrs. Roosevelt, and her talents should have full play on the air" (Gould "Television"). Others also wanted to hear more from Eleanor herself, rather than merely serving as moderator for guests. "On few air programs do American notables chew the fat over burning issues more interestingly," wrote one columnist. However, he surmised that everyone who tuned in wanted to know what she thought: "You are known all over the world as a woman with definite opinions, and as a courageous gal who never hesitates to battle for your views.... The public wants you in there as 'Battling Eleanor'" (Phillips). In an issue of the fan magazine *T-V Stars*, she was able to defend her role on the show, taking it quite seriously and stating that the "responsibility to moderate is a sacred trust" and a contribution to guarding freedom of speech. This same article also pointed out that she had added "a rather housewifely touch to the program" by using the Hyde Park tea set and referred to her as "long a militant advocate of human rights." What a contrast

The February 12, 1950, premiere episode of NBC's *Today with Mrs. Roosevelt* addressed issues surrounding the atomic bomb and nuclear energy. From left: panelists Allan Kline, American Farm Bureau Federation president; Detlev Bronk, Johns Hopkins University president; moderator Eleanor Roosevelt; David Lilienthal, former chair of the Atomic Energy Commission; and J. Robert Oppenheimer, president of Princeton University's Institute for Advanced Study (author's collection).

between housewife and militant ("Eleanor Roosevelt"). *The Billboard* reported that ER brought interesting twists to the usual forum style show with an informal setting and non-debating guests. She took a more active part in the March 12 discussion than she had on previous occasions, which was "to be welcomed since she is certainly the focal point of the show.... It's an impressive airer and one which should earn a considerable audience on its own merit as well as from the name of its hostess" (Chase).

Friend Joe Lash said that overall, "she brushed aside the criticism. Although she said she did the television and radio shows to help Anna and Elliott, she enjoyed them, too. They gave her access to a large audience, and she wanted that" (Lash *Years Alone*

Dr. Albert Einstein readies to record his first-ever television appearance from his home in Princeton, New Jersey, for the premiere of *Today with Mrs. Roosevelt* on NBC. The topic of the show airing February 12, 1950, was "The H-Bomb and Atomic Energy" (author's collection).

184–85). Son Jimmy had a different take: "In order to help Elliott, mother did radio and television shows that he produced. With her as his star, he was able to sell the shows. She didn't like appearing on radio and TV, but she did it for her son" (*My Parents* 294–95). ER did indeed do much to help her children monetarily, but throughout the 1950s, she appeared on many public affairs television shows without being paid or with fees directed to charities. She realized that television was the place to be to reach people, especially the young, with her issues and ideas. "Mrs. Eleanor Roosevelt began her first regular TV series" was listed as one of the milestones from 1950 for the celebration of NBC's 25th anniversary ("The Saga"). When highlights were released for the company's 35th anniversary, the launch of her show was mentioned again (NBC-New York "NBC Highlights"). Patricia Peabody Roosevelt, Elliott's fifth wife, remembered that the show won a Peabody Award as the best public service program on television; however, she was mistaken (204). The program did win an honorable mention award from the Institute for Education by Radio and Television ("American Exhibition").

Episodes of Today with Mrs. Roosevelt

Details gathered from television program listings, audio files located in the Franklin D. Roosevelt Library and Museum, video files in the Paley Center for

Media, and Robert Haakenson's 1952 PhD dissertation, *A Study of Major Network Discussion Programs Televised During the Period January through May 1951* (359–62).

February 12, 1950

"The H-Bomb and Atomic Energy"
Dr. Hans A. Bethe, Cornell University physicist
Dr. Detlev W. Bronk, President, Johns Hopkins University
Dr. Albert Einstein, Scientist
Allan Kline, Vice-President, American Farm Bureau Federation
David E. Lilienthal, former Chair, Atomic Energy Commission
Senator Brien McMahon, Chair, Joint Congressional Committee on Atomic Energy
Dr. J. Robert Oppenheimer, President, Institute for Advanced Study, Princeton
    University
Harry Winne, Vice-President, General Electric Corporation

February 19, 1950

"National Health Insurance"
Dr. Moses Ben Moshe, Staff Surgeon, Mount Sinai Hospital, New York
Representative Andrew J. Biemiller, Democrat, Wisconsin
Dr. Ernst Boas, Chair, Physicians' Forum; Instructor in Pathology, Columbia
    University
Dr. John F. Conlan, Member, American Medical Association
Dr. Lowell S. Goin, Physician, Los Angeles, California
Sister Elizabeth Kenny, Sister Kenny Foundation
Senator James E. Murray, Democrat, Montana
Dr. Philip Reichert, Physician, New York City

In "My Day," ER wrote:

> Today I must go back to New York City for the second in my series of television-radio programs. I hope I can succeed in getting the important people with me to discuss their points of view on the subject of medical care. This is a matter of great importance to the people of this country. It is one where both sides of the question should be heard and where people should be fully advised at all times of what they can get, under either the voluntary or compulsory insurance system, and what the costs will be to them [20 Feb. 1950].

Since archival sources are scarce, her reference to "my series of television-radio programs" helps to establish that audio files or transcripts that exist refer to both versions of the show.

February 26, 1950

"Should United States Recognize Spain?"
Senator Owen Brewster, Republican, Maine
James B. Carey, Secretary-Treasurer, CIO
John D. Hickerson, Assistant Secretary of State

Representative Eugene Keogh, Democrat, New York
James A. Wechsler, Editor, *New York Post*

March 5, 1950

"Is Our Tax System Unfair?"
Ray Blough, Professor of Economics, University of Chicago; former Director of Tax
    Research, U.S. Treasury
Leo Cherne, Executive Secretary, Research Institute of America
Vivien Kellems, Industrialist, Connecticut
Gloria Swanson, Actor

Vivien Kellems, who owned a company that manufactured cable grips, argued that as an employer, she should not be forced to withhold employee taxes and "become a tax collector." Gloria Swanson contended that her earning power as an actor had depreciated in the past 30 years, and while a car or house could be depreciated, a human being should be able to do so as well for tax purposes (Hughes). ER noted that Kellems felt beforehand that she was at a disadvantage because she had to argue against two men, Blough and Cherne, but ended up getting more airtime than they did ("My Day" 7 Mar. 1950).

March 12, 1950

"Are Rent Controls Still Necessary?"
Elsa Maxwell, columnist, radio personality
Henry G. Waltemade, Director, National Association of Real Estate Boards
Tighe Wood, Federal Housing Expediter

The Billboard reported that ER was giving some interesting twists to the usual forum style show, with an informal setting and non-debating guests on the topic of rent control. "The two main guests [Waltemade and Wood] were seated flanking Mrs. Roosevelt on a couch, making for concise if limited camerawork as the arguments began to flourish." An interesting element was the introduction of tenants and property owners stating their cases and pulling up chairs. Guests continued to talk to one another off-mic as the show wound up (Chase). It appears that the tighter set they noticed resulted from missing guests. Mary Lee and Douglas Fairbanks, Jr., are listed in the program notes sitting opposite director Stanley Kramer, but the Hollywood residents did not end up participating.

March 19, 1950

"The Republican Program"
Senator Homer Ferguson, Republican, Michigan
Senator H. Alexander Smith, Republican, New Jersey
Senator Alexander Wiley, Republican, Wisconsin

The original topic for this episode had been "The Position of the Negro in American Political Life," featuring entertainer Paul Robeson, Mississippi Republican committeeman Perry Howard, and New York Democratic representative Adam Clayton Powell. NBC canceled Robeson's appearance.

March 26, 1950

"Democrats Uphold Their Administration"
Senator Clinton P. Anderson, Democrat, New Mexico
Senator William Benton, Democrat, Connecticut
Senator Paul H. Douglas, Democrat, Illinois
Senator Theodore Francis Green, Democrat, Rhode Island

To begin the program, ER introduced Chicago and Southern Airlines pilots Captain Jack Adams and First Officer G.W. Anderson with a scale model of the flying saucer, a "strange blinking, speeding craft," they say they saw on a flight over Arkansas. She "appeared to be impressed" ("Mrs. FDR Sees"). After five minutes of flying saucers, the program notes say that ER was to introduce Lord Leighton for a 30-second spot before central discussion began.

This episode also made some news when President Truman requested a copy. There was no Kinescope made, so only a written transcription of a sound recording could be sent to the White House (Hyatt 439). Much of early television was recorded via the Kinescope process, which involved pointing a film camera at a video monitor of the live show. *Variety* noted that the president did not request a transcript of the show the week before, which had Republican senators discussing foreign policy ("Mebbe").

All four Democratic senators denounced Senator Joseph McCarthy's anticommunist campaign. Senators Green and Benton expressed resentment at the attacks against the State Department and Secretary of State Dean Acheson. Green declared the attacks reckless, unsupported by evidence, and unfair to the accused, who found it difficult to clear themselves. Senator Benton described the assaults on Acheson and Ambassador Philip C. Jessup as completely irresponsible and harmful to the U.S. abroad ("4 Senators"). Former assistant secretary of state Benton added that McCarthy was playing into the hands of the communist propaganda machine, and the "entire U.S. and its reputation is being blackened throughout the world" ("Democrats Gaining").

April 2, 1950

"Should the E.C.A. [Economic Cooperation Administration] Program Be Amended?"
Senator Harry P. Cain, Republican, Washington
Patricia Gore-Booth, wife of the Director-General of British Information Services
Paul G. Hoffman, Administrator, Economic Cooperation Administration
Paul Reynaud, former Premier of France
Hellé Zervoudaki (addressed as Mme. Henri Bonnet), wife of the French Ambassador to the United States

Announcer Ben Grauer ended the program with "Next Sunday, *Parade Magazine* will carry a feature story on *Today with Mrs. Roosevelt*." It did indeed run "Television Tea with Mrs. FDR" (program notes, Gardner).

April 9, 1950

"How Can World Peace Be Achieved?"

Ely Culbertson, Chair, Citizens' Committee for the Reorganization of the United Nations

Allen W. Dulles, Vice-Chair, American Committee on a United Europe

Cord Meyer, Jr., Chair, Executive Committee, United World Federalists

Elmo Roper, member, Board of Directors, Atlantic Union Committee

In her "My Day" column, Eleanor wrote that the panelists on this Easter Sunday program represented organizations dedicated to searching for pathways to peace:

> We do not all agree on how we can attain our coveted objectives, but it is good to know that so many people are thinking of ways and means whereby we can work together. I happen to believe that we should not rest content with a divided world. We must press on to find ways to attain some measure of confidence and co-operation, even with those in whose philosophy, both political and economic, we can not agree. The United Nations seems to me the best stepping stone in the way of machinery toward this end. I do not think we are ready to go much beyond the present type of organization, but I do think that we can constantly strive for improvement [10 Apr. 1950].

April 16, 1950

"What Should Our Future Policy Be in China?"

John King Fairbank, Director, China program, Harvard University

Patrick J. Hurley, former Secretary of War and former Ambassador to China

Richard Lauterbach, Chief, Moscow Bureau for *Time* and *Life* magazines, 1943–44

Senator Warren Magnuson, Democrat, Washington

April 23, 1950

"Statehood for Alaska and Hawaii"

Edward Raymond Burke, former Senator from Nebraska

Oscar L. Chapman, Secretary of the Interior

Representative Frederic R. Coudert, Jr., Republican, New York

Ernest Gruening, Governor of Alaska

Representative Leroy Johnson, Republican, California

This episode was also used as a platform to honor ER and Brigadier General David Sarnoff, chair of the board of the Radio Corporation of America (RCA), for their contributions to "better understanding among Americans" by the Joint Defense Appeal, which represented both the Anti-Defamation League of B'nai B'rith and the American Jewish Committee ("What's Doing").

April 30, 1950

"Mrs. Roosevelt Cross-Examines the Press"

Emma Bugbee, *New York Herald Tribune*

Mae Craig, *Portland* (Maine) *Press Herald*

Doris Fleeson, Bell Syndicate

Genevieve Herrick, formerly with *Chicago Herald Tribune*
Bess Furman, Washington, D.C. Bureau, *New York Times*

The women who were given a television platform for this episode had all covered Eleanor and her press conferences during the White House years. She wrote about it briefly in "My Day":

> We had an interesting press conference on my television program Sunday.
> One of the things that stood out was the fear on the part of one veteran press woman—Elisabeth May Craig—that the government might gradually take over and dry up the sources of the news. I think she felt that a great deal of government assistance developed government control, and that this might grow to be dangerous. However, this did not seem to bother much the other guests on the panel—Genevieve Herrick, Doris Fleeson, Bess Furman and Emma Bugbee. Some agreed with me that personal intimidation and unwillingness to express a personal opinion are more serious [2 May 1950].

May 7, 1950

"Pakistan Faces the Future"
Liaquat Ali Khan, Prime Minister of Pakistan
Ra'ana Liaquat Ali Khan, wife of the Prime Minister of Pakistan
George C. McGhee, Assistant Secretary of State

McGhee commented that the understanding reached between Pakistan prime minister Liaquat Ali Khan and Pandit Nehru of India constituted "one of the outstanding examples of statesmanship in modern times." Ali Khan reiterated his belief that peace in the world depended on peace in Asia. He also remarked that his wife Ra'ana Liaquat Ali Khan was known as the "Dynamo in Silks." She turned to ER and said, "Mrs. Roosevelt, I could tell you the dynamo in silks doesn't impress me so much as when people said I was the Mrs. Roosevelt of the East" (Parke). In "My Day," Eleanor returned the compliment by citing her leadership of Pakistani women. ER was hopeful that Pakistan and India could establish peace and trade in the region, becoming an example for the rest of the world (10 May 1950).

May 14, 1950

"Human Rights and the United Nations"
Eunice H. Carter, member, Human Rights Commission, American Association for the United Nations
René Cassin, French Representative
Dr. P.C. Chang, Chinese Representative, Human Rights Commission of the United Nations
Dr. Charles Malik, Lebanon Representative and Rapporteur, Human Rights Commission
Dr. Maurice Perlzweig, Consultant to United Nations Economic and Social Council from the World Jewish Congress

Eunice Carter, who also represented the National Council of Negro Women, took this opportunity on television to promote passage in the U.S. Senate of the Genocide Convention adopted by the UN in 1948. The Senate Foreign Relations

Committee recommended approval in 1950 with attached language outlining the understanding that genocide did not include lynching or racial segregation. The treaty was not adopted in the United States until 1986 (Carter). Eleanor's entire "My Day" column after this episode of the show was dedicated to explaining why further elaboration of the rights and freedoms identified in the original Universal Declaration of Human Rights was so important for peace in the world (16 May 1950). A trailer ran at the end of this program: "*Today with Mrs. Roosevelt* is one of the programs being recorded for use by the Voice of America for its international transmissions" (program notes).

May 21, 1950

"World Trade and the United States"
William L. Batt, President, SKF Industries
Senator George W. Malone, Republican, Nevada
Philip D. Reed, Chair of the Board, General Electric Corporation
O.R. Strackbein, Chair, National Labor-Management Council on Foreign Trade Policy

Guests and crew prepare for the May 7, 1950, episode of *Today with Mrs. Roosevelt* on the topic of "Pakistan Faces the Future." Pictured are unidentified persons on the left and right of the NBC camera, Ra'ana Liaquat Ali Khan, moderator Eleanor Roosevelt, producer Elliott Roosevelt (standing), and prime minister of Pakistan Liaquat Ali Khan (Department of State, Harry S. Truman Presidential Library & Museum).

After this episode, ER wrote in "My Day" about the importance of an international point of view, approaching the issue of world trade to see the advantages to the world, rather than from the vantage point of only one country. She encouraged not only working to increase production of raw materials for export from what is now known as the Global South, but also increasing standards of living, thereby developing markets for our own goods in those countries (23 May 1950).

May 28, 1950

"America's Role in Germany"
Senator Guy M. Gillette, Democrat, Iowa
Representative Jacob Javits, Republican, New York
Brigadier General Telford Taylor, Chief of Counsel, War Crime Trials at Nuremberg, Germany
Dorothy Thompson, Author, Foreign Correspondent

ER welcomed Countess Mazaubran of the French Resistance and Lady Hazel and Lord William Douglas of Kirtleside to the audience before greeting her guests. Lord Douglas had been the commander in chief and military governor of the British Zone in postwar Germany. Then Eleanor walked over to a second location to speak with Senator Gillette, followed by the two moving over to the main set for the program of the day with the other guests (program notes).

This was the last in the *Today with Mrs. Roosevelt* series, which went on hiatus for the summer of 1950 to accommodate ER's continued work in Paris with the United Nations. The plan had been to resume the show when she returned in the fall, but instead, the format and title were adjusted, returning as *Mrs. Roosevelt Meets the Public*.

14

Mrs. Roosevelt Meets the Public

The next NBC talk show began on October 1, 1950, after a summer in Europe, and aired weekly on Sunday afternoons from the Park Sheraton Hotel, this time without tea. *Mrs. Roosevelt Meets the Public* was packaged by Elliott; directed by Charles Christensen, the former director of *Meet the Press*; and produced by Henry Morgenthau III, with Dee Tucker as an associate producer. Morgenthau III was the son of good friends Elinor, ER's horseback riding partner, and Henry Morgenthau, Jr., and had been working for CBS on *Vanity Fair* before leaving for Roosevelt Enterprises ("Morgenthau"). Eleanor's new show had no commercials and was network sustaining, acting as the lead-in to *Meet the Press* at 4:00 p.m. It ran through July 15, 1951, including some episodes shot in London and Paris to coincide with United Nations sessions.

Morgenthau explained, "Mrs. Roosevelt likes the program—she feels she reaches many people this way. She feels it is another vehicle for her to express ideas through general discussion" (Haakenson 45). By this time, Eleanor had defined a style that differentiated her approach. In addition to an international focus, she prompted and led discussions geared toward finding solutions and resolutions to the problems and issues at hand. Participants often disagreed with one another, but her moderating style encouraged problem solving. Oftentimes guests represented differing points of view—between politicians and scientists, for example, or both federal and local officials on the same topic—but were not necessarily in direct opposition to one another, the style on other similar shows. Guests were usually on their best behavior in the presence of ER's authority, so that confrontations were not as contentious as what might be found on *Meet the Press* or *Face the Nation*, even on quite controversial topics. She also tried to represent the interests of the average viewer, rather than an expert, as she asked questions of panelists.

In an article written for *TV Screen*, Elliott explained that one of his mother's qualities was an ability to put people at ease, especially valuable in radio and television interviews:

> They are usually prominent persons with great reputations in their respective fields, but often the mere sight of a microphone or a camera makes them extremely nervous.
>
> It is seldom that my mother cannot help them to relax. Someone has suggested that people relax in her presence because she is so genuinely interested in what they have to say that they forget their fears in trying to satisfy that interest. People seem to warm to her without any

effort on her part; some, who have criticized her violently for her political and social views, have been won over at a personal meeting ["My Mother"].

Helen Gahagan Douglas observed something similar over 20 years of friend-ship, finding ER "imbued with soft but unmistakable authority" and a "disarming quality of directness that dissolved all nervousness in the people she met," drawing out even the quietest of guests (151–52). As former secretary of labor Frances Perkins recalled FDR saying of his wife, "Eleanor always makes people feel right" (132).

Elliott and Morgenthau handled inviting guests after a small research staff col-lected clippings and suggested participants for each topic. The usual number of guests was four but could range from two to six. They planned four episodes ahead of the schedule, allowing the show to react to political and international events with flexibility. Then staff members Nancy Hyatt and Robert Gill prepared the opening and closing scripts for the show, a suggested lead-in comment, questions for guests, and background information on the issues and people involved for Eleanor to read. The staff also arranged for four members of the public to appear just off stage of the sitting room setting, supplying questions for them to ask. This segment was added because ER's incredibly busy schedule could not as easily accommodate the longer rehearsal times needed when shooting *Today with Mrs. Roosevelt*. The audience par-ticipants were chosen from a pool of writers of the most interesting letters, prompt-ing an "extraordinary volume of mail" into the Park Sheraton Hotel (A. Stewart). The April 29 and May 6, 1951, shows were captured on Kinescope in London by the BBC, followed by an episode from Paris, during and after which the public questions were no longer scheduled as part of the show, even back in New York.

Guests arrived an hour beforehand for a brief rehearsal with microphone and camera checks. The episodes began with newsreel footage of ER as a world traveler and UN representative with the musical theme "Dignity" leading into the announcer Ben Grauer. It then cut to a close-up of Eleanor, who introduced the topic of the day. She did so with a combination of reading from notes on her lap and extemporane-ously speaking, until she was provided with cue cards off camera starting on April 8, 1951. Then she introduced the participants, some of whom began with a prepared statement, but most often ER supplied a directed question to kick off the discussion. Robert Haakenson, whose PhD dissertation covers public affairs television shows in 1950–51, explains that, observing the program over time in person, the ability of camera crews in these early days of television to track the conversation among guests was not always impressive, but by May 1951, on this show, "the camera work was uniformly good." One production problem was never adequately solved during the life of the show. Participants routinely directed their comments to ER rather than to the camera as directed, which had been observed on her previous program as well. Haakenson was in the audience on April 22 and noticed crew members giv-ing Nelson Rockefeller both hand signals and written notes to encourage him to turn toward the camera, rather than talking to his host or other guests (64–65).

In the next segment, four representatives from the public asked questions. ER received a cue when time was running out and had to politely find a moment to inter-rupt the conversation, however lively, often with a hand movement and uneasiness.

The camera came in for a close-up when she thanked the speakers and concluded the topic. Occasionally, with time running out, the program ended with a fade out. The credits ran, followed by the topic for the following week, the same newsreel footage of ER from the opening, and the "Dignity" musical theme. A new feature was added to the opening on January 29, 1951, when film about the topic for the day was added after the newsreel footage introducing ER.

Some guests were quite well known, while others were specialists in their fields without public name recognition. *Variety* called booking Secretary of State Dean Acheson on the premiere episode an "impressive coup" (Stal "*Mrs. Roosevelt*"). The show personnel asked Henry Wallace to appear with others who had changed their minds about Russia after events in Korea. However, he had been approached before Eleanor rejected this topic for the program, and in her letter of apology about the misunderstanding, ER said that her staff had strict orders not to approach potential guests without her approval first (Schlup 154). Wallace had been vice president during Roosevelt's third term, but was pushed out by conservative Democrats in favor of Harry Truman in the fourth. He ran for president in 1948 with the Progressive Party but resigned in 1950 over his support of UN intervention in Korea and the party's conciliatory attitude toward the Soviet Union.

When the show traveled to London, ER wrote Winston Churchill in March 1951 requesting an appearance: "It would simply be an informal discussion during which you will present matters which you believe to be of particular significance at this critical time in our history." That same month, she asked Dwight Eisenhower, who was then Commander of NATO forces in Europe, to join her on the show from Paris. She wrote, "I feel most deeply that the continuing awareness of developments in Europe by our fellow citizens in the United States is a matter of primary importance" (Schlup 155–56). Both Churchill and Eisenhower declined. Participants were not paid for appearing, but were compensated for travel and incidental expenses, and some were invited back to ER's residence in the hotel afterward.

Reviews were not as overwhelmingly positive with the new format. The conservative *Chicago Tribune* described it as "largely a parade of administration functionaries, plus figures from the New Deal era who drop in to say nice things to Mrs. Roosevelt. Now and then a Republican leader shows up—and probably wishes later he hadn't" (Wolters). In October, *Variety* lamented that "most of the charm and informality" had gone compared to the earlier show, although recognizing that participants had more time to discuss issues. "Mrs. R, still an extremely gracious video personality, has become more of a panel moderator than a hostess welcoming guests to her Sunday afternoon tea soirees." The writer also complained about the city traffic noise (Stal "*Mrs. Roosevelt*"). However, another reviewer mentioned that ER moderated her distinguished panel exceptionally well. That same columnist began with an observation of her attire, "a very becoming afternoon gown with considerable black net," and continued the "compliment": "Despite the fact that she has never been considered a handsome woman, she looked quite well and exuded a most charming personality" (Deo).

Elliott's voice opened the first episode of the season by welcoming viewers to the fall renewal of Mrs. Roosevelt's television series. Afterward, she addressed thoughts about the show in the context of the Korean situation then raging, hoping that she was able to contribute to educating the public and moving discussion forward:

> From now on I hope our telecast will be a clearinghouse for our viewers. We invite questions and later we want people from the audience to come on the program so that others can see them asking their questions either of me or of some qualified expert that I am able to get who will know more about the subject than I can find out.
>
> I am hoping too, to bring before you some of the people you see out at the United Nations when they televise the meetings…. The aim and object, of course, of interesting the citizens of the United States in both national and international situations, is to help bring about peace in the world ["My Day" 3 Oct. 1950].

She asked viewers to send in their questions on current affairs issues to be read on air, and during the second episode, the role of the public was further clarified:

> I should like to explain that in this series, we shall attempt to answer questions on current affairs, which you, through your letters, have expressed a desire to have clarified. Where I feel that I am qualified to answer, I shall be glad to give whatever information I have available. When the questions concern problems best answered by someone qualified in the particular field, I shall bring you that person. I also hope to include in this program with me many of you who write in questions [program notes].

Thus, she used the "public" to ask questions in a different way than she might have herself addressed guests on the panel.

In a notable episode in November 1950, ER declared herself neutral in the New York City mayoral race, since she was registered to vote in Hyde Park instead, and each of the four candidates for mayor of New York City outlined his campaign platform in an allotted two-minute slot ("Mrs. Roosevelt with"). Then Eleanor turned the questioning over to "newswomen," who queried the men on behalf of the public. *The New York Daily News* praised ER in a curious way: "By the ingenious planting of hecklers, she brought out all the campaign skeletons without letting the bitter rivals claw one another" (Crosson). The "hecklers" Muriel Hutchinson and Phyllis Pollack were actually the assigned questioners who broached some uncomfortable topics. This was the first time all four candidates had come face-to-face (program notes). She had recently received a letter observing that the people who asked questions showed little interest in prominent issues, but ER found in this case that "the questions put to the candidates for Mayor showed that the average public was keeping very close tabs on what was being said in this campaign" ("My Day" 7 Nov. 1950). Elliott published an article titled "Politics on TV" in which he wisely foresaw that television audiences would demand face-to-face candidate debates in the tradition of Abraham Lincoln and Stephen Douglas. He felt that this episode of his mother's show was a perfect example of how it might work in a wide variety of campaigns of the future. The hundreds of letters received after the telecast convinced him that this appearance helped Vincent Impellitteri win the election, and it was the only time the candidates appeared together. Elliott also believed that television would be the end of the traditional U.S. political machines as it educated the public.

Another episode in January 1951 focused on the educational potential of TV. After newsreel footage of ER traveling, the lead-in opens with the announcer speaking over footage of dancers performing and then what looks like behind the scenes of a drama being shot for television. After the participants and members of the public asking questions are introduced, finally there is a cut to a close-up of Eleanor looking into the camera. That much had improved in the year since her first show to bring the audience in, but after saying "Good afternoon," she looks down to read her introductory remarks, occasionally looking up and smiling:

> Television is the newest and most controversial wonder child of modern science and industrial ingenuity, and it has just really come into its own in the American scene. Although still young, it's rapidly promising to become our major medium for communications. It will eventually reach a far greater number of people than any other media. Because it appeals to both the eye and ear simultaneously, television may make the greatest possible impression on the human mind. You who watch television know that it can bring you wonderful entertainment and can be very convincing in selling you the products of various sponsors, but I wonder how often you have stopped to realize that television can also be a great teacher. On programs such as this one, we try to bring you important ideas on controversial matters through the personalities of the people who are influencing and developing.

The close-up widens to reveal ER in a living room–style chair with guests FCC commissioner Frieda Hennock and Neville Miller, president of the FCC Bar Association and former president of the National Association of Broadcasters, on either side of her. A microphone on a waist-high stand is visible in front of participants in a living room setting. After reading guest introductions from notes on her lap, ER invites Hennock to "give a brief summary of the role of television in education." The commissioner tells her, "Democracy thrives on education, totalitarianism on ignorance and darkness. Educational television will be a strong weapon in America's arsenal. Educational TV will be an investment in our country's future that will pay dividends for generations to come." Miller then speaks passionately for some time before Eleanor turns to the public questions for the show. Afterward, Hennock wrote ER with appreciation for the "opportunity to explain to your large and faithful television audience my views concerning the reservation of television channels for educators" (Brinson 130). When the FCC first appointed Hennock, Eleanor had been one of her backers for the position (Morgenthau "Donna," "FCC's").

The program moved to 5:00 p.m. ET for the final three episodes during July 1951. Plans had been to resume airing in the fall of 1951 after ER's summer United Nations work as she had the previous year, but Paris UN meetings in November interrupted the schedule. Listings note that *How Does Your Garden Grow?* (a how-to show on gardening) was a summer replacement and not a permanent substitution since she had been expected back (Ross "This Week"). At the time, Elliott said that the immediate problem was that ER was going off to Europe for an extended period, followed by visits to India and Pakistan, "so it was impossible to book a television show for this fall and winter" (Wamboldt 303–04).

Episodes of Mrs. Roosevelt Meets the Public

Details gathered from television program listings, program notes, and audio files located in the Franklin D. Roosevelt Library and Museum, video files in the Paley Center for Media, and Robert Haakenson's 1952 PhD dissertation, *A Study of*

Major Network Discussion Programs Televised During the Period January through May 1951 (362–67).

October 1, 1950

"Our Government's Plan for Our Future within the Field of International Relations"
Dean Acheson, Secretary of State
Benjamin Cohen, Assistant Secretary of State
John Sherman Cooper, former Republican Senator from Kentucky; United States
    Representative, Security Council of the United Nations
Isadora Lubin, United States Representative, Economic and Social Council of the
    United Nations

Secretary of State Acheson's interview with ER had been shot earlier, and the other guests were supplied with both the text of his comments and the planned questions from the public ahead of time. After running the Acheson film, a dissolve transitioned to ER on set with panelists. Acheson said that the United Nations reaction against aggression in Korea made world peace "infinitely more possible." He praised the UN General Assembly for its decision to intervene and further urged that the UN pool all its technical skill in the reconstruction of Korea once hostilities ceased ("Korean," "Acheson"). In her summation of the day's discussion, Eleanor asked viewers to send in their questions on current affairs issues to be read on air, and Elliott read the closing announcements (program notes).

October 8, 1950

"America's Role in Asia"
Sir Mohammed Zafarullah Khan, Foreign Minister of Pakistan
Dr. Lambertus Nicodemus Palar, Chief Indonesian Representative to the United States
Madame Vijaya Lakshmi Pandit, Indian Ambassador to the United States
General Carlos Romulo, Philippine Representative to the United Nations

October 15, 1950

"The United Nations Looks Ahead"
Dr. Ralph Bunche, Director, Division of Trusteeship, United Nations
Ambassador Ernest A. Gross, United States Deputy Representative to the United
    Nations

This show aired during United Nations Week.

October 22, 1950

"The Problem of Graft and Corruption in Government"
Judge Samuel S. Leibowitz, County Judge, Kings County, New York
Miles McDonald, District Attorney, Director of Crime Investigation, Brooklyn, New York

This week Judge Samuel Leibowitz and District Attorney Miles McDonald answered questions in letters from the public, resulting in coverage on page one of

The New York Times. Leibowitz and McDonald both called for the creation of a commission to combat rackets in all five boroughs of New York City to "serve as watchdog" over municipal departments, including the police. Leibowitz called for a pay increase for members of the police department and declared that the people must "have an honest man in City Hall." He also voiced his strong opposition to legalized gambling, especially because of its impact on young people. Eleanor asserted that one of the important problems was "keeping the youngsters busy" and suggested that the city could convert vacant lots for recreational use (Spiegel). At the end of the program, ER celebrated the fifth anniversary of the United Nations by cutting a cake and passing pieces to her guests (program notes).

October 29, 1950

"Predicting the Outcome of the Election"
Louis H. Bean, Political Analyst; Economic Advisor to the Secretary of Agriculture

November 5, 1950

"New York City Municipal Election"
Edward Corsi, Republican Candidate for Mayor
Acting Mayor Vincent R. Impellitteri, Experience Party Candidate for Mayor
Ferdinand Pecora, Democratic-Liberal Candidate for Mayor
Paul L. Ross, American Labor Party Candidate for Mayor

In "My Day," Eleanor praised the "three lovely ladies and one young male first voter who had come down from Harvard to cast this first and most important vote."

November 12, 1950

"United Nations Policy in Korea"
Senator John Sparkman, Democrat, Alabama, U.S. delegate to the United Nations
Crew of the USAAF B-29 bomber *The Spirit of Freeport*

The bomber crew had just returned home from Korea and included pilot Lt. Duane Ohmann of Minnesota, navigator Lt. Alton Reeves of Texas, and bombardier Lt. Joseph Taylor of New York (program notes).

November 19, 1950

"Personal Problems Raised by Selective Service"
William T. Collins, New York County Commander, American Legion
Major General Lewis B. Hershey, Director of Selective Service
Dr. Willard Rappleye, Dean of the College of Physicians and Surgeons, Columbia
    University
General Elliott Roosevelt, Producer of the *Mrs. Roosevelt Meets the Public* program

Major General Hershey believed that the enlistment term should be two or two and a half years for universal military training, instead of the six months proposed in pending legislation. This proposal was in lieu of continuing the draft, instead requiring all young men to serve, and Hershey saw six months as inadequate training ("Hershey").

November 26, 1950

"Internal Security Act: The McCarran Bill"
Senator Owen Brewster, Republican, Maine
Senator Homer Ferguson, Republican, Michigan
Senator Theodore Green, Democrat, Rhode Island
Crown Prince and Crown Princess of Norway

December 3, 1950

"Should the United Nations Forces Use the A-Bomb?"
Dr. Theodore Benjamin, Scientist, Columbia University
Senator Harry Cain, Republican, Washington
Major Alexander P. de Seversky, Author, Aeronautical Designer
Senator Joseph O'Mahoney, Democrat, Wyoming

In her follow-up in "My Day," Eleanor discussed the differences in philosophy between the United States and the Russians and Chinese. She was especially concerned that the U.S. was not lured into becoming the aggressor in the Korean situation and believed that the Russians were not threatening to use nuclear weapons because they would instead act without warning, like the Japanese at Pearl Harbor (5 Dec. 1950).

December 10, 1950

"Is Youth Being Deprived of Its Youth?"
Mark McCloskey, member, New York City Board of Education
Dr. Harold Taylor, President, Sarah Lawrence College
Alice Thompson, Editor, *Seventeen*

ER was especially struck by comments that in the past, war was somewhere else, not on the U.S. mainland. Now young people were afraid that missiles meant war might come directly to them. For their sake, "we must keep on doing the things that bring and hold us together and may, in the future, develop an understanding that will obviate some, if not all, of our present-day difficulties" ("My Day" 12 Dec. 1950).

December 24, 1950

"Christmas: Friendship and Good Will"
The Right Reverend Henry Knox Sherrill, Presiding Bishop of the Protestant Episcopal
    Church in the United States
Choir of the Congregational Church of Manhasset under the direction of Robbie
    Norton

Exchange students from the American Field Service and International House, Columbia University

The exchange students shared Christmas traditions and discussed promoting friendship between countries.

December 31, 1950

"End of the Year Summary and New Year Forecast"
Major George Fielding Elliot, author, columnist, and military analyst
Richard Harkness, NBC Washington, D.C., commentator
Max Lerner, *New York Post* syndicated columnist
George Sokolsky, *New York Journal-American* syndicated columnist

Korea, the Soviet Union, Communist China, and the emergence of the United Nations were the topics of discussion. Eleanor's comments in "My Day" reveal how she approached not only the problem-solving goals of this television show, but also what she wished to achieve with her never ending efforts for world peace and bettering the lives of every human being on the planet:

> On my Sunday television program, however, I found myself reacting violently against what I felt was the rather weak and fearful attitude of one of the gentlemen participating. I suppose when you have great possessions, for example, it makes you more fearful that you may lose them, even though you protest that they are of no importance to you.... Somehow down deep inside of me there is always the resentment against the attitude that the answers to our problems can not be found and that, when we face those problems honestly, our people will not meet them courageously and adequately [2 Jan. 1951].

January 7, 1951

"Rearmament of Germany and European Foreign Policy"
Senator Homer Capehart, Republican, Indiana
Frank Pace, Jr., Secretary of the Army

January 14, 1951

"Continuation of December 31, 1950 Program—End of the Year Summary and New Year Forecast"
Richard Harkness, NBC Washington, D.C., commentator
Edgar Ansel Mowrer, Washington and Foreign Correspondent, Author
George Sokolsky, *New York Journal-American* syndicated columnist

In response to many requests, the discussion from December 31 on the noteworthy events of 1950 was continued in this episode with "three famous news analysts" (program notes).

January 21, 1951

"How Can Television Best Meet Our Education Needs?"
Frieda Hennock, Commissioner, Federal Communications Commission
Neville Miller, President, Federal Communications Commission Bar Association

During discussion of one of the questions from the public, Eleanor interjected to suggest that an issue with low ratings for educational television programs might be that they were not scheduled during prime-time programming slots. "If it is regularly on the air in the usual way, a lot of people would listen who might never turn it on for an educational program."

January 28, 1951

"United States Farm Policy and Its Effect on Food Prices"
Charles F. Brannan, Secretary of Agriculture
Representative Jacob K. Javits, Republican, New York

Special guests including radio personality "Mrs. Alfred McCann," vice president of Dorset Foods Arthur Davis, and general secretary of the New York State Farm Bureau Edward S. Foster asked questions of Brannan and Javits (program notes).

February 4, 1951

"The Great Debate: United States Foreign Policy for Europe"
Henry Steele Commager, Professor of History, Columbia University
Senator George W. Malone, Republican, Nevada

In the preliminary materials sent by staff to ER prior to the show, Senator Malone was designated as "an extreme isolationist" (program notes). In "My Day" following this episode, Eleanor reacted to his overuse of the term "socialist":

> On my television program the other day Senator George W. Malone of Nevada, with whom I heartily agreed that colonialism is going to disappear more or less quickly from the world scene, made me gasp with surprise when he stated that England, being a socialist country, was not a democracy.
>   It seems to me that anyone who has visited that country since the war cannot help being impressed by the fact that it is a democratic country. We may have differences in our economic systems, it is true. But the basic conception of a democratic way of life and of government which makes the individual human being all important and government exist for the benefit of the human being, rather than the human being for the state or government, is as cherished in Great Britain as in our own country [10 Feb. 1951].

The announcer mentions at the show's end that they will be back in two weeks (program notes). There was no February 11 program.

February 18, 1951

"How Can We Best Solve the United States Military Manpower Problem?"
Harold Dodds, President, Princeton University
Marx Leva, Assistant Secretary of Defense
Senator Wayne Morse, Republican, Oregon

Press coverage of this episode included comments from Oregon Republican senator Wayne Morse as he criticized the Defense Department for appeasing American isolationism. He was concerned about educational draft deferments and encouraged the military establishment to better utilize the labor of women and civilians ("Morse").

February 25, 1951

"Civil Defense"
Millard Caldwell, Jr., Federal Civil Defense Administrator
Senator Hubert Humphrey, Democrat, Minnesota
Arthur Wallander, Director, New York City Civilian Defense

March 4, 1951

"The Voice of America"
Edward Ware Barrett, Assistant Secretary of State
Senator William Benton, Democrat, Connecticut

March 11, 1951

"Labor's Role in Economic Mobilization Plans"
James B. Carey, Secretary-Treasurer, CIO
Michael V. DiSalle, Administrator, Office of Price Stabilization

In "My Day," Eleanor included a letter she received from a reader after watching this program. The writer argued that industry was able to increase industrial efficiency annually, so that labor's argument that it could get higher wages without increasing prices was correct. However, the savings of efficiency was being passed on to management or labor and not to the public. Therefore, white-collar workers were paying higher consumer prices without commensurate salary increases received by blue-collar labor. ER suggested that this was a problem that should be studied, as labor should represent all workers (19 Mar. 1951).

Robert Haakenson, who wrote his 1952 doctoral dissertation on political affairs television shows airing in 1951 and provided eyewitness accounts from ER's television audience, most likely was one of the members of the public asking questions during this episode. "Professor Robert Harkenson instructor in speech at Temple University" is identified as one of the questioners in a transcript of the episode. Haakenson would become dean of speech and communications at Temple (*Mrs. Roosevelt* transcript).

March 18, 1951

"Status of Military Preparedness"
Thomas K. Finletter, Secretary of the Air Force
Francis P. Matthews, Secretary of the Navy
Frank Pace, Jr., Secretary of the Army

March 25, 1951

"Special Easter Broadcast"
The Reverend Dr. Franklin Clark Frye, President, United Lutheran Church of America
William Warfield, Bass
Cantata Singers
Choir of St. Luke's and St. Matthew's Episcopal Church of Brooklyn

ER was concerned that she had picked up a virus and worried about how her voice would hold out for this special Easter episode of the show. "I find these bugs unfortunately do not leave you as quickly as you wish they would; and in spite of taking the most modern pills and inhaling benzoin at intervals, I am still a little nervous about what I will sound like on my television program" ("My Day" 26 Mar. 1951).

April 1, 1951

"How Can We Best Stop Inflation?"
George B. Harrison, President, Brotherhood of Railway and Steamship Clerks, AFL
Leon Keyserling, Chairman, President's Council of Economic Advisers
Allan B. Kline, President, American Farm Bureau Federation

Leon Keyserling outlined three steps which, coupled with a more effective price and wage stabilization program, he said would enable the United States to meet the greatest international problems it faced. Allan Kline added, "If we wish to control prices, we have to control inflation at its source, the money supply." George Harrison denied that wages have "anything to do with present price levels" and said that under the Defense Production Act, targeting "retail outlets" rather than profits was the wrong approach ("3 Steps").

April 8, 1951

"Non-Military Aid Abroad"
Paul Hoffman, former Director, Economic Cooperation Administration
Nelson Rockefeller, Chair, International Development Advisory Board

April 15, 1951

"The MacArthur Controversy"
Elliott Roosevelt, substitute moderator
Senator William Benton, Democrat, Connecticut
Senator Owen Brewster, Republican, Maine
Senator Homer Ferguson, Republican, Michigan
Four college editors of women's publications from the *Mademoiselle* Forum

The press announced that Madame Vijaya Lakshmi Pandit, Indian ambassador to the United States, would be substituting for ER while she was in Geneva, joining David Lilienthal, former head of the Atomic Energy Commission, in a discussion of problems in East Asia for this episode ("Mme. Pandit"). In his journal, Lilienthal mentions that he had a conversation with Madame Pandit when he ran into her at a party at the French Embassy and agreed to go on the show with her (Vol III 135). A transcript from the previous episode also promises these guests on this show (*Mrs. Roosevelt* transcript). However, "The MacArthur Controversy," hosted by Elliott, aired, and four young women representing women's colleges across the country asked questions of the guests. In April 1951, President Harry Truman had relieved General Douglas MacArthur of his command in Korea. Eleanor was in Geneva, Switzerland, to attend a meeting of the United Nations Commission on Human Rights.

April 22, 1951

"Moral Fibre of the U.S. People"
Senator Margaret Chase Smith, Republican, Maine, substitute moderator
Senator Estes Kefauver, Democrat, Tennessee
Dr. Lawrence S. Ruble, Psychiatrist, Harvard University

Senator Margaret Chase Smith substitute hosted for ER, who was still in Geneva, in this discussion on the morality of the American people. Senator Estes Kefauver said his committee had "found a letdown in various parts of the nation," but he believed that recent campaigns urging people to "return to the teachings of their grandparents and become more religious" were encouraging ("Ramblin'").

April 29, 1951

"Report from Britain, Part I"
Location: BBC, Lime Grove Studios, London
W.J. Brown, Independent Member of Parliament
Michael Foot, Labor Member of Parliament, British Journalist

May 6, 1951

"Report from Britain, Part II"
Location: BBC, Lime Grove Studios, London
Sir Hartley Shawcross, British Attorney General; Prosecutor at Nuremberg trials
Rebecca West, British Novelist and Journalist; Author of *The Meaning of Treason*

One U.S. columnist called this episode from London "one of the most intelligent public programs that television has produced." He continued, "It is not often that television gets as much brain power on one program." Rebecca West said that it was useless to outlaw communists because the dangerous ones were the most secretive. West, Sir Hartley Shawcross, and ER agreed that nations should not alter their own bills of rights to fight those whose aim is to destroy those rights (Cotton). In "My Day," Eleanor mentioned that it was unusual for a member of the cabinet like

The April 29 and May 6, 1951, episodes of NBC's *Mrs. Roosevelt Meets the Public* were shot in London at the BBC Lime Grove Studios. Eleanor Roosevelt had been attending to United Nations work in Geneva, Switzerland, and the show followed her to London and Paris (© BBC Photo Archive).

Shawcross to participate in a television show in the U.K., and he told her that "they practically had a Cabinet meeting on the subject of his appearance." She also discusses differences in television protocols:

> It has been amusing to me to put on television make-up and to see the other guests, both men and women, being made up in France and in England. We were all given much heavier make-up in France and the lights must have been warmer there because the bald-headed gentlemen were watched over by a pretty little make-up girl who ran out in the intervals between filming to wipe off their heads and powder them again.
>
> In London the make-up was even lighter than at home. I asked a young woman who did mine whether she did not get a little weary putting stuff on people's faces. She said she didn't, that every face was different and it was something like creating a new picture each time [5 May 1951].

May 13, 1951

"Report from France"
Filmed in Paris
Robert Schuman, French Minister of Foreign Affairs
Jean Monnet, General Commander for French Reconstruction; founder of Plan Monnet

From New York:
Elliott Roosevelt, substitute moderator
Heinz Krekeler, Consul General, Federal Republic of Germany
Paul A. Porter, Assistant Administrator, Economic Cooperation Administration
Roger Seydoux, Consul General, France

Technical difficulties meant that only a small part of the interviews Eleanor conducted from Paris were successfully recorded, so Elliott presided over an added segment from New York to fill out the show. In an interview a few months later, he explained that the film shot by a French television company was a "complete failure" because of distortion of the soundtrack. They only had about seven minutes of usable footage after working for four hours under hot lights. "This was very disconcerting to Mother and to NBC because we had to do that show live and just put in the scraps we had of what had been done in France," he said (Wamboldt 309).

May 20, 1951

"Iranian Oil Crisis, Part I"
Elliott Roosevelt, substitute moderator
Dr. D.J. Abdoh, Deputy Representative from Iran to the United Nations
Sir Norman Angell, British economist; former Member of Parliament
Max Thornburg, former oil advisor to the State Department and former Vice President
    of Overseas Consultants, Inc., which handled the "7 Year Plan for Iran"

Elliott continued to moderate while ER worked at the UN in Geneva. Dr. Abdoh read an official statement on behalf of the Iranian government. Discussion centered on political developments in Iran and the oil crisis there.

May 27, 1951

"Iranian Oil Crisis, Part II"
Dr. D.J. Abdoh, Deputy Representative from Iran to the United Nations
Christopher Braswell, British subject; former Washington representative, Anglo-
    Iranian Oil Company
Ned Russell, Washington correspondent, *New York Herald Tribune*
Max Thornburg, former oil advisor to the State Department and former Vice President
    of Overseas Consultants, Inc., which handled the "7 Year Plan for Iran"

June 3, 1951

"Arab-Jewish Question"
Hussein Kamel Salim Bey, Dean of Faculty, Commerce of Fuad
Harry Zindler, member, Israeli delegation to the United Nations

Today's topic centered on political unrest and social instability in the Middle East.

June 10, 1951

"Defense Production Act"
James Carey, CIO (Congress of Industrial Organizations)
Roger Fleming, American Farm Bureau

This program focused on whether Congress should extend the Defense Production Act. First enacted in 1950 during the Korean War, the Act has been reauthorized repeatedly, including by U.S. President Joseph Biden to produce Covid-19 vaccines and in response to the 2022 infant formula shortage.

June 17, 1951

"Federal Price Controls"
Senator Blair Moody, Democrat, Michigan
Herman Steinkraus, President, Bridgeport Brass Company

June 24, 1951

"The Situation in Korea"
Y.C. Chang, Korean Ambassador
Galo Plaza Lasso, President of Ecuador

Eleanor had known President Plaza when he served as Ecuadorean envoy to Washington, and she shared some pre-show pointers with him before what was his first television appearance. *The New York Times* reported that Plaza interrupted ER to complete an anecdote about sports, when her mind was on discussing Korea. Jacob A. Malik, chief Soviet delegate to the UN, had made statements supporting a ceasefire and armistice in Korea, and ER noted that Malik's suggestions for a Korean truce had "come as a surprise to us all." His statement "must be treated with complete seriousness but as yet they are only words and it is the actions that follow that may determine the future of the world" (Teltsch). Plaza declared that Malik's ceasefire proposal should be taken very seriously as well and insisted that agreement to discuss a ceasefire in Korea did not imply appeasement. "It's just stopping the fighting, stopping the bloodshed and discussing the problem." He said that the Korean issue involved a fight to defend "our way of life" ("Ecuadorean").

July 1, 1951

"Teenage Heroin Addiction"
Harry Anslinger, Commissioner, Federal Bureau of Narcotics
Dr. Kenneth W. Chapman, Bureau of Medical Services, U.S. Public Health Service
Max Rubinstein, Principal, James Fenimore Cooper Junior High School, Manhattan

Harry Anslinger called for new legislation at the municipal level that would compel the hospitalization of narcotics addicts. He thought that this legislation would brand drug addiction as a communicable disease, thus isolating its victims from community. He also advocated for more stringent penalties for narcotics dealers and asked for added personnel for local agencies combating narcotics sales. "We in the Federal service have only 180 men to combat this evil. It's like using a blotter to try to blot up the ocean," he said. Anslinger singled out California, Pennsylvania, and Florida as the only states where local narcotics enforcement agencies were adequate. Max Rubinstein added that the use of narcotics among teenagers existed in "frightening proportions" last fall, but that its use was declining ("Law").

July 8, 1951

"Advances in Cancer Research"
Dr. C.P. Rhodes, Vice President, American Cancer Society
John H. Teeter, Head, Damon Runyon Memorial Fund

July 15, 1951

"Discussion of the Korean Situation"
Senator Paul Douglas of Illinois
Senator Harry P. Kean of Washington
Congressman John F. Kennedy of Massachusetts

Before this last episode of the series, ER lamented the end of the television season in "My Day":

> Next Sunday will be my last television program for some time, and I feel sure that even though I am looking forward to the freedom of these next few weeks I shall still be regretful not to meet the television audience every week and get its reaction to our discussions. Nevertheless, I am sure that I will hear from many of my friends who will express their feelings on what goes on in the world. I am very grateful that they are willing to share their points of view with me [10 July 1951].

She would not have guessed that there would be no regular television series presence again until 1959. Elliott, who was married again, later explained the end of the program: "She agreed to the closing up of Roosevelt Enterprises. The traveling she had done and planned to do made it hard to keep up her television and radio shows. Her need for income was less pressing nowadays when fewer cries for help were heard from her children. If I stayed, she would renew the NBC contracts solely for my sake. As it was, they were allowed to expire" (*Mother R.* 201–02).

ER often appeared on various shows across American television screens in the 1950s, but she would not have a regular program of her own again until *Prospects of Mankind* from 1959 to 1962. She and Morgenthau discussed a new project with the format of an open forum with the public as early as 1951, but it never developed. In a letter to daughter Anna in late 1952, she wrote, "I haven't got any radio or T.V. yet, the advertisers think I'm too controversial!" (Asbell 297). Eleanor's agent Tom Stix, who worked with her in the late 1950s and 1960s, recalled that she believed that most advertisers were Republicans who thought of her as "poison" (Stix "Mrs. Roosevelt").

ER engaged talent agent Ted Ashley, who had previously been with William Morris, to seek out television and radio opportunities beginning in 1953. He was involved in booking her on Garry Moore's TV program. However, ER was not happy when she ran into the manager of NBC, and he seemed surprised to hear that she was interested in another radio or TV show. Radio was preferable since she could often record the show from wherever she might be. She wrote to Ashley about that encounter in March 1954: "While he agreed I was a controversial figure, he said he would be willing to think about the matter. It has been a long time since I first asked you to try to get me something." Ashley responded that NBC management had recently changed, and "my personal desire to be of service to you and my belief that something can be accomplished is undiminished." Two months later Eleanor was ready to move on and replied, "I have waited so long for some action on a radio or TV contract that I have decided to give up considering myself tied only to you." She would enlist the help of her lecture agent W. Colston Leigh. Ashley, who also represented Marlene Dietrich and Yul Brynner, would go on to become CEO of Warner Brothers movie studio and vice president of Warner Communications (Ross "News," Ashley correspondence).

This did not stop Eleanor from using the much higher ratings of major prime-time shows and stars like Bob Hope and Ed Sullivan, as well as scores of other small programs, to continue to educate the public. Issues of race, labor, women's rights, youth, Russia, international relations, and the United Nations were just some of the topics she broached on air. Shifting from the role of moderator to guest also allowed Eleanor to speak her mind about political candidates in a way that she had not been free to do on her own two television shows.

ER's television presence had been unique in that few national political players had their own TV programs. As an exception after he left office, Truman's vice president, Alben Barkley, hosted *Meet the Veep*, a 1953 weekly NBC show that ran for 26 episodes before low ratings caused its cancellation (Libbey 110). ABC's *Adlai Stevenson Reports* broadcast on alternate Sundays from 1961 to 1963 while he served as U.S. ambassador to the United Nations, winning a Peabody Award for contributions to international understanding.

15

"Grand Old Lady
of the Democratic Party"

"The old gal was terrific," one reporter wrote lovingly (Driscoll). ABC, CBS, and NBC all broadcast the 1952 Democratic National Convention in Chicago for the first time live coast to coast, and the Democrats had learned from the mistakes of the Republican convention airing two weeks before. They delivered the first convention elaborately orchestrated for television, with direction of camera angles and special towers built for network access, in contrast to the Republicans who had unwisely relegated cameras off to the side. Nine out of 10 homes with a television tuned in an average of 26 hours between the two parties that year, and polls showed that TV coverage gave a bump to votes for Adlai Stevenson (Bogart 234). "One of the convention high points" identified by *The New York Times* was the speech by Eleanor Roosevelt on July 22. With shouts and stamping feet, the crowd gave her a full 18-minute ovation after an introduction by Speaker of the House Sam Rayburn (Hill). A short film clip of the speech was archived by the International Information Administration, the State Department institution then responsible for disseminating positive information about the United States abroad. ER said, "You often ask, 'What can I, as an individual, do to help the United Nations and to help in the struggle for a peaceful world?' I answer, make your own country the best possible country for all its citizens to live in and it will become a valuable member of the neighborhood of nations," to another standing burst of applause. ER inspired as both a symbol of the past and the New Deal and of hope for the future with her passionate words about the United Nations. Nielsen reported that her speech reached 6,677,000 homes, two million more than those who tuned in for Truman's or Stevenson's speeches later in the evening (Gray 272–73).

When she finished, the crowd burst into another two minutes of applause before India Edwards, vice chair of the Democratic Party, presented a tribute from the women delegates and alternates at the convention, citing ER's work with the United Nations and "building a world of social justice, dignity, and freedom for all" (W. Edwards). Even with the high-tech camera setups, there were some issues with television coverage. NBC convention anchor Bill Henry received multiple telegrams demanding to know why someone in the background was allowed to blow cigar smoke into Eleanor's face as she spoke. Lens compression made people behind the rostrum appear close by, when they were really 40 feet away from the speaker (NBC-New York "Sidelights"). Roosevelt favorite candidate Adlai Stevenson was chosen as the Democratic Party candidate for president, going on to lose to Republican Dwight Eisenhower.

ER has been called the "First Lady of Liberalism" and lived up to that title in an August 26, 1953, appearance on *Longines Chronoscope*. Bill Downs and Edward Morgan conducted the interview, regarding Eleanor as an expert on foreign affairs and treating her with respect and authority on the CBS political talk show, sponsored by Longines-Wittnauer watches. The hosts acknowledged her political leadership, not for just women, but for Americans in general, and her work with United Nations that made her a respected figure worldwide. Topics included questions about the view of the United States abroad, her assessment of the UN, and a request for her to define what a liberal is. She replied, "It's very hard to put in a few words what a liberal is, but I would feel that a liberal was a person who kept an open mind, was willing to meet new questions with new solutions and felt that you could move forward. You didn't have to always look backwards and be afraid of moving forward." Her definition is still inspiring to liberals today.

Wearing an Adlai Stevenson button and appearing in a television interview with the candidate, the partisan powerhouse that was Eleanor Roosevelt had an even greater impact on the 1956 Democratic National Convention in Chicago ("My Day" 16 Aug. 1956). She spoke on the evening of August 13 with an address on the responsibilities of young people, the meaning of democracy, and the nature of great leaders, but it was what was going on behind the scenes that also caught the attention of the press. Her words about not looking back to the New Deal were interpreted as support for Stevenson versus former president Truman's endorsement of New York Governor Averell Harriman. Eleanor implied that Truman related to an older generation and older political viewpoint. "There are both admirers and detractors of Mrs. Roosevelt and the old New Deal days who have always felt that it was she and not her husband who was the master Machiavellian politician. They are the ones who are making book that Mrs. Roosevelt has planted a time bomb here that will make mince meat out of the former President and Honest Ave," wrote Frank Kent. He concluded that ER had more political influence than Truman, and that "her voice is the most potent in the country among the Negro voters. And it should be." In his journal, Arthur Schlesinger, Jr., wrote that he would never forget when "Mrs. Roosevelt came to town and proceeded, in the kindest possible way, to destroy Mr. Truman" (180). Reporting shortly before the election in November, the Washington, D.C. *Evening Star* concluded that ER had "emerged from the Democratic convention this summer with towering power and prestige" (Shelton).

Tennessee governor Frank Clement, who was vying for a vice presidential nod, announced: "A Democratic convention of our time would not be a Democratic convention without the presence of a great lady. Four years ago, Sam Rayburn introduced her as the 'first lady of the world,' Mrs. Franklin Delano Roosevelt." The *Boston Globe* described her performance as "deadly earnestness." Her voice "went low, as if it were weighted down with seriousness." It started to rise and then warmed to a smile as she spoke about the promise of young people in the party who "must be allowed to meet new problems with new solutions," rather than leaning on tradition. She encouraged the crowd to bring the Democratic Party back to power with the right candidate (Cremmen). The speech was marked by an "ease of delivery" and an "intimate approach which won Mrs. Eleanor Roosevelt wide compliments on her televised address" ("Talent"). Broadcast journalist Edward R. Murrow called it "the greatest convention speech I ever heard" (R. Henry 120). The next "My Day" column was a humble record of reactions to the speech:

> I arrived in New York about midnight and have been surprised to find that wherever I go, everyone—taxi drivers, people in stores, in the bank, and, not so surprisingly, at home and in my office—tell me they listened and watched the convention on Monday night.
> One taxi driver told me that he just had to go to sleep, because I came on so late, but most of them said that their wives listened, and all of them were so kind in their expressions of interest.
> I felt myself most inadequate to follow Governor Frank G. Clement, even with an interlude between, but it certainly is pleasant to have had everyone apparently at least interested by something I had to say [17 Aug. 1956].

Stevenson lost to Eisenhower a second time in 1956.

Earlier in the summer of 1956, ER's June 10 appearance on *Between the Lines*, a local New York Dumont television show, had already revealed her choice of Stevenson. She spoke in favor of him as the Democratic Party nominee for president and called his chances "good at present" after a significant primary victory in California. ER also noted the importance of choosing a vice president with care after President Eisenhower's recent illness. Eisenhower had a heart attack in 1955, followed by surgery for a bowel obstruction in 1956.

She extended her convention influence in what broadcasting historian Douglas Gomery has called a "turning point for TV news" when her performance on *Meet the Press* played a significant role in the 1956 presidential campaign (118). This was her third appearance on the Sunday morning public affairs show with a panel consisting of producer Lawrence Spivak, journalist May Craig, John Steele, and Richard Clurman from *Newsday*, plus moderator Ned Brooks. Joe Lash observed, "She appeared on *Meet the Press* on September 16, and her answers to questions about Nixon and Eisenhower showed again her deadly capacity for setting off dynamite charges while looking and sounding her most grandmotherly" (*Years Alone* 264). The impact came from statements about why she had "no respect" for Richard Nixon, Eisenhower's running mate for vice president:

> I am told that Mr. Nixon is a very fine young man by many Republican people whom I know, particularly young people, and that he has matured and grown in many ways. I happen to remember very clearly his campaign for the Senatorship. I had no respect for the way in which he accused Helen Gahagan Douglas of being a Communist because he knew that was how he would be elected, and I have no respect for the kind of character that takes advantage and does something they know is not true. He knew that she might be a liberal, but he knew quite well, having known her and worked with her, that she was not a Communist. I have always felt that anyone who wanted an election so much that they would use those means did not have the character that I really admired in public life.

She also believed that Republicans had "a great poverty of issues" by bringing up the Alger Hiss case in this election season, since he had been convicted of perjury in 1950 ("Desegregate").

(From left) Moderator Ned Brooks, producer Lawrence Spivak, and Eleanor Roosevelt on the set of NBC's *Meet the Press* at the RCA Exhibition Hall in New York City, September 16, 1956 (Franklin D. Roosevelt Presidential Library & Museum).

Dealing with the Suez crisis, when Israeli armed forces pushed into Egypt after President Nasser nationalized the Suez Canal, she believed that the U.S. was at fault. It had declined to protest when the Egyptian government initially barred Israeli ships from using the canal over a year prior to the crisis ("Mrs. FDR Raps"). This was another area in which the Eisenhower administration did not rise to the task of world leadership. May Craig asked, "Mrs. Roosevelt, before the nominations former President Truman said that we could not risk a period of trial and error by Mr. Stevenson in the White House in the international situation. Don't you really regard President Eisenhower as better qualified to handle the Suez Canal and the Mediterranean?" ER refuted this claim. "I feel that President Eisenhower gained his knowledge of foreign affairs as a general in the European theater. He was a general carrying out the policies that were made by other people and when you are doing that you learn to be skillful in carrying out those policies. You do learn a great deal, but I do not think it is the same thing as having to think out policies for yourself, and my experience is that Mr. Stevenson has taken a great deal of trouble to inform himself on the background of Asia and Africa, with which this question is closely tied." Some journalists called her out for "unreasoned partisanship" in this claim since Eisenhower was stationed under General Douglas MacArthur for seven years in the Philippines and had been entrusted by FDR to command U.S. troops in Europe (Sokolsky 1956).

Those in the Stevenson camp were impressed. "That was the wisest, most gracious and convincing performance in my recollection," he wired (Stevenson to ER). "I thank you, I congratulate you and I bless you." Adlai wrote campaign manager James Finnegan, "I am told that her *Meet the Press* performance was masterful," especially her condemnation of Nixon and characterization of Eisenhower (Johnson 230). Democratic Party Chairman Paul Butler noted, "I have been watching this program for many years. Never has a person done a more magnificent job than you did." Katie Louchheim, Democratic National Committee Director of Women's Activities, shared that she and her husband spent the entire half hour "assuring each other you are the very ablest spokesman the Democratic party has" (Lash *Years Alone* 265).

Republicans contested the attack on Nixon. John O'Donnell accused Nixon of being "soft" by his response that Mrs. Roosevelt "had been misinformed on the subject," rather than directly challenging her, and the reporter went on to paint Gahagan Douglas specifically as a communist. He delivered a backhand compliment to ER as "even smarter than her politically gifted husband," whom he notes was a "diabolical genius," for her political acumen in the television campaign for Stevenson and "a much smarter, older and experienced politician" than the presidential candidate himself (O'Donnell 1956). Likewise, Marquis Childs was incensed that Nixon replied first by "warmly praising Mrs. Roosevelt for her efforts to spread good will for America around the world" in the presence of Indiana senator William Jenner, for whom the New Deal and World War II were both "a monstrous conspiracy to betray America to the Russian Communists" by President Roosevelt, the "conspirator-in-chief" (Childs).

A history of *Meet the Press* contends that Eleanor conceded the point (R. Ball 39), but her response in "My Day" still retained the claim that Nixon knew what he was doing by inferring that Gahagan Douglas was a communist:

> I was met here at once by the question, "Had I really meant that Mr. Nixon had called Mrs. Douglas a Communist?" I replied that Mr. Nixon has said he had never called her a Communist and that I must have been mistaken.
>
> Of course, it is obvious he never made that statement in so many words, but anyone in this state will remember a pink sheet which came from his headquarters, relating false facts and giving the impression that he believed her to be a Communist [2 Oct. 1956].

Back in 1950, ER had traveled to California to campaign for Helen Gahagan Douglas, who was running against Nixon for U.S. Senate. Helen and her husband, actor Melvyn Douglas, were friends of the Roosevelts. Helen had worked with the Works Progress Administration (WPA), National Youth Administration (NYA), and in the Office of Civilian Defense and held a seat in the U.S. House of Representatives from 1945 to 1951. The Douglases first arranged for ER to visit the California migrant labor camps full of dust bowl refugees in the 1930s (H.G. Douglas 153–56). *Screenland* would even report on Eleanor's visit to the Douglas home during a 1941 Hollywood stop (East 1941). The dirty campaign run by the Nixon team in 1950 included not just flyers on pink sheets of paper, but also anti-Semitic inferences about Melvyn. Myrna Loy was enlisted by ER to help in the fight against the red-baiting tactics, and as a vocal supporter of Helen would find herself on Nixon's long-running personal blacklist (Loy 247).

Democrat Joseph Kennedy, who had fallen out with FDR, was funding anti-communist crusader Joseph McCarthy and contributed to Nixon's Republican Senate campaign. Son John F. Kennedy also supported Nixon in the race, which may have been related to widespread misogyny, but also to his friendship with McCarthy, who visited the Kennedy compound in Massachusetts and even dated sister Patricia Kennedy (Mitchell). When ER would later talk about her mistrust of the younger Kennedy as it related to McCarthy, the Gahagan Douglas campaign must have been on her mind. *The Billboard* reported that the Democratic Party bought time on local Los Angeles television station KTTV for Eleanor to "mount the political stump," the first time she had spoken on local television for a political campaign ("Mrs. FDR on LA"). On September 11, 1950, she spoke for 15 minutes with a campaign pitch for both Gahagan Douglas and son Jimmy ("Mrs. F.D.R. Making"). James Roosevelt was running for governor of California in 1950 but lost that race. He would later serve in the House of Representatives from 1955 to 1965. Eleanor mentioned the trip in "My Day" and felt that it was important that California set an example of a liberal, forward-looking policy.

> As a nonpartisan representative on the U.N. I feel there is a special need for all of us to work within our own particular parties to get the best possible representatives in our national government. In the U.N., above all other places, we recognize the need for having in the United States Senate people with knowledge and understanding of history and of the other peoples of the world. We also value experience in the field of foreign relations [12 Sept. 1950].

She noted that September was early for an election appearance, but she could not get away from United Nations work later in the fall. However, it would be hard to categorize her campaign trip as "nonpartisan."

Around the time of ER's April 11, 1954, second appearance on NBC's *Meet the Press*, the Democratic National Committee did not endorse Jimmy, then seeking nomination for Congress, due to his widely publicized marital problems and multiple divorces. When asked on the show about the controversy, she responded, "I have no comment on political questions of that kind. I'm now working as much as I can in a nonpolitical field." In the context of her influence in the party on the national level, it was a blatant non-answer. Franklin Jr. was a potential candidate for governor of New York; asked about her endorsement, she replied, "I have always supported my children when they thought it was the right thing to do." With a note of misogyny, the *New York Daily News* called this not only an evasive answer, but "coy and kittenish" ("Mrs. R. Rewrites").

Back in the 1956 campaign, Eleanor played a huge role on *Face the Nation* after her *Meet the Press* triumph on NBC. The November 4, 1956, CBS appearance with Maine Republican senator Margaret Chase Smith is notable for two reasons. It was the first time the program included any woman, and four years before the televised Kennedy and Nixon presidential debates, ER and Smith debated the merits of Adlai Stevenson versus Dwight Eisenhower. Thus, *Face the Nation* featured the first television debate about presidential candidates, with an exchange important enough to call for a *New York Times* blow-by-blow of the two women's arguments (Drury). The panel consisted of William Hines, Jr., from the *Washington Star*, Arthur Sylvester from the *Newark News*, and Peter Lisagor from the *Chicago Daily News*, with

Eleanor Roosevelt, moderator Stuart Novins, and Maine Republican senator Margaret Chase Smith get ready to *Face the Nation* from Washington, D.C., on CBS, November 4, 1956. The two debated Adlai Stevenson versus Dwight Eisenhower for president (Franklin D. Roosevelt Presidential Library & Museum).

moderator Griffing Bancroft. Hines began by asking Eleanor what portion of the electoral vote she thought Stevenson might win. Her initial reply represented a typical self-characterization designed to make opponents underestimate her knowledge and power in the political arena: "Oh, sir, I'm not a good enough politician to have any idea about such things. I'm not a prophet, and I really would have no idea." She then continued by slamming Eisenhower's foreign policy: "It seems to me, however, that as the last few days have been developing that there can be no question in the people's minds of the failure of our policies in the Near East, which have now resulted in our making NATO weaker…. I can see, of course, nothing but anxiety in the minds of everyone who understands the situation in these areas of the world."

In "A Debate with Eleanor Roosevelt," Smith devoted an entire chapter of her autobiography to this show and her preparation. She characterized her relationship with ER as a friendship that crossed party lines, based on mutual respect, and had even served as a substitute moderator on *Mrs. Roosevelt Meets the Public* when Eleanor served the UN in Europe. She wrote, "I felt that I was far from a match for Mrs. Roosevelt in debating and in the breadth and depth of knowledge of issues." So Smith focused on appearance and style to distinguish and contrast herself with the older, taller, more experienced ER. She would not try to match her opponent's forcefulness, expecting Eleanor to speak with a tone of authority, but would instead answer briefly, deliberately, and deferentially. There was a risk that Mrs. Roosevelt might dominate the debate, but Smith preferred this to "over-extending myself to the point of vulnerability." She was confident that a strong summary statement would offset any weakness. "It was evident that Mrs. Roosevelt was caught by surprise as I refrained from tangling with her. The more that I spoke softly and smiled faintly, and the less I said in reply, the more Mrs. Roosevelt seemed to be put off balance. And this made her talk more to try to regain her composure and emotional balance." Then Smith shocked ER by changing her delivery style in the summary period to a "biting staccato." To counter Eleanor's criticisms of the Republican administration, the senator boasted that Democratic presidents had selected Dwight Eisenhower to lead NATO and had previously asked him to join the Democratic presidential ticket.

ER declined to shake hands with Smith at the end of the broadcast, angry at both the tone and the content of what had been a civil debate up to that point. Of course, it *had* been FDR and Churchill who chose Eisenhower to command the Allied Forces in Europe and Truman who asked him to join the Democrats in 1952. As she left, Eleanor asked of others, "Did you hear what she said?!" Smith did not think herself unethical, but she was not happy with the result of Eleanor Roosevelt turning her back (Smith 203–11). Four years later in 1960, when CBS took out a large advertisement for *Face the Nation* in *The New York Times* featuring the portraits of famous guests, ER and Smith were still the only two women to appear ("The Face").

In a national television broadcast on October 11, 1956, Adlai Stevenson pledged to make a nuclear test ban his first order of business if elected president. The 25-minute film *Nuclear Test Ban* was broadcast as part of this campaign, narrated by Stevenson and Eleanor, and produced by Vanessa Brown (Archerd 1956). A January 1957 article suggests that Stevenson planned to narrate a documentary called *H-Bomb Over America* about the horrors of a third World War, and it was "to be partially bankrolled by Eleanor Roosevelt." However, when the reporter checked in with both Adlai and ER, they had no such plans. "I know nothing of it, I am not backing anything," she said (Gardner "Ben"). Midway through the 1956 film, ER appears with her own message about the ban. She sits on a couch with notes on her lap, wearing pearls and a cardigan sweater, and reads much of the text, not appearing in any way extemporaneous in her remarks until the very end. New York street noise can be heard, indicating that this may have been shot in her NYC apartment. She talks about making no apologies for developing the bomb in a race with the Germans, but "I do think we have a grave responsibility for guiding the power we developed into channels which benefit rather than injure all of mankind." She disputes those who say that we should not make the threat of nuclear war or the framework of disarmament a campaign issue. "I agree with Adlai Stevenson. I think we should take the minimum risk and therefore that we should do away with the tests of the hydrogen bomb."

Before the 1956 election, ER would participate in several paid campaign television spots, including October 24 in New York with Stevenson and New York mayor Robert Wagner, "presented by the Liberal party," and another that month on ABC New York to promote Stevenson with Estes Kefauver as vice president ("Political

Broadcasts"). There she also talked about peace and disarmament. In a political broadcast on October 18, 1956, in Pennsylvania, Eleanor introduced Joseph S. Clark, Jr., Democratic candidate for the United States Senate, and discussed the presidential election, civil rights, and the integration of public schools before asking the audience to vote a straight Democratic ticket. On October 20, she appeared via closed circuit television to Democratic fundraising dinners in more than 40 cities across the country (O'Leary). On October 25, her speech to the Delaware State Education Association convention was televised locally, followed by talks by Republican and Democratic candidates for governor ("Harrington"). Presumably, there were many other local television spots. Finally, near the 1956 election eve on November 5, she and Senators John F. Kennedy, Hubert Humphrey, and Estes Kefauver joined Stevenson on a 45-minute national "television spectacular" about voting for the Democratic ticket. Press coverage notes, "There was the elder-stateswoman, Mrs. Roosevelt, saying she hoped Americans could be known as a bold and generous people, not as a fat and smug generation" (Stringer).

Although Stevenson lost again in 1956, ER's opinions on political matters continued to be sought. On her fourth appearance on NBC's *Meet the Press* on October 20, 1957, she was even asked what she thought of reports that *she* might be the next Democratic presidential candidate in 1960. She laughed: "I am 73 years old. Wake up." Marquis Childs of the *St. Louis Post-Dispatch* followed up: "Do you think we shall ever have a woman president?" She replied, "Yes, of course we will," but was unsure how soon that might be. She felt that "someday it will happen when you get to the point where you look at people in politics and in positions of political importance as people and not as either women or men." Her crystal ball might have been too forward-looking in light of continuing American political realities. ER also judged that the Democratic leadership in Congress had been "very poor" in recent years, without a clear idea of what it stood for. She believed the Eisenhower administration was a "businessman's administration" most concerned with tax and fiscal matters ("*Meet the Press* Interview"). Agent Tom Stix wrote to congratulate her on a particularly fine job in this appearance (Stix correspondence II).

In *The Mike Wallace Interview* series from 1957 to 1960, journalist Mike Wallace conducted half-hour prime-time probing interviews with politicians and celebrities for ABC, all framed in tight, tense close-ups. This predates his well-known *60 Minutes* news magazine show for CBS. The book *Mike Wallace Asks: Highlights from 46 Controversial Interviews* transcribes segments of the show that "have unquestionably pushed back the frontier of talk on television," including portions of Eleanor's November 23, 1957, interview. "Gray, serene, patient and opinionated, seventy-three-year-old Eleanor Roosevelt stands relentlessly behind her convictions. Her unyielding stamina and her single-minded determination to defend and disseminate what she believes to be best for her country have split her public into two sharply opposed camps, those who love and those who loathe. There seems to be no middle ground" (Preston 5, 108).

Variety covered her appearance on the hot seat: "Mrs. Roosevelt handled the interview well and registered her feelings and opinions with an air of dignity and sincerity." However, the writer felt that Wallace "took it easy" on her in the beginning with standard questions about present-day leadership versus wartime political leaders and the current world and domestic situations. He "got a bit rough" toward the end of the show, reading "zingers" about hatred for both her and FDR from Westbrook Pegler. "Mrs. Roosevelt parried these thrusts with a calm dignity that took most of the sting out of the digs and never lost control of the verbal gymnastics" (Silverman). Arthur Grace agreed overall and found ER "a paragon of quiet dignity, answering each question with reasonable candor" (Grace). *The Billboard* review of the show noted, "both sides of the conversation had dignity and importance for the most part" (Bernstein).

The interview with Wallace had been rescheduled from October 19, since ER had an appearance booked on *Meet the Press* the following day (Adams "N.B.C."). Wallace leads with questions about leadership, asking her what Winston Churchill, Mahatma Gandhi, and FDR all had in common. For her, great courage—mental, spiritual, and physical—is key, in addition to great patience, a deep interest in people, and intellectual ability. She remarks that Eisenhower was good at carrying out directions from others, and that he had less of an intellectual interest in a wide variety of subjects than her husband or Churchill. He wonders about her earlier criticisms of Richard Nixon. She replies, "Because I think that in great crises, you need to have deep-rooted convictions, and I have a feeling from the kind of campaigns that I have watched Mr. Nixon in in the past, that his convictions are not very strong." When Wallace asks about potential leaders, she mentions Stevenson again, but admits that it would be extremely difficult for him to run for a third time. Then he hits hard by reading Pegler's words about her, asking for a reaction: "This woman is a political force of enormous ambitions. I believe she is a menace, unscrupulous as to truth, vain and cynical, all with a pretense of exaggerated kindness and human feeling, which deceives millions of gullible persons." ER smiles at this and then turns the tables to indicate how pathetic she really believes Pegler to be. After mentioning that as far as political ambition goes, she had never run for office, she continues:

> I can see that Mr. Pegler probably believes all these things, and I'm not…. I suppose one does things unconsciously that makes you seem like that. Perhaps I do seem like that to him. I think it must be terrible to hate as many things as Mr. Pegler hates, and I would be unhappy, I think, and therefore, I'm afraid that he is unhappy. And I'm sorry for him because after all, we all grow older, and we all have to live with ourselves, and I think that must sometimes be difficult for Mr. Pegler.

Wallace then directly asks about the hatred some people had for both her and FDR. About the president she says, "I suppose that that is just the feeling that certain people had that he was destroying the thing that they held dear and felt touched them." She does not explain that statement further, but goes on to say that political campaigns were still being fought on the memory of FDR, rather than on the person running. About herself, she was now extraordinarily direct with her answer:

> I was touching something, which for some people seemed a sacred thing they had to keep hold of, and a major part of my criticism has been on the Negro question, of course. And I've had many others, but that is the major part, and I think that that is quite natural because to some people, that seems to be destroying something that to them is very dear.

One might interpret this to mean her threat to the sacredness of whiteness, the purity of femininity, American exceptionalism, or the altar of capitalism. ER clearly understood what she was challenging in her activism.

Wallace ends the program by turning to face the camera: "Because she'll fight courageously for what she believes, Eleanor Roosevelt has had to pay a certain price—bitter criticism, a lack of privacy, the infighting of partisan politics—but Eleanor Roosevelt has also reaped what must be the most satisfying of all rewards, the respect and with it the affection of hundreds of thousands of people." In his memoir years later, he said of ER and this interview, "Of all the First Ladies who have graced the White House in my lifetime, there was one who towered over all others, just as her husband towered over all other presidents who came to power over the last century" (*Between* 37). Wallace characterized this experience as "a few special hours with her" and wrote, "I made plain to her, ahead of time, how much I along with tens of millions of Americans, admired her gently phrased but nonetheless steely determination to oppose the politics of fear, to fight for civil liberties and civil rights, to bridge opposites by forging partnerships. She was within everyone's grasp yet remained always slightly detached, in the battle surely, but appealing always to our better natures" ("Introduction" VII).

On October 26, 1958, ER made her fifth appearance on the NBC public affairs show *Meet the Press* with panelists Clifton Daniel of *The New York Times*, Luke Carroll of the *New York Herald Tribune*, May Craig of the *Portland* (Maine) *Press Herald*, producer and permanent panelist Lawrence Spivak, and moderator Ned Brooks ("Mrs. FDR Is"). In a testy discussion of New York politics that was well reported in the newspapers, Spivak said that he had heard that she was she was so upset about the nomination of Frank Hogan for Senate that she had told some of her friends that she would not vote for him. She disliked his connections with Carmine DeSapio's Tammany Hall and felt that political bosses had too much influence in both parties. However, she would still vote for the Democratic Party candidate ("Mrs. Roosevelt Wary," "My Day" 29 Oct. 1958). One columnist shared the gossip that her lack of support for Hogan might have to do with a different connection. The suggestion was that Carmine DeSapio had not backed FDR, Jr., when he ran and lost the New York Democratic gubernatorial primary race, so that was what this was all about (L. Martin). Friend Gore Vidal, also known to gossip, confirms this point of view when describing the evening he, Franklin Jr., and a beaming ER celebrated victory over DeSapio and Tammany in the name of reform and civic virtue (*Palimpsest* 344). However, the Roosevelt fight against Tammany Hall political control in New York was long-standing, since FDR's first efforts back in 1911.

Journalists criticized Spivak for persistently coming back to the Hogan question during the show, since *Meet the Press* is a national program and other panelists' issues were not given as much time as New York politics. "I'm sure that most of us tuned in would much rather have heard her views on some of the current and hot national topics." In addition, Brooks "took up two or three minutes telling us who Mrs. Roosevelt was and it's difficult to be more extraneous than that. Mrs. R. could have done better in an isolation booth on *$64,000 Question*" (Humphrey "Two"). ER's statement that she thought it wrong for the Democratic Party to reinstate

Representative Adam Clayton Powell, Jr., caused additional controversy ("Mrs. Roosevelt Isn't"). He had defected to support the election of Republican president Eisenhower but had recently been reelected as a Democrat for an eighth term representing Harlem. Since Powell was the first Black member of Congress from New York, a letter published in the Black-owned *New York Amsterdam News* chided Eleanor, pointing out that there was strength in unity for a minority group who had long been divided by White politicians who paid little attention to issues of discrimination and injustice—regardless of criticisms of Powell's politics ("So Right"). Powell became a House leader, serving from 1945 to 1971. ER believed that she had not done very well in explaining her position on the air and reviewed her thoughts in "My Day" (29 Oct. 1958), but a columnist from the Black publication *Chicago Defender* thought otherwise: "Despite her age, Mrs. Roosevelt proved to be as sharp as ever in getting across her point of view when questioned by the reporters. Some of her critics insist that the former first lady can throw a political knife with more skill than any of the professionals" (L. Martin). One might counter that it would be naive not to consider her one of the "professionals" in politics at this point.

The day before ER's rock star entrance to the 1960 Democratic Party Convention in Los Angeles described in the introduction to this book, Walter Cronkite's televised coverage on CBS switched to a press conference she had organized at the Biltmore Hotel to promote a Stevenson-Kennedy ticket. The tide had already turned to the senator from Massachusetts as the presidential pick, which Stevenson acknowledged; he did not expect to be nominated himself. He admitted embarrassment at ER's last-minute maneuverings on his behalf and introduced her to the press in attendance and the viewers at home:

> I have come to think of her not alone as the best known and the best liked and the best loved American of our time but as our most distinguished and most effective ambassador to the world. That she has made common cause with me in minor endeavors of no public consequence in the past, in large endeavors of great public consequence in the more recent past, has been, I suppose, the greatest honor that has befallen me. It's been my good fortune, as some of you here well know, to have met and known and talked with and corresponded with most of the leaders of my generation throughout the world. I have yet to meet one of the moral stature, of the moral influence, of the public resonance of Mrs. Roosevelt.

The CBS commentator followed up: "It sounded more as though Governor Stevenson were presenting Mrs. Roosevelt as a candidate for nomination than vice versa. The Grand Old Lady of the Democratic Party took it in her stride, and now she's about to speak." Perhaps he meant what "grande dame" might imply, rather than "old lady." She was only 75 years old.

Wearing a casual short-sleeved dress and carrying her purse, ER made her way to the podium, complained about the Los Angeles traffic, and then asked for questions. She did not have a prepared statement and seemed extremely comfortable in this role, smiling with the group. Wearing black glasses with attached hearing aid, she asked journalists to repeat questions if she was unable to hear very well. The first question was about comments she had made about Kennedy and "the Negro vote." She explained that she felt that a Stevenson-Kennedy ticket was the strongest ticket Democrats could put in the field, and she doubted that Kennedy could carry the Black vote, a sentiment shared by the *Chicago Defender* for Kennedy's lackluster voting record on civil rights and close relationship with several Dixiecrat governors (Michaeli 357). She also feared that he would suffer from religious prejudice as a Catholic candidate. The next reporter began shouting to get her attention, addressing her as "Mrs. Kennedy" before quickly realizing his error and calling out, "Mrs. Roosevelt!" The room exploded in laughter at the mistake, and she had a good laugh as well. However, now Cronkite had to cut in to leave live coverage of the press conference to go back to the floor of the convention, which was just being called to order.

Two days later, ER experienced the intrusion of the network cameras as she shook off the hands of the men accompanying her to the convention podium. Paul Butler introduced her as the First Lady of the World: "We are honored to have you among us as the wonderful Democrat and wonderful person you are." She seconded the nomination of Adlai Stevenson in a short speech that was met with "warm emotional applause" (T. White 155). Gore Vidal, who did not favor another run for Stevenson, felt divided loyalties that evening. Eleanor served as his political mentor while he unsuccessfully ran for the House of Representatives in her district, but Vidal also worked to elect John F. Kennedy, his brother-in-law through step marriage. "Mrs. Roosevelt, a giant of a woman, in every sense, walked out into the glare of the lights and, like some ancient priestess, warned us about turning our backs on Stevenson," he wrote in 2009. "When she wanted to be, she was extraordinarily eloquent, and so she was that day" (*Snapshots* 122). It would take some effort to convince Eleanor of JFK's worthiness as the Democratic candidate for president, but she did come around.

16

Joseph Kennedy's Son

Joseph P. Kennedy was always a powerbroker. The Hollywood producer and financier backed Franklin Roosevelt early on but would become a political enemy. As Blanche Wiesen Cook described ER's point of view, "She ultimately came to despise Joe Kennedy, but in 1938 merely distrusted him" (Vol. II 501). Rather than reward his support with a coveted cabinet position, FDR appointed the Kennedy patriarch as ambassador to Great Britain in 1938 and soon found him publicly advocating not only American neutrality and isolationism, but appeasement. Noticeably pro–German and out of touch with the administration's views on the European situation, Kennedy returned to the U.S. in late October 1940. Within two weeks, Hollywood welcomed him back at a November 13 Warner Brothers lunch for 50 with studio heads Samuel Goldwyn, Louis B. Mayer, Harry Warner, and others to talk about the British Film Exchange Agreement. However, his off-the-record remarks after dessert went far beyond that topic. Feeling that Kennedy "stirred the embers of terror, isolationism, and racism," Douglas Fairbanks, Jr., wrote a hurried note to FDR saying that Kennedy told the producers and executives that they should refrain from making anti–Nazi pictures "because people would say it was because of the Jews!" (Fairbanks, Jr., 309, 366). Drew Pearson and Robert S. Allen wrote in their syndicated column that Kennedy "had the movie-moguls almost popeyed" when he expressed views that Britain was virtually defeated, the U.S. should limit its aid, and that "Hollywood producers should stop making films offensive to dictators" (Pearson). Ben Hecht opined in January 1941: "At a number of private luncheons with the jittery cinema moguls, Ambassador Joe has peddled the *sub rosa* information that anything the movies do to decry the horrors of Hitlerism will act as a boomerang and come back and knock over all the Jews." Kennedy was advising "Semitic Hollywood" not to attract attention to themselves by using the movie industry as a weapon, but to keep people from noticing them and calling them warmongers. "The fact that in gagging the great Jews of Hollywood, Joe was removing a powerful and talented weapon against the Nazis may not have occurred to him" (Hecht). President Roosevelt met with Kennedy on December 1 and accepted his resignation. Afterward, FDR wrote in a letter to son-in-law John Boettiger that Joe Kennedy "has a positive horror of any change in the present methods of life in America. To him, the future of a small capitalistic class is safer under a Hitler than under a Churchill" (Goodwin 212).

Kennedy would become enmeshed in postwar hysteria over communism, supporting his friend Joseph McCarthy. This played out in financial support of

Republican Richard Nixon's dirty campaign for the 1950 California Senate seat against Eleanor's friend, Democrat Helen Gahagan Douglas. Rising star John F. Kennedy inherited his father's friendship with McCarthy and did not speak out during the anti-communist crusades in the House and Senate. For ER, this showed a crisis of character when McCarthy was a serious threat to American free speech and democracy.

Weekly Sunday afternoon ABC program *College News Conference*, simulcast over TV and radio, featured a panel of accomplished college journalists who asked questions of a prominent political guest. Show founder Ruth Hagy produced and served as moderator from Washington, D.C., with assistant producer Peggy Whedon, who would interview Eleanor herself in 1962 on *Issues and Answers*, and director Richard Armstrong. The show's tagline was "where the leaders of tomorrow meet the leaders of today," and it received a Peabody Award in 1958 for Outstanding Television Program for Youth. On ER's December 7, 1958, appearance, Hagy began by announcing that they were extremely fortunate and proud to have such a staunch champion of human rights as a guest. The first question addressed the Democratic Party's stand on civil rights, with a follow-up asking if this would split the party. Eleanor did not believe that it would result in Democrats leaving the party; Southerners would have to accept the platform. She was even ready to accept losing the 1960 presidential election, rather than not standing up for what they believed in. ER publicly doubted the presidential potential of Senator John F. Kennedy. She praised his charm and the book *Profiles in Courage*, but "I would hesitate to place the difficult decisions that have to be taken by the next President of the United States will have to make with someone who understands what courage is and admires it but has not quite the independence to have it." On other occasions, she made clear that he would have shown the requisite courage had he spoken out against Senator McCarthy.

Eleanor was widely known to hate Joseph Kennedy by this time, largely because of his acquiescence to Hitler and support of McCarthy, and said on the show, "His father has been spending oodles of money all over the country and probably has a representative in every state by now." JFK wrote her privately in protest that this was not the case:

> Because I know of your long fight against the injudicious use of false statements, rumors or innuendo as a means of injuring the reputation of an individual, I am certain that you are the victim of misinformation; and I am equally certain that you would want to ask your informant if he would be willing to name me one such representative or one such example of any spending by my father around the country on my behalf. I await your answer, and that of your source, with great interest. Whatever other differences we may have had, I'm certain that we both regret this kind of political practice.

ER was adamant in her reply that many had told her of the money spent on JFK's behalf, although she finally acquiesced in their letter exchange to say that if asked, she would assure people that the rumors were not true (JFK to ER, ER to JFK, Lash *Years Alone* 280).

On the same show, she mentioned that she was still supporting Adlai Stevenson for the Democratic nomination but conceded that to have already lost twice in the presidential race was a greater liability than Kennedy's Catholicism. ER also praised Hubert Humphrey during the exchange about the candidates, and *The New York Times* headline from this appearance read, "Mrs. Roosevelt Lauds Humphrey." When Humphrey appeared on the program in April 1960, moderator Hagy prefaced questions with the comment, "He is a man who has been described on this very program by Mrs. Roosevelt as one of the Democrats who had the spark of greatness needed by the next president of the United States." ER noted that Humphrey had an alert mind and was as tough as Soviet premier Nikita Khrushchev. She also felt quite sure that "reactionary Republicans" had promised Richard Nixon the Republican nomination, rather than Nelson Rockefeller.

Still promoting Stevenson, ER appeared on *College News Conference* again on June 19, 1960, saying that she respected Senator Kennedy, but felt that Stevenson had "more experience and more maturity." She predicted that "if a big groundswell develops in the country" from liberal Democrats, Stevenson still had a chance of being nominated. ER suggested that Kennedy should accept the vice presidential nomination and turn his convention votes over to Stevenson, although she knew this was asking a great deal of him. Then she added that she would support Kennedy if nominated and suggested Humphrey as his vice presidential running mate. If the nominee were Senator Lyndon B. Johnson, she said, "I doubt I would be very enthusiastic." Although former president Truman was supporting Senator Stuart Symington, she commented, "I don't think it is even worth considering" ("Mrs. Roosevelt Analyzes"). Later, ER understood that Johnson's value as vice president was the work he would do to advance civil rights (Fuchs "Lady" 22). When JFK appeared on *Face the Nation* on March 30, 1958, reporter John Madigan asked about the views she had expressed, "that you had dodged the McCarthy issue in 1954, and then in 1956." JFK explained that he had been in the hospital a good deal of that time and defended his record on civil liberties (*Eleanor Roosevelt, John Kennedy*).

Kennedy was also a topic of conversation in her October 26, 1958, appearance on *Meet the Press*. An issue on the docket for the day's show was that of a potential Catholic president of the United States, and Luke Carroll of the *New York Herald Tribune* queried what ER thought. Eleanor said she was not sure that the public would accept a Catholic candidate, revealing what some interpreted as a lingering prejudice. A *Washington Post* column took her to task: "Mrs. Roosevelt has, perhaps inadvertently, added fuel to a rising anti–Catholicism by emphasizing this unrealistic issue of church and state" (Sokolsky). Lawrence Fuchs, who co-taught an international law seminar at Brandeis University with ER, served as an adviser for *Prospects of Mankind*, and wrote several of JFK's speeches for Jewish audiences, explained that he believed that Kennedy often painted liberals or progressives as anti–Catholic if they did not support his presidential bid. He did not believe this was true of Eleanor. She disagreed with Catholic Church leadership and the institution's attempts to mix issues of church and state but admired JFK for the way that he spoke out on church-state issues. "I think she had the kind of free mind that did not stereotype people," said Fuchs. He believed that, although a fine young man, "her consistent objection to Kennedy was, as far as I could make out, was he was not Adlai Stevenson" (Fuchs "Oral"). She and FDR had been supporters of Catholic Al Smith back in the 1920s.

After economist John Kenneth Galbraith, who was working for Kennedy's presidential campaign, appeared on Eleanor's new show *Prospects of Mankind*, he spoke to her afterward and convinced her to book JFK. Galbraith believed that her reluctance was about Joseph Kennedy's break with FDR over the failure to back the British prior to World War II. Morgenthau described him as "most anxious to take part with you on the program" (Morgenthau correspondence II). In a sign of how important it was that he be associated with the Roosevelt name, on January 2, 1960, the younger Kennedy announced his presidential bid at a press conference in Washington and then hopped the family plane to Boston for the *Prospects* show that afternoon. When he arrived, staffer Paul Noble took JFK aside to ask him to switch from a white shirt that glared on camera to a "TV blue" shirt that helped cameras better render skin tones. They kept an assortment of blue shirts in assorted sizes just for that purpose (Noble 13). Fuchs recalls Kennedy asking them to cancel the usual post-show press conference because "she might bring up the McCarthy business."

When approached, she replied, "You tell the Senator not to worry. Everything will be all right. I won't do anything that would embarrass him" (Fuchs "Oral"). Even though she did not call him out about McCarthy, the press conference was not exactly a tremendous success for the senator. Galbraith describes the day:

> The program a short time later went very well; both participants were interesting, even mildly eloquent. I was in a state of warm self-congratulation. The press had rallied around, and after the show Mrs. Roosevelt was asked the most pressing question of the time. Kennedy had, that very day, stated his intention of seeking the Democratic nomination. Would she support him? Leaving no one in doubt, she said she certainly would not. That, needless to say, was the principal news that came out of the meeting. Kennedy was not impressed by my role as a political strategist [53].

Eleanor Roosevelt talks with Massachusetts Democratic senator John F. Kennedy before the taping of *Prospects of Mankind* at Brandeis University, January 2, 1960. Kennedy had just announced his candidacy for the presidency that morning in Washington, D.C., before flying to Boston to appear on the NET show (courtesy Robert D. Farber University Archives & Special Collections Department, Brandeis University).

Producer Henry Morgenthau III believed that her reluctance had to do with support for Stevenson as the superior candidate and the intense dislike of Kennedy's father, but the television executive also thought that JFK assumed that his appearance would please her. "Actually, Mrs. Roosevelt could care less," Morgenthau later recalled, but regardless, he felt that in the press excitement over the younger man's announcement of his candidacy for president, her doubt that day got little coverage (Morgenthau "Eleanor"). *The New York Times* reported that she "declined to comment" on the senator's entry into the race, saying at the post-show press conference, "I am not for or against any candidate, until after the convention" ("Mrs. Roosevelt Bars"). Fuchs felt that she was being politically astute and considerate in that she did not make a political plug for Stevenson (Fuchs "Oral"). Later Galbraith, who had run the Office of Price Administration during the war, still counted Franklin and Eleanor Roosevelt as the largest political influences in his life.

Eleanor had a connection between father and son in mind that day, although she surmised that JFK was not aware of the presence of Louis Lyons at the press conference. Lyons had worked for the *Boston Globe* in 1940 when he scooped Ambassador Joseph Kennedy's pronouncement that "Democracy is finished in England." Joe protested that he thought his remarks were off the record, but did not deny that he implied that Great Britain might be better off submitting to Hitler (C. Beauchamp 368). ER said that she had stormed into Franklin's bedroom demanding that he fire Mr. Kennedy. His resignation was soon tendered. In 1960, Lyons was reporting for WGBH and asked the first question during the post-show press conference with JFK. Eleanor may have been the only one who understood the significance, which she shared with Paul Noble (Noble 13–14). She wrote Adlai Stevenson to suggest that he appear on *Prospects of Mankind* as part of the effort to win the 1960 nomination. "I am most anxious that your ideas be given full expression on this program which reaches a different, more specialized audience than the usual commercial television channels," she said (R. Henry 169). He did take part in the last episode of the season on June 5.

After Kennedy won the nomination, Eleanor came around to back JFK for president after a private meeting with him at her Val-Kill home, although some of her anti–Kennedy remarks were unfortunately incorporated into a Republican Party television commercial for Richard Nixon (Lasky). ER and the young candidate became friendly, and he named her chair of the first Presidential Commission on the Status of Women. Kennedy appeared in taped segments of *Prospects of Mankind* twice while serving as president, but Morgenthau described ER's irritation when there was no reply to the first of her invitations. The producer was able to contact JFK's press secretary Pierre Salinger, who confirmed the president's interest and direction to arrange the program when it was convenient for her. Said Morgenthau, "He could get on television all he wanted. I think it was that Mrs. Roosevelt was a challenge to him. He liked a challenge. He respected her, but to win her favor was a challenge to him. He wanted to meet that challenge" (Marc).

During the election season, Metropolitan Broadcasting Corporation launched a nonpartisan "get out the vote" campaign after Labor Day in 1960, with three-minute television and radio appeals by ER, Al Capp, James Farley, Buddy Hackett, Helen Hayes, and Cardinal Francis Spellman. Organizers wished to promote "the importance of the forthcoming presidential elections to the entire citizenry and the free world" ("Political Sidelights"). ER appeared on the October 31, 1960, NBC late-night *Jack Paar Tonight Show* discussing her recent *Redbook* magazine article, "My Advice to the Next First Lady." An assistant producer had written saying that the show would be both flattered and delighted if she would accept the invitation from Mr. Paar as one of the most outstanding guests they had ever presented (O'Malley). In this case, the main goal was to help Kennedy win the upcoming presidential election. Robert Stein, who worked for *Redbook*, described her appearance:

> On the way to the studio, I asked Mrs. Roosevelt, who had supported Adlai Stevenson during the convention and been visibly cool to JFK, what made her decide to take part in a talk show. "I want to help elect Senator Kennedy," she said. On the *Tonight* show, she did just that. As Paar sat beaming deferentially, she compared Kennedy to FDR during his first campaign in 1932, inspiring voters and responding to their enthusiasm, and predicted he would make a fine President. In Kennedy's hairline victory, her testimonial may well have been significant [Stein].

Her intention was no secret. In a piece about pre-election programming, the *New York Herald* noted Eleanor's upcoming *Jack Paar* appearance: "NBC apparently owes time to the Democrats" (Griffith). Anna wrote her mother, "People in Miami told me they'd seen you on the Jack Parr [sic] and the Dave Garraway [sic] shows—not the most desirable hours for you to be working—but they said you were wonderful!" (Asbell 345). *Paar* was on late at night, while *Today* with Garroway aired quite early in the morning. ER had been part of a *Today* interview series with "elder statesmen" and "molders of American opinion" (Parsons correspondence).

Come November, Eleanor hit the airwaves in short national television advertisements for Kennedy. Street sounds from New York City can be heard in the background as she speaks:

> When you cast your vote for the president of the United States, be sure you have studied the record. I have. I urge you to vote for John F. Kennedy, for I have come to believe that as a president, he will have the strength and the moral courage to provide the leadership for human rights we need in this time of crisis. He's a man with a sense of history. That I'm well familiar with because my husband had a sense of history. He wanted to leave a good record for the future. I think John F. Kennedy wants to leave a good record.

In another version of the campaign spot, she says:

> John F. Kennedy came to visit me at Hyde Park. We talked together, and I learned that he was truly interested in carrying on many of the things which my husband had just begun. Mr. Kennedy is a strong and determined person who as president will provide the leadership for greater Social Security benefits which the social welfare of a civilized nation demands. I urge you to study Mr. Kennedy's program to look at his very remarkable record in Congress, and I think you will join me in voting for John F. Kennedy for president.

In New York, paid political spots titled "Mrs. Eleanor Roosevelt Speaks for Kennedy" featured ER speaking to voters on ABC affiliate WABC-TV and then on WNEW-TV the following evening of November 6 for 15 minutes. Television listings called it "Political Talk: Mrs. Franklin D. Roosevelt for Kennedy" ("Television Programs"). On a December 15, 1960, educational program called *Transitions*, ER spoke on the topic of "Politics and Democracy" on WPIX in New York. The board of regents of the New York City Board of Education funded this experimental use of a commercial station to deliver educational content, and *Variety* noted that "she will become a teacher" on the afternoon half-hour show ("TV-Radio").

Like a good part of the nation, ER watched the four televised presidential debates between candidates Kennedy and Nixon in September and October 1960, calling them an "advance in the democratic process" and "the first time campaigning had been conducted on this level" (*Eye on St. Louis*, "Programming"). She also commented in "My Day" about each of the debates individually, writing after the first event that she and the small group of people with whom she watched unsurprisingly "felt honesty in Mr. Kennedy and distrustfulness in Mr. Nixon" (28 Sept. 1960). Nixon did not wear makeup for this first debate, and the press criticized him for how much the five o'clock shadow stubble of his beard was visible during the performance and how he wore a gray suit that blended into the background, while JFK had his own team apply makeup. Kennedy, who was also tan and wore a black suit that stood out, looked better on TV than his opponent, and those who watched this first debate on television swung to Kennedy in polling the following day.

Before commenting in "My Day" on the next debate, Eleanor talked to other people to get their reactions and heard quite a lot about Mr. Nixon's new pancake makeup:

> The most general opinion I get is that the make-up man and the lighting helped Mr. Nixon very much. I am not quite sure that this satisfies me completely, for I had to look at Mr. Nixon twice before I recognized him. Furthermore, it would seem to me that the objective in these debates was to get to know the two candidates as they are, not as some make-up man wishes to make them appear. This question, however, does not seem to arise with Mr. Kennedy, as I understand he decided that it was more important that people get to know him as he is.
>
> Lighting, of course, can affect both candidates greatly, but that depends entirely on the technician at the time—and when all is said and done this is not a beauty contest [12 Oct. 1960].

After the last of the four confrontations, she was impressed that the public had access to the candidates in a new way:

> Whatever our political opinions may be, I believe we can be grateful to the networks for having given us these four debates. They have been a milestone in TV usefulness, and have served to introduce the candidates and the people to each other. I would in the future far rather see debates where the two opponents were alone on the stage and where their ideas and views throughout were exchanged man to man, without the intervention of reporters. Perhaps it would be effective to have a moderator to start them off and, if they got too heated, to calm them down. Since this technique is probably here to stay, we can improve on it as the years go on and make it of ever greater value to the people who have to vote on Election Day [24 Oct. 1960].

However, there was not another presidential candidate debate until 1976, when it became an accepted tradition.

John F. Kennedy, of course, won the presidential election of 1960. When it came time for his inauguration on January 20, 1961, all three networks covered the festivities. On CBS, Howard K. Smith announced the dignitaries in the motorcade drive from the Capitol to the White House, including two women in the back of one of the open cars, "Mrs. Woodrow Wilson and Mrs. Franklin D. Roosevelt driving along the avenue past the White House. What memories they must have." A placard on the side of the car announced the occupants inside to the crowds lining the route on the cold and snowy day, and although Kennedy had invited her to sit with the family and directly behind cabinet members during the ceremony, she declined and sat outside the cameras' glare. Edith Wilson would pass away later in 1961 at the age of 89. That evening, ER was to attend the largest inaugural ball, broadcast live by CBS from the National Guard Armory in Washington, D.C., including a reading by Laurence Olivier and a performance by Frank Sinatra. Her appearance was scheduled just before the end of the program in "A Moment with Lincoln" along with Fredric March and Helen Traubel, directly before Kennedy spoke ("Inaugural Gala"). However, a letter shortly afterward to Lorena Hickok revealed that she never made it there due to the chaos of a major snowstorm and cars abandoned in the streets: "I tried to get to the gala performance but sat 4 hours in traffic & when a break came I went home!" She thought JFK's inaugural address "magnificent" (Streitmatter 286–87).

Eleanor was also an honorary chair of the Democratic Party fundraiser that celebrated Kennedy's 45th birthday in Madison Square Garden on May 19, 1962. Peter Lawford served as host, with appearances by Harry Belafonte, Jack Benny, Maria Callas, Bobby Darin, Jimmy Durante, Ella Fitzgerald, Henry Fonda, Peggy Lee, Shirley MacLaine, Miriam Makeba, Elaine May, and Mike Nichols. Other honorary chairs in attendance at the televised event with ER were James Farley, who had been head of the Democratic National Committee and FDR's campaign manager; Herbert Lehman, former governor and senator from New York; and New York mayor Robert F. Wagner. The most well-known of the performances is Marilyn Monroe's breathless rendition of "Happy Birthday."

ER continued to work in New York politics with Lehman and Wagner, including a January 1962 "Inner Glimpse of Herbert Lehman" tribute episode of *Directions '62* "A Jewish Perspective" on WOR-TV ("TV Programs"). Lehman followed FDR as New York governor from 1933 to 1942 and served in the U.S. Senate from 1949 to 1957. He worked with ER and others against Tammany Hall, finally defeating the New York political machine in 1961. On another local WNTA program, *At Your Beck and Call*, Betty Furness hosted a live phone-in talk show. The evening of June 5, 1961, Mayor Wagner and his aides took questions from the public, including one from the director of the Citizens Committee for Children, Mrs. Franklin D. Roosevelt. She asked in a written submission if the city's Welfare Department should set up a 24-hour emergency service, seven days a week, "to investigate and handle juvenile delinquency trouble before it explodes." ER was described in *New York Times* coverage of the show as a "leader in the Democratic insurgent group," since she supported Wagner's break with Tammany Hall (Grutzner).

New First Lady Jacqueline Kennedy overtook ER in the Gallup poll as the most popular American woman, but Eleanor was a supporter of her young rival. On November 30, 1962, *The World of Jacqueline Kennedy* appeared on NBC as part of a documentary series, and Leonard Bernstein, Margaret Mead, JFK's press secretary Pierre Salinger, Oleg Cassini, and ER offer their personal thoughts about Jackie. Alexander Scourby narrates the program, which includes mention of the "arduous" Democratic National Convention in 1960 over images of Eleanor and Adlai

Stevenson. Later, archival footage of ER and FDR runs as Scourby says, "Another era, another fearless man and a unique first lady. She was more at home on the road than in the White House. Her travels, her typewriter, and her visits to our troops at the war front made her a subject of controversy the world over." Near the end of the hour, "a woman who knows the house Jacqueline lives in, Eleanor Roosevelt" is interviewed about Jackie and the role of the First Lady. ER says, "I suppose there are situations which you might normally prefer to avoid, but I think on the whole a president's wife learns to meet almost any situation she has to meet and not to be annoyed and not to be upset by them." ER seems quite excited and happy when she comments, "The thing which distinguishes this administration is the fact that it is uniformly a young and vital and new administration, and she's part of it." Over footage of Jackie waterskiing, Eleanor adds, "She's full of life. Her complete naturalness makes her most appealing," a statement included in a *TV Radio Mirror* article on the new First Lady (Storm). Eleanor ends with counsel that she certainly followed while in the White House: "I would advise her to be herself because that is the best way for her to meet any development which is bound to come." One review called the overall program "bland," except for the ER and Mead segments (Harrison).

17

Anti-Communist Crusades

Richard Nixon once said that without taking the lead in the Alger Hiss hearings, he would never have become Eisenhower's vice president or been given the opportunity to run for president in 1960 (Nixon 70). Hiss was accused of spying for the Soviet Union in the 1930s and was found guilty in January 1950 not of treason, but of lying under oath in testimony to HUAC. He had worked in the U.S. State Department, attended the Yalta Conference, and played a role in creating the original United Nations Charter. Hiss maintained his innocence for the rest of his life, and by the 1990s, Russian officials revealed that there was no record of a relationship with Soviet intelligence. Senator Joseph McCarthy used the manufactured Hiss case as evidence that the U.S. State Department was "thoroughly infested" with communists (Hartshorn).

ER appeared with host Charles Collingwood and Maine Republican senator Owen Brewster to discuss the topic of "What Does Loyalty to the U.S. Mean?" on the CBS political talk show *People's Platform*, airing May 12, 1950. Brewster, who worked closely with McCarthy, attacked Eleanor for support of Hiss, reading portions of a 1949 "My Day" column in which she saw Hiss's version of events as plausible, explaining that attending a meeting with others who were later found subversive should not necessarily make one subversive by association (28 June 1949). His HUAC conviction for lying under oath, not for "communism," did not stop ER from continued support, even though warned she should regret her words and "squirm" in her chair facing Brewster (B. Henry). She discussed the show in two "My Day" columns on May 15 and 17, 1950. What especially troubled her were the senator's remarks that implied that questioning our judicial system was "doing something very wrong." ER wrote about those people found guilty who were later proven innocent and interrogated an approach that did not consider that our institutions might be improved upon:

> I think the margin of mistakes is narrower under this system than under any other, but the reason we have grown, and are growing, in this country is because our minds have remained free. We have always questioned our own wisdom; we have been ready to make experiments and to change our mind. But, it is such a remark, and coming from someone like the honorable Senator, that troubles me most. Those who say such things are so sure that they are right in their judgments, whereas I am always so conscious of the margin of error, of our lack of knowledge and understanding!

Collingwood wrote about his experience moderating *People's Platform*, comparing the role to a referee in a boxing match. "There are many special problems in television. They must be handled on the spot. Guests often get tangled up with their opponent or subject. Only once did I fail to clear the ring in this respect. When Sen. Brewster appeared to discuss with Eleanor Roosevelt 'What Does Loyalty to the United States Mean?' I attempted to restrain the senator from pursuing a personal attack on Mrs. Roosevelt's views. But the senator would not yield" (Collingwood).

ER was ambushed on her own television show *Today with Mrs. Roosevelt* by guest Patrick Hurley, Hoover's secretary of war and former ambassador to China. On the April 16, 1950, episode, he charged that a secret agreement at Yalta in 1945 had been the "Communist blueprint for the conquest of China." He blamed Hiss, President Roosevelt, and Truman for communism in China, and this was one of the few times on her own program that ER had to deal with a panelist whose comments were outside what she considered regular political discourse. She was appalled by Hurley's suggestions about what had occurred at Yalta, questioning the motives of the Roosevelt and Truman administrations. Later that year on her November 26 program, Senator Brewster joined the guest panel. Eleanor was concerned that the Internal Security Act of 1950 would be used to abridge freedom of thought, speech, or expression in its anti-communist zeal, although Republican proponents denied those implications. "In fact, Senator Brewster said that, of course, under any legislation some hardships would probably occur but the good would outweigh the bad. It seems to me that that still remains to be proved" ("My Day" 28 Nov. 1950).

In ER's April 11, 1954, appearance on NBC's *Meet the Press*, "wearing what looked very much like an Easter hat," the first subject the panel raised was that of Senator McCarthy's anti-communist crusades (Cremmen). She responded, "I object very strongly to the methods that have been used, not to trying to deal with the issue. I object to trying to use the same methods that you object to in communism and in fascism." She thought they endangered the freedoms and rights of the American people and that President Eisenhower and McCarthy's colleagues in the Senate should have done more to limit his investigating powers (R. Ball 29). When asked what the Roosevelt administration had done to curb the late Huey Long, she replied that his rebellious actions were quite different from those of Senator McCarthy, declaring that Senate investigative committees had never been used to this extent. ER also praised Roman Catholic bishop Bernard J. Sheil for denouncing McCarthy's methods ("Curb"). She was asked to explain how "so many" communists had infiltrated the government during the Roosevelt and Truman administrations, like Hiss and Harry Dexter White. Eleanor refuted this claim, saying that few were convicted, including the late White, and Hiss for lying under oath, with shaky evidence. The Republican press lambasted her for "the customary cracks" at McCarthy and charged her with slick, evasive political talk for suggesting that communism was not so much a danger when the Soviets were our allies. "During that time both homegrown and foreign Reds had virtually the run of official Washington," argued the *New York Daily News*. "What piece of U.S. history will Mrs. Roosevelt try to rewrite next?" A political cartoon with a chicken laying the egg of USSR subversion in the White House during the New Deal is placed next to the editorial ("Mrs. R. Rewrites"). Republican extremists certainly categorized ER as one of those "communists" in the Roosevelt administration.

On her September 16, 1956, *Meet the Press* appearance, she was asked about former president Truman's contention that Hiss was not a Soviet spy, even though convicted of lying under oath, and that the case was a Republican red herring. She called it an "unimportant issue" that was settled and was willing to stand by the court's decision until evidence of his innocence was presented. However, she agreed with Truman that the Republicans should not be making it an issue for Stevenson in the 1956 presidential campaign ("Mrs. FDR Raps"). "It is an indication that you have a great poverty of issues if you now have to discuss this particular question. It seems to me to be a question of the past," she said, since Hiss had been convicted in 1950 ("Desegregate").

On March 8, 1959, ER appeared on NBC's *Wisdom* series with William Attwood, senior editor of *Look Magazine*, for "A Conversation with Eleanor Roosevelt," for which she was paid $1,000 and would receive another $1,000 after costs were recovered (McCann). From her office at the AAUN in the Carnegie Foundation Building, located across the street from the UN in New York City, she discussed the United Nations, women's suffrage, Theodore Roosevelt, criticism of her views and actions, FDR's legacy, the Soviet Union, and young leaders in the United States. Beatrice Cunningham directed the episode, which was featured in NBC's full-page "Television to Remember" *New York Times* advertisement for the month of March, and a special accompanying edition of *Wisdom Magazine* honored her achievements as a world humanitarian ("Television to," *Wisdom* 70). NBC's director of special projects wrote ER afterward to express his delight at the extraordinarily successful program (D. Hyatt).

Attwood asked about McCarthy and the anti-communist hysteria of the time. Specifically, he wanted to know if ER would encourage young people to enter government service at this point. A few years prior, she would have emphatically said "No" because she "thought that we had lost our sense of really wanting people to think freely for a while." Now, she would once again like to see the younger generation in government service:

> But I think we must get over as a country the desire to see conformity. We must allow the young people of today to develop and to think over a wide field even if we disagree with them. We developed for a short time a strange phenomenon for us, namely that you couldn't change your mind. If at eighteen, you'd happened to even glance at communism with interest, you were doomed. You were going to be a communist forever. Now, that's just perfect nonsense and something that would not have happened years ago in our country where our people tolerated all kinds of thinking and of expression of thought.

She felt that the 1950s concentration on gaining material things had contributed to the loss of a sense of intellectual, moral, and spiritual character. Her answer subtly connects the Eisenhower administration and its focus on economic success to why the Red Scare flourished.

18

Khrushchev: "At least we didn't shoot at each other!"

Nikita Khrushchev did not often grant audiences to Americans, but with deep appreciation for the respect the Russians felt from and for Franklin Roosevelt, the Soviet premier agreed to meet with Eleanor Roosevelt. She very much believed that coming together at the same table was critical for the U.S. and the Soviet Union to work toward peace, and in September 1957, she traveled to Yalta, where her husband had met with Stalin and Churchill near the end of the war, to interview Khrushchev as part of a series of articles for the *New York Post*. They did not agree on very much in their three-hour meeting, and Khrushchev laughed as they parted, "At least we didn't shoot at each other!" (E. Roosevelt *On My Own* 230).

A newspaper advertisement for the October 20, 1957, episode of *Meet the Press* featured a thumbnail photo of ER: "See Eleanor Roosevelt just back from Russia where she interviewed Khrushchev." Most of the questions from panelists Marquis Childs from the *St. Louis Post-Dispatch*, Richard Clurman of *Newsday*, May Craig from the *Portland Press Herald*, and John Oakes of *The New York Times* focused on the Soviet visit. Childs began by asking her if the attention for Khrushchev did more harm than good by giving him a propaganda forum. She sized up the premier as a ruthless, power-loving figure but felt that he was "honest when he thinks that war is unthinkable." He and other Soviet leaders "have made up their minds they can win what they want without war," and the USSR "understands the value of scientific research" better than the United States. She criticized the small amount of money that the U.S. Congress had designated for cancer and heart research, for example, and Oakes also took that to imply that was why the Russians were able to put up a satellite first. ER felt that arms sent to the Middle East were "going down the drain" because no Middle Eastern country could withstand a Russian onslaught, and she did not believe there was any basis at present for peaceful coexistence, although she had hopes that there might be changes to make this possible (*"Meet the Press* Interview").

In conservative press coverage of the show, Eleanor was called to task for being "taken in by the Reds" for believing that communists could be "honest men" and suggesting that the Soviets were doing some things better than the U.S. The implication was that she was vulnerable to communist propaganda and thus naively spreading Russian lies to the American people on *Meet the Press* and in her daily column ("Mrs. Roosevelt's Visit"). ER's answer to a Craig question about how it was possible to find Khrushchev "likeable"—"How can you *like* a man who has been a murderer?"—was interpreted by another columnist to imply that she was no communist dupe, but a traitor. The fact that she could "make it sound plausible that one can dislike a person and yet find him likeable" was a sign that she had no convictions at all. In fact, it was more proof of "the growing suspicion that she was a consulting architect" in "losing the peace to that other likeable man, Josef Stalin" and allowing communists into the highest levels of the Roosevelt administration (Valentine). William Paley at CBS purposely did not give her a platform on *Face the Nation* or other network shows during this period because of the controversy surrounding the Soviet visit (Gomery 118).

The ABC *Mike Wallace Interview* on November 23 utilized the Khrushchev encounter in advertising: "Mrs. Eleanor Roosevelt on *The Mike Wallace Interview*. How will Mrs. Roosevelt answer probing questions about her recent trip to Russia?" *Variety* criticized the program because Wallace did not end up asking questions about ER's recent trip to the Soviet Union, as promised in advance (Silverman). However, he did ask her if she thought state socialism might be the wave of the future, with capitalism on the way out. She was more interested in democracy and freedom, retaining the right to shape our economy as we want, even if capitalism changed in many ways. "I'm not really much interested in capitalism," she said, but in democracy of the people. Her answer about whether she thought it would be a catastrophe if socialism came peacefully to the U.S. must have alarmed many conservatives with her lack of horror at the idea:

> To a certain extent, I don't see any real need for socialism in the United States immediately, but things change, and it may be that there will come a need for partial changes in our economy. I don't know. I'm not an economist, and I'm not a financier, but I'm not worried by that side of it. I'm intensely anxious to preserve the freedom that gives you the right to think and to act and to talk as you please. That, I think, is essential to happiness and the life of the people.

The other topics at hand were compelling, but few questions about the Soviets were discussed as advertised.

The next summer in June 1958, the NBC program *Youth Wants to Know,* in which college and high school students asked questions of politicians and business leaders, took part in an exchange with the Soviet Union. American students went to Moscow to film five episodes on "nonpolitical" matters, and Russian students visiting the U.S. interviewed Eleanor; Supreme Court justice William O. Douglas; retiring secretary of health, education and welfare Marion Folsom; Louisiana Democratic senator Allen J. Ellender; and Detlev W. Bronk, president of the National Academy of Sciences and the Rockefeller Institute. These interviews were only to be screened in the Soviet Union, while the American version was broadcast in the U.S. (Shepard "U.S."). Central Intelligence Agency (CIA) records in the National Archives hold the half-hour June 14, 1958, interview with ER conducted in Russian with an English interpreter from studio 8-H at 30 Rockefeller Plaza in New York (Marshall). After the NBC logo appears, four young Russian journalists ask questions about the issues facing American youth. They speak in Russian and a translator interprets for ER, who answers in English, and vice versa. Wearing makeup for

TV and appearing more relaxed with these young people than in most other television appearances, she tells them that she believes the most fundamental problem facing American youth today is the realization that they have far greater responsibilities in a postwar world than did previous generations. She sees living up to the ideals on which the country was founded as another challenge, including recognizing the equality of all peoples in their own country and the world. Young people were doing much better than their elders at the treatment of minorities. The rise of youthful crimes was, in her opinion, the result of growing up in the shadow of war, with violence accepted. When asked about the effects of television and the movies, she focuses on the benefits of educational television. However, "many of our ordinary Hollywood movies are very detrimental to the youth of the country." She advises adults to regulate what children watched on TV. They ask if she thought that television would replace live theater. She thinks not: "Movies are never as good as the actors on the stage." Theaters were closing because people were staying home to watch TV and going to the movies less as well, but on the other hand, she believes that television and radio made many more people familiar with wonderful music they would not have had access to in the past. The four young men are also interested in the question of opportunities for workers to attend university classes in the evenings or by correspondence as in the Soviet Union. She is familiar with these courses in New York City and guesses that other large public universities across the country also have such programs. With that, the show ends when ER tells them that she must leave to go speak to the Young Democrats of Syracuse, New York, followed by the NBC logo. One wonders what notes the CIA might have taken.

The NBC *Wisdom* series interview on March 8, 1959, also broached issues connected to the Soviet Union. William Attwood asked if she thought the Cold War inevitable or if our relationship with the Russians would have been different if FDR had lived out his term. She was unsure, but knew that Roosevelt would have been disappointed in the way Stalin's promises were not carried out, as Churchill was. However, "my husband had a very great confidence in his personal ability to contact people and win them over or make a dent, to make them understand." She believed that the Soviets had ruled out a nuclear war because they knew it would cause mutual destruction, and they had long-term goals. Khrushchev had said to ER, "It may take fifty years, but the law of the future is communism, and we are to have a communist world." She was not certain that leaders in the West recognized these Soviet objectives.

When the Soviet premier ventured to the United States, ER appeared on NBC's *Today* morning show on September 15, 1959, with host Dave Garroway and others who had previously met Mr. Khrushchev—Adlai Stevenson, Minnesota senator Hubert Humphrey, executive vice president of New York University Dr. John Ivy, Jr., and Iowa farmer Roswell Garst. The press release promoting the show included Eleanor's answer to the question, "What is Nikita S. Khrushchev really like?"

> I had a feeling, and very strongly, that this is a man who believes in research and in the people who know their own jobs, you see, and he is going to take advantage of anything that he could find out that is going to serve his purposes. I think, however, that he has an understanding of the strength of physical things but very little appreciation of the strength of a spiritual or

moral dedication…. Khrushchev, like a great many Russians, is emotional at times, and emotional on certain subjects where he wishes to be emotional [NBC-New York "What Is"].

Afterward, she wrote in "My Day" about the just-ended session of Congress in which no real civil rights legislation had been passed, blaming a group of Southern senators who were not able "to explain to their constituents that even the South is a part of a changing world." This, she felt, was "not good reading for our Communist guest" (18 Sept. 1959).

The September 18, 1959, Friday evening episode of the CBS news program *Eyewitness to History* features "Khrushchev in New York" and chronicles his trip to New York City, visits to the Empire State Building and Wall Street, and address to the United Nations. A CBS crew also provides coverage of his call on ER at Hyde Park, with correspondent Harry Reasoner on the scene. Eleanor, Mr. Khrushchev, and his wife Nina walk together to Franklin Roosevelt's gravesite and then to the presidential library, with ER between them, taking each of their arms. Soviet foreign minister Andrei Gromyko walks behind them. Reasoner speaks as they slowly make their way across the grounds: "Eleanor Roosevelt met the Russians with a fussy but unhurried pace of a confident matron having the garden club to tea." With a microphone around her neck, ER can be heard saying, "I think it might interest Mr. Khrushchev to know that the reason my husband's grave is in front of the monument is because he wanted to lie with no stone over him and the sky above him." Reasoner continues commentary over footage of placing a large wreath on the grave, noting that the Soviet premier "was with an elderly lady who has seen and been part of even more history than he…. Khrushchev stayed restrained with the air of a man who knows how to act in the presence of important old ladies." It is astounding now to hear the misogyny of Reasoner referring to Eleanor Roosevelt as a fussy garden club matron

Soviet premier Nikita Khrushchev (right) visits the Franklin D. Roosevelt Presidential Library with his wife Nina Khrushchev (left) and Eleanor Roosevelt (center), where they were shown letters from Joseph Stalin to FDR. The September 18, 1959, trip to Hyde Park was broadcast on CBS news program *Eyewitness to History* (Franklin D. Roosevelt Presidential Library & Museum).

and an old lady, failing to recognize that she was one of the few people in the country who had previously met the Soviet leader. Reasoner takes a woman's age as a cue to turn her into merely a symbol of Franklin Roosevelt and the New Deal, rather than a respected humanitarian in her own right. Although ER very often resisted gendering, as an older woman, she is put in her place and disregarded on this occasion.

Still microphoned, ER welcomed the party into the library, where they signed the guest book and examined a collection of letters from Stalin to FDR. Reasoner added, "Mrs. Roosevelt said afterwards that she thought Khrushchev enjoyed nothing at Hyde Park. He was so terribly anxious about getting back for his United Nations speech." She wrote more about the visit in "My Day," saying that Nina was enjoying the trip and glad she came. Khrushchev told her that "he felt that my husband understood the needs and aspirations of the Soviet Union" and had thus come to pay his respects to FDR's memory. She hoped that in this visit he would come to realize that Americans had convictions and beliefs, and if the time came for sacrifice for the country, they would be quite capable, rather than soft and thinking of only material comforts (19 Sept. 1959). Afterward, the Soviets produced a color film about the U.S. visit, *N.S. Khrushchev in America*, including footage with ER ("Soviet").

Dr. John Schwarzwalder, general manager of KTCA-TV Minneapolis-St. Paul, hosted *That Free Men May Live*, a series of interviews related to personal and political liberties and freedom. The National Educational Television (NET) episode airing on March 8, 1960, was produced through the facilities of United Nations Television and featured ER discussing her views on peace ("Television Log"). Others in the series included Vice President Richard Nixon, Dr. Martin Luther King, Jr., and former Republican presidential candidate Alf Landon, defeated by FDR in a landslide in 1936. An early review, a reminder that an omitted King was not yet as well respected in 1960, described the show: "Vice President Nixon, Mrs. Eleanor Roosevelt and others bluntly remind Americans that unless we work to preserve freedom in a number of fields, it will be lost" ("Educational Television"). An announcer began, "The price of freedom is constant vigilance, a vigilance which must face many threats. Direct your attention now to one who works and fights for freedom, Mrs. Eleanor Roosevelt." Schwarzwalder added that she was "among those who have most effectively through the years served in this struggle for freedom" and began the interview by asking about disarmament. She pointed out that without the rule of law through the United Nations, she did not think disarmament could take place between the U.S. and the Soviet Union. She was encouraged by more State Department officers learning Russian than in the past, but was doubtful that American tourists visiting the Soviet Union would have much impact.

ABC's 1952 New York Easter Parade coverage from Fifth Avenue highlighted the Crusade for Freedom, with the goal of raising funds for Radio Free Europe, which spread American ideals and propaganda during the Cold War. Eleanor appeared on this Easter show from the Hotel Pierre to discuss the Crusade, and John Daly and Jinx Falkenburg joined her with commentary on the parade itself (Ross "Easter," Lohman 1952). She was initially sent a cable asking her to be a "coordinating MC" for the entire broadcast, which she declined and wondered why Henry Morgenthau, Jr., was asking her to appear. The cable turned out to be from Henry Morgenthau

III, who was producing the coast-to-coast broadcast. ER donated her fee toward the Elinor Morgenthau Workshop, which was producing the work of young playwrights and had been established in honor of one of Eleanor's good friends, recently deceased (Morgenthau correspondence). Charles Underhill, head of ABC Television, wrote that the Easter presentation was "infinitely better" than the other networks and independent stations. The Crusade for Freedom and ER's presence made for a "dignified and distinguished" Easter celebration in contrast to publicity stunts and press-agented tricks by others (Underhill).

Several months earlier, she had written about the Crusade project in her "My Day" column:

> From my own point of view one of the most important steps is freedom of communication among the nations, a freedom which allows the use of every means of communication—television, radio, movies, the written and spoken word—and which allows free access to people. At present, citizens of Russia and the satellite countries cannot leave their homelands and visitors from other countries cannot get into these countries except after very careful scrutiny and the granting of visas which are exceptionally hard to obtain [1 Sept. 1951].

ER spoke on the Voice of America while in Europe, able to switch between English, French, German, Spanish, and Italian. The broadcasts were so successful that VOA asked her to continue even after returning to the United States (Wamboldt 303). It has since been revealed that the CIA was the major source of funds in the Crusade for Freedom, but this was not known at the time (Puddington 22).

In May 1960, ER signed with American Continental Telefilms as the host and narrator of *Operation Escape*, which dramatized stories of flight from behind the Iron Curtain, although real names and escape routes were not to be divulged ("Abroad"). Jayark Films Corporation in New York planned to distribute the action-adventure series of 39 episodes produced by H. Lawrence Holcomb in Munich, Germany ("New York Roundup"). The segments involving ER were to be shot in New York, and she received a payment of $5,000. However, there is no evidence that the series ever made it to air ("Religion Courses," Stix correspondence II).

She appeared on Jack Paar's late-night show for a second time on Wednesday, May 31, 1961, near the end of the program to educate the public about contributions to "Tractors for Freedom." Five hundred tractors were to be sent to Cuba in exchange for Fidel Castro's ransom of 1,200 imprisoned Cuban survivors of the Bay of Pigs invasion, and Eleanor and labor leader Walter Reuther were part of the initial committee that President Kennedy asked to negotiate with Castro. In his memoir, Paar explains that he was chosen to raise money on the show night after night, took a beating in the press, and was accused of trying to negotiate with a foreign government as a private citizen, but he raised millions. "No one defended me until Mrs. Roosevelt came on the program and wrote in her column her admiration for my courage. What no one knew was that I was asked secretly to do this by President Kennedy!" (143). In "My Day," ER wrote about the campaign:

> I am very much impressed by the courage which has been shown by Mr. Jack Paar. From the very beginning he seems to have felt that this was a cause worthy of the participation of all American people, quite regardless of party lines, and I am sure that his aid has meant a great deal in the response which has come to the committee in this country in the last few days. Ten

thousand letters, I am informed, were received on Friday in Detroit. However, none of the letters that have come in so far will be opened until we get the official confirmation from Pres. Castro [5 June 1961].

In June, it was reported that ER and others on the committee would not be traveling to Havana to negotiate, ending speculation that she might be called upon to do so ("Swap"). Castro had made demands that she and Milton Eisenhower, younger brother of President Eisenhower and then president of Johns Hopkins University, complete the arrangements in Cuba ("Castro"). Eventually, Kennedy sent money for food and medicine in exchange for the prisoners, instead of tractors.

19

Bringing Issues of Race to TV

In what has been called a watershed moment in civil rights history, opera contralto Marian Anderson was denied permission to sing at Constitution Hall in Washington, D.C., in January 1939, when the Daughters of the American Revolution (DAR) did not allow Black performers on its stage. ER pressured the organization and publicly resigned in protest, creating a national stir. Then she helped behind the scenes to arrange a concert on the National Mall for an integrated audience of 75,000 people, with hundreds of thousands more listening on the radio.

Bull Connor is most well known as the commissioner who brutally ordered dogs and firehoses to stop Martin Luther King, Jr., and peaceful protesters in Birmingham, Alabama, in 1963. However, Eleanor had first encountered Connor in November 1938 as she attended the Southern Conference for Human Welfare in Birmingham. Connor demanded segregated seating in the auditorium, and when Roosevelt intentionally sat in the Black section, police required that she move. Anyone who crossed the line was to be arrested. She picked up her chair and sat it in the middle of the aisle, straddling the designated Black and White areas for the entire session—and was not arrested.

These stories about ER's challenges to segregation and the injustices and indignities meted out to Black Americans are notable. She even had a $25,000 kidnapping bounty put on her head by the Ku Klux Klan in 1958 when conducting a civil rights workshop at Highlander Folk School in Tennessee; however, on television an initial experience may have curtailed what she felt she could address about race on air. Eleanor was made to cave to network pressure to remove Paul Robeson from the guest list of *Today with Mrs. Roosevelt*. An actor, singer, and activist, Robeson spoke out for the rights of Black Americans, often allied with socialist and pacifist philosophies, and was noticeably pro–Soviet. At the height of the Cold War, NBC would not give voice to a perceived communist who had had his passport revoked by the State Department. Robeson was scheduled on the show for March 19, 1950, representing the Progressive Party in a discussion on "The Position of the Negro in American Political Life," along with Black Republican committeeman Perry Howard from Mississippi and liberal Democratic representative Adam Clayton Powell from Harlem, the first African American elected to Congress from New York.

Robeson's appearance had been announced at the end of the show the previous week, but was quickly canceled with a statement from NBC executive vice president

Charles R. Denny, page one news in *The New York Times*: "We are all agreed that Mr. Robeson's appearance would lead only to misunderstanding and confusion, and no good purpose would be served in having him speak on the issue of Negroes in politics" ("Protests"). The conservative press, led by the Hearst newspapers, specifically the *New York Journal-American*, encouraged two to three hundred telephone calls protesting the Robeson scheduling ("Despite Censorship"). *Variety* reported that NBC was caught between public pressure and the desire not to antagonize Eleanor "in view of her standing and the fact that she's parlayed the program into considerable stature and one of the most prestige-laden in video" ("Mounting"). An editorial in the then-liberal *New York Post* blasted the ban: "We do not believe democracy would have reason to have feared such a debate. Instead the show has been called off because of ideologically wet grounds and everybody—including America—looks stupid and undignified, as though we believe the rumble of Robeson's rhetoric could shake the Republic" ("*N.Y. Post*"). The NAACP and ACLU protested the cancellation as "censorship by private pressure" ("NAACY," "Radio and Television"). The Communist Party of the United States told its members not to "bow down to this political censorship by Negro-hating white supremacists" ("Pressure Drive"). The Harlem Trade Union Council picketed NBC's New York offices and asserted, "You might find a Negro pushing a broom at NBC, but not in any other capacity." Powell also spoke out, stating that the ban on his debate with Robeson was "not in keeping with our American principles" ("Powell").

Robeson himself had this to say: "It is not surprising to me that a huge network which practically excludes colored persons from its large army of skilled professional personnel, and which is the medium of so much distortion of their lives should balk at a discussion of the colored group in American politics which professes to present all points of view." He went on to criticize both major parties and their records on civil rights. "As an American whose fathers toiled as slaves to create the wealth of the great land, I shall continue to make my voice heard for the complete liberation of colored Americans and all oppressed peoples, for security for American workers, and farmers and for world peace" ("Robeson Hits"). ER confirmed that she did not herself cancel the show, but when she met with a group of leftist youth, she would not agree to break her contract with NBC to appear on another network with Robeson, with whom she often "sharply disagreed." The Young Progressives of America (YPA) were not happy that she felt it wisest not to appear elsewhere with Robeson, which was complicated by her anger at their tactics. The YPA led ER to believe that she was speaking to representatives of the NAACP, Union Theological Seminary, Junior Hadassah, and the Wholesale Warehouse Workers Union, but "they fooled Mrs. FDR" into a meeting only attended by YPA members. She had also specifically asked that her comments were off the record for the press, and they did not honor this request ("Mrs. Roosevelt Tells Off").

ER shared her point of view in "My Day," pointing out that she often invited guests on her show with whom she did not agree, but believed that "the public should hear controversial opinions expressed by the people who hold them." There would be minority and majority points of view communicated, and she hoped that people were not afraid of listening to viewpoints with which they themselves did not agree.

I have never been afraid of the American people. I have always felt they were able to form their own judgments and in the end that the majority would think straight. I don't believe in suppressing or keeping from people points of view that are held even by minorities.

I think I will always have confidence in the common sense and clear judgment of the American people as a whole if they hear all sides of any question. Above everything else, we must guard our freedoms, and that means that all must have a right to be heard. When we begin to discriminate we can never tell where the discrimination may end [21 Mar. 1950].

In other columns, she was clear that she often disagreed with Robeson's politics, but Eleanor promoted understanding his frustrations and point of view as an educated Black man in a United States in which he did not experience equality of opportunity. The substitute topic on March 19 was, ironically, "The Republican Program," in which Republican senators criticized the Truman administration.

A February 16, 1949, *Variety* headline read, "Mrs. Eleanor Roosevelt Among Name Sponsors of Non-Profit TV Show." Nonprofit organization Torchlight Productions was working on a radio series called *Conflict*, and once off the ground, the plan had been to launch a television version of the show. ER was listed among the sponsors of the program, in addition to the NAACP's Walter White, but it does not appear that *Conflict* made it to TV ("Mrs. Eleanor Roosevelt Among"). She worked with White on a regular basis, and a letter in the Minnesota Black newspaper *St. Paul Recorder* indicates that ER spoke out to support NAACP protests of the *Amos 'n' Andy* television show debuting in 1951. Although the radio version had been long running, the TV show was considered degrading and full of extreme racial caricatures (Hedgeman). A few years later, she took part in a tribute to the by then late White on *The Brokenshire Show*. NBC affiliate host Norman Brokenshire welcomed ER, Rutgers University professor and soon to be public television host Richard Heffner, New York attorney general and soon to be senator Jacob Javits, and others to celebrate the civil rights leader's life on June 28, 1955 (Ross "Multiple" 1955). White had led the NAACP since 1929, and ER joined the Board of Directors after Franklin's death in 1945.

Eleanor mentioned a May 17, 1954, television appearance in her "My Day" column, writing, "While I was on *The Tex and Jinx Show* I was given the news of the unanimous Supreme Court decision that wiped out segregation in the schools. I am delighted this was a unanimous decision because I think it will be difficult for the states with segregated school systems to hold out against such a ruling" (20 May 1954). On that day, the Supreme Court ruled that racial segregation of schools was unconstitutional in the *Brown v. Board of Education* decision. Spouses Tex McCrary and Jinx Falkenburg had a half-hour NBC daily interview program broadcast from New York City, one of the first TV talk shows. When ER appeared on NBC's *Today* show with Dave Garroway the following day, other guests included reporter Jack Lescoulie, actor Frank Blair, chimp J. Fred Muggs, and show regular Estelle Parsons. She "found that Thurgood Marshall, counsel for the NAACP, was on just ahead of me and he seemed so happy over the Supreme Court segregation decision, which of course seems to have lifted a weight from so many of our colored citizens" ("My Day" 25 May 1954). Marshall represented the Brown family and would go on to become the first Black Supreme Court justice in 1967.

Eleanor's September 16, 1956, appearance on *Meet the Press* is remembered for her comments on Nixon and Eisenhower, but another topic on the show was "race problems." ER suggested that the North should take the lead, point the way, and move extremely quickly to desegregate New York's Harlem and sections of Chicago and Detroit. In the South, she said, "we should move slowly and with wisdom," but the first step was "the protection of all citizens and their right to vote." She added, "It can't happen overnight, and we don't want violence." ER concluded that immediately after the Supreme Court ruling on desegregation, President Eisenhower had failed to exercise leadership and should have called for meetings of Black and White leaders across the country to discuss ways to carry out the decision ("Nixon Charge," "Mrs. Roosevelt Asks"). Chicago's *Daily Defender* Black newspaper responded with editorial praise of her call for desegregation of housing and schools in the North: "Mrs. Eleanor Roosevelt was never more right" ("Segregation"). However, the *St. Paul Recorder*, Minnesota's Black newspaper, thought she demonstrated "fuzzy thinking" by not focusing on the legal segregation of the South as opposed to the economic and social conditions behind school segregation in the North ("Eleanor Roosevelt and Segregation").

The CBS June 16, 1957, episode "Segregation and the South" on Edward R. Murrow's *See It Now* news magazine documentary series includes footage of a White student expelled from the University of Alabama "as he indulged in a sardonic and irrelevant denunciation of Mrs. Franklin D. Roosevelt" (Shanley "Documentary"). Murrow's program was critical to the downfall of Senator Joseph McCarthy and his communist witch hunt; it won four Emmy Awards. ER would vehemently disagree with Truman on the June 19, 1960, episode of *College News Conference*. She mentioned a statement he had made on the show the previous week in which he charged that communists were inspiring sit-in protests at segregated lunch counters in the South. "I dislike differing with Mr. Truman, because I'm very fond of Mr. Truman," she said, "but in his assertion which he has made a number of times that the sit-ins in the South among students are entirely communist-inspired, I think he does not watch very carefully the way in which communists ordinarily organize." She continued, "I would not for a minute say that you wouldn't find some communists among this movement, because they would be very stupid if they didn't put some among them. But they don't inspire or incite to passive resistance. That's not the way the communists organize" ("Mrs. Roosevelt Analyzes").

In the summer of 1962, the Rev. Robert L.T. Smith became the first Black candidate to run for the U.S. House of Representatives from Mississippi since Reconstruction. Jackson, Mississippi, television channel WLBT repeatedly refused to sell him television campaign airtime, and manager Fred Beard threatened that if he appeared at the station, "They would find my body floating upside down in the river." Appeals to the FCC went nowhere, and complaints never made it to FCC chair Newton Minow. A week before the primary, ER responded to a letter she received from Smith and gave a call to Minow, who had appeared on *Prospects of Mankind* in May. The FCC leader had been a clerk at the U.S. Supreme Court during the *Brown v. Board of Education* case and immediately pressured the station. Smith was able to buy 30 minutes of airtime the day before the primary election, which he lost to incumbent segregationist John Bell Williams. Myrlie Evers, whose husband, civil rights activist Medgar Evers, would be murdered the following year, recalled that Smith's appearance on television "was like the lifting of a giant curtain. He was saying things that had never before been said by a Negro to whites in Mississippi." Eleanor visited Minow in Washington, D.C., soon afterward, along with his wife and three daughters, who were all excited to meet her. WLBT was sued for failure to service its Black viewers, and it became the only television station to lose its license for not serving the public interest. Ironically, Smith's campaign manager Aaron Henry, who was then president of the Mississippi chapter of the NAACP, would later become chair of WLBT (Minow *Inside* 3–6, Minow "How"). Even after leaving the FCC, Minow was extremely influential in telecommunications law and served on the boards of NET and its successor, the Public Broadcasting Service (PBS), and as president of the Carnegie Corporation, among many other roles. He received the Presidential Medal of Freedom in 2016 from President Barack Obama, who had worked for Minow's law firm. ER likely agreed with Minow's speech in 1961 in which he referred to the "vast wasteland" of commercial television, a phrase that would often be repeated (Minow "Television").

In the fall of 1962, one of the last letters ER would ever write was to Martin Luther King, Jr., asking him to appear on a television show devoted to civil rights. Historian Allida Black tells a related story: "A year before she died, she came into breakfast humming. Her secretary asked her why she was so cheerful. And ER replied, 'I dreamed I was marching and singing and sitting in with students in the South'" (Conroy).

20

The UN: "Naïveté and cunning gracefully blended"

TV Guide ranked *What's My Line?* number nine on its list of greatest game shows ever. Running from 1950 to 1975 on CBS and then in syndication, the half-hour shows featured host John Daly and panelists Dorothy Kilgallen, Arlene Francis, and Bennett Cerf, who quizzed a contestant each week with the goal of finding out that person's occupation. Then a celebrity mystery guest appeared while the panelists were blindfolded, and the object was to figure out the visitor's identity. The program won three Emmys for Best Quiz or Audience Participation Show in the 1950s and a Golden Globe for Best TV Show in 1962.

It seems an unlikely arena for ER, but she appeared as the celebrity invitee on October 18, 1953, to promote United Nations Week. Instead of paying her the usual $500 as the mystery guest, the production made a $1,000 donation to UNICEF. Guests sat in the control room as a measure to ensure secrecy and were given the protocols by director Franklin Heller—no talking allowed. Producer Gil Fates remembered that when they turned to tell ER that she was on next, she was nowhere to be found. Heller found her in the hallway all alone. "I heard what you said about noise while you were working. I suddenly had this uncontrollable desire to cough, so rather than take a chance at disturbing you, I thought it better that I wait outside," she explained. "She was that kind of lady," Fates said, especially compared to the behavior of many other celebrities (39–44).

The panelists, this time including comedian Steve Allen, were blindfolded as ER entered and signed her name "Eleanor Roosevelt" on the blackboard to thunderous applause. She carried her purse and sat down next to Daly behind a "Mrs. Roosevelt" placard. Because her voice was so recognizable and not easily disguised, ER whispered answers to Daly, who repeated what she said aloud. Kilgallen began the questioning but was tripped up by supposing the guest had a regular television program. Allen used the male pronoun "he," so it was on to Francis, who assumed the mystery person lived in Washington, D.C. Cerf was then ready to ask about the United Nations but thought this must be someone who was a citizen of another country. That set the stage for Kilgallen to figure it out. Daly told the audience about United Nations Week, followed by Eleanor talking about United Nations Day, which was being launched that evening. Said Daly, "Well, I think to get that week off to a good start, you're the best spokesman that anyone could possibly hope to have, and more than that, this is a banner day for *What's My Line*. We will always remember very fondly that you honored us by being our mystery guest, and I'm sure that the panel would love very much to shake your hand." Eleanor was given screen time to discuss the United Nations on a show that did not often stray from the comic. Kilgallen and Francis rose from their chairs, as did Cerf and Allen, to shake her hand—the only guest, male or female, for whom the female panelists stood up in the entire history of the show.

ER's other appearances on television to discuss the UN are a bit more routine but reflect her serious commitment. As she once noted, "If I can reach only one person with my message about the importance of the United Nations, I feel that my efforts were rewarded and my time not wasted" (A. Black 174 fig. 6). A 1947 Gallup poll showed that 85 percent of the American public favored the United Nations. Both NBC and CBS aired sessions of the General Assembly from New York, helping to fill their daytime schedules at low cost. In 1948, NBC cosponsored UN Week, and in 1949, CBS contracted for exclusive daily coverage, 11:00 a.m. to 1:00 p.m. and 3:00

The United Nations' temporary home from 1946 to 1951 was in a former defense plant on Lake Success on Long Island, New York. Here actor Gary Cooper meets with Eleanor Roosevelt at Lake Success on April 3, 1950 (Franklin D. Roosevelt Presidential Library & Museum).

p.m. to 4:00 p.m., sponsored by Ford Motor Company. NBC added the children's program *UN Stamp Club* in 1951 on Saturday afternoons. However, as other daytime programming was developed that attracted advertisers and more viewers, both networks soon aired little from the UN except special news reports (Baughman 224).

Truman appointed ER as a delegate to the first United Nations General Assembly in 1946, and she became chair of the Commission on Human Rights and a major author and primary driver in the passage of the Universal Declaration of Human Rights. Perhaps Hollywood had a hand in the initial decision. *Film Daily* reported in April 1945 that 50 "members of [the] film colony" wired the president proposing that he appoint ER to "a place in the councils of the nation." Joe E. Brown, Eddie Cantor, Bette Davis, and Groucho Marx were among signers who urged that it would be a "double loss" to the nation to lose both FDR's and ER's "presence, influence and understanding" ("Want Mrs. Roosevelt"). When Eisenhower came into office as a Republican and filled official delegation seats with new appointees, ER continued her work through the AAUN, eventually becoming chair of the board of directors. John F. Kennedy reappointed her to the official U.S. delegation in 1961. Promoting the UN and educating the American public on why they should support the efforts of the United Nations toward the goal of world peace were a primary impetus for many of her television appearances over the years.

The UN experience provided ample practice in the arts of persuasion, debate, and discussion—skills that served her well on TV. *New York Times Magazine* recounted how effectively she used the crack of the gavel to quiet Russian delegates who were out of order. After a disagreement in a meeting over U.S. State Department policy in the Middle East, a colleague was overhead to say, "That was the most effective 'damn' I ever heard" (Janeway). A 1948 *New Yorker* article pinpointed how she often maneuvered in the UN, the same tactics that may be observed in her television appearances. In what the columnist recognized as "performance" at the UN, ER went out of her way not to appear opinionated, sometimes even mentioning that as a woman, she might not understand. Instead, she offered her opinion hesitantly, stating that she was sure that there was a good deal to be said for other arguments, but suggesting that it might be a promising idea to … xyz. She got others to say "yes" or "maybe" by working around the issue, not directly contradicting. "A State Department career man, after watching her artfully maneuver her way through a delicate discussion, once murmured, 'Never have I seen naïveté and cunning so gracefully blended'" (Kahn Jr.). It is the same kind of technique Joe Lash saw when she critiqued Nixon on *Meet the Press*—dynamite charges disguised in a grandmotherly tone.

A notable appearance with ER discussing the UN is the ABC public affairs program *Perspective* on November 20, 1953. It illustrates her strategy to educate on the issues, trying to come to an understanding among participants and work out issues, rather than arguing. There are still disagreements, but the goal is to constructively move forward and find solutions. During the show, she answers questions effectively while talking about strategies to move ahead with the Universal Declaration of Human Rights, all with her black purse sitting in her lap. She is well respected in the discussion and is obviously the expert on the topic, interjecting when necessary to correct the others. Those others are Dana C. Backus, counsel for the American Association for the UN and chair of the International Law Committee of the Association of the Bar of the City of New York; James M. Landis, former dean of Harvard Law School; and Limon M. Tandel (name unclear), chair of the international law section of the American Bar Association, who all sit around a coffee table. The three men ask her questions, and she is the one speaking for most of the half hour. As the group sits together talking, the announcer says, "Well, I'm very glad you're able to join us because here in our study are some of the most distinguished persons in world affairs. Mrs. Eleanor Roosevelt is just starting to tell us about some the accomplishments of the United Nations Commission on Human Rights." The camera zooms in for a close-up on ER, wearing a black, short-sleeved dress with elaborate lace on the top and pearls with a fleur de lis brooch, as well as a hat. "You know, she's a member of the Commission and a United States delegate to the UN." They talk about the Universal Declaration in a global context, and she notes issues with discrimination based on sex or race that the United States does not do so well with itself.

From March 31 to April 2, 1949, representatives from over 800 national organizations convened in Cleveland, Ohio, for the second National Conference on UNESCO (United Nations Educational, Scientific and Cultural Organization). The ABC affiliate in Cleveland canceled all its regular programming on the evening of April 1 from 8:00 to 10:00 p.m. to cover the convention but ran up against a U.S. State Department ban on telecasting the sessions. The "ban" turned out to be concern over Hollywood actors scheduled on stage who did not have clearance to appear on television, but they were replaced by New York actors with television rights instead. That just left the approval of speaker Eleanor Roosevelt. "If anybody should want the program to reach the greatest number of people, Mrs. Roosevelt should," wrote the television editor of the *Cleveland Press*. "Her record as a UN worker should work against a refusal. As a matter of fact, she should ask for television coverage," he continued ("TV Ban"). As predicted, ER did consent to the local television broadcast of her speech ("UNESCO").

On June 7, 1949, Eleanor, French Professor René Cassin, Dr. P.C. Chang from China, and Dr. Charles Malik of Lebanon, all members of the UN Commission on Human Rights, participated in a CBS discussion on "You and Human Rights" ("Radio and Television"). ER began the program by saying, "This is Eleanor Roosevelt. And so our goal has been to set a standard of achievement, a bill of human rights for peoples of all nations, a light to guide them as they emerge from recent terrors of fascism and war." A short documentary played next, featuring footage of Nazi concentration camps, the attack on Pearl Harbor, other horrors of war, and starvation in India, before the formation of the United Nations brought hope to millions. The panel discussion then followed ("You"). In July, she appeared on *The People's Platform* on CBS in a special program devoted to worldwide human rights initiatives endorsed by the UN (Conway 310). A few months later, NBC broadcast a celebration of the Declaration from Carnegie Hall on December 10, 1949. ER joined the Boston Symphony Orchestra, Brigadier General Carlos P. Romulo, and UN secretary general Trygve Lie ("Programs").

CBS broadcast the March 27, 1950, United Nations meeting on human rights from Lake Success, New York, the temporary home of the UN in the United States. Television listings announced the coverage with "Mrs. Franklin D. Roosevelt and others" ("Programs" 27 Mar. 1950). On April 27, "Mrs. Franklin D. Roosevelt speaking at American Association for the United Nations, Newark, N.J." was broadcast on WATV, now WNET, the New York City area's primary PBS television station ("On Television" 27 Apr. 1950). CBS ran *The Four Freedoms Award* television special in which Eleanor was presented with the honorary scroll for 1950 on May 11 ("Radio and Television"). The awards are given each year to individuals who have demonstrated a commitment to the four freedoms outlined by FDR in a speech to Congress on January 6, 1941: freedom of speech and expression, freedom of worship, freedom from want, and freedom from fear. The honor was announced by New York state Supreme Court justice Ferdinand Pecora, who was chair of the selection committee. ER spoke at the Waldorf-Astoria Hotel at a dinner for 600 in her honor and had received the most nominations for the award that year, especially for her work as chair of the Human Rights Commission ("My Day" 11 May 1950, "Mrs. Roosevelt Wins"). She devoted much of her talk to freedom from fear: "We must make up our minds that we are not going to make our decisions and act because of fear. We must try to find a way to be afraid and yet unafraid." In "My Day," she wrote:

> The award in itself is a beautiful citation, with paintings in the four corners illustrating the different freedoms. When it was finally presented to me there was little for me to say except to express my humble gratitude and assure those present that I knew only too well that we would achieve the realization of the Four Freedoms and of the peace which must be based upon them only through the vision and the courage and the determination of the people of the United States, themselves. They, alone, can be the architects of peace [13 May 1950].

Other speakers were Pecora, Attorney General J. Howard McGrath, Senator Brien McMahon, and Aubrey Eban, head of the Israeli delegation to the United Nations ("Freedoms").

A May 1950 article in *Variety* reported that ER was to serve as a technical adviser in Los Angeles to MGM on its "proposed filmization" of the Declaration of Human Rights. MGM's head of production Dore Schary, who would make *Sunrise at Campobello* in 1960, met with Eleanor when he was in New York to discuss the project. Schary's model was Norman Corwin's dramatization of the Declaration of Independence, and Corwin spent six months researching and writing the UN version. Schary was delighted with the manuscript by November and asked ER to wire with a "commendatory message" to impress the MGM board into backing the project. However, there is no record of its completion. Corwin would later script the first three episodes of ABC's 1965 26-part documentary mini-series on FDR ("Mrs. FDR as Pic," Lewis).

Eleanor appeared on the *Marshall Plan in Action* series of documentaries on ABC with her short film *My Trip Abroad* on October 22, 1950, before it was released in theaters in December by *The March of Time* ("Today's"). Included were her visits to Denmark, England, Finland, France, Holland, Norway, and Sweden, with a focus on projects receiving Marshall Plan funds. These were U.S.-funded resources to help Europe rebuild after World War II. The other three short films for the Economic Cooperation Administration covered Bing Crosby's trip to Paris, a 4-H farm club tour, and a French comedy about the role of American tourism in European recovery ("Crosby").

CBS produced a television special in celebration of the second anniversary of United Nations Human Rights Day on Sunday, December 10, 1950, from New York's Metropolitan Opera House. ER and Ambassador Nasrollah Entezam of Iran, president of the UN General Assembly, were the two speakers. Others performing included Chilean pianist Claudio Arrou, Marian Anderson, Sir Thomas Beecham conducting the Royal Philharmonic Orchestra of England, and the Schola Cantorum. *Variety* reported that CBS picked up $10,000 in production and talent costs for the UN ("10G"). Eleanor said, "Human rights must be applied to all human beings regardless of race or creed or color. When they are applied, it will mean a growing understanding among the peoples of the world. Freedom can never be absolute because it must be consistent with the freedom of others. But the more observance there is of human rights the more freedom the individual will have." Actor Judith Anderson read several articles of the Declaration, followed by actor Charles Boyer reading other pieces in French. Entezam also spoke briefly in French ("U.N. Celebrates").

A six-part NBC Sunday afternoon series, *Assembly VI*, focused on the Paris meetings of the sixth United Nations General Assembly with commentary by Arthur M. Schlesinger, Jr., from film put on a plane to New York at the end of each day in Paris. On November 10, 1951, Eleanor took part in the opening ceremonies, and over footage of the U.S. delegation entering state cars with small U.S. flags identifying them, Schlesinger read from visible notes: "From around the world, delegates arrive by airplanes, cars, and railroad carriages. The United States has a veteran delegation, Secretary of State Acheson, Eleanor Roosevelt, Warren Austin, a former Republican Senator from Vermont, now the permanent US delegate to the UN." On December 8, 1951, she gave a speech concerning Korea and peace, freedom, security, and individual well-being for the world. Said Schlesinger, "Mrs. Roosevelt in my judgment was absolutely right when she suggested that wars generally came about through miscalculation. That is why weakness may lead to war by giving the enemy confidence that he can get away with aggression." He found in the UN the best hope that there would not be another Pearl Harbor.

ER was the guest on the February 12, 1952, episode of *United or Not?*, an ABC show that featured visitors from the United Nations to discuss issues of the day with host John MacVane, who served as press consultant to the United States delegation to the UN and produced this program ("On Television"). Ben Grauer moderated the NBC talk show *It's a Problem*, and Eleanor appeared on August 5, 1952, to discuss "What Are Human Rights?" Others on the panel were feminist novelist Fannie Hurst, who was a friend of ER and had served on the National Advisory Committee for the WPA, and Mousheng Lin from China, the senior officer of the Division of Human Rights for the UN ("On Television"). ER and John Foster Dulles, who had worked with Eleanor as a U.S. delegate to the UN, were on *The Hot Seat* on the October 12, 1952, political interview program on NBC in New York. *Hot Seat* questioners were host Stuart Scheftel and Thomas Hamilton, chief UN correspondent for *The New York Times*. On December 2, 1952, she appeared on the DuMont

Television Network's *Keep Posted* public affairs show with New York University philosophy professor James Burnham, moderator Martha Rountree, and Lawrence Spivak, who headed a "citizens' panel" to pose questions to the two guests. This was not a panel of the public as might be assumed, but well-known people in the field, even members of Congress. On this occasion, May Craig served as a questioner. They discussed "Has the U.N. Been Worth While?" in an argument one columnist described as frightening and dramatic ("Tonight," Russell). Beforehand, ER consulted with a UN public affairs officer to ask if she should accept the invitation. He thought it useful, but warned that "questions sometimes are heated and loaded" and that Spivak himself might seem antagonistic, although equally sharp to all guests. The UN staff member predicted that her opponent would represent the "Bricker viewpoint," that of Ohio Republican senator John Bricker, who promoted limiting the treaty power of the president and the Congress. Spivak wrote ER afterward to say that she had done a "fine job," and they had had a wonderful response to the program (G. Stewart, Spivak correspondence).

On October 19, 1952, ER appeared on the premiere episode of *Inside Israel* on WABD, an independent New York station. Host Bartley Crum, former appointee to the Anglo-Palestine Commission of Inquiry, was making the switch from radio to television. *Variety* was none too happy at what happened, charging Crum with "lack of sufficient preparation," talking at length about the purpose of the show and economic aspects of Israel, with a film clip of Prime Minister David Ben-Gurion and a long in-house commercial for Scrip for Israel, sponsor of the show. The lack of time available forced Crum to "give almost a brushoff to Mrs. Eleanor Roosevelt, his guest," with time for her to answer only two brief questions. The reviewer added, "It left viewers feeling cheated that she could not have spoken more" (Stal "*Inside*"). Advance publicity for the show had promised that she would talk about her recent trip to the Middle East (Shalit).

The University of Minnesota Audio–Visual Education Service distributed *Youth and the United Nations*, a short "pictorial presentation of the 1952 Youth Pilgrimage to the United Nations sponsored by the International Order of Odd Fellows." The religious organization Independent Order of Odd Fellows and Rebekahs took a group of high school students from across the U.S. and Canada to travel by bus to New York to visit the United Nations headquarters. While there, they observed the dedication of a fountain paid for by contributions from schoolchildren. A review of the short complained, "The one statement of Mrs. Roosevelt at the dedication of the fountain was dubbed in with rather poor-quality sound on the preview print" (Williams). The University of Southern California also distributed a short 1953 film, *Model United Nations*, featuring ER speaking with students about setting up a model UN with debate opportunities (Library 451).

Host and producer Jack Barry wrote in January 1953 inviting ER to participate as a panel member on *Wisdom of the Ages*, a DuMont Network show on Tuesday evenings. The program, which combined younger and older panelists, "received wonderful critical notices and is seen by an extremely large audience Coast to Coast each week," Barry communicated. He was a longtime, ardent supporter of both ER and the president and would consider it a deep privilege to welcome her. Because of the rigors of her schedule, he recognized that it would be difficult for her to become a permanent panel member, but he hoped she would spare the time for one episode. They would be happy to consult with her on the script so that she was able to answer a question designed to effectively present information about the United Nations. With no rehearsal, the program planned to take up only an hour of her time, and she would be paid (Ashley correspondence). There is, however, no record that she appeared on the show, which only aired through June.

NBC's *Today* show literary editor Estelle Parsons booked ER for August 7, 1953, to talk about her recent world tour and then again on November 4 to discuss her new book, *UN: Today and Tomorrow*, coauthored with William DeWitt (Parsons correspondence). Bill Downs and Edward Morgan regarded ER as an expert on foreign affairs when they interviewed her on the CBS political talk show *Longines Chronoscope* on August 26, 1953. The United States image abroad and her assessment of the United Nations were major topics of conversation, and Morgan asked about what he interpreted as a great deal of "suspicion" from people in the United States about the UN and its effectiveness. ER explained this by referencing the programs other countries had received to eradicate malaria or tuberculosis, for example, but those kinds of actions were not visible on the ground in the U.S. as they were in many other areas. ER also felt that the Soviets had misused the veto, but identified the major issue around expectations:

> I think that like everything else that we started out expecting that the United Nations would solve every difficulty right just by being the United Nations. We didn't realize that the United Nations was only all the nations gathered in one place, but all the troubles remained just as they were before, and therefore, we had to work to make the United Nations work. And we didn't want to work, and we didn't expect to have to do this work, and now we know we have to, which is healthy, I think.

This interview gave her an opportunity to provide complex explanations, rather than what might be the usual short answer format on many programs. She also briefly mentioned her new book, *India and the Awakening East*. When it was time to say goodbye to the *Longines Chronoscope* program, they gathered the best moments for rebroadcast, and the April 25, 1955, episode included the segment of ER's interview from the paragraph above.

On September 10, 1953, Virgilia Peterson moderated the ABC book discussion panel *Author Meets the Critics*, in which ER talked about her recently published work on India and the Middle East with Lady Dhanvanthi Rama Rau, Dr. Lin Yutang, and Dr. Charles Malik ("On Television"). The book focused on her impressions and experiences in travels to India, Israel, Jordan, Lebanon, Nepal, Pakistan, and Syria. Lady Rama Rau founded the Family Planning Association of India and would become president of the International Planned Parenthood Federation. Her daughter Santha Rama Rau appeared years later as a guest on ER's *Prospects of Mankind* television show. Dr. Yutang was an important Chinese philosopher and linguist, while Dr. Malik served as Lebanese ambassador to the United Nations, helped draft the Universal Declaration of Human Rights, and succeeded Eleanor as the UN Human Rights Commission chair. Malik commented that he felt the book missed a point because it only dealt with material factors, and Yutang agreed that the spiritual and moral order could not be disregarded. Malik also noted that goodwill from Americans was often lost because of the types of individuals overseeing programs that lent technical assistance to developing countries ("From the Managing"). On June 20, 1954, ER was back on the show to discuss *Ladies of Courage*, coauthored with Lorena Hickok ("Today's TV"). They covered women who worked in the political arena, including tips on breaking into politics and a chapter from Hick on Eleanor herself. ER also served as one of the critics on October 7 for former UN secretary general Trygve Lie, who had just published *In the Cause of Peace: Seven Years in the UN*. Thai foreign minister Prince Wan Waithayakon appeared as the second critic, with Peterson as moderator ("TV Programs").

NBC broadcast an official celebration of United Nations Day on Sunday, October 24, 1954, from the General Assembly Hall at UN headquarters in New York. Secretary General Dag Hammarskjöld welcomed guests who heard performances from the Symphony of the Air. ER introduced the preamble to the United Nations charter, which was then spoken by the chorus, and New York mayor Robert Wagner also participated in the show ("TV Programs"). CBS Sunday news program *The American Week* hosted by Eric Sevareid wrapped up events and interviewed newsmakers, broadcasting June 19, 1955, from San Francisco, where the UN session was convening. His guest was ER, appearing for the United Nation's 10th anniversary to talk about the past and future of the UN and its effect on U.S. policy. Others on the program included General George Marshall, former U.S. ambassador to the UN Warren Austin, and his Republican replacement, Henry Cabot Lodge, Jr. ("Today's Best").

Arlene Francis hosted *The Arlene Francis Show*, which lasted less than a year on NBC as a daily midmorning talk show from New York featuring celebrities and friendly chat. ER appeared on the program on October 24, 1957, to promote the United Nations along with actor Myrna Loy, who also volunteered with the UN. Hugh Downs served as announcer (Ross "Multiple ... October 21–October 25"). Francis notes that a wonderful result of her career was meeting people like Eleanor Roosevelt. The host authored a book about charm and wrote ER asking for her definition. "Instead of telling me to get lost and that she had no time for such nonsense—or ignoring my letter, which was also a possibility—she wrote a gracious reply, saying she'd given the subject matter much thought and had concluded that the only thing that matters in the relationship between two human beings is kindness, and that she wasn't, therefore, qualified to comment on charm" (Francis 158).

Broadcasting from New York, ER appeared on the popular CBS *Ed Sullivan Show* on May 11, 1958. In addition to performers like Connie Francis that Sunday evening, Eleanor was the season's political guest, and she paid tribute to Israel's 10th anniversary. Her agent Tom Stix reported trying to arrange for two paid appearances, one before and one after her trip to Israel, but the deal fell through when she insisted on making appeals as part of the presentations (Stix "Mrs. Roosevelt"). After the Holocaust and seeing hundreds of thousands of refugees after the war in Europe, ER was committed to the cause of Israel. She entered Sullivan's stage in a black, short-sleeved gown, her hair coiffed, with an elaborate necklace and no glasses. She held notes, but did not look at them, instead making eye contact with the camera and the studio audience, making her words that much more effective. She reminded listeners that Israel "has been the great example of rehabilitation of people. They have taken in more than a million refugees and tried to feed them, find work for them, and develop the country, and I think we in the non-communist world owe Israel a debt of gratitude. And so I'm glad to be part of this celebration, and I thank you Mr. Sullivan for giving us this opportunity." Sullivan took both her hands in his, clearly treating ER as an honored guest as he walked her off the stage. Nearly a year after her death in November 1962, this footage was rebroadcast on October 13, 1963. Sullivan introduced the clip in response to a suggestion from Adlai Stevenson, mentioning the groundbreaking ceremonies of the Eleanor Roosevelt wings at the FDR Library in Hyde Park. Her words about Israel and refugees were an illustration of "the concern for human beings that always animated Mrs. Roosevelt."

On June 10, 1958, ER was the guest of host Evelyn Echols on *It's Fun to Travel*, a New York–based television show that often featured delegates and visitors to the United Nations ("TV-Radio"). She spoke about her work with the United Nations and recent trip to Russia on the October 19, 1958, CBS Sunday program *UN in Action* ("Television Programs," "Today's TV"). The December 27, 1959, episode of the same show featured her as a special guest to help observe Human Rights Sunday, and Marlon Brando narrated over one hundred photographs to illustrate the welfare work of the UN across the world. ER discussed the origin and significance of UN Human Rights Day, tracing the development of the movement for human rights worldwide ("Mrs. Roosevelt to Appear," "Mrs. Roosevelt Discusses"). Industry journal *Television* listed her appearance on the special Human Rights Day broadcast as one of the television highlights of the year ("United Nations"). A December 2 telegram from ER to Harry Truman asking him to appear on the show the following weekend when he visited New York indicates that she may have been more than casually involved in this series. She stressed, "It would be very important for the AAUN if you could do this in your capacity

Harry Lasky interviews Eleanor Roosevelt for the December 27, 1959, episode of the CBS television series *UN in Action*. She discussed United Nations Human Rights Day and the UN's work to promote human rights across the globe (author's collection).

as AAUN honorary national membership chairman. This will be the last opportunity as the series ends shortly" (Telegram). Earlier that year on behalf of the AAUN, she presented *UN in Action* moderator Larry LeSueur with a special citation of merit "for distinguished programming in the public interest" on the show's 10th anniversary ("Mrs. Eleanor Roosevelt Cites").

On November 13, 1959, ER appeared on the independent channel WPIX *Insight* show to talk about her work at the United Nations and comment on both domestic and international issues. ER and former governor of Minnesota Harold Stassen discussed "Our Foreign Policy" on *Search for America*, an NET show moderated by MIT philosophy professor Dr. Huston Smith on December 6 ("*Globe's*"). Later in December on the same program, she talked with Professors Elspeth and Walt Rostow on the topic of "Relations with our Western Allies," including the status of relationships with NATO allies and the problem of colonialism ("Monday," "Relations"). Walt was a foreign policy adviser to John F. Kennedy and would become national security advisor to Lyndon B. Johnson, as well as a key influencer on U.S. policy in Vietnam. Elspeth wrote the book *European Economic Reconstruction* in 1948 and would serve as dean of the LBJ School of Public Affairs at the University of Texas at Austin.

When appearing on Quebec, Canada, show *Premier Plan* on February 14, 1960, United Nations Day, ER discussed the UN with journalist and politician René Lévesque in a conversation in French. When asked if she thought the UN would result in a world government if there were an accepted world legal system, she replied, "No, I don't think so. Because we limit it to things that we find are necessary to be resolved in this way, and we keep domestic matters within their governments" (translated from French). She thought that many agreed-upon UN processes and procedures were still required before disarmament might occur. These topics were also relevant to her March 8, 1960, interview on *That Free Men May Live*. A major issue for her was the establishment of a police force within the United Nations to carry out the decisions of the UN legal system. This was dependent on universal membership to replace the rule of force with the rule of law. She felt that the major issue was how much sovereignty each nation was willing to yield:

> We must not frighten people by telling them that they will have to give up all their sovereignty. That, I think, is a thing that might delay us very much. If we begin to talk about an overall world government, we will lose an enormous number of adherents. Whereas if we talk about building a law to replace force and gradually discussing what has to be submitted to that law, I think we may work out a very workable and acceptable procedure. I do think from the earliest possible days, as soon as we have certain things that we agree to submit to international law, we should set up our enforcement police force within the United Nations.

Host John Schwarzwalder asked what she thought was the most important thing that the UN had done. She replied that bringing together people from all areas of the world and increasing their understanding of one other was critical. She hoped that strong nations like the U.S. and the Soviet Union would remember that we should sometimes act through the United Nations, rather than unilaterally.

She was back on NBC's early morning *Today* show on June 27, 1960, for a "U.N. Anniversary salute" with former president Truman, AAUN president Clark

Eichelberger, and host Dave Garroway ("Television Programs," Ross "Multiple" 1960). Also in June 1960, ER received $1,000 for appearing on *This Week*, an ITV current affairs program in the U.K., shot during the UN Summit Conference (Stix correspondence II). Airing on New Year's Day, January 1, 1961, she narrated an NBC program about the children of United Nations delegates (Shepard "Adlai"). The United Nations and international relations were the major focus for her own television show *Prospects of Mankind* from 1959 to 1962.

21

Reminiscing and Inspiring

Sarah Churchill, daughter of British prime minister Winston Churchill, hosted a short-lived weekly CBS talk show sponsored by Hallmark Cards on Sundays. The October 7, 1951, premiere episode of *The Sarah Churchill Show* featured ER as the very first guest, later joined by Antony Beauchamp, celebrity photographer and Sarah's husband. Churchill seems extremely comfortable, talking into camera, an actor who does not look as if she is constantly reading from cue cards or notes, unlike Eleanor on her own programs. Here ER also seems relaxed and replies naturally. She looks at Sarah, not worried about her next line, except a moment when given a signal that it is time for the interview to end. This is perhaps the best available example of Eleanor Roosevelt on television as a relatable person, rather than a subject expert. The show itself is also more like a modern talk show than other early appearances. She laughs more than we ever see her on any other appearance, and it really does seem like a conversation between friends.

Sarah enters and says, "In just one moment, you're going to meet a very famous person who nearly had me court-martialed during the war." This is followed by a Hallmark card commercial that transitions into the opening credits of the show. "Now, I don't have to tell you about Mrs. Roosevelt, but to me she seems a woman who has embraced three careers, that of wife, mother, and humanitarian, with that wise understanding and her heartwarming personality." The message seems to be that after marriage and children, a woman may step outside of the domestic sphere into the public realm. Upon introduction, Eleanor welcomes Sarah "to the ranks of those women who have programs of their own on television. I think you'll enjoy it. I enjoyed mine." The two casually reminisce about ER's visit to London during the war, cold appearances on battleships, and both being reprimanded at times around issues of security. Sarah was threatened with court-martial for some information she was assumed to have repeated when it was really her father, and ER was reprimanded for leaving paperwork in her room unattended. After that chat ends, Churchill says, "Well, she really is magnificent, and I can't tell you how wonderful it was of her to come today … and as you know, Mrs. Roosevelt is a very busy lady." *Motion Picture Daily* was kind to Eleanor, but not as much to her host. "Miss Churchill got off to a good, lively start a couple of weeks ago, with Mrs. Roosevelt on her program. Since then, the show has deteriorated," wrote the reviewer (Hift). "Unlike other media, TV demands more than just a pretty face and an illustrious name." *The Billboard* had similar things to say about what they called a "celebrated-female-in-the-living-room show" with Winston Churchill's daughter. "Then Mrs. Roosevelt was there, a great lady, truly charming, vibrant, self-assured." However, the conversation had a "Bundles-for-Britain-Destroyers-for-Bases flavor" (Wexler). ER mentioned the show in her "My Day" column:

> At 5 o'clock I had the pleasure of being a guest on Sarah Churchill's new television program. She is one of the most charming young women I know. Her husband, who is an expert photographer, is working with her in the lighting of this show. She told her audience that she hoped to give them a pleasant 15 minutes, and I think it will not only be a pleasant but an interesting program…. Sarah should be a success on television. There is a warmth about her personality that cannot fail to get through to her audiences. She has a zest for life and the television audiences will enjoy "being with her" [9 Oct. 1951].

Churchill would soon move to NBC to become the first host of *Hallmark Hall of Fame* in 1952 (McNeil 661).

In her memoir, Sarah writes about ER's appearance on the television premiere: "Though she was warm, friendly, and generous, neither of us could forget the strain and training of our respective positions, one as the widow of an illustrious President, and the other as the daughter of an illustrious Prime Minister. Despite Eleanor's previous involvement in my 'security breach,' we both still seemed bound by wartime conventions and could hardly find a topic we felt suitable to discuss in public." Churchill went to the producer afterward and told him that she was unhappy. "I felt it was not the right use of my father's name, or the possible use of connections with people I had known all my life." They agreed that she should switch to interviewing actors and writers, rather than political figures (218–19).

Eleanor did exist in the world as a nostalgic reminder of Franklin Delano Roosevelt, the New Deal, and the days of World War II. As she got older, others began to celebrate her legacy and accomplishments after decades of humanitarian and activist work. Many of these television appearances were about the responsibility of citizens, hope in the world in a time of nuclear fears, and a message of her belief in the American people. *The Rootie Tootie Club* children's show featured a puppet named Rootie Kazootie controlled by Paul Ashley, along with human friends, and ran on an NBC New York affiliate. The "Rootie Tootie Club Thanksgiving Day Party" aired on November 23, 1950, with "a very special Thanksgiving message by Mrs. Eleanor Roosevelt." She told the audience that she wanted to speak seriously to the young people watching this program and read part of FDR's address to the Young Democratic Club in Baltimore, Maryland, on April 13, 1936:

> You ought to thank God today if, regardless of your years, you are young enough in spirit to dream dreams and see visions, dreams and visions about a greater and finer America there is to be—that poverty can be lessened, that class hatred can be done away with, and that peace at home and peace abroad can be maintained, and that one day a generation may possess this land, blessed beyond anything we now know, left with those things material and spiritual, which make man's life abundant. If that is the fashion of your dreaming, then I say, hold fast to your dreams. America needs them.

She said that life goes by quickly, and that they would soon enough be in the positions in which they now saw adults in their lives.

It was page one news in *Variety* announcing Eleanor's guest appearance on

NBC's *The Colgate Comedy Hour* with host Eddie Cantor on December 3, 1950. She joined Cantor in his "Maxie the Taxi" sketch in which the comic drove a makeshift cab with a celebrity passenger in the back. This was to promote the "Give a Gift to the Yank Who Gave" campaign, in which the public donated Christmas presents for hospitalized armed services members ("Mrs. F.D.R. Rides"). Additionally, Cantor planned to drop by *Mrs. Roosevelt Meets the Public* on both November 26 and December 24 as part of the promotion ("Week's TV"). She also participated in the *Bob Hope Christmas Special* on December 24, introduced by Hope as "one of the world's greatest women … the mother of one of America's best-known families, and also the wife of one of history's greatest men." ER's role on this program is clearly to represent the past, defined by husband and family, rather than as a leader valued for her own political acumen. Wearing a large corsage, ER joins Hope on stage to great applause, and is clearly reading cue cards as she speaks. Hope greets her with a "Merry Christmas" and shares that he finds that many people these days are confused and afraid of what the future may hold. For this occasion in troubled times, she reaches back to the message sent by George Washington to those fighting for independence. In part, she reads:

> The time is near at hand, which most probably determine whether Americans are to be free men or slaves, whether they are to have any property they can call their own, whether their houses are to be pillaged and destroyed and themselves consigned to a state of wretchedness from which no human efforts will deliver them. The fate of unborn millions will now depend, under guard, on the courage and conduct of the American people. Our enemy leaves us only the choice of a brave resistance or the most abject submission. We have, therefore, to resolve to preserve our own. Our country's honor calls upon us for a vigorous and manly exertion, and if we now shamefully fail, we shall become infamous before the whole world.

She hoped and prayed that with the same self-sacrifice and devotion to freedom, Americans could win world peace and goodwill without the use of arms. *Variety* approved of the performance: "Mrs. Roosevelt finaled the show with her reprise of a Yuletime message of peace and goodwill, a message once read by George Washington himself, and while this was not entertainment per se, it lent the proper spiritual quality to the program" ("Tele Follow-Up"). *The Billboard* review, calling the special "spotty" overall, still concluded, "Mrs. Eleanor Roosevelt closed proceedings with an effective reading" ("Another Look").

The January 1951 issue of *Radio and Television Mirror* included a similar short piece written by ER titled "A Message for the New Year." Her inspirational message reads:

> In these troubled times, with so much uncertainty in everybody's mind about the future, we should all remember that much of our hope for the security of ourselves and our children, depends on our all working together to find the solutions to the problems that lie ahead. This can only be done if we all think about the problems which we face and bring ourselves to a greater awareness of the issues. I feel that war is not inevitable; destruction in not inevitable; solutions can be found and peace is possible throughout the world.

This was a message that she was committed to throughout her work with the United Nations, and she brought this philosophy repeatedly to television screens as well. She was eager to communicate these ideals to young people, and appeared as a guest on *Youth Wants to Know* on August 13, 1952, and in October 1953 ("On Television," O. Adams). This NBC program based in Washington, D.C., featured high school students asking questions of prominent political and business figures, modeled on a *Meet the Press* format with moderator Alma Walker ("What's On"). On a Lancaster, Pennsylvania, local program, she also participated in a February 21, 1955, *Junior Press Conference* program with high school journalists ("TV Programs"). However, she rejected an October 1956 appeal from the Buffalo Junior Chamber of Commerce to participate on a television panel focused on "Integration and Related Problems." Tom Stix felt that her time was more valuable than traveling all the way to Buffalo to appear on local television (Stix correspondence). Targeted to even younger children, Roosevelt Enterprises had a series of 52 half-hour children's marionette tales in color and black and white under option as *Once Upon a Time*. ER was to perform the narration, but the project never made it to the screen ("Elliott").

In May 1952, the Congress of Industrial Organizations-Political Action Committee (CIO-PAC) launched *Issues of the Day*, a weekly documentary film series that local unions paid nearby television stations to air in 13 cities. The interview segments featured Washington correspondent Willard Shelton interviewing experts like Eleanor Roosevelt, who spoke about the Great Depression. The goal was to spread the message of organized labor to union members and the public ("Labor"). Henry Morgenthau III collaborated with others on a pilot for *Visit*, a show that looked in on celebrities, "lensed in their homes and showing their personalities and ways of living." Arlene Francis, who was one of the producers of the project, served as host, and Eleanor was lined up in August 1952 with an interview from Hyde Park ("Francis"). She appeared on the WABD *Barry Gray Show* on August 11, 1953, and did a local San Francisco ABC affiliate television show in November 1953 ("On Television," "My Day" 19 Nov. 1953).

The Anti-Defamation League celebrated its 40th anniversary on November 23, 1953, with a ceremony broadcast on all three networks from Washington, D.C. The program was staged by Richard Rodgers and Oscar Hammerstein with President Dwight D. Eisenhower, Bernard Baruch, and ER as special guests ("Telecasting Notes"). Eisenhower accepted the America's Democratic Legacy award in recognition of his views and actions since assuming the presidency, as well as his service in combating Nazism during World War II. Eleanor had already received this award in a previous year ("President"). The show's theme was considered an answer to charges by communists that the U.S. was a country of bigotry and intolerance ("R&H"). On NBC, the American Jewish Committee and YMCA had sponsored a similar 1951 television show, *Unfinished Business, U.S.A.*, and honored ER in addition to Baruch, Eisenhower, singer Al Jolson, and baseball great Jackie Robinson (Clemenko).

Comedian Garry Moore hosted *The Garry Moore Show*, a sketch comedy/variety talk show on which Eleanor appeared on January 21, 1954 ("TV and Radio"). In his initial pitch to ER, agent Ted Ashley wrote: "Your appearance would take the form of a ten minute period during which members of the studio audience would be invited to ask questions concerning matters of interest to you. I am reasonably certain that arrangements can be made with the producers of the program to make certain that you have the opportunity of discussing the United Nations and, of course, to curtail, within reason, any unreasonable questions from the audience, etc." She would receive $500, the maximum fee paid by the show, and ER's assistant Maureen Corr had a conversation with the producer beforehand about expected topics (Ashley correspondence). Eleanor held what was called an "Open Forum" with the studio audience, answering their questions on the United Nations, the White House, and her world travels (Sanford 61).

Legendary CBS journalist Edward R. Murrow interviewed ER in her new Manhattan apartment on January 22, 1954, during the first season of *Person to Person*. Murrow pioneered the celebrity interview with a format in which he is in his New York studio while the interviewee is at home. Notably, ER herself calls attention to the role she plays as the woman by whom others will be judged. First, viewers get a walk-through of her five-room duplex apartment on East 62nd Street. She was still receiving 100 letters a day in 1954, and he asks if the critical mail bothers her, to which she says, "No sir, no. You have to do the best you can in this world, and if you've done that, that's all you can do." He wants to know what she considers her most satisfying achievement. She is not sure that she would call anything an achievement; however, she continues:

> I've just done whatever came along to do, but the thing I remember giving me the greatest pleasure was at the end of the first session in London of the United Nations. I had gone in fear and trembling, and I had felt that I had to walk very carefully because I was the first woman on the delegation, and a woman must do well, or it hurts all women.... Mr. Dulles and Senator Vandenberg were kind enough to follow me up in saying goodbye to say that they were glad that I had been on the delegation. And while they had opposed me and begged the President not to appoint me, they had found it good to work with me, and I think that pleased me almost more than anything that could have happened.

Murrow asks why she works so hard, to which she replies, laughing, "What else would I do?" She lived alone and liked to keep busy. The other guest on this episode was Captain Donald W. Sorrell, skipper of the *Queen Mary* ("On Television"). A few years later, Eleanor would write, "Edward R. Murrow is one of my favorite people" ("My Day" 25 June 1958).

The concept of the *Where Were You?* syndicated television program, produced, directed, and narrated by Ken Murray, was to speak to people who remembered major events on a specific day (Murray). Each show also featured a mystery guest, and ER is mentioned in *Screenland* with an upcoming appearance in March 1954 (McNellis). Alf Landon, Ty Cobb, Bobby Jones, Douglas "Wrong Way" Corrigan, and Sgt. Alvin York were also profiled, among others ("BCE"). On the April 4, 1954, Saturday special program *The Challenge*, ER moderated a panel discussion on WNBT, New York's local NBC station, on the topic of "Is New York Doing an Adequate Job in Combating Juvenile Delinquency?" Guests included New York City commissioner of correction Anna Kross, president of New York City's Youth Board Judge Nathaniel Kaplan, and Mary O'Neil Hawkins, authority on adolescent psychology. The program also featured a tribute to the 92nd Street "Y" 80th anniversary (Ross "Local").

In her April 11, 1954, second appearance on NBC's *Meet the Press*, ER faced questions about Admiral Robert Theobald's new book *The Final Secret of Pearl Harbor: The Washington Background of the Pearl Harbor Attack*. May Craig asked,

"Admiral Theobald says that President Roosevelt invited the attack. Are you aware of any of this?" ER replied, "The whole Pacific area was alerted to the danger two weeks before the attack took place." After further questioning, she continued, "Secretary of State Cordell Hull had urged the continuance to Japan of scrap metal as an attempt to turn them from waging war." She added firmly, "My husband made every attempt to keep Japan from war ... at the time of attack he was just as surprised as everyone else" (Cremmen). On June 20, 1954, *Adventure* on CBS featured Eleanor narrating "The Story of Marco Polo" and talking to Charles Collingwood about her recent experiences in Asia, since she had covered much of the same ground in her travels as had the medieval explorer ("TV Topics"). James Abbe predicted that the American Museum of Natural History, which produced the show with CBS, "never just drag in somebody with a big name to help publicize their Sunday program, so we may expect that Eleanor Roosevelt will justify her role on today's program." The "unusual French film" shown illustrated Marco Polo's travels through illuminated manuscripts of Japanese, Persian, and Italian origin (Abbe, Devane). ER mentioned shooting the program in "My Day":

> Sunday morning I drove back to New York because, in the early afternoon, rehearsals had to begin for the *Adventure* TV show for which I had been asked to do some of the narration. This was fun to do and I enjoyed very much the picture of Marco Polo's travels.
> I have traveled to some of the same places; but it is far less adventurous today than it was in the days of Marco Polo, who traveled for so many years and went over so much completely unknown and uncharted territory. When you know nothing about a specific area, you are apt to people it with all kinds of imaginary terrors, and that is what the people of the 13th century did. It therefore must have taken great courage, which we modern travelers do not require, for we know fairly well what we are apt to find wherever we go [21 June 1954].

Afterward, the show received complimentary reviews for its "usual nice job" with notes that Eleanor served as a fitting principal narrator, since she had traveled much farther around the world than Polo (Cotton).

The impact of the women's vote was the major topic of ER's interview with the BBC's *Panorama* television program on March 9, 1955, in London. The U.K. was celebrating the anniversary of women's right to vote, leading Malcolm Muggeridge to open with a question about women and the vote in the U.S. He did not think it extraordinarily successful, since it had not produced large numbers of women elected to office. Eleanor disagreed. She said, "I find that the women having the vote has made a great difference in the interests of the men, and there were far fewer men who were concerned about social reforms before the women got the vote. But since they have to win the women's vote, they have got to be interested in things that will attract the women." She regarded this as far more important overall than the number of women in Congress or state legislatures. There was little social legislation before the women's vote. Muggeridge asked if ER missed being at the center of power in the White House. She did not feel nostalgic about the house itself but missed knowing the reasons and motives behind actions taken by the government or in foreign affairs. Now she got her news from the papers, like everyone else, but "I know enough about it to know that some of that is not true" (*Panorama* transcript). *The New York Times* only reported that ER criticized the U.S. press, a last short topic of conversation during the *Panorama* interview. She noted that journalists here did not know "where to draw the line" in coverage of the private lives of public figures. "Where it is not a matter of public interest, where what the public figure does is going to affect his own life and own interests, but not public interests, then I would say privacy should be observed" ("Mrs. Roosevelt on").

The Radio and Television Section of the American Cancer Society ran advertisements in industry publications in March 1955 to promote free television and radio materials to local stations. Two 15-minute educational films, among other promotions, were offered to help raise funds for the organization, and all featured well-known entertainers and stars like Nat King Cole, Bing Crosby, Cecil B. DeMille, Frank Sinatra, and an extensive list of others, including Eleanor ("This Hamster"). On April 2, 1955, ABC aired *Imprint of a Man*, the "heart-warming human story of the late CIO President Philip Murray and his contribution to American life" ("Today on"). The film emphasized Murray's role in labor struggles after 1930 and events that the Congress of Industrial Organizations (CIO) helped to shape. ER, Adlai Stevenson, and others appeared in short tributes ("New Materials"). It is hard to imagine it this early in the Golden Age of Television, but the FCC was deliberating in May 1955 over authorizing subscription television, or pay TV. Among the "big names" writing in favor of allowing a "toll TV" subscription model were director Cecil B. DeMille, poet Carl Sandburg, and Eleanor Roosevelt ("Broadcasters").

In her second appearance on the CBS *Adventure* show on June 19, 1955, ER joined Sandburg and anthropologist Dr. Harry L. Shapiro to comment on photographer Edward Steichen's "Family of Man" photography exhibit at New York's Museum of Modern Art. Sandburg recited portions of his book length poem "The People Yes," from which the title of the exhibit came, over select images from the five hundred photographs of people from around the world. Eleanor's segment was noted as particularly interesting and came midway through the television program ("Television Highlights," "Today's Best"). She sits on a striped couch in her New York apartment with both pearls and a microphone around her neck, reading cue cards off camera right and trying to look into the camera occasionally. ER is introduced as a humanitarian and says, in part:

> We are reminded that all of us, wherever we may live, belong to the first family, the family of man. An old truth is retold. At the right time, it strikes home. What makes us brothers? What makes us all members? Through the years, wherever I've traveled, wherever I've served, a simple fact has been confirmed for me. Cultures, languages, manners, may differ. The passions of people are alike. All have the need for love, warmth, understanding. All are passionately against hunger, isolation, and fear. From the large family of mankind, we draw faith and obstinacy. Our own personal families are the factories to nourish the world in repayment. When our children, our inheritors, are reared with love, they can but spread respect for man, their stubborn love for the world. We take and we must give love.

This *Adventure* episode won second prize for TV films at the Venice Film Festival in 1955 ("Two TV").

She rejected an offer in October 1955 to appear on the ABC game show *Masquerade Party* in which famous people appeared in disguise and attempted to stump the panel trying to identify them. ER would receive $800–$900, plus a charity donation, for dressing up as Whistler's Mother, but Tom Stix advised that it would be an "undistinguished performance" and she did not need to prove that she had a sense of humor. Franklin Jr. appeared instead as "Mr. Hyde" and raised $300 for the National Foundation to Fight Polio. The clue was the "Hyde" in "Hyde Park," but none of the panel members were able to guess who he was (Stix correspondence). In 1958, Stix would recommend that ER not go on NBC's *Hi Mom* show, hosted by puppeteer Shari Lewis. He did not think that the program for children with advice for young mothers "carries any distinction" and appearing on commercial programming without recompense damaged her own prospects as a "commercial property." He received 10 percent of her television and radio income (Stix correspondence II).

To start off the new year on January 2, 1956, ER appeared on *Tex McCrary's M.I.P.* (Most Important Persons), a 10-minute show on local WABD-TV in New York. McCrary, of Tex and Jinx, interviewed interesting guests from all levels of society and all occupations ("On Television"). Arlene Francis served as both host and managing editor of the *Home* daily talk show series, and an NBC press release touted the success of *Home* in its third season, listing "outstanding guests" that year such as Chief Justice William O. Douglas, Billy Graham, Fannie Hurst, Dr. Alfred Kinsey, and ER. She appeared on the show on April 6, 1956: "Mrs. Eleanor Roosevelt, winner of a number of teenage popularity polls, discusses the future with teenage panel." Other guests were cooking contest winner Kit Kinne and Lucille Rivers with a demonstration on making slipcovers (NBC-New York "*Home*," "Friday Morning").

On January 6, 1957, Dave Garroway hosted NBC's *Wide Wide World* episode titled "A Woman's Story" featuring interviews with six prominent American women: Maine senator Margaret Chase Smith, anthropologist Dr. Margaret Mead, singer Marian Anderson, disability activist Helen Keller, actor Katharine Cornell, and ER. This was Keller's first live television appearance. Prior to broadcast, a newspaper article described Eleanor's role: "Speaking from apartment in New York, Mrs. Eleanor Roosevelt, widow of President Franklin D. Roosevelt, will comment on women's role in international affairs. She recently was named in a Gallup Poll as the 'most admired woman in the world today.' The Roosevelt National Historic Site at Hyde Park, N.Y. will be shown, with Garroway commenting on momentous events which occurred during the Roosevelt administrations" ("Woman's Story"). The program begins with the host addressing a male audience: "Today we have a story to tell that is close to every man's heart—women." The lead-in to Eleanor's appearance includes FDR's life story with footage from Hyde Park, none of it specifically about ER. The show defines her by her marriage, rather than by her own accomplishments. After Margaret Chase Smith, Garroway introduces ER: "Another woman resides in a modest apartment in New York City, but her home is the world, Eleanor Roosevelt, first choice in a survey of the American public as the woman they admire most in the world today." The camera looks out to a patio from her apartment building and pans to someone handing ER her mail for the day. She smiles broadly and looks friendly and approachable.

Garroway continues after the commercial: "'She walked with kings but never lost the common touch.' This was said by a British paper about an American woman. She is known and loved all over this world, both by kings and commoners, by citizens of democracies and dictatorships, by Eskimos beyond the timberline and by natives below the equator. Name your countries in between, she's been there and gave them help and courage to help themselves." The camera cuts from Garroway to Eleanor speaking to a woman outside before she turns and enters the apartment. "Her modest apartment in New York City faces a small patio, but her travels throughout the geographical world and the world of ideas are as wide as her heart is wide." She wears a conservative gray suit and skirt with a white blouse and pearls, a microphone hanging around her neck. Before sitting on her striped couch, ER passes a portrait of FDR, and behind her on a table, photos of all four sons in military dress are visible. "This is her story, and her name is Eleanor Roosevelt." ER puts on her glasses. Garroway asks what her personal goal is with all the work she has done over the years. She replies that it is "to increase the work done for peace among the peoples of the world, to achieve a better understanding of our own problems at home and better solutions to those problems." After a brief chat about Hyde Park, for several minutes Garroway tells the story of FDR's parents and his birth and young life. On a program devoted to women, it seems quite odd, as if ER is only and completely defined by Franklin's story. She is not even mentioned during this eight-and-a-half-minute segment out of a total of 15 minutes, so one suspects that this footage was originally prepared for another use. Finally, they get to the marriage, and then the program continues to focus on FDR and the house and his gravesite. Garroway says, "From a rose garden in Hyde Park to a patio on East Sixty-Second Street in New York City, a span of ninety-five miles and eleven years in time, and the living link is a woman." Again, it is reinforced that that the only reason ER is on this program is because of her marriage to FDR.

Incongruously, the next question is about her own experience and points of view. Garroway asks, "Mrs. Roosevelt, why is a knowledge of world affairs so important to every American?" She tells him and the audience, reading from cue cards off camera left:

> A knowledge of world affairs is important to every American because there is hardly a single domestic question that touches the interest of the people in this country that at some point does not also touch our attitude on foreign affairs. Take, for instance, our farm surplus question, which may seem of purely local interest, but, as a matter of fact, these surpluses can be used as a diplomatic weapon and wisely handled throughout the world via change in our surpluses and by growing such things as are needed by people in areas of the world where they now go to bed hungry every night.

He follows up with a question about the UN, and ER tells him that she does believe that we are closer to peace and better understanding than we were years ago. She is also keen that the U.S. show intellectual and moral leadership to demonstrate the benefits of freedom. Afterward, *The New York Times* called the program "generally informative and entertaining" (Gould "A Study"). Because of the show's focus on "women," Eleanor's usual ability to transcend the category of female, defined as wife, mother, and grandmother, was stifled in large part.

In April 1957, the BBC introduced a *Portraits of Power* series on the nature of power with individual episodes focused on Hitler, Gandhi, Stalin, and Franklin Roosevelt. The episode on FDR aired on April 23 and included footage of Eleanor.

A history of the BBC notes that the four programs "had a wide impact on the viewing audience" (G. Ross 114). On a visit to the U.K., ER also appeared on the Granada Television program *Youth Wants to Know*, which featured high school and college students asking questions of business and political leaders. On the May 8 British version of the show, she answered questions on the theme "What the future holds in store for the youth of today" from students from a high school in the North of England ("Mrs. FDR on Brit"). ER briefly mentioned an early morning appearance on the *Today* show with Dave Garroway on June 3 ("My Day" 5 June 1957). Local KCMO-TV, Kansas City, Missouri, news covered the dedication of the Harry S. Truman Presidential Library on July 6, 1957. Harry and Bess Truman, former president Herbert Hoover, Texas senator Lyndon Johnson, Missouri senator Stuart Symington, New York governor Averell Harriman, former secretary of state Dean Acheson, and Chief Justice Earl Warren all attended with ER. From the podium, she said that she was sure that the library would bring an "immeasurable degree of education and pleasure" to young and old ("Key").

In addition to a variety of other topics on the November 23, 1957, *Mike Wallace Interview*, Wallace asked about her views on the American people. Architect Frank Lloyd Wright had been on the show with him a few weeks back and had said that the U.S. was in danger of declining as a world power because of the obsession with "bigger and better tail fins on automobiles, westerns on television, sex drenched movies, fur coats, and push buttons." Alcoholism was on the increase. Mental institutions were full. What did she think about that assessment?

> I think that estimate of the American people is completely wrong. I feel quite sure that what the American people lack is knowledge. I feel quite sure that the American people, if they have knowledge and leadership, can meet any crisis just as they've met it over and over again in the past. I can remember the cries of horror when my husband said we had to have fifty thousand airplanes in a given period, but we had them. The difference was that the people were told what the reason was and why, and I have complete faith in the American people's ability if they know and if they have leadership. No one can move without some leadership.

Eleanor always communicated her faith in the people, if they had access to information and direction. For her, the problem was that the United States lacked leadership to show its denizens the way.

The 1958 new year began in Warm Springs, Georgia, as Dave Garroway and NBC's *Today* show traveled south with ER for the 20th anniversary celebration of the National Foundation for Infantile Paralysis. The January 2 broadcast featured the dedication of a Polio Hall of Fame at the Warm Springs Foundation. On the program, Eleanor praised the speed with which the polio vaccine had been developed, and the audience was given a tour of President Roosevelt's cottage, the "Little White House" where he went to rest and regain strength and where he passed away on April 12, 1945 (Furman). Long-running Canadian show *Front Page Challenge* included a panel of journalists who guessed the news story with which a challenger was associated. ER took part on January 28, 1958, as "by far the most prestigious figure to appear on the show," and producers credit her early sign-on with allowing them to book other internationally known individuals. "The panelists were awed by Mrs. Roosevelt, if only because of her international stature," but Tony Robins was relieved at her apparent nervousness beforehand. Gordon Sinclair noted that "the panelists, himself included, became so tongue-tied that Mrs. Roosevelt had to save the show by virtually interviewing herself." Eleanor's challenge was a headline about FDR's 1932 election as president of the United States. Rather than taking payment, the production donated the usual guest's fee to the March of Dimes at her request (Barris *Front* 22–23, 53, 63–64). Marguerite Higgins, a "famous American guest panelist" in the show's early days, shared the flight back to New York with ER ("My Day" 1 Feb. 1958). In February 1958, Eleanor was off to Miami to appear on *First Federal Presents*, a local, live NBC affiliate public affairs show hosted by Harry Cain (C. Smith 262). A former Republican senator from Washington, Cain had been a guest on *Today with Mrs. Roosevelt* twice back in 1950.

ER appeared in a series of four half-hour *Heritage* television documentaries on NET affiliate stations across the country. Produced by WQED in Pittsburgh, Pennsylvania, and filmed there in March 1958 with Henry Morgenthau III and Dean Clarence Cramer of Western Reserve University conducting the interviews, the first episode aired in April. It addressed her life after the death of Franklin, including a touching story about Fala, FDR's Scottish terrier. Following the president's death, one day Fala jumped to attention and began yipping as the rarely used main gate of Hyde Park swung open at the sound of sirens. But the little dog was disappointed that the motorcade contained not his beloved owner, but General Dwight D. Eisenhower, who was there to place a wreath on FDR's grave ("Mrs. Roosevelt Is"). She also discussed Senator Joseph McCarthy, the "Negro situation," and reevaluating the American educational system ("Today's Programs"). In a second episode, ER talked about her early life and education at Allenswood, while the third program focused on Franklin's personality as a young man, their first meeting and the wedding, and his political beginnings. For the last program in the series, "Mrs. Roosevelt talks of her husband and his philosophy, religion, friendships and courage. She tells of D-Day in the White House and what happened after the attack on Pearl Harbor." She also covered the topics of communism, war, and leadership in the world today ("Sunday Television").

A March 1958 *Variety* article on local successful programming mentions KPIX CBS San Francisco's *New Horizons*, a show targeted toward retirees. The program "consists of discussions and lectures on what California's senior citizens are doing to maintain useful, productive, happy lives," and well-known people active in their 60s, 70s, and up appeared as inspiration. Eleanor was noted as an example of a recent guest (Traube). For her 74th birthday, *McCall's Magazine* produced both a 15-minute film and a nine-page story using photographs of ER and her family in the October 1958 issue. *Eleanor Roosevelt: Her Life in Pictures* was shot on August 27, 1958, and she looks through pictures that tell the story of her life. The unnamed interviewer begins, "Regardless of political sentiment, most people agree that Eleanor Roosevelt is the outstanding woman of our time." She talks about the fashions of her youth and appreciates how much more comfortable the styles are in 1958. A shot with her sitting next to columnist Westbrook Pegler, who had many horrible things to say about the Roosevelts, prompts a chuckle: "I'm surprised that Mr. Pegler ever let himself go in that way." They talk about criticism, which does not really bother her, but if it was "really truthful criticism," she thinks about it very carefully. "I'm afraid I did some things which were not usual for the lady in the White House." And what would she say to her great-grandchildren if she had them all together to offer advice in growing up?

> I think I would say that they have a greater opportunity because they're born in a less rigid mold. They have more opportunity to shape their lives. They will, of course, I believe, have many disappointments because in life, you always have disappointments, but if you have the character which makes you go on striving, I think the young people of today have greater opportunity than ever before.

The FDR Library has made this full interview available online.

In her October 26, 1958, *Meet the Press* appearance, in addition to New York politics and issues with JFK, ER discussed right-to-work laws, stating that their true aim was to destroy unions and collective bargaining. May Craig prompted her, "In your column, Mrs. Roosevelt, in 1941—March 13—you said: 'I do not believe that every man and woman should be forced to join a union.'" ER replied, "No, I don't. I don't think you should be forced to join a union, but that means, then, you go to work where there is no union." Conservative journalists attacked this point of view, that a worker with "conscientious beliefs" about joining a union would have to leave a job in lieu of becoming a union member in a union shop. "What a travesty on American freedom and the bill of rights," charged one such columnist, who believed that she had misinterpreted the real issue (Lawrence). ER would have countered that the real issue was union busting.

In February 1959, Eleanor earned $35,000 for appearing in her first television commercial for Lever Brothers' Good Luck Margarine, running on both CBS and NBC. The money went to the Wiltwyck School for Boys, located across the Hudson River from the Roosevelt home and serving Black boys from New York City with emotional and behavioral problems, and the Citizens Committee for Children of New York, which served disadvantaged children in the city. Her secretary Maureen Corr and friends Trude and Joe Lash were very much opposed to the idea, but agent Tom Stix believed that if the commercial was successful, then she would no longer be "poison" to advertisers. A few years earlier, agent Ted Ashley had advised her not to do two one-minute Zenith hearing aid commercials that were to be aired on NBC's Sid Caesar's *Your Show of Shows* for a fee of $3,500. He wired in October 1953, "Consider your appearance on program solely with respect to such commercial announcement undignified and recommend against acceptance," and she did not accept that offer (Ashley correspondence).

ER had a positive attitude about the power of commercials: "Very little can be said in a commercial, but there is time to put one thought across and one reaches far more people than can possibly be reached in any other way. No matter how much I travel or lecture, I can reach only a few people. The idea which I wish to stress is that we should give from our overabundance to the underfed peoples of the world. The money which I shall receive from these commercials I shall put into my charity account" (Adams "Godfrey"). She told Stix, "With the amount of money I am to be paid I can save over six thousand lives. I don't value my dignity that highly.

Go ahead and make the arrangements." He reported that instead of a flood of protests, the sponsor received fewer than one hundred letters (Stix "Mrs. Roosevelt"). In terms of a few adverse letters, *Newsweek* reported that ER said, "I get those no matter what I do" ("Newsmakers").

The Good Luck commercials were placed in the full network lineup, including daytime shows *Haggis Baggis*, *County Fair*, and *Treasure Hunt* on NBC and reruns of *I Love Lucy* on CBS. Twenty-three CBS radio stations ran the audio version ("New Lever"). Produced by advertising, public relations, and marketing agency Ogilvy and Mather, David Ogilvy later wrote about the ad spot in his seminal book *Ogilvy on Advertising*, addressing what are sometimes the negative impacts of celebrity endorsements. "Viewers have a way of remembering the celebrity while forgetting the product. I did not know this when I paid Eleanor Roosevelt $35,000 to make a commercial for margarine. She reported that her mail was equally divided. 'One half was sad because I had damaged my reputation. The other half was happy because I had damaged my reputation.' Not one of my proudest memories" (109). When he appeared on the *Late Show with David Letterman* to promote the book, Ogilvy even showed the ER commercial as an example of what he had done wrong in the past. However, Lever Brothers itself seemed quite happy with all the attention the commercial received at the time. "We are delighted," commented product manager Tom Drohan, although it was too soon to see if the spot actually sold margarine ("Criticism"). Ogilvy had also been pleased while watching the initial rushes and wrote ER that her "performance was *marvelous*." They were all incredibly grateful that her work was "exactly the right combination of seriousness and charm" (Ogilvy to ER).

Three versions of the commercial were recorded in the New York studios of MPO Productions. *The New York Times* television editor included the text of one he watched on February 16, 1959, during NBC game show *Haggis Baggis*:

> ANNOUNCER: Ladies and Gentlemen, Mrs. Franklin D. Roosevelt.
> ER: When you sit down to breakfast, don't you often think of the starving people of the world? I wish we could share our abundance with them, wholesome foods like Good Luck Margarine. Years ago, we never dreamed of eating margarine. But nowadays, you can get margarine like Good Luck, which tastes delicious. I really enjoy it!
> ANNOUNCER: The margarine Mrs. Roosevelt has just recommended is new Good Luck, the light margarine that leaves no oily aftertaste.

The columnist excused ER for what he saw as a lapse in judgment but blamed the advertising agency for not lending more guidance. "The sight of her raising her eyes to the camera and linking her concern for the world's needy with the sale of a food product at the retail counter was disquieting in the extreme" (Gould "Dubious"). A reviewer for *The Family Digest*, a Christian publication, wrote that the commercial "irks" him, in part because she laughs and says that no one would have dreamed of eating margarine years ago. That was all that his family could afford, so he was offended by her characterization, which did not fit ER's usual concern for the poor and working class (Francis). Despite the criticism, one television executive was quoted as saying that the commercials were "the biggest thing to hit TV since Bert and Harry Piel," popular animated spokespeople for Piels Beer ("Advertising").

Eleanor saw this move as a means to book a television series in an era in which shows were directly sponsored by brands. She explained, "You know as well as I do that every program sells something, whether the person featured sells it or it is done by the announcer. I don't see the difference between doing the commercial directly or indirectly." She added that she felt that if the commercials were successful, they might lead to an opportunity to reach people on a regular program. "Time and time again I have been told that I am too controversial for a sponsored program" ("Criticism").

In a slightly different version of the commercial, she wears makeup and effectively reads cue cards:

> **ER**: I wonder if you realize than more two-thirds of the people in the world are underfed. I certainly wish that we could find more ways to use the tremendous capacity of our American farmers to produce vast quantities of food. I'm confident that America could lead the way in helping to feed the starving people of the world. I hope that more ways can be found to send them good, nutritious foods like the new Good Luck Margarine. Years ago, most people never dreamed of eating margarine, but times have changed. Nowadays, you can get a margarine like the new Good Luck, which really tastes delicious. That's what I've spread on my toast. Good Luck, I thoroughly enjoy it.
>
> **Announcer:** The margarine Mrs. Roosevelt has just recommended is new Good Luck, the light margarine. Good Luck is light on flavor, light on your tongue, and leaves no oily aftertaste.

It is a more natural performance than many of her other television appearances. One columnist joked, "Ever since Eleanor Roosevelt started commercials for oleomargarine, Jack Kennedy eats nothing but butter" (Knebel). In a tongue-in-cheek column, a *Variety* writer took on the suggestion that television needs more "culture," but depicted viewers leaving in droves over signs of culture in commercials. One of the examples: "How would the dial twister react if Jimmy Roosevelt would run towards his mother, suddenly put the brakes on and breathlessly gush, 'Look Eleanor, no cavities'" (Lipscott).

A decade earlier, ER had stepped into a mess by accepting an advertising deal with the American Television Dealers and Manufacturers, who represented 22 TV companies. On November 13, 1950, the group ran a full-page ad in 502 newspapers across 358 cities in the U.S. In homes that did not own a television set, a girl was depicted crying, with implications that children would be ostracized from others and considered underprivileged, and their personalities would be inhibited. The public backlash was swift for the advertising firm Ruthrauff and Ryan, and child psychologist Angelo Patri, who supplied a statement about children's well-being to run in the advertisement, lost his syndicated column in the huff. The Newspaper Guild of New York voted to urge newspapers not to accept comparable ads, and the FTC was prompted to investigate accuracy in advertising aimed at children (Farrant). The problem for Eleanor was that she had also given the group a statement scheduled to run nationwide the following week. Hers was part of a five-part series about the benefits of television, although none as controversial. The Roosevelt response was proactive, with a *New York Times* headline declaring, "TV Ad Deplored by Mrs. Roosevelt" and in the *Washington Post*, "Mrs. Roosevelt Hits TV Ad on Children."

She told the press, "I thought it was horrible and immediately asked Elliott to check the use of my statement." The Roosevelts asked that her words not be used unless she was able to check the entire sequence of ads, but the agency responded that the contract with ER did not require prior approval and that they had already run a radio version. There were assurances, though, that the next advertisement would promote "positive joys of TV set ownership" ("TV Ad"). Originally, the plan had not been to start the positive campaign until the third or fourth ad.

"I thought the ad was dreadful and I didn't want to have anything to do with it," she said. Elliott shared ER's prepared statement with the press, indicating that she "feels the television industry has a great responsibility to the children of the Nation in providing good programs." In addition, it was "equally important for parents to supervise what a child sees on television as the books a child reads" ("Mrs. Roosevelt Hits"). The new November 20 advertisement featuring her endorsement was a positive spin: "You'd give them the world if you could…. This Christmas you can! … With TV this magic world is theirs to enjoy every day." Unlike Patri, there were no cancellations of ER's column. The following text appeared:

> Mrs. Franklin D. Roosevelt, United States Delegate to The General Assembly of the United Nations says:
>
> To me television offers a magnificent opportunity to increase the education which we make available to the children of today. If parents will supervise carefully the type of show and the time spent by children watching television, they can see the best that television has to offer, which can bring much enjoyment and much that will be valuable in their education. Of course, I am a firm believer of the supervision of children's reading habits, and now that we have television, I think the same thing should be true for television. It is a parent's duty to see to it that the children get the best in books and the best in television entertainment and education.

This was accompanied by a thumbnail photo of ER.

A March 18, 1959, front-page headline in *Variety* read, "Experienced Lady (1st) Invites Bids to Make Her a Television Star." The tongue-in-cheek article revealed in what high regard ER was held for her vast experience. It read, "WANTED: A TV show. Have traveled widely. Broad experience as social worker, politician, First Lady, lecturer, author, diplomat, and tv commercial announcer. No guarantee against controversy. If interested, please contact Eleanor Roosevelt, Hyde Park, N.Y." Eleanor pointed out that she was welcome on occasional appearances, but "no one wants me to be on a steady program because I am controversial and it doesn't sell their programs" ("Experienced"). Several weeks later, the following item appeared: "Eleanor Roosevelt may be interested in tv, but doesn't crave an acting career." Stix turned down an offer with a generous salary for her to appear in *White Oaks* at Drury Lane Theatre in Chicago, a part once played by Ethel Barrymore on Broadway ("And That's That").

Fifty thousand people gathered in New York, Chicago, Boston, Los Angeles, Washington, D.C., and other cities across the country for Harry Truman's 75th birthday, and the celebration full of celebrities and notables was broadcast via closed-circuit television to 16 of the 75 participating locations for the Democratic Party fundraiser. *Variety* called it a "glittering show business shindig" with Jack Benny, Leonard Bernstein, Jimmy Durante, Danny Kaye, and Peggy Lee, joined by political figures like ER, Adlai Stevenson, Lyndon B. Johnson, Dean Acheson, and Sam Rayburn, with Melvyn Douglas as host. Douglas told the story of Eleanor informing Truman about FDR's death and their exchange in which the vice president asked if there was anything he could do. She replied, "Is there anything we can do for you, for you are the one in trouble now?" Douglas said, "The greatness and goodness of this remarkable lady showed even in that moment of sorrow." ER appeared on camera in the tribute and gave a speech *The New York Times* called "dramatic" (Alden). She referenced the encounter with Truman on the day of Franklin's death, following up with:

> And I can answer by saying that the character of my friend was proved on that terrible day. He was frightened, as he should have been, for no man had ever been placed so abruptly in such a seat of responsibility, and yet there was never in him the slightest hint that he would try to evade what fate had thrust upon him. I knew then he was a good man. Later I thrilled to watch him grow to greatness. With every decision he grew, until to the entire world he was a towering figure. The decisions he made then shaped the very world we live in today. Those were the years of decision, a thrilling record.

The technology shifting back and forth between cities was considered innovative for the time and a demonstration of what could be carried out over 16 separate locations. The film was produced by Teleprompter Corporation, later bought by Westinghouse (Woodstone).

ER shot a TV pilot for *Thinking Things Through* in New York on July 17, 1959, for a television series discussing world affairs with a group of four American and international students who were to comment on "typical news clips" while gathered in a replica of the den at Hyde Park ("Networks," "Eleanor Roosevelt at 75"). This was backed by the Alexander Film Company and Flamingo Films as a mid-season network replacement or syndicated show with 39 episodes ("Mrs. Roosevelt in," "Programming"). The company planned to shop the program to advertisers and networks, but the series did not materialize after shooting the pilot. *Prospects of Mankind* was already in the works and debuted in October 1959 with a panel of experts, rather than students. The backers of *Thinking Things Through* found it impossible to compete with ER's public television show that was also offered free for broadcast on commercial stations ("Flamingo").

The NBC documentary series *Project Twenty* covered 20th-century American life and was fundamental in creating the style of archival footage, still photos, narration, and musical scoring for the now-familiar television documentary. The September 13, 1954, "Three Two One Zero" episode counts down the birth of the atomic age by surveying the hours before the first atomic bomb test in the New Mexican desert in July 1945. Narrator Alexander Scourby relays the day's events, including: "At Hyde Park, Mrs. Roosevelt broadcasts in support of the UNO [United Nations Organization]," over archival footage as she speaks over the radio. The "Life in the Thirties" episode airing on October 16, 1959, examined the decade of the Great Depression, with just one sentence referencing ER. Scourby says: "The president of the United States is the first man in history to achieve world stature without the ability to walk. His affliction, says his wife Eleanor, gave him strength and courage he had not had before."

In the October 17, 1959, issue of *TV Guide*, ER wrote the first in a series of articles by "outstanding Americans" on "Television as I See It." Her article, "Television's Contribution to the Senior Citizen," does not reflect Eleanor's experience of TV, but what she thinks it might provide to others of her age. She begins:

> I do not happen to be one of the people who are fortunate enough to have a great deal of time to watch and analyze what television is now presenting to the public, but I find that many of my contemporaries get a great part of their information from television programs and that many of their interests stem from what they have seen and heard on television.
>
> I have, as you know, reached 75 and know many of the limitations that come with age. TV can supply many pleasant hours as well as much information. No matter what one's age, one can develop new interests and TV will help older people to develop these interests.

She addresses issues of older people being ignored and forgotten, feeling that television could bring them information that might prompt conversations in the household.

Stars and politicians came together on the NBC variety show *Sunday Showcase* to honor ER on her 75th birthday and raise funds for the Eleanor Roosevelt Cancer Research Foundation in "A Tribute to Eleanor Roosevelt on Her Diamond Jubilee" on October 25, 1959. Arthur Godfrey hosted the program, which included participation by Marian Anderson, Lauren Bacall, Ralph Bellamy, Israeli prime minister David Ben-Gurion, Gertrude Berg, Milton Berle, Eddie Cantor, Art Carney, Jimmy Durante, Henry Fonda, Sir Alec Guinness, Sir Cedric Hardwicke, Helen Hayes, Bob Hope, Ghanaian prime minister Kwame Nkrumah, Vice President Richard Nixon, Sidney Poitier, Elizabeth Taylor, and Harry Truman. Eleanor discussed the purpose of her work in the cancer field to close out the program, although several months earlier she had told *The New York Times* that she would not be taking part in the observance of her birthday (Shepard "TV").

One Washington columnist called it a "rich, impressive hour," with ER herself noted as engaging (Lowery "TV Show"). NBC announced that thousands of women were getting together to watch the program together in gatherings organized by the Eleanor Roosevelt Institute for Cancer Research, AAUN, and various civic and philanthropic organizations (NBC-New York "*Sunday,*" "TV Network"). On November 20, ER appeared on WPIX independent show *Insight* to talk "about the personal beliefs and attitudes of the late President Roosevelt" ("Television"). She took part in the *Celebrity Parade for Cerebral Palsy* telethon on independent WOR-TV in January 1960 along with Frankie Avalon, Pat Boone, Dick Clark, Jimmy Dean, Henry Fonda, Arlene Francis, Eartha Kitt, Sarah Vaughn, Andy Williams, and Henny Youngman ("Great Entertainment").

In his third television special for ABC, Frank Sinatra welcomed guests Lena Horne, Juliet Prowse, and Eleanor Roosevelt to *The Frank Sinatra Timex Show: Here's to the Ladies*. Pre-show publicity photos show Horne visiting ER in her New York apartment with a caption that reads, "They're discussing their forthcoming appearance together on ABC-TV's *The Frank Sinatra Timex Show*" ("Lena"). The two had known one another since Horne joined the effort supporting anti-lynching laws in the 1940s, but they do not actually appear together on stage on the program. Another publicity photo showing Sinatra and ER at rehearsal suggests that they would be singing a duet together, although Eleanor certainly did not sing ("Singing"). Near the end of the February 15, 1960, broadcast, Sinatra introduces ER, who recites the lyrics to the song "High Hopes"—"Whoops, there goes another rubber tree plant…. Kerplunk." One columnist called it, out of the many unlikely spots Eleanor had turned up in in her travels, "possibly the most curious spot of all" (Lowery). *The New York Times* commented that she was "not noted as a guest star on television variety shows" and described her appearance as "an unusual interlude" (V. Adams "WBAI," "Mrs. Roosevelt Among"). However, another reviewer explained to viewers wondering about her appearance that the former First Lady had just been chosen again in a Gallup Poll as the most admired woman in the country, so it made sense for this program honoring "the ladies" (Gardella). Eleanor dominated this poll from its inception in 1948 through 1961, when Jackie Kennedy usurped her number one spot. Sinatra, who had been pictured with her at Democratic Party fundraisers, called ER personally on the phone to ask her to take part, and she noted, "I like Mr. Sinatra" (Torre "Mrs. FDR"). "High Hopes" songwriter Sammy Cahn described going over a list of the most admired women with Sinatra: "Believe me, I would never dare to presume to call Mrs. Roosevelt. He gets on the phone. Next thing I know I'm writing her into the show" (Schumach "Money"). ER left for California on February 8, and the show was taped on February 9 and 10.

Sinatra begins with an introduction of "a lady whose friendship I treasure very much. Ladies and gentlemen, the most admired woman of our time, Mrs. Eleanor Roosevelt." In some scripted chitchat, he asks ER about the reasons for her travels around the world, to which she replies, "That's because my interest in people and the dignity of the individual seems more important to me than material things." If she could leave one word with the television audience, what would that be? "Hope," which she felt was "the most neglected word in our language." Eleanor then performs a spoken-word rendition of "High Hopes":

> Once there was a silly old ant who thought he'd move a rubber tree plant. Anyone knows an ant can't move a rubber tree plant. But he had high hopes, high apple pie in the sky hopes. So any time you're getting low, instead of letting go, just remember that ant. Whoops, there goes another rubber tree plant. So keep your high hopes, those high apple pie in the sky hopes…. Whoops, there goes another problem, kerplunk.

The script reads "ker-plop" rather than "kerplunk," but that does not sound like what she is saying. A version of "High Hopes" with different lyrics would become John F. Kennedy's 1960 presidential campaign song.

She is clearly reading cue cards during the on-screen conversation with Sinatra, and although one reviewer referred to it as "chatting coyly," another reviewer aptly called it a "stilted exchange of compliments." However, he added, "Mrs. FDR … never looked lovelier" (Humphrey "Video," Danzig). She wears an elegant evening gown to match the white silk underfoot, with hair and makeup unlike her usual more natural appearance and simple dresses. Cahn asked ER to bring two gowns to the show, prompting her to respond, "but you know I don't have any low-cut ones." *Variety* noted that there was not a dry eye in the house among cast or crew members after taping her performance (Archerd Feb. 1960). Critical reception of her reading of the song varied widely, from a "delightful recitation" to blame for assigning her the "questionable chore" of reciting the lyrics (Torre *Frank*," Barnes). While she "rang down the curtain" positively for *The Hollywood Reporter*, a *Newsday* critic published a scathing review calling the script "ill-prepared," the rendition badly done, and her guest spot "ill-advised." "She certainly should have known better," the anonymous writer complained, but a *Variety* reporter saw it at least a little more positively: "It was a routine that only Mrs. Roosevelt's tremendous stature saved from being embarrassing" (Grant, "Sinatra," Herm).

ER mentioned the performance in a letter to daughter Anna: "I went on Frank Sinatra's show in Hollywood (the pay for 5 minutes was fantastic & my part rather nice) but I'm not very good at 'entertainment.' I have never had so many compliments however & I found watching the mechanics amusing!" (Asbell 330). She was paid $12,500 for the appearance (Stix correspondence II). A few days later, one report said that because of the "painful [almost embarrassing]" reception, "Mrs. F.D.R. now will nix any more such outings" (Lyon). Another entirely contradicted this, saying that ER enjoyed her experience on the show so much that she "would not be averse to further forays in strictly entertainment shows" (Torre "Best"). Whatever Eleanor's thoughts about reviews, the offers did not come rolling in to perform on other such programs. Agent Tom Stix recalled traveling with her to Los Angeles for the show, noting that she had studied her part and was done in 10 minutes. The production later sent her the silk she walked across on the set, after she requested it so that it would not be thrown away. Afterward, they went to a party at the home of screenwriter Jack Roche and his Dutch wife Jean, who had fought in the resistance against the Nazis, with additional guests Alice and Ralph Bellamy. What neither ER nor Stix understood was that she was being used. Beforehand, Stix told a reporter that he made the trip with Eleanor "to make sure that Hollywood doesn't bite her" (Stix "Mrs. Roosevelt," Torre "Mrs. FDR"). However, he failed in this endeavor, and some inside the industry cried foul. Sinatra had sung "High Hopes" in the 1959 movie *A Hole in the Head* and was nominated for an Oscar for Best Original Song. *The Hollywood Reporter*

Frank Sinatra and Eleanor Roosevelt rehearse for her spoken-word rendition of his song "High Hopes" on the ABC television special *The Frank Sinatra Timex Show: Here's to the Ladies*, airing February 15, 1960 (author's collection).

described Roosevelt's performance as a promotion for the Oscar candidate, saying that thousands of Democrats across the country were irritated that "Eleanor Roosevelt Oscar-plugged a song candidate" (Connolly). *THR* checked with her, and "Eleanor didn't realize it was a plugola." Others like Fred Danzig matter-of-factly reported, "Mrs. FDR helped launch the campaign" for the Oscar (Danzig). "High Hopes" did end up winning Best Original Song at the Academy Awards that year for its writers, who were also the producers of the television special.

The syndicated 1960 television series *Reading Out Loud* featured celebrities reading to children from their favorite books. ER was one of those readers, as were Harry Belafonte, Pearl Buck, Julie Harris, Senator John F. Kennedy, and Vice President Richard Nixon (Editors 521). The show was produced by Westinghouse Broadcasting Company (WBC) and offered free to educational stations or others who put it on in prime time without commercials (Crosby *"Reading"*). Eleanor appears in the WBC advertisement in industry publications, saying, "It is very important, I think, that you should read aloud fairly often because we really enjoy it more when we do it together—and remember it more" ("TV Viewers"). She read segments of Rudyard Kipling's "The Butterfly Who Stamped" from his *Just So Stories* in the episode airing on April 26, 1960. Years earlier in 1955 she had turned down a request to perform two televised Bible readings for the DuMont Network, with no compensation involved (Stix correspondence).

For her 76th birthday, the October 7, 1960, *Eleanor Roosevelt's Diamond Jubilee Plus One* NBC celebration honored ER and raised money for the Eleanor Roosevelt Cancer Research Foundation. Bob Hope hosted performers and telethon commentators Lucille Ball, Jack Benny, General Omar Bradley, George Burns, Carol Channing, Nat King Cole, Jimmy Durante, Mahalia Jackson, Senator John F. Kennedy, Mary Martin, Paul Newman, Vice President Richard Nixon, Richard Rodgers, and Joanne Woodward, among others. Nixon made an appeal for

Days before her 76th birthday, Eleanor Roosevelt appears on *Eleanor Roosevelt's Diamond Jubilee Plus One* to raise money for the Eleanor Roosevelt Cancer Research Foundation. The NBC celebratory fundraiser aired October 7, 1960 (author's collection).

funds but did not mention Eleanor herself. *Variety* assessed the program as "emi-nently successful" as a public service and as entertainment. "A brief distinguished appearance by Mrs. Roosevelt" and a spiritual by Mahalia Jackson "rounded out an excellent 60-minutes" (Art "*Eleanor*"). In the Friday night ratings, the show came in second after *77 Sunset Strip* ("Dinah"). Hope begins with a brief introduction:

> I'm not about to make a speech honoring Eleanor Roosevelt. The deeds of her lifetime so far outshine whatever words I could find to describe them that a speech would be superfluous. It's enough to say that we who perform tonight at this second annual tribute to Mrs. Roosevelt, her diamond jubilee plus one, are honored to be here. Now, what do we hope to accomplish tonight? Well, first let me explain that Mrs. Roosevelt has given her name, her time, and her endless energies to the Eleanor Roosevelt Cancer Foundation. We are here to serve that foundation.

Throughout the show, celebrity participants wish her a Happy Birthday while asking for donations to fight cancer. Hope later jokes that she is the only Democrat with more hair than Kennedy and refers to her as "Adlai Stevenson's agent."

Viewers were to write a check or money order payable to the Eleanor Roosevelt Cancer Foundation and addressed to Eleanor Roosevelt, Box 4, Hyde Park, New York. ER herself makes an appeal near the end of the program, thanking the entertainers giving of themselves, as well as "all of you who honor me by watching at this very moment":

> Somewhere we know there is a cure for this mysterious illness, which knows no difference among people, which attacks the white, the yellow, and the black, no matter what god they love or what language they speak. The Foundation which bears my name has begun to honor a pledge made one year ago that it will strive to destroy the scourge of cancer for the benefit of all of the people who live in our one small world. We know no boundaries where human suffering is concerned. We work for the health of all people, and we believe that international concern for the welfare of human beings everywhere is a beginning in the struggle to bring peace to the world. With your help, we have begun our fight against cancer. With your help, we will finish it.

Mahalia Jackson closes out the program with a song and "May God bless Mrs. Roosevelt and always keep her in thy care."

Walter Cronkite hosted the CBS documentary series *The Twentieth Century* that looked at events and personalities since 1900. "The White House Story" episode on November 6, 1960, chronicles the history of the structure with drawings and photographs, including FDR's new swimming pool, as well as his open press conferences and cluttered desk. In a brief reference to Eleanor, Cronkite says, "Mrs. Roosevelt, in addition to family duties, becomes one of the most active First Ladies in White House history." The November 5, 1961, episode of this series focuses on former governor of New York and presidential candidate Al Smith. Both FDR and ER were included in archival footage ("TV Time Previews"). *The Finest Hours* documentary airing December 12, 1960, on independent WNET-TV in New York features Winston Churchill. Quentin Reynolds narrates over archival footage, and ER appears briefly to talk about Churchill's wartime visits to the White House. Her segment was mentioned in the press as one of the highlights of the program ("Tele Follow-Up," Torre "TV"). The *National School Telecasts* were shown in Canadian classrooms, and the December 4,

1962, broadcast deals with the New Deal. In filmed segments, Eleanor, Columbia University Professor Moley, and Roosevelt administration critic Hamilton Fish discuss President Roosevelt, his personality, and policies ("Program Notes").

The August 30, 1961, episode of *Understanding Our World* offered "A Portrait of Eleanor Roosevelt" ("Television"). This interview series was produced at the University of Michigan and brought visitors like ER, extreme right-wing novelist Ayn Rand, and poet Robert Frost to campus while broadcasting across the country (Barritt 6). In the next several months, she also guested on local program *Face the Community* for NBC affiliate WHEC-TV in Rochester, New York. Others scheduled on the show included New York governor Nelson Rockefeller, Ambassador Henry Cabot Lodge, U.S. Supreme Court justice William O. Douglas, and California governor Pat Brown ("In Rochester"). On November 3, *The Chevrolet Golden Anniversary Show* celebrated a half century of car manufacturing with a musical variety show on CBS featuring host James Arness, Art Carney, Nanette Fabray, and Tony Randall. *TV Guide* noted a symposium spoof near the end of the program, including a panelist who was "a woman of the world, described as a cross between Eleanor Roosevelt and Zsa Zsa Gabor," played by Fabray ("Chevrolet"). The U.K. version of the popular U.S. show *This Is Your Life* surprised guests by presenting the story of their lives in the form of interviews with family, friends, and colleagues. The program was broadcast by the BBC, and host Eamonn Andrews surprised Father Mano Borrelli in Naples, Italy, in the episode of October 9, 1961. Borrelli was known for his work supporting homeless children in Italy after World War II and establishing "The House of the Urchins." ER was part of the group who honored Father Borrelli's work with poor children. She was a fan of the U.S. version of the program, and host Ralph Edwards shared that she sent in a 1959 story suggestion. Eleanor wrote, "I have followed your program from time to time with the greatest of interest, for it seems to me that you are presenting a panoramic view of the American people which has considerable social importance and I have admired the things that you stood for." Edwards kept her suggestion a secret (NBC-New York "Ralph").

Dick Schneider directed the April 1, 1962, ABC television variety show telethon *At This Very Moment* for the American Cancer Society and the Eleanor Roosevelt Cancer Foundation. The show inaugurated Cancer Control Month and celebrated 25 years of progress in cancer research. Along with ER, guests include a long list of celebrities, including Harry Belafonte, Richard Chamberlain, Bobby Darin, Jimmy Durante, Connie Francis, Greer Garson, Charlton Heston, Bob Hope, Lena Horne, Rock Hudson, Vice President Lyndon B. Johnson, President John F. Kennedy, the Kingston Trio, Paul Newman, Jack Paar, Jane Powell, Edward G. Robinson, Dinah Shore, Danny Thomas, and Joanne Woodward. More celebrities offered their time than could be scheduled in the show, including Milton Berle, Pablo Casals, Sammy Davis, Jr., Kim Novak, Richard Rodgers, and Rosalind Russell, among others. All the stars on the show donated their time for the cause, and Robinson wrote afterward that he was simply grateful to participate in one of ER's humanitarian projects (Robinson). Burt Lancaster hosted the program and worked from 11:00 a.m. to 9:00 p.m. without stopping for meals. Belafonte faced a host of technical problems, singing his song at least 20 times. He and ER worked together on issues of civil rights,

President John F. Kennedy prepares to record a message from the White House Oval Office on February 15, 1962. The spot was televised as part of *At This Very Moment*, the April 1, 1962, ABC special benefiting the American Cancer Society and the Eleanor Roosevelt Cancer Foundation. To the right of JFK is White House Army Signal agency staff member Harold Haley. Others are unidentified (Cecil Stoughton, White House Photographs, John F. Kennedy Presidential Library and Museum, Boston).

including supporting the Freedom Riders in the south. She had written President Kennedy, enclosing a letter from Belafonte, and asked for his support: "You and I must keep faith with those who suffered. We must not stop until buses and terminal facilities are open to all—everywhere in our country" (ER to JFK).

Kennedy had memorized his two-and-a-half-minute speech, refusing to use cue cards, and was done in five to 10 minutes of shooting from the White House (Schumach "Many"). He called on all Americans to help in the struggle against disease as well as other national challenges and targeted 1962 as a year of progress in the fight against cancer. He added, "I'm proud to be able to pay tribute to one special volunteer who has made this cause very much her own, Mrs. Eleanor Roosevelt. The Cancer Foundation that bears her name is now affiliated with the American Cancer Society in a great national effort. I hope that all of you will be part of it. This deserves our most earnest and sympathetic consideration" ("Remarks"). *Daily Variety* described ER as "another pro" who relaxed in front of the camera and ably utilized cue cards (Kaufman). ER wrote JFK afterward with her deep appreciation for his "gracious participation." She had been informed "that the crusade got off to a very good start this year" in part because of his support (Schlup 275).

22

Prospects of Mankind

> Most people buy television sets in anticipation of light
> entertainment, just as most theatergoers prefer bright musical
> comedy and shun serious themes. Yet there are TV producers—
> chiefly in the educational television field—who believe that
> (1) television is a medium that can be used to sharpen awareness
> of basic issues, and (2) informational programs can be made
> attractive enough to win and hold audiences. One of the newest
> program entries springing from these twin convictions is called
> *Prospects of Mankind*."—Frederick Guidry, *Christian Science Monitor*

Recorded at the Slosberg Music Center at Brandeis University in Waltham, Mass-achusetts, Eleanor hosted the *Prospects of Mankind* public affairs talk show series for NET from October 11, 1959—her 75th birthday—through June 3, 1962, in front of a live audience of 250 educators, students, and invited guests. Executive producer Henry Morgenthau III helmed the monthly show on behalf of WGBH, underwritten by a Ford Foundation grant and donations from individuals like Dore Schary. An advisory group that included Henry Kissinger from Harvard made recommendations for participants, and ER was paid $1,500 per episode, plus expenses. At this time, she also taught as a visiting lecturer of international relations at Brandeis, where she had been the Jewish-sponsored university's first commencement speaker and a member of the board of trustees. However, the television show was her priority. She did not want to teach if she did not have the television commitment in Boston as well (Stix correspondence II, Morgenthau correspondence II). Brandeis president Abram Sachar believed it an impressive achievement for the university to host ER and her prestigious guests in what became a high point in early educational television programming (Sachar 267–68). The show was recorded on Sunday, and she stayed overnight in Boston to teach a seminar on Monday.

The program's stated purpose, which had begun with the tentative title *The Eleanor Roosevelt Diamond Jubilee Series: Involved in Mankind*, was "to stretch the imagination of American citizens through greater awareness of the problems of other countries and thus to achieve an international outlook that is relevant to this era of revolution, confusion, and conflict." ER's wide knowledge and indefatigable efforts on behalf of mutual understanding among nations contributed to the importance of the show in an era in which "to be well-informed is no longer a luxury." Fundraising appeals referred to "what Mrs. Roosevelt's influence and leadership mean to this country" in the context of television as the most modern and effective way to educate the public (NET papers, "ER Diamond"). Ratings data was difficult to ascertain, but the WNEW-TV New York broadcast on Sunday evenings at 9:00 p.m. garnered an average of 400,000 viewers. The program manager of KQED San Francisco wrote that they were "terribly impressed" with the number of viewers watching *Prospects*. If every public television program were half as popular, he felt that the station would be a phenomenon. When NET sent out a viewer diary to member viewers, 29 percent said they watched *Prospects* in April 1961, 19 percent usually viewed the program, and 26 percent occasionally viewed it. Those who watched were composed of 43 percent 45–65 years old, 28 percent 30–45, and 20 percent 65+. The educational background of viewers showed 40 percent had a graduate school education, 17 percent were college graduates, and 20 percent had some college (NET papers). In a 1961 letter to President Kennedy requesting his appearance to talk about the Peace Corps, Eleanor mentioned that the program was carried by over 50 educational stations as well as commercial stations in New York and Washington (Schlup 259).

To view the series now, which is available streaming online from the American Archive of Public Broadcasting, is to observe some of this era's most important political and cultural influencers. In three years, ER interviewed Zbigniew Brzezinski, Ralph Bunche, John Kenneth Galbraith, Hubert Humphrey, John F. Kennedy (as senator and president), Henry Kissinger, Luis Muñoz Marín, Edward R. Murrow, Julius Nyerere, Nelson Rockefeller, Bertrand Russell, Arthur Schlesinger, Jr., Adlai Stevenson, Paul Tillich, and many more names we still recognize. Its focus was on the international issues that made up her major interest later in life, and she ended each program in a close-up, telling her audience *au revoir*. With the French expression of good wishes, this subtle message invited viewers to come back repeatedly. Morgenthau wrote her a handwritten note after the first episode to say that all involved were "tremendously enthusiastic and felt that the series has gotten off the ground in great style" (Morgenthau correspondence II).

Morgenthau describes briefing ER in her New York apartment with producers Diana Tead Michaelis and Dr. Beatrice Braude before each program: "Paul Noble, our director, worked with her on the style and pacing of her performance. We learned to value Mrs. Roosevelt's ideas and made it our business not to try to impose our own. The more the programs were really hers, the better they were. She was always herself and completely at ease, confident in what she wanted to say and what she didn't want to say" ("ER at Brandeis"). On the day of taping, they met with her again before a noon rehearsal in front of the cameras. Panelists for the day met over lunch at 1:00 p.m., running through the outline of the show, and each person took turns at a makeup table in the same room. Thus, the guests could continue the conversation uninterrupted. Everyone went in for lighting and camera tests at 3:00 p.m., then to the green room before the telecast began at 4:00 p.m. After the taping, usually done a week before air, there was a question-and-answer period with the press, often followed by a cocktail party, reception, and formal dinner. There appears to have been some dissatisfaction with the press conference held on the day of taping, since a newsmaker might be covered by the printed press a week before the actual episode aired across the country. Some NET stations saw this as advantageous for

WGBH and Brandeis publicity, but not for other broadcasters who could not cash in on the news for a week (NET papers).

Commenting on the first episode, Frederick Guidry observed that ER was the central figure of the program, but she did not dominate the show. "She sometimes injects a personal opinion, indicating that she regards her role as not that of a mere moderator. But Mrs. Roosevelt is on screen much less often than her guests, and her remarks clearly aim at keeping the focus primarily on their ideas rather than hers" (Guidry). Physically, ER sat on the left in a semicircle of guest chairs, rather than in the center as she had done in her early 1950s television programs, this time with less formality. This show did not carry her name in the title, and the set design carried out this emphasis on the guests, with a map of the world behind them and a focus on international issues and ideas, rather than a portrait of FDR and an older politics. Initially, she played roles of both host and moderator, but Saville Davis, managing editor of *The Christian Science Monitor*, was soon added as a second moderator so that Eleanor could participate more freely in discussions. Morgenthau perceived that ER was a good interviewer, but "she wasn't really a very good M.C. She was at her best when she was talking herself, when she could express her own views" (Marc). The addition of Davis allowed Eleanor's personality to shine, as she was able to interject into conversations more freely without worrying about keeping the entire program and other participant contributions constantly on her mind. They also began feeding discussion sound directly into her hearing aid. "In the control room, if we ever felt she wasn't engaged, we'd just boost up the sound a little," said Noble (qtd in Michaelis).

As was the case with her earlier shows in the decade, dramatic conflict was not a significant part of discussions, something that was encouraged on other similar network public affairs shows, which some felt was missing from this one. Guidry also criticized the lack of "visual interest beyond the faces of the four participants" and their "rather consistently bland expressions." The simple set design with very inexpensive chairs gains warmth only from ER's smile in close-up during the introduction and conclusion of the show, and through the guests' contributions. Notes of enthusiasm or disagreement add interest, but sometimes Guidry's observation of viewers being served up a series of serious White male faces cannot be escaped. Bob Jones served as announcer throughout the run, and he narrated the opening of each episode over an image of Leonardo da Vinci's "Vitruvian Man" drawing, considered to be a synthesis of both science and art. Related news footage followed with information on the topic for the day before each guest was introduced in close-up. Then as the camera moved from a wide view of the panelists to a close up of ER, Jones cued the start of the conversation: "Now, here is Mrs. Roosevelt."

After being off for the summer, *Variety* reviewed the second season opener on September 25, 1960, which was produced at the BBC Studios in London with the topic "Britain: Ally or Neutral?" ER's British guests were philosopher and social critic Bertrand Russell, independent Lord Boothby, and socialist member of Parliament Hugh Gaitskell. In a slightly patronizing tone, *Variety* described the show: "Mrs. Eleanor Roosevelt, the hostess, left the boys, for the most part, to their own verbal devices which were always well articulated. When she did come in with her own ideas on the subject, the points were well-taken and served to develop the American point of view." The reviewer ended by predicting that based on this performance, the "viewing prospects for *Prospects* are extremely good" (Gros). NET president John White wrote to express his genuine pride in "truly an excellent hour" and a program that provided significance and meaning to educational television across the country (J. White). ER had hoped that these episodes from London and Paris would give the show a "new look" and separate her from the "feverish political climate" at the time (Hillman 1960). It was also the first time an NET program had been produced overseas ("News of the World"). The new season promised three guests in each discussion: an outstanding American public official or well-known authority on some aspect of foreign policy; an equally representative individual from another country; and a journalist or writer whose field of interest coincided with that of a particular subject for the day (NET papers).

Topics, guests, and air dates for each *Prospects of Mankind* show are noted below, transcribed from the episodes.

Prospects of Mankind *Episodes*

October 11, 1959

"New Possibilities for Coexistence"
Robert Bowie, Director of the Harvard Center for International Affairs; former
　　Assistant Secretary of State for Policy Planning
V. K. Krishna Menon, Indian Defense Minister; Head of the Indian Delegation to the
　　United Nations General Assembly
Harrison Salisbury, *New York Times* correspondent

November 15, 1959

"What Hopes for Disarmament?"
Saville Davis, Managing Editor, *Christian Science Monitor*
Trevor Gardner, former Assistant Secretary of the Air Force; President of Hycon
　　Manufacturing Company
Jules Moch, French representative to the United Nations General Assembly

In "My Day," she told readers, "I think you will find this an informative and lively program" (11 Nov. 1959).

December 5, 1959

"Foreign Aid and Economic Policy"
Rajendra Coomaraswamy, Delegate from Sri Lanka to the United Nations; former
　　President of the Colombo Plan Council
John Kenneth Galbraith, author of *The Affluent Society;* Harvard University Professor
　　of Economics
Dr. Arthur Lewis, Deputy Director of the United Nations Special Fund

Recorded January 2, 1960; aired January 3, 1960

"Europe Faces East and West"

Erwin D. Canham, Editor of *Christian Science Monitor*; President of the United States Chamber of Commerce

Senator John F. Kennedy of Massachusetts, member of the United States Senate's Foreign Relations Committee

Paul Rosenstein-Rodan, Professor of Economics at the MIT Center for International Studies

Senator Kennedy had just announced his candidacy for president of the United States earlier in the day in Washington, D.C., before flying to Boston to appear on the show.

February 14, 1960

"Latin America: Neglected Neighbors"

Benjamin Cohen, Chilean Ambassador to the United Nations General Assembly

Saville Davis, Managing Editor, *Christian Science Monitor* (additional moderator)

Luis Muñoz Marín, Governor of Puerto Rico

Nelson Rockefeller, Governor of New York; President Roosevelt's Coordinator of Inter-American Affairs

In January, Morgenthau traveled to Puerto Rico to interview Luis Muñoz Marín to prepare for the show and shared several pages of notes on the governor's political philosophy, attitudes toward the American and Cuban governments, and ideas around Latin American economic development with the television team. He began:

> It is clear that Governor Munoz considers his appearance on PROSPECTS an important event. He is coming from San Juan to Boston primarily for this purpose (with a secondary stop-over in Washington). The trip itself is distasteful to him and since he dislikes flying in bad weather, he will entrain from New York, Washington, or even possibly Miami. He is also generally apprehensive about appearing on television. His reasons for accepting are his strong affection and admiration for Mrs. Roosevelt, his concern for deteriorated U.S.-Latin American relations, and a desire to use his influence to better them, and his desire to create a favorable image on the "continent" of Puerto Rico and Puerto Ricans [program notes].

Recorded March 6; aired March 13, 1960

"Africa: Revolution in Haste"

Ralph Bunche, Nobel Peace Prize winner; United Nations Undersecretary for Special Political Affairs

Saville Davis, Managing Editor, *Christian Science Monitor* (additional moderator)

Julius Nyerere, President of the Tanganyika [Tanzania] African National Union

Barbara Ward (Lady Jackson), resident of Ghana; Lecturer at Harvard University

In "My Day," ER supplied more valuable information about this topic. Julius Nyerere brought a new and challenging point of view to the show:

> Mr. Nyerere … has earned the reputation of being the most moderate of the African leaders who have visited our shores. He is young, as are nearly all the people who are founding

the new nations on the African continent. I have a feeling that he will be an astute and wise leader. What is more, he will have wit and humor. His eyes can sparkle and smile, and he is not slow to take up any challenge…. If the truth were told, I think every one of my guests was a little impatient that the United States did not have more interest than we have shown so far. I hope that the television audience, when it sees this particular *Prospects of Mankind* show, will find it as exciting and interesting as I did in participating in it [9 Mar. 1960].

Harper's Magazine called this episode "positively triumphant" ("News of the World").

Recorded April 10; aired April 17, 1960

"The American Image Abroad"
Denis Brogan, "leading British authority on America"
Harlan Cleveland, Dean of Syracuse University's Maxwell Graduate School of
     Citizenship and Public Affairs
Saville Davis, Managing Editor, *Christian Science Monitor* (additional moderator)
Santha Rama Rau, author of *A Passage to India* [a stage adaptation of E.M. Forster's novel]

This episode received mention in *Television* magazine's review of recent world affairs programming, including a photo from the show, and a review in *The New York Times* called it a "worthwhile hour, stimulating and informative" ("World Affairs"). The program was overall "a welcome addition to Sunday-night viewing" (Gould "Golf").

May 15, 1960

"China: Shadow on the Summit"
Zbigniew Brzezinski, Associate Professor of Government at the Columbia University
     Russian Institute; author of *The Soviet Bloc: Unity and Conflict*
Saville Davis, Managing Editor, *Christian Science Monitor* (additional moderator)
Blair Fraser, Editor of *Maclean's*
Charles Porter, Democratic Representative from Oregon

A newspaper advertisement for this episode promised "a TV first—the award-winning photography of Communist China by Henri Cartier-Bresson," and the program began with a series of his photographs ("China").

Recorded June 5, 1960; aired June 12, 1960

"The Future of Democracy Abroad"
Saville Davis, Managing Editor, *Christian Science Monitor* (additional moderator)
Mohammad Hatta, former Prime Minister and Vice President of Indonesia
Henry Kissinger, Associate Director of Harvard University Center for International
     Affairs; author of *Nuclear Weapons and Foreign Policy*
Adlai Stevenson, twice Democratic candidate for President; recently a traveler in
     Africa, Asia, and Latin America

New York Times coverage of the program included Stevenson's contention that Russia's failure to expand its territory in a period of rapid economic and scientific growth was a prime factor in its shift to a more aggressive foreign policy ("Stevenson Weighs"). A letter from Morgenthau to Stevenson indicates that the latter was unhappy with the outcome of this episode, likely because of the time taken up for translation to and for Hatta, who did not reply in English. ER invited Stevenson to appear to gain more exposure before the Democratic Party Convention, but it was Hatta and his translator who held the floor most prominently (R. Henry 169). In a handwritten note to ER, Morgenthau told her that he was "sorry we didn't give both of you more chance to talk together, but it was nonetheless most worthwhile" (Morgenthau correspondence II). Stevenson appeared two more times later in the series, but always in a one-on-one interview with ER, not on a panel.

September 25, 1960

"Britain: Ally or Neutral?"
On location, Lime Grove BBC Studios, London
Lord Boothby, independent in the House of Lords, former Conservative member of
    Parliament
Hugh Gaitskell, Socialist member of Parliament, leader of Her Majesty's Opposition
Robert McKenzie, London School of Economics and Political Science (additional
    moderator)
Lord Russell (Bertrand Russell), philosopher and mathematician

In "My Day," ER briefly mentioned arriving in London:

> We had a comfortable flight from New York on Monday and on hand to greet me and Miss Corr here were Henry Morgenthau III, Diana Michaelis and Paul Noble, all from the educational TV team in Boston.
> Inevitably the BBC was set up on my arrival and requested a short interview. These interviews are always promised to take "just a minute." But something usually goes wrong either with the photography or the sound and they usually consume at least half an hour [24 Aug. 1960].

Morgenthau had written to warn her about the 10-minute interview on arrival, also explaining why they were shooting two programs in London, rather than a second in Paris. The guests were all in the U.K. or coming from other places in Europe, not France, and while the BBC allowed them to use their facilities for free, WGBH was charged $3,000 in Paris (Morgenthau correspondence II).

ER was especially active in the *Prospects* discussion from the BBC studios. They broadcast the episode on September 29, and *The Listener*, the BBC weekly magazine that included transcripts of selected radio and television talks and interviews, reproduced five and half pages of the panel's conversation ("*Prospects of Mankind*"). Bertrand Russell, addressed as Lord Russell, advocated that Britain should leave NATO and not hold independent nuclear weapons of its own. When ER replied, "That puts a good deal of responsibility on the United States," he spoke of Western European countries as "satellites" of the U.S. that could be wiped out by the Soviet Union with nuclear weapons without causing a general nuclear war. Eleanor objected to the use of the term "satellites" in the West and was incredulous that he believed that an American president would not do anything about a Russian attack on Britain. The group debated Russell's contention that it was safer for Britain to be neutral, rather than a NATO member. Specifically at issue were American bases in the U.K. Eleanor became animated in her opposition to Russell's statement that worldwide domination of the Soviets would be better than going through a nuclear war. She believed that most people in the United States would rather be wiped out than submit to a Russian invasion. ER also stated that she felt that people in Europe were far safer from targeted Soviet attack than was the United States. "In that case," she said, "you in Europe would not have to be destroyed, but you would become slaves."

In his autobiography, Russell calls this a "disappointing TV occasion." He writes, "I was horrified to hear Mrs. Roosevelt enunciate the belief that it would be better, and that she would prefer, to have the human race destroyed than to have it succumb to Communism. I came away thinking that I could not have heard all right. Upon reading her remarks in the next morning's papers I had to face the fact that she really had expressed this dangerous view" (B. Russell 107–08). Russell was shocked at her "better dead than red" philosophy, since his was quite the opposite, "better red than dead." In ER's thank-you note addressing him as "My Lord," she merely says, "It was a lively and exciting discussion and I feel the result was satisfying" (B. Russell 135).

October 23, 1960

"European Unity: Obstacles and Goals"

On location, Riverside BBC Studios, London

Denis Healy, journalist, Labour member of Parliament, and Foreign Affairs Spokesman of Her Majesty's Opposition

Robert McKenzie, London School of Economics and Political Science (additional moderator)

Anthony Nutting, Minister of State for Foreign Affairs; author of *Europe Will Not Wait*

Maurice Schumann, President of the Commission of Foreign Affairs for the French National Assembly; member of the First and Second Assemblies of Europe at Strasbourg

November 20, 1960

"The Changing Shape of the United Nations"

Raymond Aron, Sorbonne Professor of Sociology; columnist for the Paris *Figaro*; author of *The Century of Total War*

Lawrence Fuchs, Dean of the Brandeis University faculty (additional moderator)

Senator Mike Mansfield, Democrat from Montana

General Carlos Romulo, Philippines Ambassador to the United States; President of the United Nations Fourth General Assembly

Of note in this episode was Raymond Aron's attempt to bait ER into discussing Soviet Premier Khrushchev when she clearly wanted to keep the subject on track about the United Nations. Aron was much more provocatively negative about the topic at hand than was usual for the show, as he found fault in the UN from the perspective of nations observing the battles between the U.S. and Soviet Union.

December 18, 1960

"The Scientist and World Politics"
Saville Davis, Managing Editor, *Christian Science Monitor* (additional moderator)
Max Lerner, *New York Post* columnist; Brandeis University Professor of American Civilization; author of *America as a Civilization*
Sir Charles Snow, C.P. Snow, British novelist, scientist, and former wartime government administrator
Dr. Jerome Wiesner, Director of the Research Laboratory of Electronics at MIT; member of the President's Scientific Advisory Committee

January 15, 1961

"Rethinking Our Alliances"
Richard Crossman, member of Parliament; chair of the British Labor Party
Saville Davis, Managing Editor, *Christian Science Monitor* (additional moderator)
General Alfred Gruenther, Supreme Allied Commander in Europe, 1953–56; Director of the United States Joint Chiefs of Staff, 1947–49; President of the American Red Cross
Hans Morgenthau, University of Chicago Professor of Political Science; author of *Politics Among Nations* and *The Purpose of American Politics*

February 12, 1961

"Nuclear Test Ban: First Step to Arms Control"
Congressman Chet Holifield, chair of the Joint Congressional Atomic Energy Committee
Henry Kissinger, Harvard Center for International Affairs; Director of the Harvard Defense Studies Program; author of *Nuclear Weapons in Foreign Policy* and *The Necessity for Choice*
Laurence Martin, MIT political scientist, Institute of Strategic Studies in London (additional moderator)
Right Honorable John Strachey MP, former Secretary of State for War under the Labor government; author of *The Prevention of War*

March 12, 1961

"Peace Corps: What Shape Shall It Take?"
Samuel Hayes, Professor, Department of Economics of the University of Michigan; author of the Peace Corps Task Force Report
Senator Hubert Humphrey, Democrat from Minnesota; chair of the Disarmament Subcommittee of the Senate Foreign Relations Committee
Senteza Kajubi, Makerere College, University of East Africa
President John F. Kennedy
R. Sargent Shriver, Director of the Peace Corps

This episode begins with ER interviewing President John F. Kennedy on the ground floor of the White House for 10 minutes about the new Peace Corps program.

From Brandeis University in Waltham, Massachusetts, panelists for the "Peace Corps: What Shape Shall It Take?" episode of NET's *Prospects of Mankind*, March 1961. From left: moderator Eleanor Roosevelt; R. Sargent Shriver, director of the Peace Corps; Senteza Kajubi, University of East Africa; Minnesota Democratic senator Hubert Humphrey; and University of Michigan professor Samuel Hayes (Franklin D. Roosevelt Presidential Library & Museum).

The only room that was soundproofed and thus easily used for television proved to be the very room in which FDR had broadcast his fireside chats, but Jackie Kennedy had filled it with hated furniture left by Mamie Eisenhower. The *Prospects* staff had to carry it all out and construct a set from other furniture found in the White House (Noble 15–16). Afterward, JFK gave a tour of the family quarters, where Eleanor had not been since 1945. Three-year-old daughter Caroline Kennedy accompanied them, plus Morgenthau and Metropolitan Broadcasting Corporation (MBC) executive vice president Bennet Korn. They peeked in on little John, Jr., in the nursery as well (Thomas). In her letter of thanks afterward, ER was also grateful for her nomination as a United Nations delegate, noting that Adlai Stevenson believed that she might be especially helpful to U.S. relationships with the delegates from new African countries (ER to JFK). She would soon accept Kennedy's invitation to join the National Advisory Council of the Peace Corps. A panel discussion filmed at WTTG-TV in Washington, D.C., follows the segment with JFK.

WTTG-TV held a special reception honoring ER. Also in attendance were Minnesota senator Hubert Humphrey and John Kluge, president of MBC, which filmed both segments of the show for NET ("Mrs. Roosevelt Honored"). The *Variety* review of this episode was glowing in its praise, calling it "proof that a tired format can come to life under proper circumstances." Camera close-ups of speakers were done well, but it was the reveal of the new Peace Corps program and the ideas behind it that kept viewers wanting more information when the show concluded. "There is nothing new about a group of experts discussing a global subject. But the viewer never lost interest in this production because the moderator, Eleanor Roosevelt, is a skilled lets-not-waste-a-word performer (and who understands better than Mrs. R what the prospects of mankind are?)" (Liz). *The New York Times* featured coverage of the show on page one, since the president released current information on the just-announced Peace Corps program (Schmidt). Sargent Shriver's wife, JFK's sister Eunice Kennedy Shriver, was upset that Shriver had used the non-word "irregardless" on the air. Noble assured her that he could "bloop" out the "ir" so that no one would ever know (Noble 17).

Eleanor followed up in "My Day" by describing current programs in place while the Peace Corps developed:

> It is impressive to see that such carefully planned projects are now being worked out by individual groups throughout this country. It shows how much real spirit of adventure exists, particularly among young people in the United States today. They are excited at the thought of seeing new things and being of service, and I think it will be one of the ways in which we will grow up to a mature understanding of the world in which we live [10 Apr. 1961].

NET officials followed up with a letter to ER about the warm praise received for this program, including a tremendous amount of mail requesting Peace Corps application forms (Pfister).

April 9, 1961

"Congo: Challenge to the UN"
Location: United Nations, New York City
Rajeshwar Dayal, special representative of Secretary Dag Hammarskjöld in the Congo; India's High Commissioner to Pakistan
William Frye, United Nations correspondent, *Christian Science Monitor*; author of *The United Nations Peace Force*
Adlai Stevenson, U.S. Ambassador to the United Nations
G. Mennen Williams, Assistant Secretary of State for African Affairs; former Governor of Michigan
Jaja Wachuku, chair of the UN Congo Conciliation Commission; Nigerian Minister of Economic Development

This episode begins with ER interviewing Adlai Stevenson, then United States ambassador to the United Nations, on location at the UN. Then it moves to a panel discussion. *The New York Times* covered Stevenson's remarks on page one as he overcame an earlier reluctance to comment on the situation in the Congo and said that he "saw no other solution" than a federated Congo. His statement emphasizing the importance of the end of military interference, including that of the Belgian colonizers, went further than the U.S. delegation to the UN had yet gone in public debate. Stevenson envisioned the federation, made up of 10 or more units, as the "best hope" for the Congo (Frankel).

May 7, 1961

"The New Aid Policy in Action"
On location, State Department auditorium, Washington, D.C.
Chester Bowles, Under Secretary of State
Paul Hoffman, Managing Director, United Nations Special Fund
Max Millikan, Director, MIT Center for International Studies
B.K. Nehru, India's Commissioner General for Economic Affairs
Barbara Ward (Lady Jackson), resident of Ghana; visiting lecturer at Harvard
    University; author of *Five Ideas that Shaped the World* and *India and the West*

NET program associate Donald S. Hillman wrote Morgenthau after this episode with criticisms, suggesting that the team of Roosevelt and Davis were more effective than ER alone at directing the conversation. He wrote, "There has been a lot of stumbling and mumbling" in which guests were saying the first things that crossed their minds. Hillman felt that more control by the moderators and less passivity was required. "*Prospects* has developed into a distinguished NET series and by and large has provided an effective model for the disciplined and informed consideration of public affairs," but viewers needed to be provided with probable courses of action. He had also heard on the grapevine that Edward R. Murrow was "quite aggravated by the snubbing he was getting" by not being invited into inner strategy meetings for the upcoming May episode in which he appeared (Hillman).

May 26, 1961

"America's Propaganda Capabilities"
Roscoe Drummond, Washington columnist, *New York Herald Tribune* (additional
    moderator)
Edward R. Murrow, Director, United States Information Agency
Chancal Sarkar, Assistant Editor of India's *The Statesman*; Nieman Fellow at Harvard
    University
Arthur Schlesinger, Jr., special assistant to President Kennedy

The New York Times covered the show, calling it a "stimulative and informative hour." Drummond was commended for asking some particularly good questions of the panel, while Murrow, in his first television appearance since assuming the government post, seemed especially relaxed and spoke with his familiar directness. "The Washington environment has not hurt his TV effectiveness" (Gould "U.S."). Another review found Murrow's manner too congenial, reporting that he spoke about "we" as in the people of the United States, forgetting that he now spoke for the administration (Zeitlin). *Variety* enjoyed Murrow's presence, calling him articulate, sensible, and frank, but complained that the "utter civility" of participants made for a sometimes-dull show. ER was judged "not always articulate but gentle and probing," and the reviewer seemed pleased that the program would be returning for another season in the fall (Art "*Prospects*" 1961). Morgenthau observed that she was able to pin Murrow down during the show using her "deceptively lady-like way," which was the practiced "naïveté and cunning" that she so often utilized at the UN and on television. The Voice of America rebroadcast the audio of this episode (Morgenthau "ER at Brandeis," NET papers).

September 17, 1961

"American Capitalism: Challenged at Home and Abroad"
Erwin Canham, Editor, *Christian Science Monitor* (substitute moderator)
Eric Johnston, President, Motion Picture Association of America
Robert McKenzie, political sociologist, London School of Economics
Victor Reuther, United Auto Workers official
Paul Samuelson, Professor of Economics, MIT

Eleanor was not present for this first episode of the third season. In September 1961, diagnosed with aplastic anemia, she needed two blood transfusions and struggled with high fever and chills (Lerner). Saying that she was "too busy to be sick," even with anemia, ER was able to come back to host the following episode in October 1961 and the rest of the shows in this season, the last in June 1962. Substitute moderator Erwin Canham, editor of the *Christian Science Monitor,* told the audience, "I'm sure everybody watching will be very pleased to learn that on the next program, Mrs. Roosevelt most confidently expects to be back with you just as strong and forceful as ever."

October 15, 1961

"Berlin: What Choice Remains"
Max Freedman, Washington correspondent for Britain's *Manchester Guardian*
   (additional moderator)
Henry Kissinger, Harvard University Director of Defense Studies; author of *Nuclear*
   Weapons in Foreign Policy and *The Necessity for Choice*
James Reston, Chief, *New York Times* Washington bureau
Dean Rusk, Secretary of State
Paul Tillich, philosopher and theologist, Professor at Harvard University

The episode begins with ER interviewing Secretary of State Dean Rusk at the State Department in Washington, D.C., before moving into the panel format. *The New York Times* covered the show, reporting that "the ethical, political and military problems posed by the Berlin crisis elicited a diversity of opinion that not only underscored the complexities of the issues but also the succinct clarity of Secretary Rusk's prologue" (Gould "*Intertel*"). In another piece in the *Times*, James Reston, who had also been a panelist on the show, wrestled with the positions of President Kennedy and others and the point of view expressed by Paul Tillich. The philosopher said it was likely "impossible" to defend Berlin from the overwhelming ground forces of the Soviet Union, but this did not warrant use of atomic weapons: "A war fought with atomic weapons can ethically not be justified, for it produces destruction without the possibility of a creative new beginning: it annihilates what it is supposed to defend." Reston contended that such statements might be an exercise in philosophy, but were dangerous in suggesting that the U.S. would easily give up Western Europe (Reston). *Variety* criticized the show for not presenting fresh perspectives from the extraordinarily strong personalities present. Instead, the industry publication referred to it as an "hourlong egghead chinfest" ("Pit"). The *Department of State Bulletin* published the transcript of the Rusk interview in its entirety ("Secretary").

November 12, 1961

"United Nations: Future Endangered"
Location: United Nations, New York City
Harlan Cleveland, Assistant Secretary of State in charge of United Nations affairs; editor and publisher of *The Reporter* magazine
William Frye, United Nations correspondent, *Christian Science Monitor* (additional moderator)
Stanley Hoffman, Professor of Government at Harvard University
C. S. Jha, India's permanent Ambassador to the United Nations

December 10, 1961

"South Asia in Crisis"
Leo Cherne, chair of International Rescue Committee sent to Vietnam in 1954; Executive Director of the Research Institute of America
Tillman Durdin, *New York Times* editorial expert for Asian affairs (additional moderator)
Senator Jacob Javits, Republican from New York
Vu Van Thai, former Director General of the Budget and Foreign Aid in the Diệm government

January 14, 1962

"Latin America Looks at Cuba"
Location: United Nations, New York City
Roberto Campos, Brazilian Ambassador to the United States
Theodore Draper, journalist, historian, and editor specializing in international affairs, American foreign policy, and the American Communist movement
Adlai Stevenson, U.S. Ambassador to the United Nations
Tad Szulc, Latin American affairs correspondent, *New York Times* (additional moderator)

   This episode begins with a spirited discussion between ER and Adlai Stevenson one on one, followed by the panel.

February 11, 1962

"Russia and China: What Does the Future Hold?"
Allen Dulles, former Director of the Central Intelligence Agency
Seymour Freidin, *New York Herald Tribune*'s Executive Editor for Foreign News; author of *The Forgotten People*
Lord Lindsay of Birker, head of the program of Far Eastern Studies at American University

Reinhold Niebuhr, Visiting Professor of Government at Harvard University; author of
  The Structure of Nations and Empires
Marshall Shulman, Associate Director of the Russian Research Center of Harvard
  University; Professor of International Politics at the Fletcher School of Law and
  Diplomacy (additional moderator)

The recording of this episode is damaged at the beginning, so it is not possible to discern the announcer's introduction or Eleanor's opening words. The topic for the day is the conflict between Russia and China, and the program begins with ER discussing this with Allen Dulles, former director of the CIA, before moving to the panel.

February 25, 1962

"The Future of France"
Location: Paris, France
Raymond Aron, editorial writer for *Le Figaro,* Sociology Chair at the Sorbonne
Alfred Grosser, Professor of Political Science at the University of Paris; Visiting
  Professor at the Johns Hopkins University Center in Bologna, Italy (additional
  moderator)
Stéphane Hessel, Director, Office of International Cultural Exchanges in the French
  Ministry of National Education
Maurice Schumann, Chair, Foreign Affairs Committee of the French National
  Assembly

ER mentioned arriving in Paris in her "My Day" column:

> My secretary, Miss Maureen Corr, and I left by Air France for Paris at midnight and had a most delightful trip—smooth and comfortable. We are now at the Crillon Hotel, where I always feel at home because of the many months I've stayed here when we used to hold meetings of the General Assembly of the United Nations in Paris.
> Henry Morgenthau III met us at Orly Airport and told us of the plans made for doing two educational television programs, and a little later we were joined at the hotel by Professor Alfred Grosser for discussion of our joint responsibilities on the programs. By this time it was 7 p.m. Paris time, though only 1 p.m. New York time, and after a delightful dinner we felt well adjusted to the change and feel well prepared for busy days ahead [16 Feb. 1962].

Morgenthau wrote afterwards from Boston that they received many, many enthusiastic letters and telephone calls after this program on the Future of France. "It was an unquestioned success" (Morgenthau correspondence II).

Paris segment recorded February 16, 1962; aired April 8, 1962

"Our Relationship with the Common Market"
Locations: Paris, France and Washington, D.C.
George Ball, Under Secretary of State
Edwin Dale, European Economic Correspondent, *New York Times* (additional
  moderator)
Albert Kervyn, Director, Belgium's National Planning Office
Robert Marjolin, Vice President, Commission of the European Economic Community

The show begins in Paris, followed by the segment with George Ball in Washington, D.C. Ball watched the others before his interview and thought the discussion "really good." Producer Beatrice Braude also wrote a friend saying that she thought "we put out two very good shows" in France, especially this one (Braude).

When she traveled to Paris to record the two episodes of *Prospects of Mankind* in English with French experts, ER was interviewed in French on February 17 for the television news magazine *Cinq colonnes à la une*. She commented that she was glad to have successfully made it through the difficulty of being interviewed in French. She also received $500 for appearing on a show with Associated Television in London (Stix correspondence II).

May 7, 1962

"New Vistas for Television"
Irving Gitlin, Executive Producer Creative Projects, NBC News and Public Affairs
Marya Mannes, television and theater critic, *The Reporter* (additional moderator)
Newton Minow, Chair, Federal Communications Commission
John White, President, National Educational Television and Radio Center

This episode is somewhat of an anomaly, as Marya Mannes not only serves as an additional moderator, but also asks questions directly of ER and actively engages her in the discussion. Mannes, who had been a television interviewer with her own show *I Speak for Myself* in 1959, stated her goal on that program of proving to people "that women do exist from the neck up" (Sanders 31). Here, she queries Eleanor about what she hopes to see on educational TV. "What would give you pleasure?" ER responds that she would like "more information about what our own government is doing throughout the world." After more discussion, Mannes wants to know how she envisages uses of the new communications satellite. Eleanor hopes that "we will stop trying to create *an* image of America because America is many images." Rather, she wishes that the satellite will contribute to showing many distinct aspects of American lives, in the plural.

The broadcasting industry was extremely interested in FCC Chairman Minow's appearance, and *Television Digest* published the promotional photo session with ER, Minow, and former FCC Commissioner Clifford Durr ("Personals"). *New York Times* coverage of the show reported that "Mrs. Roosevelt expressed the hope that the international satellite would not become a propaganda tool and that whatever body supervised United States participation should not try to offer 'the American image.' This country is composed of too many different images to permit such simplification," she noted (Gould "Control"). *Variety* was not so kind in its review, pointing out that the participants had all expressed these ideas before, and the discussion held nothing new for those in the industry. However, it was the production itself that came in for the worst critique. "It becomes difficult convincing viewers that 'those people there' know what they're doing when the producers of the program cannot assure that the vidtape keeps voice and picture in synchronization. Through nearly all the hour, the lips were a fraction of a second behind the picture, making Gitlin, White, Mannes and Minow look like actors in a dubbed Italo film" (Art "*Prospects*" 9 May 1962).

June 3, 1962

"What Status for Women"
Location: Washington, D.C.
Arthur Goldberg, United States Secretary of Labor
President John F. Kennedy
Mirra Komarovsky, Professor of Sociology at Barnard College and Columbia
    University; author of *Women in the Modern World: Their Education and Their*
    Dilemmas (additional moderator)
Thomas Mendenhall, President, Smith College for Women
Agda Rossel, Sweden's permanent representative to the United Nations

    This episode was recorded in Washington, D.C., and begins with ER interviewing President John F. Kennedy in the White House for 10 minutes before the panel discussion. Morgenthau later remembered, "Kennedy had appointed her Chairman of the Commission on the Status of Women, and she was pleased again to go to the White House and to talk with the President as an introduction to the program. In some ways, this program seems dated. In other ways it seems prophetic" (Morgenthau "ER at Brandeis"). Betty Friedan's *The Feminine Mystique* would be published the following year. Eleanor ends the hour by saying, "This is our last program for the season, so I want to thank all of our faithful audience and say goodbye, and I hope we will have you all together joining us next year." She did not say "*au revoir*" to viewers, which was her habit to indicate that she would see them again, but spoke a more resolute "goodbye" instead. As scheduled, this was the last *Prospects of Mankind* show for the season, but ER's voice seems quieter and lower than usual. She expected to be back again in the fall; however, her health took a turn for the worse.

23

Signing Off

NBC's *Today* show celebrated its 50th anniversary in 2002, and on January 14 host Katie Couric welcomed Florence Henderson, Lee Meriwether, Estelle Parsons, and Betsy Palmer back on the air. They were all former "*Today* Girls" who handled interviews, book reviews, weather, and fashion in the early years of the show. Parsons began as a production assistant and would become the first female political reporter on television for *Today*. They reminisced about on-air moments, and Couric encouraged Parsons to talk about the occasion when Eleanor Roosevelt fell asleep during an interview. Although this was a time for laughs about the past, Parsons responded, "Well, she was very old. She died shortly thereafter."

In the summer of 1962, ER received periodic blood transfusions for aplastic anemia and experienced feverish reactions, but something else was wrong. Her condition worsened; she was increasingly weak and in pain with an undiagnosed condition. Still, she tried to keep working as much as she could, expecting to power through as she always had. ER told David Lilienthal that it was important not to concentrate on the increasing aches and pains of getting older: "If you pay much attention to them, the first thing you know, you're an invalid" (Lilienthal Vol. IV 298). In a May 1962 letter to agent Tom Stix, she talked about more television and confessed, "I am afraid I must reluctantly admit that I am not quite as young as I was…. I think I shall have to give up lecture trips," except those within one day of New York (Stix correspondence II).

Following a similar project on Winston Churchill, from January 8 to September 10, 1965, ABC aired a 26-part documentary mini-series *F.D.R.* narrated by Arthur Kennedy, with Franklin voiced by actor Charlton Heston reading excerpts from his writings. Initially the half-hour episodes aired in a prime-time evening slot, followed by reruns in an earlier spot to reach school-age viewers. Numerous key participants in the New Deal administration are interviewed about the president during the White House years, including Lorena Hickok. ER served as a consultant and wrapped up approximately one hundred hours of interviews and commentary in July 1962, and her voice is heard in each of the episodes with thoughts and memories (Adams "Mrs. Roosevelt"). Harper and Row published an *F.D.R.* paperback book to accompany the television program, and 14 hours of the audio interviews with Eleanor became the basis of two long-playing Columbia records ("1965"). In the planning stages, ER said, "I think [the series] will be very interesting from an historical point of view. When I speak at colleges today, I find I have to explain what a depression

216

was" ("Programming"). It makes one wonder about what she might have to explain to audiences today! She received $26,000 for her participation (Stix correspondence II).

Eleanor's voice begins the entire series as she says of Franklin, "He wanted to be remembered in history as having served the actual betterment of mankind." The first interview in the program is with Frances Perkins, FDR's secretary of labor and the first woman to serve in a cabinet post. Six minutes in, "Lorena Hickok, Assistant to Harry Hopkins" appears to tell the audience, "I never knew anyone who had a more mischievous sense of humor than Franklin Roosevelt had. He was an unmerciful tease." An extensive list of associates is also interviewed, from secretary Grace Tully to anti–Roosevelt columnist Westbrook Pegler, who says that it is unfortunate that the assassin's bullet did not hit his mark when Giuseppe Zangara shot at FDR prior to the first inauguration. ER's comments are used throughout the series to give background on much of the biographical information presented. During the first episode, ER talks about their wedding with Uncle Teddy Roosevelt giving her away on St. Patrick's Day in New York. Then she reminisces about their three-month honeymoon in Europe. In the second episode, ER mentions that FDR had a moral courage as well as physical courage in combating the effects of polio. FDR's cousin Laura Delano says, "He had great help that I sometimes don't think people realize in that his wife Eleanor really was his legs." Eleanor discusses Louis Howe's plan to keep the Roosevelt name alive in political circles, including encouraging her to become active with Democratic women's organizations. She attributes all of this to Howe in one of the oft-repeated stories that ignore her own ambitions. Her story is more central to these first two episodes that focus on the pre–White House years than other segments of the series.

Later she will comment on topics like FDR's relationship with Al Smith, putting the preinaugural assassination attempt out of their minds, Franklin's religious beliefs and his skills with radio communications, and the strategic move to have her speak to the Bonus Army that Hoover had previously burned out. She talks about Harry Hopkins coming to her for help with messaging around the Civilian Conservation Corps (CCC) so that it did not look like they were forming something akin to the Hitler Youth. ER speaks about FDR's love of the land and the country life, while Hick adds commentary on how farmers seemed ready to revolt early in the Depression. In the seventh episode, the series credits Eleanor with the beginning of FDR's social conscience. She explains, "It didn't surprise him to find that there were things that he didn't know anything about. He'd never been inside a tenement until I took him. He never had the feeling of superiority that I think people expected of someone of his economic and social background." Narrator Arthur Kennedy ends this segment: "The Hyde Park squire has traveled far since his first visit to a tenement brought the awakening of his social conscience. He has made it possible for organized labor to become a powerful political force. He has brought dignity and acceptance to the labor movement." ER talks about FDR's belief in private enterprise, and how New Deal programs such as the National Industrial Recovery Act (NIRA) were the means they developed to save private enterprise during the Great Depression. It was an emphasis on humanity first and profits afterwards. He also believed that you could not legislate morals, which was a major reason behind his support for the repeal of Prohibition on alcohol. Her comments in later episodes cover topics related to World War II, including Franklin's high regard for the Chinese people and his "great bitterness and anger" that he had hardly finished talking to the Japanese envoys when the Pearl Harbor bombing occurred. She believed that he did not have any idea that an attack was on the horizon.

Eleanor signed an exclusivity agreement with ABC indicating that she would not participate in any radio, television, or theatrical film concerning the life of Franklin Roosevelt from the date of the contract on December 28, 1960, through one year after the series broadcast, which was planned for September 1963 through the spring of 1964 (Graff). Although she finished her contribution that July of 1962, the series did not actually air until 1965. Considering this agreement, Morgenthau was working on plans for *Mrs. Roosevelt at Hyde Park*, which would not be released for television or in theaters until the lapse of the exclusivity clause for the *F.D.R.* program. He taped a conversation with her at the "Big House" at Hyde Park on July 23, 1962, and transcribed it to serve as an informal production guide to the flavor and content they might develop. He imagined recollections and reminiscences of people and events, using the house and grounds to prompt her personal and intimate memories: "Mrs. Roosevelt's warm, anecdotal style can enhance the visual effect of being on a very special tour.... A flexible and fluid account is given as she passes from the grounds through the house." From election nights to genealogy inspired by numerous portraits and tales of European royal families visiting during the war, "the whole story would be presented in Mrs. Roosevelt's voice." ER on camera, ideally in color, and in voiceover would be combined with footage and stills available from the presidential library. She had expressed her interest in the program, and Brandeis University president Abram Sachar and WGBH general manager Hartford Gunn both indicated that they would support the project. In the July transcript, Eleanor does not talk about herself for the most part, but in commentary on the British royal visit, she relays the story of Franklin's mother Sara suggesting that the King have tea, rather than a cocktail. He told FDR that his mother would say the same thing, but he would prefer a drink. Said ER, "I was always amused by this because Queen Mary always reminded me *very* much of my mother-in-law. I was equally afraid of both of them. They filled me with terror" (Morgenthau "*Mrs. Roosevelt*," "Tour").

Morgenthau wrote a detailed August 1 memo to Eleanor and those involved at NET, WGBH, and Brandeis to outline educational television plans for the 1962–63 season. ER was cutting down on her lecture schedule, eliminating extended travel, and wanted to increase her television activities to be produced in New York, Boston, and Washington, D.C. Four projects were proposed, including the Brandeis-sponsored *Mrs. Roosevelt at Hyde Park*. Eleanor was enthusiastic, and Sachar and Dean Clarence Berger planned to visit with her and Morgenthau at Hyde Park on August 27. While *Prospects of Mankind* would not be coming back, she agreed to serve as moderator for four episodes of NET's *Perspectives* series, which aired on what were now 60 member stations. "Negro Leadership in the United States" would be produced in Boston featuring "important factions in the Negro community," either in October or March. In December, "Foreign Students in the United States" was also to be produced from Boston. "Prospects for Peace" would involve ER traveling to London for a week in late January, utilizing BBC facilities as one of the *Perspectives* "Decisions 1963" programs. She would then go to the Television Francaise studios in Paris for a second "Decisions 1963" program on "The Future of France." She wanted to book the same panel of guests from the February 1962 *Prospects of Mankind* episode: Raymond Aron, Alfred Grosser, Stéphane Hessel, and Maurice Schumann. ER had agreed to this travel, although there is no mention of the contradictory nature of her desire to stay home more versus the demands of shows in London and Paris.

Also on the agenda was a contemporary affairs book series featuring Eleanor as host of 15 episodes with authors and another subject matter expert. There was to be a particular emphasis on biographies and other books relating to people and subjects from the present day and recent past with which she had personal acquaintance. Live from Boston, WGBH Boston and WNDT in New York would both broadcast simultaneously on Friday evenings at 8:30 p.m., although they might also record a second program on Fridays for later release. She further described the project to Stix:

> I envision a program in which I might read enough of a book or story or a series of poems to invite more interest in the works of the author. If he were a current author, perhaps I could interview him for a few minutes at the end of the program. If, on the other hand, I were reading from Sinclair Lewis and were reading parts of *It Can't Happen Here*, which is certainly vital today, I might have Mr. Mark Schorer, whose *Sinclair Lewis* is such a magnificent work. This is the basic idea and I wonder if you could pursue it [Stix correspondence II].

ER said that she had been interested in a program on books for some time but had spoken to Faye Emerson earlier in the year about a book show her former daughter-in-law had in development. Although Emerson was now divorced from Elliott, Eleanor asked that Morgenthau speak to her to make sure no conflict existed between the two projects.

Bennet Korn at Metropolitan Broadcasting Television was also interested in producing a program like *Prospects of Mankind* from their WNEW New York and WTTG Washington, D.C., studios. Since neither New York nor D.C. had NET stations, Metro Media had been airing *Prospects* as a public service, the only commercial stations to do so. With Morgenthau as executive producer, the new show would include commercial breaks, to which ER did not object if they were reasonably spaced without beer, wine, or cigarette advertising. However, she would consider this commercial program only as the alternative to the educational television projects she preferred. Morgenthau, Stix, and Eleanor would soon meet to discuss the options (Morgenthau "Educational").

ER's current promotional biography told the story about the role she wished to expand on TV:

> She has been particularly eager to arouse a new generation of post-war Americans to more active interest in the problems abroad that will determine their own destiny.... Recently, she has found through television she could reach and affect more people at one time than through any other medium. She found that educational television could afford to provide enough time and the right atmosphere for the thorough, penetrating, and continuing examination that

serious world problems demand…. She has fashioned a format which permits her to function in turn as commentator, interrogator, and hostess ["Mrs. Roosevelt" Biography].

Meanwhile, on August 3, her fever reached 105 degrees, and an ambulance was called. By August 6, she was asking for the mail from her hospital bed, and secretary Maureen Corr brought in a letter from Stix about the commercial series for which she would receive $1,000 per episode. She gave instructions to call and let him know she was in the hospital. Eleanor was released after five days, but doctors still struggled to diagnose her condition as she became wearier and ailing (Lash *Years Alone* 325).

Issues and Answers was ABC's entry into the political news magazine arena to compete with NBC's *Meet the Press* and *Face the Nation* on CBS. The long-running show was created and produced by Peggy Whedon, the first woman to regularly produce a news series on television. In her memoir, Whedon notes that she rarely appeared on camera, but chose to interview Eleanor herself on August 26, 1962, to discuss the President's Commission on the Status of Women and the hope of passing an equal pay for equal work bill in Congress. Assistant Secretary of Labor Esther Peterson also appeared on the show ("TV Programs"). This was the last television interview of Eleanor Roosevelt, and she does not look well in ABC photos from that day. Whedon describes her as "very tired and very frail," refusing to remove her hat because she had been ill, and her hair was not looking its best. "As we sat on the set, and I looked at the white hat and her weary appearance, my heart sank. She would never hold up for a half-hour interview. The show would not be the great tribute to the opinions of a strong woman that I had hoped…. I was wrong. The minute that little red light flashed on, and she realized she was on camera, the old pro took over. She straightened up, she smiled, and in a strong voice she gave the answers we were waiting for on all the issues."

Eleanor predicted opposition to the bill promoting job equality between women and men. "There will be opposition," especially "in the south," she added. ER discussed combining a career and family: "I think it depends on the person. If they have a real desire to develop, they will find ways. But they will have to do it in cooperation with the husband, and later in cooperation with the children … then it will be very satisfying." Whedon believed that "she was a lady way ahead of her time." ER blamed industry and big business for not expanding and including women in the workforce, fearing change. They had not faced the fact "that we live in a revolutionary period where not just military things are in revolution, but where your whole industrial and educational worlds are in revolution." She was looking for acceptance of this by industrialists and warned, "The minute you see a change, everybody draws back and says, 'Oh, let's go back to the good old days.'"

Whedon concludes, "I marvelled at this remarkable woman. Under that ghastly white hat, her face was luminous, her mind was so facile, and her ideas were so far ahead of her time that we listened, and learned, avidly." She was immensely proud that *Issues and Answers* "had had an opportunity to pay tribute to a very great lady and that her ideas on women and the state of the world had been presented to millions of people who would think about what she had said" (Whedon 156–58). Esther Peterson also remembered Eleanor's contribution fondly: "Toward the end of the

President's Commission on the Status of Women, we were pressing to get the equal pay bill through Congress…. and I fumbled a question very badly. They were asking me about why we were having trouble in a Senate Labor Committee, and I didn't want to answer it honestly because I didn't want to annoy the Senator I had to work with…. He was a Southern Senator, by the way, and she said, 'Well, I think he just does not like that word equal'" (*We Remember*).

ER spent the Friday before Labor Day in New York City and met with Stix about the new television show. She was not strong enough to travel any longer and signed a contract effective September 15 to host 10 or 12 hour-long discussion programs for the Metro Media series from New York that now had a name, *The American Experience*. She would receive $1,000 per episode, plus 10 percent of net revenues from syndication after distribution fees, exclusive to the network in terms of a show of her own, and she would be expected to be available for television specials at the same price (Lash *Years Alone* 326, Korn "Recollections," Korn to ER). The show would feature guests who were "the shapers of America's destiny" from the perspective of those intimately involved in the major events of the times. "The mood is reflexive, analytical, probing," emphasizing understanding rather than controversy, not avoiding differences of opinion, but shunning acrimony to encourage new and meaningful insights. Events of the past would be explored in terms of consequences for the present and future. Initial potential topics included "The First 100 Days of the New Deal" (and its continuing relevance), "The Limited War in the Nuclear Age," "Lenin/Stalin/Khrushchev" (personality as a factor in Soviet politics), "The Court and Desegregation," "America's Commitment to Internationalism: The United Nations," "The Great Depression" (Could it happen again?), "The Legacy of Hiroshima," "The McCarthy Era," "The Good Neighbor Policy," "The Labor Union in the American Economy," "The Presidency," "Our Future in Space," "The Truman Years" (ER interviews Truman one on one), and "The Eisenhower Years" (ER interviews Eisenhower one on one) (Barron).

Eleanor sent Morgenthau a copy of the June 1962 issue of "CORE-Lator," the newsletter of the Congress of Racial Equality, noting that they might want to do a program on the topic reported on the front page. She was heading a Committee of Inquiry into the Administration of Justice in the Freedom Struggle, hearing testimony about how Southern law enforcement officials were abusing "justice" (Rich). "The Court and Desegregation" became "The Negro and Civil Rights," and director Paul Noble outlined ideas for the first show, tentatively scheduled for taping on October 26 and airing on November 4. He was concerned, however, that it would be considered "too political" with both ER and potentially Attorney General Robert Kennedy on the program so close to Election Day. His September 15 memo includes detailed notes on potential guests, including an "ideal panel" of Kennedy, Martin Luther King, Jr., Thurgood Marshall, plus perhaps either Ralph McGill or Harry Ashmore. The plan was to have a "negro-white guest balance" (Noble Letter).

On September 21, Eleanor invited Martin Luther King, Jr., with whom she had an active correspondence and whom she had supported on many occasions, to be a guest on the inaugural episode of the new show focusing on civil rights. This was one of the last letters she would write, and did not mention her illness:

Dear Dr. King:

I would like to invite you to appear with me on the first program of my new series of one-hour discussions for Metropolitan Broadcasting. In *The American Experience*, we will examine contemporary issues in historical perspective. The subject of the first program is "The Negro and Civil Rights," and we plan to record it on Tuesday afternoon, October 23, in the New York studios of WNEW-TV.

I would especially like to have you join me for this discussion because of your leadership in the field of civil rights [Schlup 280].

An honorarium of $50 plus expenses was offered. On the same day, she also wrote Robert Kennedy inviting him to appear on the show, with no mention of compensation. Others asked to take part were John Hope Franklin, author of *Civil Rights in the United States, 1863 to 1963*, and Barry Bingham, publisher of the *Louisville Courier-Times*. As usual, staff members typed the letters, and she signed her name to them.

From her New York apartment, ER sent for Morgenthau to discuss the series, yet found that she could only speak to him from her bed. They earnestly talked about the future, but after 10 minutes, she dropped off to sleep. This was the last time he saw her (Morgenthau "ER at Brandeis"). With a persistent fever, coughing, and passing blood, ER was back in the hospital on September 26. Tuberculosis was now suspected, dating back to a dormant condition from 1919 and reactivated by the side effects of taking prednisone for anemia, which made the immune system less able to combat infection. The Kennedys sent flowers, and Eleanor's thank-you note of October 2 reveals her continued optimism for the future:

Dear Mr. President:

I want to thank you and Mrs. Kennedy for the lovely flowers and for your thought of me. It was more than good of you to have me on your mind and I am deeply appreciative.

The cause of my fever has been discovered and I should shortly be back on my regular schedule [Schlup 282].

However, her body did not respond to tuberculosis medications, and her fever hit 105 degrees again on October 12. A nurse noted on the chart, "Patient very miserable with temperature rising." ER was adamant that she did not want to die in the hospital and returned home on October 18, passing away on November 7. The autopsy revealed that she had a severe and rare form of tuberculosis that did not respond to treatments available in 1962 (Lerner). Eleanor Roosevelt was 78 years old.

When she was laid to rest on November 11 in the Rose Garden at Hyde Park next to Franklin, President John Kennedy; former presidents Dwight Eisenhower and Harry Truman; Vice President Lyndon Johnson; singer Marian Anderson; broadcaster Edward R. Murrow; First Lady Jacqueline Kennedy; former First Lady Bess Truman; future First Lady Bird Johnson; Supreme Court chief justice Earl Warren; Supreme Court justice Arthur Goldberg; labor leaders Walter Reuther and David Dubinsky; Secretary of State Dean Rusk; New York governor Nelson Rockefeller; New York City mayor Robert Wagner; United Nations under secretary general Ralph Bunche; United Nations ambassador Adlai Stevenson; Kennedy special assistant Arthur Schlesinger, Jr.; and New Dealers Henry Wallace, Jim Farley, Tommy Corcoran, Henry Morgenthau, Jr., and Frances Perkins were just a few of the 250

Journalist May Craig (center in flowered coat) attends funeral services for Eleanor Roosevelt in Hyde Park, New York, on November 10, 1962. Craig had been one of Eleanor Roosevelt's White House press conference attendees, would interview her on *Meet the Press* several times, and participated as a panelist on an episode of *Today with Mrs. Roosevelt* (Cecil Stoughton, White House Photographs, John F. Kennedy Presidential Library and Museum, Boston).

invited. Paul Noble recalled standing between Faye Emerson and Dore Schary (Noble 29). The family received messages of condolence from Russian premier Nikita Khrushchev, French president Charles de Gaulle, West German chancellor Konrad Adenauer, Yugoslav president Josip Tito, and Martin Luther King, Jr., among many others. Hundreds lined the streets of Hyde Park. It has been called the first "power funeral" of an American woman (Peyser). "The world has suffered an irreparable loss," said the Rev. Gordon Kidd of St. James's Church in Hyde Park during the service. "The entire world becomes one family orphaned by her passing."

Conclusion

On the CBS year in review broadcast, *1962: A Television Album*, the Cuban missile crisis, Vietnam, John Glenn's space flight, nuclear testing, and the Berlin Wall are all topics as they "run the time machine back." Before President John F. Kennedy appears near the end of the hour to sum up the year, host Eric Sevareid says: "Most people everywhere know the difference. They can recognize goodness in a regime as they recognize it in a person, and that is why one death this year gave to millions a sense of loss, the passing of Mrs. Eleanor Roosevelt." In a file interview, she tells a fascinating story of her early life and emerging awareness. At 18, when she returned from school in Europe and "came out into society as you did in those days and was not a success," ER began teaching in a Rivington Street settlement. She worked for the Consumer's League and learned about sweat shops and conditions of labor:

> I was very much embarrassed because I was very shy, and I was sent around with an experienced person to inspect, and I remember now thinking that it was terrible to have to ask how many people they employed and what chances there were for a restroom and what it looked like. And it always looked awful. And I didn't know how much space you should have for people to work with machines. I was being educated, and then when we went on into the homes of people where they made artificial flowers and feathers and I saw little children who worked hours on end until they fell off the benches, just asleep. This was all completely new to me.

Learning about the empathy and activism origins of the woman who would become the First Lady of the World in the year of her death certainly seems fitting.

Many years later in 1984, on the one hundredth anniversary of her birth, WNEW in New York broadcast *We Remember Eleanor*, a television special interweaving reminiscences, memories, and personal perspectives on the life of Eleanor Roosevelt, hosted by Harry and Bess Truman's daughter Margaret Truman Daniel. Sons and grandsons talk about her great contributions, but a surprising interview with Henry Kissinger—Jewish refugee from the Nazis, Harvard political science professor, panelist on *Prospects of Mankind*, and U.S. secretary of state under Nixon and Ford—clearly encapsulates her approach on television and to her life's work. ER led in a way that respected individuals and their struggles, encouraging everyone to take part in the full life of their country. Hers was a distinctive style of persuasion and respect, not disregarding one's political opponent, but educating all in the interests of every participant.

Kissinger remembered coming to the United States as a teenage exile in 1938 and shared what it meant to him at the time to have a president and First Lady who clearly cared about individuals. As an adult, he came to respect Eleanor Roosevelt and her approach to politics, although they did not always agree completely. She was open to negotiating with the Russians, but he respected that she did not think that talk was its own justification. She wanted to see concrete results and was not "starry-eyed":

> I was on a number of television programs with her called *Prospects of Mankind*, and she of course had her own point of view, but she was technically the moderator. And she played the devil's advocate in a very gentle, unobtrusive manner and in a way in which it sometimes seemed as if she were putting her own point of view. But what she was attempting to do was to bring out from the people, from the participants, all aspects of the problem. On any particular issue, she might sound hardline. On some others, she might sound excessively liberal, but in fact, her role was to bring out the best of which we were all capable, which I also believe was her role in the society.

Kissinger said it perhaps better than anyone else. Eleanor Roosevelt's role was to bring out the best of others on her television show and in the world. Respect, admiration, and the art of diplomacy cemented her place in the life of her country and in the world community.

Appendix

*Film and Television Appearances
and References During
Eleanor Roosevelt's Lifetime*

1933

> *The Fighting President*—newsreel footage

1934

> *Massacre*—possible reference

1939

> April 30—World's Fair (NBC)—appears in background
> *Babes in Arms*—impersonation
> *Mr. Smith Goes to Washington*—reference

1940

> *Hobby Lobby*—appearance
> *Pastor Hall*—prologue appearance

1941

> *Blondie Goes Latin*—possible impersonation
> *Louisiana Purchase*—reference
> *Women in Defense*—scriptwriter

1942

> *The Man Who Came to Dinner*—reference
> *Training Women for War Production*—appearance
> *Woman of the Year*—reference
> *Yankee Doodle Dandy*—reference

1943

> *The More the Merrier*—reference

They Got Me Covered—reference
Women at War—inspired by

1944

Booby Hatched—reference
Broadway Rhythm—impersonation
The Doughgirls—reference
Meet the People—reference
That's My Baby!—reference

1945

May 9—VE Day special (NBC)—appearance
Bring on the Girls—reference
Great Day—character

1947

A Greater Tomorrow—appearance
The Roosevelt Story—newsreel footage

1948

May 6—*CBS Television News*—appearance
May 8—Anti-Defamation League special (CBS)—appearance

1949

April 1—National Conference on UNESCO (ABC)—appearance
April 8—*Meet the Press* (NBC)—appearance
May–June—*McCall's Magazine* commercials for *This I Remember*—appearance
June 7—*You and Human Rights* (CBS)—appearance
June 16—*Crusade in Europe* (ABC)—appearance
June 21—*Vanity Fair* (CBS)—appearance
October 13—*Freedom House Awards* (CBS)—appearance
December 10—United Nations Declaration of Human Rights celebration (NBC)—
    appearance
December 13—*Baking Contest Awards* (CBS)—appearance
His Fighting Chance—narrator

1950

February 9—*Author Meets the Critics* (ABC)—appearance
February 12—*Today with Mrs. Roosevelt* (NBC)—moderator
February 19—*Today with Mrs. Roosevelt* (NBC)—moderator
February 26—*Today with Mrs. Roosevelt* (NBC)—moderator
March 5—*Today with Mrs. Roosevelt* (NBC)—moderator
March 12—*Today with Mrs. Roosevelt* (NBC)—moderator
March 19—*Today with Mrs. Roosevelt* (NBC)—moderator

March 26—*Today with Mrs. Roosevelt* (NBC)—moderator
March 27—United Nations Commission on Human Rights (CBS)—appearance
April 2—*Today with Mrs. Roosevelt* (NBC)—moderator
April 9—*Today with Mrs. Roosevelt* (NBC)—moderator
April 16—*Today with Mrs. Roosevelt* (NBC)—moderator
April 23—*Today with Mrs. Roosevelt* (NBC)—moderator
April 27—American Association for the United Nations (WATV)—appearance
April 30—*Today with Mrs. Roosevelt* (NBC)—moderator
May 7—*Today with Mrs. Roosevelt* (NBC)—moderator
May 11—*The Four Freedoms Awards* (CBS)—appearance
May 12—*People's Platform* (CBS)—appearance
May 14—*Today with Mrs. Roosevelt* (NBC)—moderator
May 21—*Today with Mrs. Roosevelt* (NBC)—moderator
May 28—*Today with Mrs. Roosevelt* (NBC)—moderator
September 11—Political endorsement (KTTV Los Angeles)—appearance
October 1—*Mrs. Roosevelt Meets the Public* (NBC)—moderator
October 8—*Mrs. Roosevelt Meets the Public* (NBC)—moderator
October 15—*Mrs. Roosevelt Meets the Public* (NBC)—moderator
October 22—*Marshall Plan in Action* (ABC)—appearance
October 22—*Mrs. Roosevelt Meets the Public* (NBC)—moderator
October 29—*Mrs. Roosevelt Meets the Public* (NBC)—moderator
November 5—*Mrs. Roosevelt Meets the Public* (NBC)—moderator
November 12—*Mrs. Roosevelt Meets the Public* (NBC)—moderator
November 19—*Mrs. Roosevelt Meets the Public* (NBC)—moderator
November 23—*Rootie Tootie Club Thanksgiving Day Party* (NBC)—appearance
November 26—*Mrs. Roosevelt Meets the Public* (NBC)—moderator
December 3—*The Colgate Comedy Hour* (NBC)—appearance
December 3—*Mrs. Roosevelt Meets the Public* (NBC)—moderator
December 10—*Mrs. Roosevelt Meets the Public* (NBC)—moderator
December 10—United Nations Human Rights Day (CBS)—appearance
December 24—*Bob Hope Christmas Special* (NBC)—appearance
December 24—*Mrs. Roosevelt Meets the Public* (NBC)—moderator
December 31—*Mrs. Roosevelt Meets the Public* (NBC)—moderator
My Trip Abroad—appearance

1951

January 7—*Mrs. Roosevelt Meets the Public* (NBC)—moderator
January 14—*Mrs. Roosevelt Meets the Public* (NBC)—moderator
January 21—*Mrs. Roosevelt Meets the Public* (NBC)—moderator
January 28—*Mrs. Roosevelt Meets the Public* (NBC)—moderator
February 4—*Mrs. Roosevelt Meets the Public* (NBC)—moderator
February 13—*Texaco Star Theater* (NBC)—impersonation
February 18—*Mrs. Roosevelt Meets the Public* (NBC)—moderator
February 25—*Mrs. Roosevelt Meets the Public* (NBC)—moderator
March 4—*Mrs. Roosevelt Meets the Public* (NBC)—moderator
March 11—*Mrs. Roosevelt Meets the Public* (NBC)—moderator

March 18—*Mrs. Roosevelt Meets the Public* (NBC)—moderator
March 25—*Mrs. Roosevelt Meets the Public* (NBC)—moderator
April 1—*Mrs. Roosevelt Meets the Public* (NBC)—moderator
April 8—*Mrs. Roosevelt Meets the Public* (NBC)—moderator
April 15—*Mrs. Roosevelt Meets the Public* (NBC)—not present, substitute moderator
April 22—*Mrs. Roosevelt Meets the Public* (NBC)—not present, substitute moderator
April 29—*Mrs. Roosevelt Meets the Public* (NBC)—moderator
May 6—*Mrs. Roosevelt Meets the Public* (NBC)—moderator
May 13—*Mrs. Roosevelt Meets the Public* (NBC)—moderator
May 20—*Mrs. Roosevelt Meets the Public* (NBC)—not present, substitute moderator
May 27—*Mrs. Roosevelt Meets the Public* (NBC)—moderator
June 3—*Mrs. Roosevelt Meets the Public* (NBC)—moderator
June 10—*Mrs. Roosevelt Meets the Public* (NBC)—moderator
June 17—*Mrs. Roosevelt Meets the Public* (NBC)—moderator
June 24—*Mrs. Roosevelt Meets the Public* (NBC)—moderator
July 1—*Mrs. Roosevelt Meets the Public* (NBC)—moderator
July 8—*Mrs. Roosevelt Meets the Public* (NBC)—moderator
July 15—*Mrs. Roosevelt Meets the Public* (NBC)—moderator
October 7—*The Sarah Churchill Show* (CBS)—appearance
November 10—*Assembly VI* (NBC)—appearance
December 8—*Assembly VI* (NBC)—appearance
The African Queen—character inspired by
Unfinished Business, U.S.A (NBC)—appearance

1952

February 12—*United or Not?* (ABC)—appearance
April 13—New York Easter Parade (ABC)—appearance
May—*Issues of the Day* (syndicated)—appearance
July 22—Democratic National Convention (ABC, CBS, NBC)—appearance
August 5—*It's a Problem* (NBC)—appearance
August 13—*Youth Wants to Know* (NBC)—appearance
August—*Visit*—appearance
October 12—*The Hot Seat* (NBC)—appearance
October 19—*Inside Israel* (DuMont)—appearance
December 2—*Keep Posted* (DuMont)—appearance
The Member of the Wedding—reference
Youth and the United Nations—appearance

1953

August 7—*Today* (NBC)—appearance
August 11—*Barry Gray Show* (DuMont)—appearance
August 26—*Longines Chronoscope* (CBS)—appearance
September 10—*Author Meets the Critics* (ABC)—appearance

October 18—*Quiz Kids* (CBS)—appearance
October 18—*What's My Line?* (CBS)—appearance
October—*Youth Wants to Know* (NBC)—appearance
November 4—*Today* (NBC)—appearance
November 19—KGO-TV San Francisco show—appearance
November 20—*Perspective* (ABC)—appearance
November 23—Anti-Defamation League anniversary (ABC, CBS, and NBC)—
    appearance
Model United Nations—appearance

1954

January 21—*The Garry Moore Show* (CBS)—appearance
January 22—*Person to Person* (CBS)—appearance
March—*Where Were You?* (syndicated)—appearance
April 4—*The Challenge* (NBC)—appearance
April 11—*Meet the Press* (NBC)—appearance
May 17—*The Tex and Jinx Show* (NBC)—appearance
May 18—*Today* (NBC)—appearance
June 20—*Adventure* (CBS)—appearance
June 20—*Author Meets the Critics* (ABC)—appearance
September 13—*Project Twenty*, "Three Two One Zero" (NBC)—newsreel footage
October 7—*Author Meets the Critics* (ABC)—appearance
October 24—United Nations Program (NBC)—appearance

1955

February 21—*Junior Press Conference*—appearance
March 9—*Panorama* (BBC)—appearance
April 2—*Imprint of a Man* (ABC)—appearance
April 25—*Longines Chronoscope* (CBS)—review of 1953 appearance
June 19—*Adventure* (CBS)—appearance
June 19—*The American Week* (CBS)—appearance
June 28—*The Brokenshire Show* (NBC)—appearance
American Cancer Society educational film—appearance

1956

January 2—*Tex McCrary's M.I.P* (DuMont)—appearance
April 6—*Home* (NBC)—appearance
June 10—*Between the Lines* (DuMont)—appearance
August 13—Democratic National Convention (ABC, CBS, NBC)—appearance
September 16—*Meet the Press* (NBC)—appearance
October 18—Political endorsement (Pennsylvania)—appearance
October 20—Closed-circuit Democratic fundraiser—appearance
October 24—Political endorsement (ABC New York)—appearance
October 25—Delaware State Education Association speech—appearance
November 4—*Face the Nation* (CBS)—appearance
Nuclear Test Ban (aka *H-Bomb Over America*)—appearance

1957

January 6—*Wide Wide World*, "A Woman's Story" (NBC)—appearance
April 23—*Portraits of Power* (BBC)—newsreel footage
May 8—*Youth Wants to Know* (Granada, U.K.)—appearance
June 3—*Today* (NBC)—appearance
June 16—*See It Now* (CBS)—reference
July 6—Dedication of Truman Library (KCMO-TV, Kansas City, MO)—
    appearance
October 20—*Meet the Press* (NBC)—appearance
October 24—*The Arlene Francis Show* (NBC)—appearance
November 23—*The Mike Wallace Interview* (ABC)—appearance
The Joker Is Wild—newsreel footage

1958

January 2—*Today* (NBC)—appearance
January 28—*Front Page Challenge* (Canada)—appearance
February—*First Federal Presents*—appearance
March—*New Horizons* (CBS San Francisco)—appearance
March 30—*Face the Nation* (CBS)—reference
April—*Heritage*, four episodes (NET)—appearance
May 11—*The Ed Sullivan Show* (CBS)—appearance
June 10—*It's Fun to Travel* (WOR-TV New York)—appearance
June 14—*Youth Wants to Know* (Soviet Union)—appearance
August 27—*Eleanor Roosevelt: Her Life in Pictures*—appearance
October 19—*UN in Action* (CBS)—appearance
October 26—*Meet the Press* (NBC)—appearance
December 7—*College News Conference* (ABC)—appearance

1959

February—Good Luck Margarine commercials—appearance
March 8—*Wisdom* (NBC)—appearance
April 5—*Kaleidoscope*, "Blueprint for Biography: The Story of *Sunrise at
    Campobello*" (NBC)—major character
May 8—*Truman's Diamond Jubilee*—appearance
July 17—*Thinking Things Through* (pilot)—appearance
August 19—*The Sam Levenson Show* (CBS)—appearance
September 15—*Today* (NBC)—appearance
September 18—*Eyewitness to History* (CBS)—appearance
October 11—*Prospects of Mankind* (NET)—moderator
October 16—*Project Twenty*, "Life in the Thirties" (NBC)—reference
October 25—*Sunday Showcase*, "A Tribute to Eleanor Roosevelt on Her Diamond
    Jubilee" (NBC)—appearance
November 13—*Insight* (WPIX New York)—appearance
November 15—*Prospects of Mankind* (NET)—moderator
November 20—*Insight* (WPIX New York)—appearance

December 5—*Prospects of Mankind* (NET)—moderator
December 6—*Search for America* (NET)—appearance
December 21—*Search for America* (NET)—appearance
December 27—*UN in Action* (CBS)—appearance
N.S. Khrushchev in America—appearance

1960

January 3—*Prospects of Mankind* (NET)—moderator
January 9—*Celebrity Parade for Cerebral Palsy* (WOR-TV New York)—appearance
February 14—*Premier Plan* (Canada)—appearance
February 14—*Prospects of Mankind* (NET)—moderator
February 15—*The Frank Sinatra Timex Show: Here's to the Ladies* (ABC)—
    appearance
March 8—*That Free Men May Live* (NET)—appearance
March 13—*Prospects of Mankind* (NET)—moderator
April 17—*Prospects of Mankind* (NET)—moderator
April 26—*Reading Out Loud* (WBC)—appearance
May 15—*Prospects of Mankind* (NET)—moderator
June—*This Week* (U.K., ITV)—appearance
June 12—*Prospects of Mankind* (NET)—moderator
June 19—*College News Conference* (ABC)—appearance
June 27—*Today* (NBC)—appearance
July 11–13—Democratic National Convention (ABC, CBS, NBC)—appearances
September—Get Out the Vote campaign (Metromedia)—appearance
September 25—*Prospects of Mankind* (NET)—moderator
October 2—*Candid Camera* (CBS)—reference
October 7—*Eleanor Roosevelt's Diamond Jubilee Plus One* (NBC)—appearance
October 23—*Prospects of Mankind* (NET)—moderator
October 31—*The Jack Paar Tonight Show* (NBC)—appearance
November—John F. Kennedy campaign commercials—appearance
November 1—*Eye on St. Louis* (CBS, St Louis)—appearance
November 5—*Mrs. Eleanor Roosevelt Speaks for Kennedy* (ABC New York)—
    appearance
November 6—*Mrs. Eleanor Roosevelt Speaks for Kennedy* (WNEW New York)—
    appearance
November 6—*The Twentieth Century*, "The White House Story" (CBS)—appearance
November 20—*Prospects of Mankind* (NET)—moderator
December 12—*The Finest Hours* (WNET New York)—appearance
December 15—*Transition* (WPIX New York)—appearance
December 18—*Prospects of Mankind* (NET)—moderator
Sunrise at Campobello—major character
Wild River—reference

1961

January 1—Children of UN Delegates (NBC)—narrator
January 15—*Prospects of Mankind* (NET)—moderator

January 20—John F. Kennedy inauguration (ABC, CBS, NBC)—appearance
February 12—*Prospects of Mankind* (NET)—moderator
March 12—*Prospects of Mankind* (NET)—moderator
April 9—*Prospects of Mankind* (NET)—moderator
May 7—*Prospects of Mankind* (NET)—moderator
May 26—*Prospects of Mankind* (NET)—moderator
May 31—*The Jack Paar Tonight Show* (NBC)—appearance
June 5—*At Your Beck and Call* (WNTA New York)—letter read on air
August 30—*Understanding Our World* (syndicated)—appearance
September 17—*Prospects of Mankind* (NET)—not present, substitute moderator
October 9—*This Is Your Life* (BBC)—appearance
October 15—*Prospects of Mankind* (NET)—moderator
November 3—*Chevrolet Golden Anniversary Show* (CBS)—reference
November 5—*The Twentieth Century* (CBS)—newsreel footage
November 12—*Prospects of Mankind* (NET)—moderator
December 10—*Prospects of Mankind* (NET)—moderator
Pocketful of Miracles—reference

1962

January 14—*Prospects of Mankind* (NET)—moderator
January 21—*Directions '62* (WOR-TV New York)—appearance
February 11—*Prospects of Mankind* (NET)—moderator
February 17—*Cinq colonnes à la une* (France)—appearance
February 25—*Prospects of Mankind* (NET)—moderator
February or March—Associated Television (UK)—appearance
April 1—*At This Very Moment* (ABC)—appearance
April 8—*Prospects of Mankind* (NET)—moderator
May 7—*Prospects of Mankind* (NET)—moderator
June 3—*Prospects of Mankind* (NET)—moderator
July—*F.D.R.* (ABC)—recorded narration airing in 1965
August 26—*Issues and Answers* (ABC)—appearance
November 30—*The World of Jacqueline Kennedy* (NBC)—appearance
   (prerecorded)
December 4—National School Telecast—appearance (prerecorded)
Face the Community (NBC Rochester NY)—appearance

Filmography

Films accessible to screen

Abe Lincoln in Illinois. Directed by John Cromwell, performances by Raymond Massey, Gene Lockhart, and Ruth Gordon, RKO Radio Pictures, 1940.

The African Queen. Directed by John Huston, performances by Humphrey Bogart, Katharine Hepburn, and Robert Morley, United Artists, 1951.

Assignment Children. Directed by Danny Kaye, performances by Danny Kaye, Vijaya Lakshmi Pandit, and Dag Hammarskjöld, Paramount Pictures, 1955. www.loc.gov/item/ihas.2001 98131.

Babes in Arms. Directed by Busby Berkeley, performances by Mickey Rooney, Judy Garland, and Charles Winninger, MGM, 1939.

The Battle of Midway. Directed by John Ford, performances by Henry Fonda, Jane Darwell, and Logan Ramsey, United States Navy, 1942. youtube.com/watch?v=7OBw0r28qC0.

The Beginning or the End. Directed by Norman Taurog, performances by Brian Donlevy, Robert Walker, and Tom Drake, MGM, 1947.

Blondie Goes Latin. Directed by Frank R. Strayer and Robert Sparks, performances by Penny Singleton, Arthur Lake, and Larry Simms, Columbia Pictures, 1941.

Booby Hatched. Directed by Frank Tashlin, performances by Sara Berner and Mel Blanc, Warner Bros., 1944.

The Bridge (*Die Brücke*). Directed by Bernhard Wicki, performances by Folker Bohnet, Fritz Wepper, and Michael Hinz, Fono Film, 1959.

Bring on the Girls. Directed by Sidney Lanfield, performances by Veronica Lake, Sonny Tufts, and Eddie Bracken, Paramount Pictures, 1945.

Broadway Rhythm. Directed by Roy Del Ruth, performances by George Murphy, Ginny Simms, and Charles Winninger, MGM, 1944.

David and Bathsheba. Directed by Henry King, performances by Gregory Peck, Susan Hayward, and Raymond Massey, Twentieth Century–Fox, 1951.

The Defiant Ones. Directed by Stanley Kramer, performances by Tony Curtis, Sidney Poitier, and Theodore Bikel, United Artists, 1958.

The Desperate Hours. Directed by William Wyler, performances by Humphrey Bogart, Fredric March, and Arthur Kennedy, Paramount Pictures, 1955.

The Diary of Anne Frank. Directed by George Stevens, performances by Millie Perkins, Shelley Winters, and Joseph Schildkraut, Twentieth Century–Fox, 1959.

The Doughgirls. Directed by James V. Kern, performances by Ann Sheridan, Alexis Smith, and Jack Carson, Warner Bros., 1944.

The Fighting President. Directed by Allyn Butterfield, performance by Franklin D. Roosevelt, Universal Pictures, 1933. youtube.com/watch?v=2QTYvd4thns.

The Forgotten Village. Directed by Herbert Kline and Alexander Hammid, performance by Burgess Meredith, Pan-American Films Inc., 1941. youtube.com/watch?v=H7-lx78PrHY

Gone with the Wind. Directed by Victor Fleming, George Cukor, and Sam Wood, performances by Clark Gable, Vivien Leigh, and Thomas Mitchell, MGM, 1939.

Great Day. Directed by Lance Comfort, performances by Eric Portman, Flora Robson, and Sheila Sim, RKO Radio Pictures, 1945.

His Fighting Chance. Directed by Geoffrey Innes, performances by Eleanor Roosevelt and Michael Redgrave, Crown Film Unit, 1949. youtube.com/watch?v=ZrIi_MUaiIs.

The Jazz Singer. Directed by Michael Curtiz, performances by Danny Thomas, Peggy Lee, and Eduard Franz, Warner Bros., 1952.

The Joker Is Wild. Directed by Charles Vidor, performances by Frank Sinatra, Mitzi Gaynor, and Jeanne Crain, Paramount Pictures, 1957.

Louisiana Purchase. Directed by Irving Cummings, performances by Bob Hope, Vera Zorina, and Victor Moore, Paramount Pictures, 1941.

Mädchen in Uniform. Directed by Leontine Sagan and Carl Froelich, performances by Dorothea Wieck, Hertha Thiele, and Emilia Unda, Deutsche Film-Gemeinschaft, 1931.

The Man Who Came to Dinner. Directed by William Keighley, performances by Bette Davis,

Ann Sheridan, and Monty Woolley, Warner Bros., 1942.

Massacre. Directed by Alan Crosland, performances by Richard Barthelmess, Ann Dvorak, and Dudley Digges, Warner Bros., 1934.

Meet the People. Directed by Charles Reisner, performances by Lucille Ball, Dick Powell, and Virginia O'Brien, MGM, 1944.

Melody Ranch. Directed by Joseph Santley, performances by Gene Autry, Jimmy Durante, and Ann Miller, Republic Pictures, 1940.

The Member of the Wedding. Directed by Fred Zinnemann, performances by Ethel Waters, Julie Harris, and Brandon De Wilde, Columbia Pictures, 1952.

Men of Two Worlds. Directed by Thorold Dickinson, performances by Robert Adams, Eric Portman, and Orlando Martins, Two Cities Films, 1946.

Mr. Smith Goes to Washington. Directed by Frank Capra, performances by James Stewart, Jean Arthur, and Claude Rains, Columbia Pictures, 1939.

The More the Merrier. Directed by George Stevens, performances by Jean Arthur, Joel McCrea, and Charles Coburn, Columbia Pictures, 1943.

My Trip Abroad. Performance by Eleanor Roosevelt, *The March of Time,* 1950. c-span.org/video/?507381-1/my-trip-abroad-eleanor-roosevelt.

Not Wanted. Directed by Elmer Clifton and Ida Lupino, performances by Sally Forrest, Keefe Brasselle, and Leo Penn, Emerald Productions Inc., 1949.

Nuclear Test Ban (aka *H-Bomb Over America*). Performances by Adlai Stevenson and Eleanor Roosevelt, Stevenson campaign film, 1956. youtube.com/watch?v=VLld7htLce8.

Our Daily Bread. Directed by King Vidor, performances by Karen Morley, Tom Keene, and Barbara Pepper, United Artists, 1934.

Our Very Own. Directed by David Miller, performances by Ann Blyth, Farley Granger, and Joan Evans, Samuel Goldwyn Company, 1950.

Pastor Hall. Directed by Roy Boulting, performances by Wilfrid Lawson, Nova Pilbeam, and Seymour Hicks, United Artists, 1940. (Prologue not included in DVD or Blu-ray releases.)

Pocketful of Miracles. Directed by Frank Capra, performances by Glenn Ford, Bette Davis, and Hope Lange, United Artists, 1961.

Pot o' Gold. Directed by George Marshall, performances by James Stewart, Paulette Goddard, and Horace Heidt, James Roosevelt Productions, 1941.

The Price of Victory. Directed by William H. Pine, performance by Henry Wallace, Paramount Pictures, 1942. youtube.com/watch?v=CAKrIdSPkHI.

Priorities on Parade. Directed by Albert S. Rogell, performances by Ann Miller, Johnny Johnston, and Jerry Colonna, Paramount Pictures, 1942.

The River. Directed by Jean Renoir, performances by Patricia Walters, Nora Swinburne, and Esmond Knight, United Artists, 1951.

The Roosevelt Story. Directed by Lawrence M. Klee, performances by Franklin D. Roosevelt, Eleanor Roosevelt, and Kenneth Lynch, United Artists, 1947.

Stage Door Canteen. Directed by Frank Borzage, performances by Cheryl Walker, William Terry, and Judith Anderson, United Artists, 1943.

Stella Dallas. Directed by King Vidor, performances by Barbara Stanwyck, John Boles, and Anne Shirley, Samuel Goldwyn Company, 1937.

Storm Center. Directed by Daniel Taradash, performances by Bette Davis, Brian Keith, and Kim Hunter, Columbia Pictures, 1956.

Sunrise at Campobello. Directed by Vincent J. Donehue, performances by Ralph Bellamy, Greer Garson, and Hume Cronyn, Warner Bros., 1960.

That's My Baby! Directed by William Berke, performances by Richard Arlen, Ellen Drew, and Leonid Kinskey, Republic Pictures, 1944.

They Got Me Covered. Directed by David Butler, performances by Bob Hope, Dorothy Lamour, and Lenore Aubert, RKO Radio Pictures, 1943.

They Shall Have Music. Directed by Archie Mayo, performances by Jascha Heifetz, Joel McCrea, and Andrea Leeds, Samuel Goldwyn Company, 1939.

This Is the Army. Directed by Michael Curtiz, performances by George Murphy, Joan Leslie, and George Tobias, Warner Bros., 1943.

The Time of Your Life. Directed by H.C. Potter, performances by James Cagney, William Bendix, and Wayne Morris, United Artists, 1948.

Training Women for War Production. Performance by Eleanor Roosevelt, National Youth Administration, 1942. youtube.com/watch?v=rEJOkrdf1Rg.

The Unconquered. Directed by Nancy Hamilton, performances by Katharine Cornell, Helen Keller, and Polly Thompson, Nancy Hamilton, 1954.

Wasn't That a Time? Directed by Michael Burton and Philip Burton, performances by Anne Braden, Carl Braden, and Pete Seeger, 1962.

Wild River. Directed by Elia Kazan, performances by Montgomery Clift, Lee Remick, and Jo Van Fleet, Twentieth Century–Fox, 1960.

Woman of the Year. Directed by George Stevens, performances by Spencer Tracy, Katharine Hepburn, and Fay Bainter, MGM, 1942.

Women at War. Directed by Jean Negulesco, performances by Faye Emerson, Dorothy Day, and Marjorie Hoshelle, Warner Bros., 1943. (Released as extra on *Air Force* DVD, 1943.)

Women in Defense. Performance by Katharine Hepburn, Office of Emergency Management, 1941. youtube.com/watch?v=tRH70pR_oCo.

Wuthering Heights. Directed by William Wyler, performances by Merle Oberon, Laurence Olivier, and David Niven, Samuel Goldwyn Company, 1939.

Yankee Doodle Dandy. Directed by Michael Curtiz, performances by James Cagney, Joan Leslie, and Walter Huston, Warner Bros., 1942.

Youth Runs Wild. Directed by Mark Robson, performances by Bonita Granville, Kent Smith, and Jean Brooks, RKO Radio Pictures, 1944.

Television Episodes

Television episodes accessible to screen

Assembly VI. 10 Nov. 1951, NBC, Paley Center for Media, T78:0778.

Assembly VI. 8 Dec. 1951, NBC, Paley Center for Media, T78:0782.

At This Very Moment. 1 Apr. 1962, ABC, UCLA Film and Television Archive, VA20582T.

"Bob Hope Christmas Special." *The Bob Hope Show,* 24 Dec. 1950, NBC, www.youtube.com/watch?v=1yUwURjPyvE.

Dedication of Truman Library. 6 July 1957, "MP77–23 KCMO-TV News Segments from 1957 through 1962," youtube.com/watch?v=p-MxZ-ij1GM&t=404s.

Democratic National Convention. "Eleanor Roosevelt at Convention," 22 July 1952, National Archives and Records Administration; Records of the U.S. Information Agency, 1900–2003; Moving Images Relating to U.S. Domestic and International Activities, 1982–1999; ARC Identifier 48424.

Democratic National Convention. 11 July 1960, CBS, Paley Center for Media, T83:0625.

Democratic National Convention. 12 July 1960, CBS, Paley Center for Media, T83:0632.

Democratic National Convention. 13 July 1960, CBS, Archival Television Audio, 866.

The Ed Sullivan Show. 13 Oct. 1963, NBC, Paley Center for Media, T82:0413.

Eleanor Roosevelt: Her Life in Pictures. McCall's Magazine, 1958, youtube.com/watch?v=rn4WenJ9QfI.

Eleanor Roosevelt's Diamond Jubilee Plus One. 7 Oct. 1960, NBC, Archival Television Audio, 7112.

Face the Nation. 4 Nov. 1956, CBS, Archival Television Audio, 13061.

"The Family of Man." *Adventure,* 19 June 1955, CBS, Paley Center for Media, T77:0267.

F.D.R. series, 1965, ABC, Paley Center for Media and Franklin D. Roosevelt Presidential Library and Museum.

The Frank Sinatra Timex Show: Here's to the Ladies, 15 Feb. 1960, ABC, DVD.

Good Luck Margarine commercial 1. Ogilvy and Mather, 1959, Paley Center for Media, AT:23607.033.

Good Luck Margarine commercial 2. Ogilvy and Mather, 1959, youtube.com/watch?v=6HY8vxYX78s.

"The H-Bomb and Atomic Energy." *Today with Mrs. Roosevelt,* 12 Feb. 1950, NBC, Paley Center for Media, T77:0362.

"How Can Television Best Meet Our Education Needs?" *Mrs. Roosevelt Meets the Public,* 21 Jan. 1951, NBC, Paley Center for Media, T77:0363.

John F. Kennedy campaign commercial 1. 1960, youtube.com/watch?v=8k-xaWK2-74.

John F. Kennedy campaign commercial 2. 1960, c-span.org/video/?153415-1/kennedy-1960-campaign-ad.

John F. Kennedy inauguration. 20 Jan. 1961, CBS, Paley Center for Media, T81:0470.

"Khrushchev in New York." *Eyewitness to History,* 18 Sept. 1959, CBS, Paley Center for Media, T:25369.

"Life in the Thirties." *Project Twenty,* 16 Oct. 1959, NBC, VHS.

Longines Chronoscope. 26 Aug. 1953, CBS, DVD.

Masquerade Party, date unknown 1954–56, ABC, Paley Center for Media, T:23550.

Meet the Press. 16 Sept. 1956, NBC, nbcnews.com/video/eleanor-roosevelt-on-why-she-had-no-respect-for-nixon-316612163859.

The Mike Wallace Interview. 23 Nov. 1957, ABC, c-span.org/video/?288489-1/mike-wallace-interview-eleanor-roosevelt.

1962: A Television Album. 30 Dec. 1962, CBS, Paley Center for Media, T77:0461.

Person to Person. 22 Jan. 1954, CBS, *The Best of Person to Person* DVD.

Perspective. 20 Nov. 1953, ABC, Paley Center for Media, T80:0483.

Premier Plan, 14 Feb. 1960, Canada, clip, facebook.com/watch/?v=10155933559981052.

"Premiere." *The Sarah Churchill Show,* 7 Oct. 1951, CBS, Paley Center for Media, T76:0024.

Prospects of Mankind series. 1959–62, NET, americanarchive.org/special_collections/prospectsofmankind.

Rootie Tootie Club Thanksgiving Day Party. 23 Nov. 1950, NBC, archive.org/details/RootieTootieParty11231953.

Texaco Star Theater. 13 Feb. 1951, NBC, Paley Center for Media, T:05554.

That Free Men May Live. 8 Mar. 1960, NET, pbs.org/video/march-3-2013-25753.

"Three Two One Zero." *Project Twenty,* 13 Sep. 1954, NBC, youtube.com/watch?v=SWr5kPmwiMA&t=129s.

Today. 14 Jan. 2002, NBC, Paley Center for Media, T:71128.

Truman's Diamond Jubilee. 8 May 1959, "Motion Picture MP77-8 Truman Diamond Jubilee-Happy Birthday, Mr. Truman," Harry S. Truman Presidential Library and Museum.

We Remember Eleanor. 1984, WNEW, Paley Center for Media, T85:0195.

What's My Line? 18 Oct. 1953, CBS, youtube.com/watch?v=0Ew82Ae_N9g.

"The White House Story." *The Twentieth Century,* 6 Nov. 1960, CBS, Paley Center for Media, T81:0031.

Wisdom. 8 Mar. 1959, NBC, youtube.com/watch?v=tAe2olgJPcI.

"A Woman's Story." *Wide Wide World,* 6 Jan. 1957, NBC, Paley Center for Media, T80:0189.

The World of Jacqueline Kennedy. 30 Nov. 1962, NBC, Paley Center for Media, T78:0102.

Youth Wants to Know. National Archives and Records Administration; Records of the Central Intelligence Agency, 1894–2002; Moving Images Relating to Intelligence and International Relations, 1947–84; Interview with Mrs. Eleanor Roosevelt by Russian Journalists, 1958; ARC Identifier 646586.

Works Cited

Abbe, James. "On the Air." *Oakland Tribune*, 20 June 1954, p. 4B.

"*Abe Lincoln* Showing at White House." *Variety*, 22 Jan. 1940, p. 1.

"Abroad in Brief." *Broadcasting*, 6 June 1960, p. 100.

"Acheson Asks Pooling of Technical Skill by U.N. to Aid in Reconstructions of Korea." *New York Times*, 2 Oct. 1950, p. 3.

Adams, Olive. "Straight Ahead." *Arizona Sun*, 30 Oct. 1953, p. 8.

Adams, Val. "Godfrey Will Do Murrow Program." *New York Times*, 18 Feb. 1959, p. 67.

_____. "Mrs. Roosevelt Helped TV Series." *New York Times*, 9 Nov. 1962, p. 52.

_____. "N.B.C. Bars Star from A.B.C. Show." *New York Times*, 17 Oct. 1957, p. 51.

_____. "Self-Taught Distaff Spellbinder." *New York Times*, 28 Oct. 1951, p. 101.

_____. "WBAI-FM's Shift Is Slated Sunday." *New York Times*, 6 Jan. 1960, p. 71.

"Advertising." *Weekly Television Digest*, 28 Feb. 1959, p. 12.

"Advise Mrs. FDR Not to Sue M-G." *Variety*, 26 Feb. 1947, pp. 1, 6.

Albert, Dora. "Bubbling Billie." *Modern Screen*, Aug. 1938, pp. 38–39, 83.

Alden, Robert. "Truman Is Toasted at 75 at Dinners Coast to Coast." *New York Times*, 9 May 1959, pp. 1, 9.

Alicoate, Jack. "Sanity and a Situation." *Film Daily*, 3 July 1934, pp. 1–2.

"All Studios to Join Mexican Festival." *Motion Picture Daily*, 3 Apr. 1941, p. 6.

Allen, Kelcey. "Amusements." *Women's Wear Daily*, 5 Aug. 1947, p. 63.

Alpert, Hollis. "*SR* Goes to the Movies: The Twenties Revisited." *Saturday Review*, 24 Sept. 1960, p. 30.

Altschuler, Bruce. *Seeing Through the Screen: Interpreting American Political Film*, Lexington Books, 2018.

"American Exhibition of Educational Radio Awards." *Broadcasting Telecasting*, 8 May 1950, p. 46.

"The American Theatre Wing Presents *Stage Door Canteen*" script. 17 Dec. 1942, Franklin D. Roosevelt Presidential Library and Museum, Anna Eleanor Roosevelt Papers, Part 2, Series 50, Box 1413.

"And That's That." *Variety*, 6 May 1959, p. 55.

Anna's Sin advertisement. *Box Office*, 31 July 1961, p. NC-4.

"*Anne* Bow to United Nations." *Motion Picture Daily*, 11 Feb. 1959, p. 8.

"Anniversary, ILGUW." *Educational Film Guide*, 1959 Annual Supplement, p. 4.

"Another Look." *The Billboard*, 6 Jan. 1951, p. 28.

"Anti-Defamation Awards Wrapped into CBS Show." *Variety*, 5 May 1948, p, 35.

Archerd, Army. "Just for Variety." *Daily Variety*, 6 Nov. 1956, p. 2.

_____. "Just for Variety." *Daily Variety*, 12 Feb. 1960, p. 2.

_____. "Just for Variety." *Daily Variety*, 7 June 1960, p. 2.

"*Are These Our Children?* as April Release by RKO." *Film Daily*, 10 Mar. 1944, p. 6.

"Argentines Ban *Pastor Hall*." *New York Times*, 8 June 1941, p. 40.

Arnold, Sarah. *Gender and Early Television: Mapping Women's Role in Emerging US and British Media, 1850–1950*, Bloomsbury Academic, 2021.

Art. "*Eleanor Roosevelt's Diamond Jubilee Plus One*." *Variety*, 12 Oct. 1960, p. 32.

_____. "*Prospects of Mankind*." *Variety*, 31 May 1961, pp. 30, 44.

_____. "*Prospects of Mankind*." *Variety*, 9 May 1962, p. 39.

Arthur, Phyllis Marie. "Gals & Gab." *Daily Variety*, 19 Mar. 1938, p. 3.

"As the Press Views the Inquiry." *Film Daily*, 31 Oct. 1947, p. 1.

Asbell, Bernard, ed. *Mother and Daughter: The Letters of Eleanor and Anna Roosevelt*, Coward, McCann and Geoghegan, 1982.

Ashley, Ted. Correspondence with ER. Franklin D. Roosevelt Presidential Library and Museum, Anna Eleanor Roosevelt Papers, Part 3, Series 54, Box 1672.

"At Screening of Paramount Victory Short." *Showmen's Trade Review*, 2 Jan. 1943, p. 40.

Bahn, Chester B. "*Rebecca* Wins Critics' Poll." *Film Daily*, 14 Jan. 1941, pp. 1, 4.

Ball, Elizabeth. "Dreams Do Come True." *TV and Radio Mirror*, Oct. 1957, p. 79.

Ball, Rick. *Meet the Press: 50 Years of History in the Making*, McGraw-Hill, 1997.

Ballesteros, Kirpi Uimonen. "HFPA in Conversation: Stanley Kramer's Legacy is Alive." Hollywood

Foreign Press Association Golden Globe Awards, 8 Aug. 2018, www.goldenglobes.com/articles/hfpa-conversation-stanley-kramers-legacy-alive.

Barnes, Aleene. "Sinatra's 35–1 Is a Winner by Longshot." *Los Angeles Times*, 16 Feb. 1960, p. A11.

Barris, Alex. *Front Page Challenge: History of a Television Legend*, Macmillan Canada, 1999.

———. *Front Page Challenge: The 25th Anniversary*, CBC Merchandising, 1981.

Barritt, Marjorie Rabe, Doris Attaway, and Gregory Kinney. *The University of Michigan on the Air: The Audio-Visual Education Center, the Television Center, and Michigan Media*, University of Michigan, 1992.

Barron, Arthur. Letter to Bennet Korn and Jack Lynn. Undated. Franklin D. Roosevelt Presidential Library and Museum, Henry Morgenthau III, Papers Relating to the Television Series: Eleanor Roosevelt: *Prospects of Mankind* (1959–1962), Series 1: Eleanor Roosevelt: *Prospects of Mankind*, Box 1, Proposed Series "The American Experience": Proposals, Program Ide, 1962–1963.

Barrymore, Lionel. As told to Cameron Shipp. "We Barrymores! Conclusion." *Saturday Evening Post*, 23 Sept. 1950, pp. 34, 172–74.

Baughman, James L. *Same Time, Same Station: Creating American Television, 1948–1961*, Johns Hopkins University Press, 2007.

"BCE Sets UTP on Ken Murray Series." *Variety*, 10 Mar. 1954, p. 45.

Beasley, Maurine H. *Eleanor Roosevelt and the Media: A Public Quest for Self-Fulfillment*, University of Illinois Press, 1987.

Beauchamp, Angela. "I Will *Not* Be Your Little China Doll: Representations of Eleanor Roosevelt in Film and Television." *Americana: The Journal of American Popular Culture (1900–Present),* Spring 2020, Volume 19, Issue 1.

Beauchamp, Cari. *Joseph P. Kennedy Presents: His Hollywood Years*, Vintage Books, 2009.

Beaufort, John. "Ralph Bellamy Stars in *Sunrise at Campobello*." *Christian Science Monitor*, 6 Oct. 1960, p. 11.

Bellamy, Ralph. *When the Smoke Hit the Fan*, Doubleday, 1979.

Berg, A. Scott. *Goldwyn: A Biography*, Ballantine Books, 1989.

Berle, Milton. "The Berle-ing Point." *Variety*, 2 July 1941, p. 2.

Bernstein, Bob. "*Mike Wallace Interview* (Net)." *The Billboard*, 2 Dec. 1957, p. 16.

"Beverly Hills." *Cincinnati Enquirer*, 21 Oct. 1940, p. 16.

Black, Allida, ed. *Courage in a Dangerous World: The Political Writings of Eleanor Roosevelt*, Columbia University Press, 1999.

Black, Ruby. *Eleanor Roosevelt: A Biography*, Duell, Sloan and Pearce, 1940.

"Bob Hope-*Jones* Wins B.O. Stakes for July; *Neptune, Steal* Follow." *Variety*, 3 Aug. 1949, pp. 5, 20.

Boettiger, John, Jr. *A Love in Shadow*, Norton, 1978.

Bogart, Leo. *The Age of Television*. Frederick Ungar, 1956.

Brady, Thomas. "Forecast for 1942." *New York Times*, 4 Jan. 1942, p. X5.

———. "Hollywood Briefs." *New York Times*, 4 May 1947, p. X5.

———. "Hollywood Slack." *New York Times*, 23 Feb. 1947, p. X5.

———. "Metro's Atomic Headache." *New York Times*, 16 June 1946, p. X1.

Braude, Beatrice. Letter to Loretta. 26 Feb. 1962. Franklin D. Roosevelt Presidential Library and Museum. Henry Morgenthau III Papers Relating to the Television Series: Eleanor Roosevelt: *Prospects of Mankind*, 1959–1962, Series 1: Eleanor Roosevelt: *Prospects of Mankind*, Box 1, Correspondence—Beatrice Braud [sic], 1962.

Breen, Joseph I. Letter to M.J. Siegel. 23 Sept. 1940. Motion Picture Association of America, Production Code Administration Records, *Melody Ranch*, 1940, Margaret Herrick Library, Academy of Motion Picture Arts and Sciences.

Brinson, Susan L. *Personal and Public Interests: Frieda B. Hennock and the Federal Communications Commission*, Praeger, 2002.

"Broad Changes on Schedule for U.S. Film Fare." *New York Herald Tribune*, 1 Feb. 1942, p. E5.

"Broadcasters Quiet on Pay-See Issue." *Broadcasting Telecasting*, 16 May 1955, p. 114.

"Broadcasting Pulls on the Newstand." *Sponsor*, 26 Sept. 1949, pp. 21–23, 42, 47.

"Broadway Bows for 3 from 20th Cet." *Motion Picture Daily*, 8 Aug. 1951, p. 2.

Broeske, Pat H. "Telling It Like It Was." *Los Angeles Times*, 12 Aug. 1990, latimes.com/archives/la-xpm-1990-08-12-ca-693-story.html.

Burnup, Peter. "*Great Day*." *Motion Picture Herald*, 12 May 1945, p. 59.

Cagney, James. *Cagney by Cagney*, Pocket Books, 1976.

Carter, Stephen L. *Invisible: The Forgotten Story of the Black Woman Lawyer Who Took Down America's Most Powerful Mobster*, Henry Holt, 2018.

"Castro Is Offered 100 Tractors in Two Weeks, Rest Later." *Philadelphia Inquirer*, 9 June 1961, p. 2.

"Celebs in Socko Performance for F.D.R. Despite Weather, Driving Ban." *Variety*, 3 Feb. 1943, p. 4.

Chapple, John B. Letter to Motion Picture Censorship Bureau. 3 Feb. 1949, Motion Picture Association of America, Production Code Administration Records, *Not Wanted*, 1949, Margaret Herrick Library, Academy of Motion Picture Arts and Sciences, digitalcollections.oscars.org/digital/collection/p15759coll30/id/10585.

Chase, Sam. "*Today with Mrs. Roosevelt*." *The Billboard*, 25 Mar. 1950, p. 12.

"Chatter." *Variety*, 10 Nov. 1954, p. 70.

"The Chevrolet Golden Anniversary Show" record. UCLA Film and Television Archive. search.library.ucla.edu/permalink/01UCS_

LAL/1hnia1h/alma991968763506533. Accessed 8 Oct. 2022.

Childs, Marquis W. "Washington Calling." *Newsday* (Long Island, NY), 20 Sept. 1956, p. 46.

China: Shadow on the Summit advertisement. *Evening Star* (Washington, D.C.), 15 May 1960, p. B-6.

Churchill, Sarah. *Keep on Dancing: An Autobiography*, Coward, McCann & Geoghegan, 1981.

"Cinema: *The Roosevelt Story*." *Time*, 15 Oct. 1951, content.time.com/time/magazine/article/0,9171, 815567,00.html.

"CIO and NAM Both Have Same Idea." *Variety*, 15 Oct. 1947, pp. 1, 48.

Clem. "Plays Abroad." *Variety*, 18 Apr. 1945, p. 50.

Clemenko, Harold B. "The Armchair Spectator." *TV Guide*, 30 June 1951, p. 25.

College News Conference transcript. 7 Dec. 1958, John F. Kennedy Presidential Library and Museum, Theodore Sorensen Papers, Box 25, Eleanor Roosevelt.

Collier, Lionel. "Shop for Your Films." *Picturegoer*, 7 July 1945, p. 12.

Collier, Peter. *The Roosevelts: An American Saga*, Simon & Schuster, 1994.

Collingwood, Charles. "The Third Man." *Variety*, 3 Jan. 1951, p. 110.

"The Congress: Black's White." *Time*, 24 Jan. 1938, content.time.com/time/magazine/article/0,9171, 758933,00.html.

Connolly, Mike. "Rambling Reporter." *Hollywood Reporter*, 17 Feb. 1960, p. 2.

Conroy, Sarah Booth. "In Eleanor Roosevelt's Orbit." *Washington Post*, 11 Mar. 1996, washingtonpost.com/archive/lifestyle/1996/03/11/ in-eleanor-roosevelts-orbit.

"Controversy Keynotes *Storm Center* Campaign." *Film Bulletin*, 20 Aug. 1956, p. 26.

Conway, Mike. *The Origins of Television News in America: The Visualizers of CBS in the 1940s*, Peter Lang, 2012.

Cook, Blanche Wiesen. *Eleanor Roosevelt, Volume 1: The Early Years, 1884–1933*, Penguin Books, 1992.

_____. *Eleanor Roosevelt, Volume 2: The Defining Years, 1933–1938*, Penguin Books, 1999.

_____. *Eleanor Roosevelt, Volume 3: The War Years and After, 1939–1962*, Viking, 2016.

Cotton, Paul. "On Television." *Des Moines Register*, 8 May 1951, p. 9.

_____. "On Television." *Des Moines Register*, 22 June 1954, p. 9.

Courageous Mr. Penn advertisement. *Evening Star* (Washington, D.C.), 28 Sept. 1945, p. A-11.

Cremmen, Mary. "Clement's Fiery Speech Ended Convention Apathy." *Boston Daily Globe*, 14 Aug. 1956, p. 37.

_____. "TV Notebook." *Daily Boston Globe*, 12 Apr. 1954, p. 7.

"Criticism of Her TV Commercials Fails to Trouble Mrs. Roosevelt." *Hartford* (CT) *Courant*, 2 Mar. 1959, p. 16A.

Croce, Arlene. "*Sunrise at Campobello*." *Sight and Sound*, Vol. 30, No. 2, Spring 1961, p. 89.

Crosby, John. "*Reading Aloud* Credit to TV." *Daily Colonist* (Victoria, BC), 30 Jan. 1960, p. 25.

_____. "Sidelights on History." *New York Herald Tribune*, 14 Feb. 1950, p. 17.

"Crosby, Mrs. FDR as Pic Envoys for ECA." *Variety*, 16 Aug. 1950, p. 1.

Crosson, John, and Dick Lee. "Mayoral Boys Do Their Acts on Mrs. R.'s TV." *New York Daily News*, 6 Nov. 1950, pp. 2C, 12C.

Crowther, Bosley. "Cinematic Close-Up: *Sunrise at Campobello* Play versus Film." *New York Times*, 2 Oct. 1960, p. X1.

"Curb on M'Carthy Put Up to Senate." *New York Times*, 12 Apr. 1954, p. 10.

C.V.L. "Motherhood and the Home." *Oklahoma News*, 31 Oct. 1937, p. B7.

Daly, Phil M. "Along the Rialto." *Film Daily*, 30 Oct. 1944, p. 4.

_____. "Make Way for *Midway*!" *Film Daily*, 10 Sept. 1942, p. 6.

Daniels, Jonathan. *The Time Between the Wars*, Doubleday, 1966.

Danzig, Fred. "Sinatra Gives Nice Salute to Ladies of U.S." *Courier-Post* (Camden, NJ), 16 Feb. 1960, p. 23.

Darnton, Charles. "Roosevelts Merry as Marx Bros.!" *Screenland*, Sept. 1938, pp. 20–21, 86–87.

"David Ogilvy on *David Letterman*." Facebook, facebook.com/ogilvy/videos/1015633152 5927994. Accessed 21 Sept. 2022.

"Demand War Pix Accessories in Probe." *Film Daily*, 5 Sept. 1941, pp. 1, 3.

"Democrats Gaining GOP Support for Defense of Acheson." *Greenville Daily Advocate* (Greenville, OH), 27 Mar. 1950, p. 10.

"Democrats Hit Leadership." *Christian Science Monitor*, 21 Oct. 1957, p. 3.

Deo, V. "*Meet the Press* TV Program Recommended Highly for H.S. Students as well as Adults." *Times Journal* (Vineland, NJ), 18 Jan. 1951, p. 15.

"Desegregate Harlem, Mrs. FDR Bids." *Newsday* (Long Island, NY), 17 Sept. 1956, p. 2.

"Despite Censorship Protest, Robeson TVer Won't Be Rescheduled." *Variety*, 5 Apr. 1950, p. 34.

Devane, James. "Marco Polo Goes Exploring on Two Shows at 4 P.M." *Cincinnati Enquirer*, 20 June 1954, pp. 4–11.

"Dinah Shore and Jackie Gleason Shows Tie for Arbitron Weekend Honors." *Daily Variety*, 11 Oct. 1960, p. 8.

Doan, Dorothy. "How to Be a Hostess." *Radio and Television Mirror*, Vol. 36, No. 3, Aug. 1951, p. 74.

"Documentary F.D.R. Biog. Preeming in N.Y. Apr. 12." *Hollywood Reporter*, 10 Mar. 1947, p. 4.

Doherty, Thomas. *Pre-Code Hollywood: Sex, Immorality, and Insurrection in American Cinema, 1930–1934*, Columbia University Press, 1999.

Douglas, Helen Gahagan. *A Full Life*, Doubleday, 1982.

Douglas, Melvyn, and Tom Arthur. *See You at the Movies: The Autobiography of Melvyn Douglas*, Lanham, 1986.

Driscoll, Joseph. "Convention Sidelights." *St. Louis Post-Dispatch*, 23 July 1952, p. 4A.

Drury, Allen. "Hall Cries Foul! at Rivals' Blows." *New York Times*, 5 Nov. 1956, p. 38.

Durant, Alta. "Gab." *Daily Variety*, 23 Mar. 1939, p. 3.

Dyer, Peter John. "Sunrise at Campobello." *Monthly Film Bulletin*, Vol. 28, No. 324, 1 Jan. 1961, p. 96.

"East Meets West Down South." *Box Office*, 11 Feb. 1939, p. 36.

East, Weston. "Here's Hollywood." *Screenland*, July 1941, p. 65.

_____. "Here's Hollywood." *Screenland*, Oct. 1946, p. 11.

Eastman, Arthur A. Letter. "Hating for Pleasure." *South Bend* (IN) *Tribune*, 3 Dec. 1940, p. 6.

"Ecuadorean Chief Visits Birthplace." *New York Times*, 25 June 1951, p. 17.

Editors of *TV Guide*. *TV Guide: Guide to TV*, Barnes & Noble Books, 2004.

"Educational Television Highlights." *Tampa Bay Times Sunday TV-Radio Dial*, 1 May 1960, p. 5.

Edwards, Catherine C. "Family Movie Guide." *Parents' Magazine*, Apr. 1947, p. 84.

Edwards, Willard. "Here's Story on Second Day at Convention." *Chicago Tribune*, 23 July 1952, p. 1.

"Einstein Warns Bomb Race Threatens Annihilation." *Daily News* (Los Angeles, CA), 13 Feb. 1950, p. 10.

"Eleanor and Anna Roosevelt Broadcast Over KECA" transcript. 18 Feb. 1949. Motion Picture Association of America, Production Code Administration Records, *Not Wanted*, 1949, Margaret Herrick Library, Academy of Motion Picture Arts and Sciences, digitalcollections.oscars.org/digital/collection/p15759coll30/id/10600.

"The Eleanor and Anna Roosevelt Program." The Eleanor Roosevelt Papers Project, George Washington University, erpapers.columbian.gwu.edu/eleanor-and-anna-roosevelt-program. Accessed 29 Dec. 2020.

"Eleanor Gets OCD Jobs for Rhythmic Dancer, Film Actor." *Imperial Valley Press* (El Centro, CA), 6 Feb. 1942, p. 1.

"Eleanor Roosevelt." *T-V Stars*, Apr. 1951, pp. 54–55.

"Eleanor Roosevelt and Segregation." *St. Paul Recorder*, 21 Sept. 1956, p. 2.

"Eleanor Roosevelt at 75 Embarks on 39-Wk. Series for Flamingo." *Variety*, 16 Sept. 1959, p. 1.

"Eleanor Roosevelt Becomes Glamor Girl for Sake of Movies." *Tampa Morning Tribune*, 22 July 1940, p. 7.

"Eleanor Roosevelt Commends Industry as V Drive Opens." *Motion Picture Daily*, 30 Oct. 1945, p. 1.

"The Eleanor Roosevelt Diamond Jubilee Series: Involved in Mankind" proposal. Franklin D. Roosevelt Presidential Library and Museum, Anna Eleanor Roosevelt Papers, Part 3, 1884–1964, Series 55: Correspondence, 1957–1962, Box 1854, Morgenthau, Henry, III.

"Eleanor Roosevelt in Living Room Set." Getty Images, gettyimages.com/detail/news-photo/former-first-lady-eleanor-roosevelt-sits-in-an-armchair-on-news-photo/2412785. Accessed 18 Sept. 2022.

Eleanor Roosevelt, John Kennedy, and the Election of 1960: A Project of the Eleanor Roosevelt Papers, ed. by Allida Black, June Hopkins, John Sears, Christopher Alhambra, Mary Jo Binker, Christopher Brick, John S. Emrich, Eugenia Gusev, Kristen E. Gwinn, and Bryan D. Peery. Model Editions Partnership, 2003. Electronic version based on unpublished letters. Accessed 28 Dec. 2020.

"Eleanor Roosevelt Scores Senate Probe of Films on Radio Broadcast." *Motion Picture Daily*, 20 Oct. 1941, p. 1.

"Elliott Forms TV Company for Roosevelts." *Statesman Journal* (Salem, OR), 20 June 1951, p. 3.

Emanuel, Jay. "*Midway* Terrific." *The Exhibitor*, 9 Sept. 1942, p. 8.

"Emphasis on S.A. in Jukepix Made East." *Variety*, 25 Dec. 1940, p. 4.

Entin, Jack. "Screenings: *Sunrise at Campobello*." *The Clearing House*, Vol. 35, No. 4, Dec. 1960, p. 253.

"Experienced Lady (1st) Invites Bids to Make Her a Television Star." *Variety*, 18 Mar. 1959, p. 1.

"The Face Is Familiar." *New York Times*, 14 Nov. 1960, p. 12.

Fairbanks, Douglas, Jr. *The Salad Days*, Doubleday, 1988.

Farrant, Lawrence. "Ad Says Children Need TV; Public Calls Admen Addled." *Editor and Publisher*, 25 Nov. 1950, pp. 5, 56.

Fates, Gil. *What's My Line? The Inside History of TV's Most Famous Panel Show*, Prentice-Hall, 1978.

"FCC's Wall St. Glamor Gal." *Variety*, 26 May 1948, p. 23.

"F.D.R. Film Brings Tears and Cheers." *Los Angeles Times*, 22 Aug. 1947, p. 1.

"FDR Story Royal Gift." *Hollywood Reporter*, 20 Nov. 1947, p. 15.

"FDR's Widow Escapes Movie Bulb Explosion." *The Times* (San Mateo, CA), 6 Nov. 1954, p. 1.

"Film Dramatizes Work of Women in Defense Program." *Women's Wear Daily*, 8 Dec. 1941, p. 3.

"Film of *Midway* Released by Navy." *New York Times*, 15 Sept. 1942, p. 19.

"Film on Home-Fronters." *Variety*, 3 Feb. 1943, p. 4.

"Films Must 'Keep Them Laughing.'" *Film Daily*, 19 Dec. 1941, p. 1.

FilmStruck UK. "Martin Scorsese on Jean Renoir's *The River*." YouTube video, 9 May 2018, youtube.com/watch?v=2w7H9pEby0M.

"First Documentary for African Gold Coast." *Film Daily*, 18 Dec. 1947, p. 7.

"The First Lady Hears Heifetz." *Box Office*, 29 July 1939, p. 33.

"First Lady Opposes Film Censorship in Chi. Talk." *Film Daily*, 18 Mar. 1940, p. 2.

"Flamingo Drops Plans for Eleanor's TV Show." *Variety*, 17 Feb. 1960, p. 23.

Flannery, Harry. "As It Looks to Flannery." *Daily Variety*, 25 Sept. 1947, p. 3.

"Foundation President Starts Dimes March on Thursday Night." *Evening Star* (Washington, D.C.), 9 Jan. 1944, p. C-10.

"4 Senators Denounce McCarthy's Charges." *New York Times*, 27 Mar. 1950, p. 8.

Francis, Arlene. *Arlene Francis: A Memoir*, Simon & Schuster, 1978.

Francis, Dale. "Guide to Family Entertainment." *The Family Digest*, June 1959, p. 40.

"Francis *Visit* Pilot Pic Readied with Lindsays; Prep Young Monolog." *Variety*, 20 Aug. 1952, p. 27.

The Frank Sinatra Timex Show: Here's to the Ladies script. Franklin D. Roosevelt Presidential Library and Museum, Anna Eleanor Roosevelt Papers, Part 2, Series 50, Box 1423.

Frankel, Max. "Stevenson Backs Federated Congo." *New York Times*, 31 Mar. 1961, p. 1.

"Freedom from Fear to Be Theme of Roosevelt Movie." *Austin Statesman*, 19 Mar. 1947, p. 5.

"Freedoms Award to Mrs. Roosevelt." *New York Times*, 12 May 1950, p. 40.

"Friday Morning." *New York Herald Tribune*, 1 Apr. 1956, p. P45.

"From the Managing Editor's Desk." *The Tablet* (Brooklyn, NY), 19 Sept. 1953, p. 11.

Fuchs, Lawrence H. "The Lady and the Senator." *Brandeis Review*, Fall 1984, Vol. 4, No. 1, p. 8.

_____. "Oral History Interview—JFK #1, 11/28/1966." John F. Kennedy Presidential Library and Museum. jfklibrary.org/asset-viewer/archives/JFKOH/Fuchs,%20Lawrence%20H/JFKOH-LAHF-01/JFKOH-LAHF-01.

Furman, Bess. "New Hall of Fame Hails Polio Fight." *New York Times*, 3 Jan. 1958, p. 25.

Galbraith, John Kenneth. *Name-Dropping: From FDR On*, Houghton Mifflin, 1999.

Gannon, Mary. "Television: The Local Businessman's Most Powerful Sales Medium." *Television*, Feb. 1950, p. 22.

Gardella, Kay. "Sinatra's Valentine Special Soars with Lena Horne." *New York Daily News*, 16 Feb. 1960, p. 46.

Gardner, Hy. "Ben Hecht Is Biographer for Pal Charles MacArthur." *Oakland Tribune*, 9 Jan. 1957, p. S-11.

_____. "Television Tea with Mrs. FDR." *Parade Magazine*, 9 Apr. 1950, p. 18.

Garson, Greer. Letter to Dore Schary. 8 Aug. 1960. Wisconsin Historical Society, Dore Schary Papers, G, General, 1941 October–1974 January, undated Box 98, folders 7–9, Garson, Greer.

Gerckhen, Richard. "Production Report: *Sunrise at Campobello*." *Film Quarterly*, Vol. 14, No. 2, Winter 1960, p. 62.

Gill, Brendan. "The Current Cinema." *New Yorker*, 8 Oct. 1960, p. 107.

"The *Globe*'s Complete Television Schedules for this Week." *Daily Boston Globe*, 6 Dec. 1959, p. A16.

"Goldwyn on Duals and U.S. Salzburgs." *Motion Picture Herald*, 29 July 1939, p. 58.

Gomery, Douglas. *A History of Broadcasting in the United States*, Wiley-Blackwell, 2008.

Goodwin, Doris Kearns. *No Ordinary Time, Franklin and Eleanor Roosevelt: The Home Front in World War II*, Touchstone, 1994.

"GOP Hitches its Satiric Donkey Serenade to Oscar." *Daily Variety*, 5 Apr. 1961, p. 3.

Gould, Jack. "*Intertel* Program Shows Clash Between the Old and the New in England." *New York Times*, 16 Oct. 1961, p. 59.

_____. "Television in Review." *New York Times*, 19 Feb. 1950, p. X11.

_____. "TV: A Study of Clinton." *New York Times*, 7 Jan. 1957, p. 53.

_____. "TV: Control of Satellites." *New York Times*, 7 May 1962, p. 63.

_____. "TV: Dubious Judgment." *New York Times*, 17 Feb. 1959, p. 63.

_____. "TV: Golf Mystery." *New York Times*, 18 Apr. 1960, p. 59.

_____. "TV: U.S. Propaganda." *New York Times*, 29 May 1961, p. 37.

Grace, Arthur. "Eleanor Dignified; *Turn of Fate* Bad." *Miami News*, 25 Nov. 1957, p. 6B.

Graff, Robert. Letter to Henry Morgenthau III. 6 Sept. 1962. Franklin D. Roosevelt Presidential Library and Museum, Henry Morgenthau III Papers Relating to the Television Series: Eleanor Roosevelt: *Prospects of Mankind*, 1959–1962, Series 1: Eleanor Roosevelt: *Prospects of Mankind*, Box 1, Proposed Series *The American Experience*: Proposals, Program Ide, 1962–1963.

Grant, Hank. "Television Reviews." *Hollywood Reporter*, 17 Feb. 1960, p. 11.

Gray, Gordon L. *Television and the National Nominating Conventions of 1952*, PhD dissertation, Northwestern University, 1957.

"The *Great Day*." *Picturegoer*, 28 Apr. 1945, p. 10.

"Great Entertainment." *New York Times*, 9 Jan. 1960, p. 43.

Green, Abel. "*The Beginning or the End*." *Variety*, 19 Feb. 1947, p. 8.

Griffith, Ann W. "Networks Get Ready for Election Results." *New York Herald Tribune*, 30 Oct. 1960, p. D9.

Gros. "*Prospects of Mankind*." *Variety*, 28 Sept. 1960, p. 36.

Grutzner, Charles. "Mayor and Aides Hear Complaints in a 2D TV Show." *New York Times*, 6 June 1961, p. 24.

"The Guiding Hands of the Bigger Hits: Directors." *Box Office Barometer*, 22 Feb. 1941, p. 54.

Guidry, Frederick H. "Mrs. Roosevelt's *Prospects of Mankind*." *Christian Science Monitor*, 22 Dec. 1959, p. 5.

"Guild and Schary Buy Out Bellamy Ante in *Sunrise*." *Variety*, 18 Mar. 1959, p. 89.

Gurewitsch, Edna P. *Kindred Souls: The Devoted*

Friendship of Eleanor Roosevelt and Dr. David Gurewitsch, Penguin Group, 2003.

Gwin, Yolande. "Mrs. Roosevelt's Maid Visits Here, but White House Talk Is Taboo." Atlanta Constitution, 30 July 1937, p. 9.

Gwynn, Edith. "Rambling Reporter." Hollywood Reporter, 28 Dec. 1942, p. 2.

Haakenson, Robert. A Study of Major Network Discussion Programs Televised During the Period January through May, 1951, PhD dissertation, State University of Iowa, 1952.

"Harrington School News." Milford Chronicle (DE), 26 Oct. 1956, p. 25.

Harris, Radie. "Broadway Runaround." Daily Variety, 21 June 1946, p. 8.

Harrison, Bernie. "The Wall Lake Bit Is Out, Says Andy." Evening Star (Washington, D.C.), 6 Dec. 1962, p. B-9.

Hartshorn, Lewis. Alger Hiss, Whittaker Chambers and the Case That Ignited McCarthyism, E-book, McFarland, 2013.

"Headliners." New York Times, 2 Apr. 1939, p. 125.

Hecht, Ben. "A Diplomat Spikes a Cannon." 1001 Afternoons in New York, Viking Press, 1941, pp. 25–28.

Hedgeman, Ann. "Letter to the Editors." St. Paul Recorder, 27 July 1951, p. 4.

"Heirs Authorize FDR Film Story." Variety, 15 Dec. 1954, p. 1.

Henry, Bill. "By the Way." Los Angeles Times, 17 May 1950, p. 29.

Henry, Richard. Eleanor Roosevelt and Adlai Stevenson, Palgrave Macmillan, 2010.

Hepburn, Katharine. Me: Stories of My Life, Random House, 2011.

Herm. "Tele Follow-up Comment." Variety, 17 Feb. 1960, p. 31.

"Hershey for 2 Years as U.M.T. Minimum." New York Times, 20 Nov. 1950, p. 16.

Heyn, Ernest. Letter to George T. Bye. 18 Mar. 1938, Franklin D. Roosevelt Presidential Library and Museum, Anna Eleanor Roosevelt Papers, Part 2, Series 50, Box 1406.

Hift, Fred. "Television-Radio Comment and Opinion." Motion Picture Daily, 24 Oct. 1951, p. 4.

Hill, Gladwin. "Convention Limps to Dispirited End." New York Times, 27 July 1952, p. 26.

Hillman, Donald S. Letter to Robert B. Hudson. 9 June 1960. Wisconsin Historical Society, National Educational Television Papers, Series 3, Vice President for Development Records, 1957–1966, Box 6, Folder 5, Prospects of Mankind 1959–1961.

_____. Letter to Henry Morgenthau III. 9 May 1961. Wisconsin Historical Society, National Educational Television Papers, Series 3, Vice President for Development Records, 1957–1966, Box 6, Folder 5, Prospects of Mankind 1959–1961.

Hobby Lobby advertisement. Box Office, 28 Sept. 1940, p. 13.

Hobson, Harold. "Great Day, Irene, Will Hay." Christian Science Monitor, 7 Apr. 1945, p. 10.

Hoffman, Irving. "Roosevelt Story Splits Press into 2 Political Camps." Hollywood Reporter, 27 Aug. 1947, p. 11.

_____. "Tales of Hoffman." Hollywood Reporter, 26 July 1937, p. 3.

_____. "Tales of Hoffman." Hollywood Reporter, 17 Mar. 1947, p. 3.

"Hollywood's Atomic Dud." Newsweek, 3 Mar. 1947, p. 81.

Hopper, Hedda. "Hedda Hopper's Hollywood." Los Angeles Times, 19 Mar. 1938, p. A7.

_____. "Hollywood." New York Daily News, 21 Feb. 1947, p. 13C.

_____. "Looking at Hollywood." Chicago Daily Tribune, 25 Mar. 1947, p. 21.

_____. "Looking at Hollywood." Chicago Daily Tribune, 11 Nov. 1954, p. C4.

_____. "Studios Theater Gossip." Los Angeles Times, 26 Mar. 1939, p. C3.

The Hot Seat advertisement. New York Times, 12 Oct. 1952, p. X13.

Hughes, Alice. "A Woman's New York." Journal Herald (Dayton, OH), 15 Mar. 1950, p. 23.

Humphrey, Hal. "Two Hits and a Miss." Mirror News (Los Angeles, CA), 28 Oct. 1958, p. 4.

_____. "Video Tape—TV's Biggest Weapon." Detroit Free Press, 1 Mar. 1960, p. 32.

"Hurley Holds Yalta Opened China to Reds." New York Times, 17 Apr. 1950, p. 3.

"H'wood Victory Caravan Set for Washington Bow." Film Daily, 30 Apr. 1942, pp. 1, 6.

Hyatt, Donald B. Letter to ER. 2 Oct. 1959. Franklin D. Roosevelt Presidential Library and Museum, Anna Eleanor Roosevelt Papers, Part 3, 1884–1964, Series 55: Correspondence, 1957–1962, Box 1856, National Broadcasting Company.

Hyatt, Wesley. The Encyclopedia of Daytime Television, Billboard Books, 1997.

"If FDR Biopic Okayed, Terms Are Called Private by President's Widow." Variety, 23 Mar. 1955, p. 5.

"In Rochester, New York ... P.S. Stands for Public Service at WHEC-TV." Sponsor, 22 Oct 1962, p. 54.

"In the Newsreels." The Exhibitor, 26 Jan. 1944, p. 34.

"The Inaugural Gala." Variety, 25 Jan. 1961, p. 64.

"India-U.S. Ties Aided by Movie Premiere." New York Times, 4 Mar. 1952, p. 3.

"Indian Film Delegation to Arrive Mon. for US Tour." Motion Picture Daily, 10 Sept. 1952, p. 2.

"Inside Television." Variety, 22 Feb. 1950, p. 35.

"ITOA Asks Trade Practice Parley." Motion Picture Herald, 22 June 1946, p. 14.

"It's Corn ... but Sponsors Love It." Broadcasting Telecasting, 19 Dec. 1949, pp. 28–29, 50.

Janeway, Elizabeth. "First Lady of the U.N." New York Times Magazine, 22 Oct. 1950, p. SM-7.

"Jazz Opening Here Launches New Season." Motion Picture Daily, 13 Jan. 1953, p. 2.

Jedlicka, Al, Jr. Letter. "Sheds Tear for Maligned Nazis." Cicero (IL) Life, 18 Sept.1940, p. 6.

John Huston: The Man, the Movies, the Maverick,

directed by Frank Martin, Turner Home Entertainment, 1989, VHS.

Johnson, Walter, ed. *The Papers of Adlai E. Stevenson*, Little, Brown, 1972.

Johnston, Laurie. "Einstein Sees Bid to Annihilation in Hydrogen Bomb." *New York Times*, 13 Feb. 1950, p. 1.

Judkis, Maura. "Lincoln biopics go back to the 'talkies.'" *Washington Post*, 14 Nov. 2012, washingtonpost.com/blogs/going-out-gurus/post/lincoln-biopics-go-back-to-the-talkies/2012/11/14/7c725f30-2e83-11e2-9ac2-1c61452669c3_blog.html.

Kahn, E.J., Jr. "The Years Alone." *The 40s: The Story of a Decade, The New Yorker*, E-book, Random House, 2014. Reprinted from 12 June 1948.

Kauffmann, Stanley. "Movies: Two Versions of the Truth." *New Republic*, 17 Oct. 1960, p. 21.

Kaufman, Dave. "On All Channels." *Daily Variety*, 28 Feb. 1962, p. 8.

Kelley, Andy. "After the Ball Is Over." *Variety*, 3. Feb. 1943, p. 4.

Kent, Frank R. "Mrs. FDR and Truman Put on a Good Show but Carried Little Weight at Chicago." *Lebanon* (PA) *Daily News*, 18 Aug. 1956, p. 6.

"Key to Dynamic Period." *Kansas City Times*, 7 July 1957, p. 9A.

Keyishian, Harry. "The 'Confidence' President: Franklin D. Roosevelt in Film." *Presidents in the Movies: American History and Politics on Screen*, edited by Iwan W. Morgan, Palgrave Macmillan, 2011, pp. 109–31.

_____. *Screening Politics: The Politician in American Movies, 1931–2001*, Scarecrow Press, 2003.

Knebel, Fletcher. "Potomac Fever." *Evening Star* (Washington, D.C.), 26 Feb. 1959, p. A-21.

Koppes, Clayton. *Hollywood Goes to War: How Politics, Profits, and Propaganda Shaped World War II Movies*, Free Press, 1987.

"Korean War Aided Peace—Acheson." *Atlanta Constitution*, 2 Oct. 1950, p. 2.

Korn, Bennet. Letter to ER. 7 Sept. 1962. Franklin D. Roosevelt Presidential Library and Museum, Bennett [sic] H. Korn Papers, 1960–1962, Box 1.

_____. "Recollections of Mrs. Roosevelt." Franklin D. Roosevelt Presidential Library and Museum, Bennett [sic] H. Korn Papers, 1960–1962, Box 1.

Kramer, Stanley. *A Mad, Mad, Mad, Mad World: A Life in Hollywood*, Harcourt, 1997.

"Labor Eyes TV." *Broadcasting Telecasting*, 25 Aug. 1952, p. 60.

Lake, Veronica. *Veronica: The Autobiography of Veronica Lake*, Dean Street Press, 2020.

Lamour, Dorothy. *My Side of the Road*, Prentice-Hall, 1980.

Lash, Joseph. *Eleanor and Franklin*, Norton, 1971.

_____. *Eleanor Roosevelt: A Friend's Memoir*, Doubleday, 1964.

_____. *Eleanor: The Years Alone*, New American Library, 1972.

_____. *A World of Love: Eleanor Roosevelt and Her Friends, 1943–62*, McGraw-Hill, 1984.

Lasky, Victor. "G.O.P. Campaign Film Uses Democratic Cast." *Evening Star* (Washington, D.C.), 26 July 1960, p. A-3.

"Law for Isolation of Addicts Urged." *New York Times*, 2 July 1951, p. 10.

Lawrence, David. "Wide Confusion Is Noted on Right to Work Issue." *New York Herald Tribune*, 28 Oct. 1958, p. 21.

"Lena Horne Visiting Eleanor Roosevelt." Getty Images, gettyimages.ie/detail/news-photo/ladies-social-although-their-fields-are-widely-different-news-photo/515257332. Accessed 17 Sept. 2022.

Lerner, Barron H. "Final Diagnosis." *Washington Post*, 8 Feb. 2000, washingtonpost.com/archive/lifestyle/wellness/2000/02/08/final-diagnosis/ea7e466f-8846-443f-affd-bfb4cc5f8cca.

"Let's See What the Pipe Line Has to Say." *Box Office Digest*, 16 Sept. 1940, p. 4.

Lewis, Dorothy. Letter to ER. 10 Nov. 1950. Franklin D. Roosevelt Presidential Library and Museum, Anna Eleanor Roosevelt Papers, Part 3, 1884–1964, Series 53: Correspondence, 1945–1952, Box 1594, Lewis, Dorothy.

Libbey, James K. *Dear Alben: Mr. Barkley of Kentucky*, University Press of Kentucky, 1979.

Library of Congress Catalog, Motion Pictures and Filmstrips, The National Union Catalog, 1958–1962, Vol. 53, Rowman & Littlefield, 1963.

Lilienthal, David E. *The Journals of David E. Lilienthal, Volume II, The Atomic Energy Years 1945–1950*, Harper & Row, 1964.

_____. *The Journals of David E. Lilienthal, Volume III, Venturesome Years 1950–1955*, Harper & Row, 1964.

_____. *The Journals of David E. Lilienthal, Volume IV, The Road to Change 1955–1959*, Harper & Row, 1964.

Lipscott, Alan. "Yeh, Let's Have Culture in TV." *Variety*, 4 Feb. 1961, p. 87.

"Literati." *Variety*, 27 Aug. 1941, p. 55.

Liz. "*Prospects of Mankind* (The Peace Corps)." *Variety*, 15 Mar. 1961, p. 35.

Lohman, Sidney. "News from the Studios." *New York Times*, 2 Apr. 1950, p. 105.

_____. "News of TV and Radio." *New York Times*, 6 Apr. 1952, p. X13.

Lonergan, Phil. "First Lady in Filmland." *Picturegoer*, 23 Apr. 1938, pp. 6–7.

Lowery, Cynthia. "Mrs. R. Has High Hopes." *Daily Home News* (New Brunswick, NJ), 16 Feb. 1960, p. 15.

_____. "TV Show Honoring Mrs. Roosevelt Lauded." *Evening Star* (Washington, D.C.), 26 Oct. 1959, p. B-23.

Loy, Myrna. *Being and Becoming*, Knopf, 1987.

Luraschi, Luigi. Carbon of memo to Sol C. Siegel. 26 Feb. 1942, ID# 71548334, Paramount Pictures Production Records, Margaret Herrick Library, Academy of Motion Picture Arts and Sciences.

Lyon, Herb. "Tower Ticker." *Chicago Daily Tribune*, 21 Feb. 1960, p. 14.

Lyons, Leonard. "Gossip of the Nation." *Philadelphia Inquirer*, 12 June 1950, p. 17.

Lytell, Bert. "Stage Door Canteen." *Variety*, 6 Jan. 1943, p. 9.

"Makes It Official." *Variety*, 12 Mar. 1941, p. 4.

"Man Hours." *Motion Picture Herald*, 6 Nov. 1943, p. 9.

"Many Celebrities at Roosevelt Film." *New York Times*, 22 Aug. 1947, p. 11.

Marc, David. "Behind the TV Scenes with JFK and Eleanor Roosevelt." *Television Quarterly*, Vol. 33, No. 1, Spring 2002, p. 61.

Marshall, Sylvan M. Letter to ER. 29 May 1958. Franklin D. Roosevelt Presidential Library and Museum, Anna Eleanor Roosevelt Papers, Part 3, 1884–1964, Series 55: Correspondence, 1957–1962, Box 1856, National Broadcasting Company.

Martin, Louis. "Off the Cuff." *Daily Defender* (Chicago, IL), 30 Oct. 1958, p. 8.

Martin, Mildred. "British Anti-Nazi Film in a Special Category." *Philadelphia Inquirer*, 25 Aug. 1940, p. 8.

_____. "*Pacific Blackout* at Stanton." *Philadelphia Inquirer*, 2 Mar. 1942, p. ad13.

"May Craig to Interview Mrs. Roosevelt on Air." *Portland* (Maine) *Press Herald*, 7 Apr. 1949, p. 17.

"*McCall* Campaign on Roosevelt Memoirs." *Broadcasting Telecasting*, 23 May 1949, p. 74.

McCann, James. Letter to ER. 2 June 1958. eBay auction listing, ebay.com/itm/120669505852. Accessed 19 Nov. 2022.

McDuffie, Elizabeth. *The Back Door of the White House*, unpublished memoir. Elizabeth and Irvin McDuffie papers, Robert W. Woodruff Library, Atlanta University Center, Box 2, Folder 3.

_____. Letter to Mrs. Marsh. 1 Jan. 1938. University of Georgia Special Collections Libraries, Margaret Mitchell family papers, Box 52, File 37.

McGilligan, Patrick. "Feminist Movie from 1931 Is Hit of Women's Film Series." *Boston Globe*, 4 May 1974, p. 15.

McNeil, Alex. *Total Television: A Comprehensive Guide to Programming from 1948 to the Present*, Penguin Books, 1991.

McNellis, Maggi. "Maggi's Private Wire." *Screenland*, Mar. 1954, p. 73.

McPartlin, R.F. "TV Diary." *Boston Daily Globe*, 14 Feb. 1951, p. 31.

McPherson, J.J. "As Personal as Possible." *Educational Screen*, May 1954, p. 178.

"Mebbe He's Prejudiced." *Variety*, 29 Mar. 1950, p. 33.

"*Meet the Press*." *Capital Times* (Madison, WI), 15 Sept. 1956, p. 17.

"*Meet the Press* Interview." *What I Hope to Leave Behind: The Essential Essays of Eleanor Roosevelt*, Allida Black, ed, Carlson, 1995, pp. 447–55.

"Metro Dickering to Film FDR's Career." *Variety*, 19 Feb. 1947, pp. 1, 48.

Michaeli, Ethan. *The Defender: How the Legendary Black Newspaper Changed America*, Houghton Mifflin Harcourt, 2016.

Michaelis, David. *Eleanor: A Life*, E-book, Simon & Schuster, 2020.

Miller, Llewellyn. "Important Pictures." *Hollywood*, Vol. 29, No. 10, Oct. 1940, pp. 20–21.

"Miniature Reviews." *Variety*, 2 May 1945, p. 27.

Minow, Newton N. "How We Should Remember John F. Kennedy." *The Atlantic*, 21 Nov. 2013, theatlantic.com/politics/archive/2013/11/how-we-should-remember-john-f-kennedy/281665/.

_____. *Inside the Presidential Debates: Their Improbable Past and Promising Future*, University of Chicago Press, 2008.

_____. "Television and the Public Interest." Address to the National Association of Broadcasters, Washington, D.C., 9 May 1961. americanrhetoric.com/speeches/newtonminow.htm.

Mitchell, Greg. *Tricky Dick and the Pink Lady*, Random House, 1998.

"Mme. Pandit to Sub for Mrs. FDR; Lady Astor to Meet the Press Sunday." *Atlanta Constitution*, 15 Apr. 1951, p. 12B.

"Monday." *Brattleboro* (VT) *Daily Reformer*, 19 Dec. 1959, p. 14.

Morgenthau, Henry, III. "Donna Quixote: The Adventures of Frieda Hennock." *Television Quarterly*, Vol. 26, No. 2, Spring 1992, pp. 62–63.

_____. "Educational Television Programs and Plans for Mrs. Eleanor Roosevelt 1962–63." 1 Aug. 1962. Franklin D. Roosevelt Presidential Library and Museum, Henry Morgenthau III, Papers Relating to the Television Series: Eleanor Roosevelt: *Prospects of Mankind* (1959–1962), Series 1: Eleanor Roosevelt: *Prospects of Mankind*, Box 1, Proposed Series "The American Experience": Proposals, Program Ide, 1962–1963.

_____. "Eleanor Roosevelt at Brandeis: A Personal Memoir." *Brandeis Review*, Fall 1984, Vol. 4, No. 1, p. 3.

_____. Letter to Adlai Stevenson. Feb. 1961. Franklin D. Roosevelt Presidential Library and Museum, Henry Morgenthau III, Papers Relating to the Television Series: Eleanor Roosevelt: *Prospects of Mankind* (1959–1962), Box 2, Folder 4, Season Correspondence.

_____. Morgenthau III, Henry correspondence. Franklin D. Roosevelt Presidential Library and Museum, Anna Eleanor Roosevelt Papers, Part 3, 1884–1964, Series 53: Correspondence, 1945–1952, Box 1606, Morgenthau, Henry, III.

_____. Morgenthau III, Henry correspondence II. Franklin D. Roosevelt Presidential Library and Museum, Anna Eleanor Roosevelt Papers, Part 3, 1884–1964, Series 55: Correspondence, 1957–1962, Box 1854, Morgenthau, Henry, III.

_____. "*Mrs. Roosevelt at Hyde Park*: A Television Program Proposal." 12 Sept. 1962. Franklin D. Roosevelt Presidential Library and Museum, Henry Morgenthau III, Papers Relating to the Television Series: Eleanor Roosevelt: *Prospects of Mankind* (1959–1962), Series 1: Eleanor Roosevelt: *Prospects of Mankind*, Box 1, Proposed Series "The American Experience": Proposals, Program Ide, 1962–1963.

_____. "A Tour of Hyde Park, Mrs. Franklin D.

Roosevelt." 23 July 1962. Franklin D. Roosevelt Presidential Library and Museum, Henry Morgenthau III, Papers Relating to the Television Series: Eleanor Roosevelt: *Prospects of Mankind* (1959–1962), Series 1: Eleanor Roosevelt: *Prospects of Mankind*, Box 1, Proposed Series "The American Experience": Proposals, Program Ide, 1962–1963.

"Morgenthau, Roosevelt in Teamup as History Repeats—This Time for AM-TV." *Variety*, 11 Oct. 1950, p. 1.

"Morse Claims Armed Forces Wasteful in Use of Manpower." *Oregon Statesman*, 19 Feb. 1951, p. 1.

"Mounting Squawks Cause Nix of Robeson on Mrs. Roosevelt's Airer." *Variety*, 15 Mar. 1950, p. 31.

"Movie Debut Made by Mrs. Roosevelt." *New York Times*, 3 May 1940, p. 23.

"*Movie-Radio Guide* Applauds Wendell Willkie." *Movie-Radio Guide*, Oct. 1941, p. 2.

"Movies Find New Mammy." *Philadelphia Inquirer*, 3 Jan. 1938, p. abd7.

"Mrs. Eleanor Roosevelt Among Name Sponsors of Non-Profit TV Show." *Variety*, 16 Feb. 1949, p. 35.

"Mrs. Eleanor Roosevelt Cites *U.N. in Action*." CBS Photo Division Press Information. ebay.com/itm/394300287620. Accessed 20 Nov 2022.

"Mrs. Eleanor Roosevelt Set for TV Guest Spot." *Variety*, 5 May 1948, p. 42.

"Mrs. Eleanor Roosevelt Speaks for Kennedy." *New York Times*, 5 Nov. 1960, p. 47.

"Mrs. Eleanor Roosevelt Speaks for Kennedy." *New York Times*, 6 Nov. 1960, p. 20X.

"Mrs. FDR as Pic Advisor?" *Variety*, 24 May 1950, p. 4.

"Mrs. FDR Is *Meet the Press* Guest." *Capital Times* (Madison, WI), 25 Oct. 1958, p. 19.

"Mrs. F.D.R. Making KTTV Pitch for Son." *Daily Variety*, 7 Sept. 1950, p. 1.

"Mrs. FDR Okays 82-Min Film on Roosevelt's Life." *Variety*, 5 Mar. 1947, pp. 1, 54.

"Mrs. FDR on Brit TV." *Variety*, 8 May 1957, p. 20.

"Mrs. FDR on LA TV to Plug for Jimmy." *The Billboard*, 16 Sept. 1950, p. 3.

"Mrs. FDR Raps Bias in North." *Daily Defender* (Chicago), 17 Sept. 1956, p. 2.

"Mrs. F.D.R. Rides Maxie's TV Hack." *Variety*, 22 Nov. 1950, p. 6.

"Mrs. FDR Says Arms to Mideast Go Down Drain." *Atlanta Constitution*, 21 Oct. 1957, p. 7.

"Mrs. FDR Says Demo Leadership Is Poor." *Ft. Lauderdale Daily News*, 21 Oct. 1957, p. 6C.

"Mrs. FDR Sees a 'Flying Saucer.'" *Philadelphia Inquirer*, 27 Mar. 1950, p. 3.

"Mrs. FDR Tops N.Y. $8,076,625 Bond Show." *Variety*, 5 Dec. 1945, p. 20.

"Mrs. FDR Will Buy First Bond Via WAC." *Film Daily*, 9 Oct. 1945, p. 1.

"Mrs. R. Rewrites Some History." *New York Daily News*, 13 Apr. 1954, p. C11.

"Mrs. Roosevelt Among Guests of Sinatra." *New York Times*, 16 Feb. 1960, p. 75.

"Mrs. Roosevelt Analyzes Trend." *New York Times*, 20 June 1960, p. 16.

"Mrs. Roosevelt Asks North Take Desegregation Lead." *Daily Boston Globe*, 17 Sept. 1956, p. 5.

"Mrs. Roosevelt Bars Any Endorsement Now." *New York Times*, 3 Jan. 1960, p. 45.

"Mrs. Roosevelt" biography. Franklin D. Roosevelt Presidential Library and Museum, Henry Morgenthau III, Papers Relating to the Television Series: Eleanor Roosevelt: *Prospects of Mankind* (1959–1962), Series 1: Eleanor Roosevelt: *Prospects of Mankind*, Box 1, Series Proposal.

"Mrs. Roosevelt Discusses Rights." *Atlanta Daily World*, 3 Jan. 1960, p. 2.

"Mrs. Roosevelt Hits TV Ad on Children." *Washington Post*, 20 Nov. 1950, p. 11.

"Mrs. Roosevelt Honored by WTTG (TV)." *Broadcasting*, 13 Mar. 1961, p. 44.

"Mrs. Roosevelt in Pilot." *Broadcasting Telecasting*, 15 June 1959, p. 79.

"Mrs. Roosevelt Is Surprised at Reaction to Kennedy Views." *Pittsburgh Press*, 16 Mar. 1958, p. 10, Section 2.

"Mrs. Roosevelt Isn't Sure She's for Hogan." *New York Herald Tribune*, 27 Oct. 1958, p. 1.

"Mrs. Roosevelt Lauds Film Industry Efforts." *Film Daily*, 11 July 1934, p. 7.

"Mrs. Roosevelt Lauds Humphrey." *New York Times*, 8 Dec. 1958, p. 34.

Mrs. Roosevelt Meets the Public program notes. Franklin D. Roosevelt Presidential Library and Museum, Anna Eleanor Roosevelt Papers, Part 2, Series 50, Box 1420.

Mrs. Roosevelt Meets the Public transcripts. The Eleanor Roosevelt Papers Project, George Washington University, erpapers.columbian.gwu.edu/mrs-roosevelt-meets-public. Accessed 14 Oct. 2022.

"Mrs. Roosevelt Not for Harriman." *New York Herald Tribune*, 11 June 1956, p. 8.

"Mrs. Roosevelt on British TV." *New York Times*, 10 Mar. 1955, p. 15.

"Mrs. Roosevelt One of the TITA First Nighters in Wash." *Daily Variety*, 3 Aug. 1943, p. 9.

"Mrs. Roosevelt Preview Guest." *Los Angeles Times*, 25 Mar. 1939, p. A1.

"Mrs. Roosevelt Says Indochina Issue for U.N." *Morning Call* (Allentown, PA), 12 Apr. 1954, p. 7.

"Mrs. Roosevelt 'Tells Off' Pro-Robeson YPA Group." *New York Amsterdam News*, 25 Mar. 1950, p. 1.

"Mrs. Roosevelt to Appear on TV." *New York Times*, 4 Dec. 1959, p. 63.

"Mrs. Roosevelt to Write Ads for Goldwyn Picture." *New York Times*, 20 July 1937, p. 18.

"Mrs. Roosevelt Wary on Hogan." *New York Times*, 27 Oct. 1958, p. 21.

"Mrs. Roosevelt Wins Award." *New York Times*, 18 Apr. 1950, p. 33.

"Mrs. Roosevelt with Rivals." *The Gazette* (Montreal), 7 Nov. 1950, p. 9.

"Mrs. Roosevelt Wrote Which About What for Goldwyn and for How Much?" *Motion Picture Herald*, 24 July 1937, pp. 10, 18.

"Mrs. Roosevelt's Tea Party." *New Yorker*, 25 Feb. 1950, pp. 94–95.

"Mrs. Roosevelt's Visit to the Soviet Union." *Montana Standard* (Butte), 22 Oct. 1957, p. 4.

Murray, Ken. *Life on a Pogo Stick: Autobiography of a Comedian*, Holt, Rinehart and Winston, 1960.

Muscio, Giuliana. *Hollywood's New Deal*, Temple University Press, 1996.

"NAACP Sees Robeson Ban as Free Speech Denial." *Miami Times*, 1 Apr. 1950, p. 7.

National Educational Television Papers. Wisconsin Historical Society, Series 3, Vice President for Development Records, 1957–1966, Box 6, Folder 5, *Prospects of Mankind* 1959–1961.

NBC-New York. "*Home* Reaches its Third Birthday March 1." *NBC Trade Releases*, 26 Feb. 1957.

_____. "NBC Highlights 1926–1961." *NBC Trade Releases*, 29 Nov. 1961.

_____. "Noted Personalities Praise *Meet the Press*." *NBC Trade Releases*, 22 Oct. 1962.

_____. "Participants and Credits for 'Blueprint for Biography' the Story of *Sunrise at Campobello* on *NBC Kaleidoscope*." *NBC Trade Releases*, 30 Mar. 1959.

_____. "Polaroid to Sponsor Half of Two Entertainment Specials on *NBC Kaleidoscope*." *NBC Trade Releases*, 30 Mar. 1959.

_____. "Ralph Edwards Gets a Suggestion and Praise from Mrs. Roosevelt." *NBC Trade Releases*, 16 Nov. 1959.

_____. "Rep. James Roosevelt, Eldest Son of F.D.R., to Join Dore Schary in Telling Story Behind *Sunrise at Campobello*, Broadway Hit, on *NBC Kaleidoscope*." *NBC Trade Releases*, 19 Mar. 1959.

_____. "Sidelights on NBC's Convention Coverage." *NBC Trade Releases*, 24 July 1952.

_____. "*Sunday Showcase*, World Leaders and Top Showbusiness Personalities Participate in 'A Tribute to Eleanor Roosevelt on Her Diamond Jubilee.'" *NBC Trade Releases*, 19 Oct. 1959.

_____. "What Is Nikita S. Khrushchev Really Like?" *NBC Trade Releases*, 16 Sept. 1959, pp. 2–3.

"Negroes Picket Abe Lincoln Picture Demanding Civil Rights in Capital." *Imperial Valley Press* (El Centro, CA), 23 Jan. 1940, p. 8.

"Networks." *Sponsor*, 4 July 1959, p. 68.

Neuberger, Richard L. "Young Man with Two Horns." *Saturday Evening Post*, 8 July 1939, pp. 25, 38–39, 42.

"Never a Candidate." *Daily Oklahoman*, 11 Apr. 1949, p. 18.

"New Lever Bros. Spot Has Mrs. FDR." *Broadcasting Telecasting*, 23 Feb. 1959, pp. 41–42.

"New Materials." *Educational Screen*, Feb. 1956, p. 74.

"New Picture." *Time*, Vol 76, No. 15, 10 Oct. 1960, p. 75.

"New York Roundup." *Weekly Television Digest*, 13 June 1960, p. 6.

"New York Sound Track." *Variety*, 1 Mar. 1961, p. 5.

"News Capsules." *Motion Picture Exhibitor*, 11 Mar. 1959, p. 9.

"The News of Radio." *New York Times*, 3 Mar. 1948, p. 42.

"News of the World on NET." Franklin D. Roosevelt Presidential Library and Museum, Anna Eleanor Roosevelt Papers, Part 3, 1884–1964, Series 55: Correspondence, 1957–1962, Box 1858, National Education Television.

"*News* Pulls Sullivan Column on Film Probe." *Motion Picture Daily*, 12 Sept. 1941, pp. 1, 7.

"Newsmakers." *Newsweek*, Vol. 53, Issue 9, 2 Mar. 1959, p. 49.

"Newsreel Clip Causes Flurry." *The Exhibitor*, 13 Oct. 1943, p. 7.

"1965: Big Year for Character Licensing." *Sponsor*, 9 Nov. 1964, p. 35

Nixon, Richard. *Six Crises*, Pocket Books, 1962.

"Nixon Charge of Red Hit by Eleanor." *Austin Statesman*, 17 Sept. 1956, p. 3.

Noble, Paul. Letter to Art Barron and Henry Morgenthau III. 15 Sept. 1962. Franklin D. Roosevelt Presidential Library and Museum, Henry Morgenthau III, Papers Relating to the Television Series: Eleanor Roosevelt: *Prospects of Mankind* (1959–1962), Series 1: Eleanor Roosevelt: *Prospects of Mankind*, Box 1, Proposed Series "The American Experience": Proposals, Program Ide, 1962–1963.

_____. *My First 83 Years*, Polo, 2018.

Nonamaker. "*Blondie Goes Latin* Music Adds Lustre to Series." *Film Bulletin*, 22 Feb. 1941, p. 6.

"Notables to Attend *Jazz* Premiere." *Motion Picture Daily*, 12 Jan. 1953, p. 2.

"Note from Mrs. Roosevelt in Eisler Red Hearing." *Daily Variety*, 25 Sept. 1947, pp. 1, 10.

Nugent, Frank S. "Reflections of Passing Events in the Screen World." *New York Times*, 22 Oct. 1939, p. X5.

_____. "The Screen in Review." *New York Times*, 20 Oct. 1939, p. 30.

"*N.Y. Post* Laments Banning of Robeson." *Baltimore Afro-American*, 25 Mar. 1950, p. 3.

O'Donnell, John. "Capitol Stuff." *New York Daily News*, 22 July 1947, p. 4C.

_____. "Capitol Stuff." *New York Daily News*, 19 Sept. 1956, p. 4C.

Ogilvy, David. Letter to ER. 26 Jan. 1959. Franklin D. Roosevelt Presidential Library and Museum, Anna Eleanor Roosevelt Papers, Part 3, 1884–1964, Series 55: Correspondence, 1957–1962, Box 1893, Stix, Thomas L.

_____. *Ogilvy on Advertising*, Crown, 1983.

O'Hara, John. "*Pastor Hall*—Not by Beethoven." *Newsweek*, 12 Aug. 1940, p. 41.

O'Leary, J.A. "Top Democrats Rip into G.O.P." *Evening Star* (Washington, D.C.), 21 Oct. 1956, pp. 1, A-9.

O'Malley, Tom. Letter to ER. 19 Mar. 1958. Franklin D. Roosevelt Presidential Library and Museum, Anna Eleanor Roosevelt Papers, Part 3, 1884–1964, Series 55: Correspondence, 1957–1962, Box 1856, National Broadcasting Company.

"On Television." *New York Times*, 27 Apr. 1950, p. 42.

"On Television." *New York Times*, 12 Feb. 1952, p. 34.

"On Television." *New York Times*, 5 Aug. 1952, p. 27.

"On Television." *New York Times*, 13 Aug. 1952, p. 29.

"On Television." *New York Times*, 2 Dec. 1952, p. 44.

"On Television." *New York Times*, 11 Aug. 1953, p. 24.

"On Television." *New York Times*, 10 Sept. 1953, p. 35.

"On Television." *New York Times*, 22 Jan. 1954, p. 36.

"On Television." *New York Times*, 2 Jan. 1956, p. 35.

"Our Respects to Oliver Archibald Unger." *Broadcasting Telecasting*, 4 Nov. 1957, p. 20.

Our Very Own advertisement. *Cosmopolitan*, Vol. 129, No. 1, July 1950, p. 121.

Our Very Own advertisement. *Motion Picture Daily*, 12 June 1950, p. 4.

Our Very Own advertisement. *New York Daily News*, 23 July 1950, p. 5.

Our Very Own advertisement. *Redbook*, Vol. 95, No. 3, July 1950, p. 16.

Paar, Jack. *P.S. Jack Paar*, Doubleday, 1983.

Panorama transcript. 9 Mar. 1955. Franklin D. Roosevelt Presidential Library and Museum, Anna Eleanor Roosevelt Papers, Part 2, Series 50, Box 1422.

"Papers Denounce Ban on *Pastor Hall*." *Box Office*, 14 Sept. 1940, p. 85.

Parke, Richard H. "Pakistani Assails U.S. Peace Policy." *New York Times*, 8 May 1950, p. 5.

Parrish, Robert. *Growing Up in Hollywood*, Harcourt Brace Jovanovich, 1976.

_____. *Hollywood Doesn't Live Here Anymore*, Little, Brown, 1988.

Parsons, Estelle, correspondence. Franklin D. Roosevelt Presidential Library and Museum, Anna Eleanor Roosevelt Papers, Part 3, 1884–1964, Series 54: Correspondence, 1953–1956, Box 1753, *Today* NBC.

Parsons, Harriet. "All-star Casts Make Comeback in Hollywood." *Philadelphia Inquirer*, 20 July 1937, p. 6

Parsons, Louella O. "First Lady of the Land Aids Cook Get Film Job." *Dayton Herald*, 7 Jan. 1938, p. 14.

"*Pastor* Benefits Fund." *Hollywood Reporter*, 23 Sept. 1940, p. 1.

"*Pastor Hall*." *Motion Picture Reviews*, Vol. 15, No. 8, August 1940, p. 6.

"*Pastor Hall* Is Powerful Drama of Nazi Indictment." *Hollywood Reporter*, 29 July 1940, p. 3.

"*Pastor Hall* Philly Preem a Roosevelt Family Proposition." *Variety*, 28 Aug. 1940, p. 8.

Pastor Hall pressbook. United States Holocaust Memorial Museum, accession number 2018.590.36, collections.ushmm.org/search/catalog/irn693026. Accessed 25 Sept. 2022.

"*Pastor Hall* Smash at Phila. Premiere." *Hollywood Reporter*, 26 Aug. 1940, p. 3.

"Pay-Hurray for Dubinsky!" *New York Daily News*, 13 June 1957, p. 24.

Pearson, Drew, and Robert Allen. "Merry-Go-Round." *Honolulu Star-Bulletin*, 7 Dec. 1940, p. 8.

Pegler, Westbrook. "Eleanor Roosevelt Bad Security Risk." *Muncie* (IN) *Evening Press*, 12 Apr. 1950, p. 4.

_____. "Empress Eleanor Meets Her Critics." *Knoxville Journal*, 17 Mar. 1950, p. 6.

_____. "Why Is Eleanor the Great So Quiet About Mrs. Rutherford being with FDR When He Died at Warm Springs?" *Dixon* (IL) *Evening Telegraph*, 22 Dec. 1949, p. 4.

Perkins, Frances. *The Roosevelt I Knew*, Viking Press, 1946.

"Personals." *Television Digest*, Vol. 2, No. 14, 2 Apr. 1962, p. 8.

Peyser, Marc, and Timothy Dwyer. "Eleanor Roosevelt's Anything-but-Private Funeral." *The Atlantic*, 4 Nov. 2012, theatlantic.com/national/archive/2012/11/eleanor-roosevelts-anything-but-private-funeral/264460/.

Pfister, Ed. Letter to ER. 16 Mar. 1961. Franklin D. Roosevelt Presidential Library and Museum, Anna Eleanor Roosevelt Papers, Part 3, 1884–1964, Series 55: Correspondence, 1957–1962, Box 1858, National Education Television.

Phillips, H.I. "The Once Over." *Marion* (OH) *Star*, 3 Mar. 1950, p. 6.

"Photography of the Month." *American Cinematographer*, Oct. 1942, pp. 456–57.

Pit. "Prospects of Mankind." *Variety*, 18 Oct. 1961, p. 39.

"Pix in UN Global Bill of Rights." *Film Daily*, 4 Feb. 1947, p. 1.

Platt, David. "Movies, TV and ...." *Daily Worker* (New York, NY), 23 Oct. 1957, p. 4.

"Political Broadcasts." *New York Times*, 24 Oct. 1956, p. 28.

"Political Dualer." *Variety*, 1 Feb. 1950, p. 6.

"Political Sidelights." *Broadcasting Telecasting*, 29 Aug. 1960, p. 33.

"Powell Attacks Robeson TV Cancellation." *Jackson* (MS) *Advocate*, 25 Mar. 1950, p. 8.

"Pres. Truman, Mrs. FDR to 0.0. Metro's Atomic Pic for their Final OK." *Variety*, 1 Jan. 1947, p. 3.

"President Eisenhower Accepts Democratic Legacy Award of ADL." *JTA Daily News Bulletin*, Vol. 20, No. 175, 9 Sept. 1953, p. 1.

"President's Mother Backs Anti-Nazi Film; Brands Attacks on Willkie as 'Disgusting.'" *New York Times*, 3 Oct. 1940, p. 22.

"Press vs Censors." *Film News*, Vol. 2, No. 7, Oct. 1941, p. 3.

"Pressure Drive on NBC Started." *The Tablet* (Brooklyn, NY), 18 Mar. 1950, p. 3.

Preston, Charles, and Edward A. Hamilton, eds. *Mike Wallace Asks: Highlights from 46 Controversial Interviews*, Simon & Schuster, 1958.

"Program Notes, December 4." *C.B.C. Times*, 1–7 Dec. 1962, p. 15.

"Programming." *Television Digest*, Vol. 15, No. 36, 7 Sept. 1959, p. 7.

"Programming." *Television Digest*, Vol. 16, No. 40, 3 Oct. 1960, p. 6.

"Programming." *Television Digest*, Vol. 17, No. 12, 6 Mar. 1961, p. 7.

"Programs on the Air." *New York Times*, 21 June 1949, p. 50.

"Programs on the Air." *New York Times*, 13 Oct. 1949, p. 48.

"Programs on the Air." *New York Times*, 10 Dec. 1949, p. 28.

"Programs on the Air." *New York Times*, 13 Dec. 1949, p. 62.

"Programs on the Air." *New York Times*, 27 Mar. 1950, p. 38.

"Prospects of Mankind." The Listener, 6 Oct. 1960, pp. 543–48.

Prospects of Mankind program notes. Franklin D. Roosevelt Presidential Library and Museum, Anna Eleanor Roosevelt Papers, Part 2, Series 50, Box 1423.

"Protest First Lady's Move at Theatre Ban." *The Michigan Chronicle*, 3 Feb. 1940, p. 1.

"Protests Block Robeson as Guest on Mrs. Roosevelt's TV Program." *New York Times*, 14 Mar. 1950, p. 1.

Pryor, Thomas M. *"Sunrise at Campobello." Variety*, 26 Sept. 1960, p. 6.

Puddington, Arch. *Broadcasting Freedom: The Cold War Triumph of Radio Free Europe and Radio Liberty*, University Press of Kentucky, 2000.

"Radio and Television." *New York Times*, 1 Apr. 1949, p. 48.

"Radio and Television." *New York Times*, 1 June 1949, p. 62.

"Radio and Television." *New York Times*, 3 Apr. 1950, p. 27.

"Radio and Television." *New York Times*, 11 May 1950, p. 42.

"Ramblin' Round." *Daily Republican* (Millville, NJ), 23 Apr. 1951, p. 4.

"Rambling Reporter." *Hollywood Reporter*, 25 Mar. 1939, p. 2.

"Reading Out Loud; 6; Eleanor Roosevelt." 1960, American Archive of Public Broadcasting, americanarchive.org/catalog/cpb-aacip-516-rf5k932895.

"Red Channels: The Report of Communist Influence in Radio and Television." *Counterattack*, 1950, p. 120.

"Redo Truman Bomb Role." *Daily Variety*, 25 Nov. 1946, pp. 1, 9.

"Regents to Hear Film Board Appeal." *New York Daily News*, 2 Nov. 1941, p. 83M.

"Relations with Our Western Allies." *Educational Film Guide*, 1959 Annual Supplement, p. 45.

"Religion Courses Scheduled on TV." *New York Times*, 30 May 1960, p. 31.

"Remarks Recorded for Television for the Eleanor Roosevelt Cancer Foundation, 15 February 1962." John F. Kennedy Presidential Library and Museum, jfklibrary.org/asset-viewer/archives/JFKWHA/1962/JFKWHA-072-007/JFKWHA-072-007.

Reston, James. "Washington: Kennedy in the Middle on German Debate." *New York Times*, 25 Oct. 1961, p. 36.

Rich, Marvin. "Mrs. FDR's Committee Hears about 'Southern Justice.'" *CORE-Lator*, June 1962, p. 1. Franklin D. Roosevelt Presidential Library and Museum, Henry Morgenthau III, Papers Relating to the Television Series: Eleanor Roosevelt: *Prospects of Mankind* (1959–1962), Series 1: Eleanor Roosevelt: *Prospects of Mankind*, Box 1, Proposed Series "The American Experience": Proposals, Program Ide, 1962–1963.

"Robeson Hits NBC Decision." *Baltimore Afro-American*, 25 Mar. 1950, p. 7.

Robinson, Edward G. correspondence. Franklin D. Roosevelt Presidential Library and Museum, Anna Eleanor Roosevelt Papers, Part 3, 1884–1964, Series 55: Correspondence, 1957–1962, Box 1875, Robinson, Edward G.

Rogers, Ginger. *Ginger: My Story*, Headline, 1991.

Rooney, Mickey. *Life Is Too Short*, Villard Books, 1991.

"Roosevelt Attends Play." *New York Times*, 26 Feb. 1941, p. 17.

Roosevelt, Eleanor. "American Television Dealers and Manufacturers advertisement." *New York Times*, 21 Nov. 1950, p. 19.

_____. *The Autobiography of Eleanor Roosevelt*, Harper & Brothers, 1961.

_____. "Democracy on the Screen." *Modern Screen*, Sept. 1947, pp. 27, 105.

_____. "Educational Value of the Movies" draft. Franklin D. Roosevelt Presidential Library and Museum, Anna Eleanor Roosevelt Papers, Part 2, Series 50, Box 1397.

_____. "The Eleanor Roosevelt Program, Episode 26, November 15, 1950." The Eleanor Roosevelt Papers Project, George Washington University, www2.gwu.edu/~erpapers/radiotv/doc.cfm?_p=erprg&_f=erprg_026.

_____. "Eleanor Roosevelt Sees Films as Force for Culture." *Daily Variety*, 30 Oct. 1939, p. 5.

_____. "Film Folk I Have Known." *Photoplay*, Vol. 52, No. 1, Jan. 1939, pp. 10–11, 83.

_____. "Film Folk I Have Known" drafts. Franklin D. Roosevelt Presidential Library and Museum, Anna Eleanor Roosevelt Papers, Part 2, Series 50, Box 1406.

_____. "Hobbies in the White House." *Radio and Television Mirror*, Jan. 1940, p. 24.

_____. "How the Movies Can Help Keep Us Out of War." *Photoplay*, Feb. 1940, pp. 15, 76.

_____. "If You Ask Me, April 1955." *McCall's*, Vol. 82, The Eleanor Roosevelt Papers Project, George Washington University, www2.gwu.edu/~erpapers/iyam/iyam_1955_04.cfm.

_____. "If You Ask Me, August 1959." *McCall's*, Vol. 86, The Eleanor Roosevelt Papers Project, George Washington University, www2.gwu.edu/~erpapers/iyam/iyam_1959_08.cfm.

_____. "If You Ask Me, February 1952." *McCall's*, Vol. 79, The Eleanor Roosevelt Papers Project, George Washington University, www2.gwu.edu/~erpapers/iyam/iyam_1952_02.cfm.

_____. "If You Ask Me, September 1941." *Ladies' Home Journal*, Vol. 58, The Eleanor Roosevelt Papers Project, George Washington University, https://www2.gwu.edu/~erpapers/iyam/iyam_1941_09.cfm.

_____. "If You Ask Me, September 1960." *McCall's*, Vol. 87, The Eleanor Roosevelt Papers Project, George Washington University, www2.gwu.edu/~erpapers/iyam/iyam_1960_09.cfm.

_____. "Introduction." *The Diary of Anne Frank*, by Anne Frank, Bantam, 1993, pp. xii–xiv.

_____. Letter to Dore Schary. 1 Apr. 1958. Wisconsin Historical Society, Dore Schary Papers, Box 20, Folder 5, Roosevelt collection, 1957–1958.

_____. Letter to John F. Kennedy. 2 Mar. 1961. John F. Kennedy Presidential Library and Museum, jfklibrary.org/asset-viewer/archives/JFKPOF/032/JFKPOF-032-007.

_____. Letter to John F. Kennedy. Undated, Received 22 July 1961. John F. Kennedy Presidential Library and Museum, jfklibrary.org/asset-viewer/archives/JFKPOF/032/JFKPOF-032-007.

_____. "A Message for the New Year." *Radio and Television Mirror*, Jan. 1951, p. 19.

_____. "Movies We Roosevelts Enjoy" drafts. Franklin D. Roosevelt Presidential Library and Museum, Anna Eleanor Roosevelt Papers, Part 2, Series 50, Box 1406.

_____. "Mrs. Roosevelt Text." *St. Louis Post-Dispatch*, 23 July 1952, p. 4A.

_____. "My Day, April 8, 1937." The Eleanor Roosevelt Papers Project, George Washington University, www2.gwu.edu/~erpapers/myday/displaydoc.cfm?_y=1937&_f=md054611.

_____. "My Day, April 5, 1961." The Eleanor Roosevelt Papers Project, George Washington University, www2.gwu.edu/~erpapers/myday/displaydoc.cfm?_y=1961&_f=md004934.

_____. "My Day, April 10, 1950." The Eleanor Roosevelt Papers Project, George Washington University, www2.gwu.edu/~erpapers/myday/displaydoc.cfm?_y=1950&_f=md001562.

_____. "My Day, April 10, 1961." The Eleanor Roosevelt Papers Project, George Washington University, www2.gwu.edu/~erpapers/myday/displaydoc.cfm?_y=1961&_f=md004936.

_____. "My Day, April 13, 1957." The Eleanor Roosevelt Papers Project, George Washington University, www2.gwu.edu/~erpapers/myday/displaydoc.cfm?_y=1957&_f=md003775.

_____. "My Day, April 20, 1948." The Eleanor Roosevelt Papers Project, George Washington University, www2.gwu.edu/~erpapers/myday/displaydoc.cfm?_y=1948&_f=md000945.

_____. "My Day, August 17, 1956." The Eleanor Roosevelt Papers Project, George Washington University, www2.gwu.edu/~erpapers/myday/displaydoc.cfm?_y=1956&_f=md003565.

_____. "My Day, August 7, 1945." The Eleanor Roosevelt Papers Project, George Washington University, www2.gwu.edu/~erpapers/myday/displaydoc.cfm?_y=1945&_f=md000096.

_____. "My Day, August 16, 1956." The Eleanor Roosevelt Papers Project, George Washington University, www2.gwu.edu/~erpapers/myday/displaydoc.cfm?_y=1956&_f=md003564.

_____. "My Day, August 16, 1946." The Eleanor Roosevelt Papers Project, George Washington University, www2.gwu.edu/~erpapers/myday/displaydoc.cfm?_y=1946&_f=md000419.

_____. "My Day, August 25, 1939." The Eleanor Roosevelt Papers Project, George Washington University, www2.gwu.edu/~erpapers/myday/displaydoc.cfm?_y=1939&_f=md055354.

_____. "My Day, August 24, 1960." The Eleanor Roosevelt Papers Project, George Washington University, www2.gwu.edu/~erpapers/myday/displaydoc.cfm?_y=1960&_f=md004832.

_____. "My Day, August 22, 1947." The Eleanor Roosevelt Papers Project, George Washington University, www2.gwu.edu/~erpapers/myday/displaydoc.cfm?_y=1947&_f=md000738.

_____. "My Day, August 26, 1958." The Eleanor Roosevelt Papers Project, George Washington University, www2.gwu.edu/~erpapers/myday/displaydoc.cfm?_y=1958&_f=md004207.

_____. "My Day, August 23, 1947." The Eleanor Roosevelt Papers Project, George Washington University, www2.gwu.edu/~erpapers/myday/displaydoc.cfm?_y=1947&_f=md000739.

_____. "My Day, December 15, 1949." The Eleanor Roosevelt Papers Project, George Washington University, www2.gwu.edu/~erpapers/myday/displaydoc.cfm?_y=1949&_f=md001463.

_____. "My Day, December 5, 1950." The Eleanor Roosevelt Papers Project, George Washington University, www2.gwu.edu/~erpapers/myday/displaydoc.cfm?_y=1950&_f=md001770.

_____. "My Day, December 2, 1941." The Eleanor Roosevelt Papers Project, George Washington University, www2.gwu.edu/~erpapers/myday/displaydoc.cfm?_y=1941&_f=md056050.

_____. "My Day, December 6, 1941." The Eleanor Roosevelt Papers Project, George Washington University, www2.gwu.edu/~erpapers/myday/displaydoc.cfm?_y=1941&_f=md056054.

_____. "My Day, December 12, 1950." The Eleanor Roosevelt Papers Project, George Washington University, www2.gwu.edu/~erpapers/myday/displaydoc.cfm?_y=1950&_f=md001776.

_____. "My Day, February 1, 1958." The Eleanor Roosevelt Papers Project, George Washington University, www2.gwu.edu/~erpapers/myday/displaydoc.cfm?_y=1958&_f=md004028.

_____. "My Day, February 4, 1958." The Eleanor Roosevelt Papers Project, George Washington University, www2.gwu.edu/~erpapers/myday/displaydoc.cfm?_y=1958&_f=md004030.

_____. "My Day, February 9, 1950." The Eleanor Roosevelt Papers Project, George Washington University, www2.gwu.edu/~erpapers/myday/displaydoc.cfm?_y=1950&_f=md001511.

_____. "My Day, February 16, 1962." The Eleanor Roosevelt Papers Project, George Washington University, www2.gwu.edu/~erpapers/

myday/displaydoc.cfm?_y=1962&_f=md005070.

_____. "My Day, February 10, 1951." The Eleanor Roosevelt Papers Project, George Washington University, www2.gwu.edu/~erpapers/myday/displaydoc.cfm?_y=1951&_f=md001828.

_____. "My Day, February 20, 1950." The Eleanor Roosevelt Papers Project, George Washington University, www2.gwu.edu/~erpapers/myday/displaydoc.cfm?_y=1950&_f=md001520.

_____. "My Day, February 27, 1961." The Eleanor Roosevelt Papers Project, George Washington University, www2.gwu.edu/~erpapers/myday/displaydoc.cfm?_y=1961&_f=md004918.

_____. "My Day, February 23, 1942." The Eleanor Roosevelt Papers Project, George Washington University, www2.gwu.edu/~erpapers/myday/displaydoc.cfm?_y=1942&_f=md056116.

_____. "My Day, January 18, 1950." The Eleanor Roosevelt Papers Project, George Washington University, www2.gwu.edu/~erpapers/myday/displaydoc.cfm?_y=1950&_f=md001492.

_____. "My Day, January 15, 1962." The Eleanor Roosevelt Papers Project, George Washington University, www2.gwu.edu/~erpapers/myday/displaydoc.cfm?_y=1962&_f=md005056.

_____. "My Day, January 2, 1951." The Eleanor Roosevelt Papers Project, George Washington University, www2.gwu.edu/~erpapers/myday/displaydoc.cfm?_y=1951&_f=md001794.

_____. "My Day, January 24, 1940." The Eleanor Roosevelt Papers Project, George Washington University, www2.gwu.edu/~erpapers/myday/displaydoc.cfm?_y=1940&_f=md055484.

_____. "My Day, January 23, 1940." The Eleanor Roosevelt Papers Project, George Washington University, www2.gwu.edu/~erpapers/myday/displaydoc.cfm?_y=1940&_f=md055483.

_____. "My Day, July 11, 1938." The Eleanor Roosevelt Papers Project, George Washington University, www2.gwu.edu/~erpapers/myday/displaydoc.cfm?_y=1938&_f=md055002.

_____. "My Day, July 10, 1951." The Eleanor Roosevelt Papers Project, George Washington University, www2.gwu.edu/~erpapers/myday/displaydoc.cfm?_y=1951&_f=md001956.

_____. "My Day, July 30, 1940." The Eleanor Roosevelt Papers Project, George Washington University, www2.gwu.edu/~erpapers/myday/displaydoc.cfm?_y=1940&_f=md055645.

_____. "My Day, June 11, 1956." The Eleanor Roosevelt Papers Project, George Washington University, www2.gwu.edu/~erpapers/myday/displaydoc.cfm?_y=1956&_f=md003507.

_____. "My Day, June 5, 1957." The Eleanor Roosevelt Papers Project, George Washington University, www2.gwu.edu/~erpapers/myday/displaydoc.cfm?_y=1957&_f=md003820.

_____. "My Day, June 5, 1961." The Eleanor Roosevelt Papers Project, George Washington University, www2.gwu.edu/~erpapers/myday/displaydoc.cfm?_y=1961&_f=md004959.

_____. "My Day, June 9, 1960." The Eleanor Roosevelt Papers Project, George Washington University, www2.gwu.edu/~erpapers/myday/displaydoc.cfm?_y=1960&_f=md004767.

_____. "My Day, June 28, 1949." The Eleanor Roosevelt Papers Project, George Washington University, www2.gwu.edu/~erpapers/myday/displaydocedits.cfm?_y=1949&_f=md001317.

_____. "My Day, June 25, 1958." The Eleanor Roosevelt Papers Project, George Washington University, www2.gwu.edu/~erpapers/myday/displaydoc.cfm?_y=1958&_f=md004154.

_____. "My Day, June 21, 1954." The Eleanor Roosevelt Papers Project, George Washington University, www2.gwu.edu/~erpapers/myday/displaydoc.cfm?_y=1954&_f=md002886.

_____. "My Day, June 27, 1949." The Eleanor Roosevelt Papers Project, George Washington University, www2.gwu.edu/~erpapers/myday/displaydoc.cfm?_y=1949&_f=md001316.

_____. "My Day, March 14, 1956." The Eleanor Roosevelt Papers Project, George Washington University, www2.gwu.edu/~erpapers/myday/displaydoc.cfm?_y=1956&_f=md003431.

_____. "My Day, March 19, 1951." The Eleanor Roosevelt Papers Project, George Washington University, www2.gwu.edu/~erpapers/myday/displaydoc.cfm?_y=1951&_f=md001859.

_____. "My Day, March 19, 1938." The Eleanor Roosevelt Papers Project, George Washington University, www2.gwu.edu/~erpapers/myday/displaydoc.cfm?_y=1938&_f=md054905.

_____. "My Day, March 9, 1960." The Eleanor Roosevelt Papers Project, George Washington University, www2.gwu.edu/~erpapers/myday/displaydoc.cfm?_y=1960&_f=md004688.

_____. "My Day, March 7, 1950." The Eleanor Roosevelt Papers Project, George Washington University, www2.gwu.edu/~erpapers/myday/displaydoc.cfm?_y=1950&_f=md001533.

_____. "My Day, March 21, 1950." The Eleanor Roosevelt Papers Project, George Washington University, www2.gwu.edu/~erpapers/myday/displaydoc.cfm?_y=1950&_f=md001545.

_____. "My Day, March 27, 1939." The Eleanor Roosevelt Papers Project, George Washington University, www2.gwu.edu/~erpapers/myday/displaydoc.cfm?_y=1939&_f=md055224.

_____. "My Day, March 26, 1951." The Eleanor Roosevelt Papers Project, George Washington University, www2.gwu.edu/~erpapers/myday/displaydoc.cfm?_y=1951&_f=md001865.

_____. "My Day, May 15, 1950." The Eleanor Roosevelt Papers Project, George Washington University, www2.gwu.edu/~erpapers/myday/displaydoc.cfm?_y=1950&_f=md001592.

_____. "My Day, May 5, 1951." The Eleanor Roosevelt Papers Project, George Washington University, www2.gwu.edu/~erpapers/myday/displaydoc.cfm?_y=1951&_f=md001900.

_____. "My Day, May 4, 1940." The Eleanor Roosevelt Papers Project, George Washington University, www2.gwu.edu/~erpapers/myday/displaydoc.cfm?_y=1940&_f=md055571.

_____. "My Day, May 2, 1950." The Eleanor Roosevelt Papers Project, George Washington University, www2.gwu.edu/~erpapers/myday/displaydoc.cfm?_y=1950&_f=md001581.

_____. "My Day, May 17, 1950." The Eleanor Roosevelt Papers Project, George Washington University, www2.gwu.edu/~erpapers/myday/displaydoc.cfm?_y=1950&_f=md001594.

_____. "My Day, May 10, 1950." The Eleanor Roosevelt Papers Project, George Washington University, www2.gwu.edu/~erpapers/myday/displaydoc.cfm?_y=1950&_f=md001588.

_____. "My Day, May 13, 1950." The Eleanor Roosevelt Papers Project, George Washington University, www2.gwu.edu/~erpapers/myday/displaydoc.cfm?_y=1950&_f=md001591.

_____. "My Day, May 20, 1954." The Eleanor Roosevelt Papers Project, George Washington University, www2.gwu.edu/~erpapers/myday/displaydoc.cfm?_y=1954&_f=md002859.

_____. "My Day, May 25, 1954." The Eleanor Roosevelt Papers Project, George Washington University, www2.gwu.edu/~erpapers/myday/displaydoc.cfm?_y=1954&_f=md002863.

_____. "My Day, May 23, 1950." The Eleanor Roosevelt Papers Project, George Washington University, www2.gwu.edu/~erpapers/myday/displaydoc.cfm?_y=1950&_f=md001599.

_____. "My Day, November 8, 1954." The Eleanor Roosevelt Papers Project, George Washington University, www2.gwu.edu/~erpapers/myday/displaydoc.cfm?_y=1954&_f=md003008.

_____. "My Day, November 11, 1959." The Eleanor Roosevelt Papers Project, George Washington University, www2.gwu.edu/~erpapers/myday/displaydoc.cfm?_y=1959&_f=md004586.

_____. "My Day, November 19, 1953." The Eleanor Roosevelt Papers Project, George Washington University, www2.gwu.edu/~erpapers/myday/displaydoc.cfm?_y=1953&_f=md002703.

_____. "My Day, November 7, 1950." The Eleanor Roosevelt Papers Project, George Washington University, www2.gwu.edu/~erpapers/myday/displaydoc.cfm?_y=1950&_f=md001746.

_____. "My Day, November 28, 1950." The Eleanor Roosevelt Papers Project, George Washington University, www2.gwu.edu/~erpapers/myday/displaydoc.cfm?_y=1950&_f=md001764.

_____. "My Day, November 24, 1948." The Eleanor Roosevelt Papers Project, George Washington University, www2.gwu.edu/~erpapers/myday/displaydoc.cfm?_y=1948&_f=md001132.

_____. "My Day, October 9, 1951." The Eleanor Roosevelt Papers Project, George Washington University, www2.gwu.edu/~erpapers/myday/displaydoc.cfm?_y=1951&_f=md002034.

_____. "My Day, October 2, 1956," The Eleanor Roosevelt Papers Project, George Washington University, www2.gwu.edu/~erpapers/myday/displaydoc.cfm?_y=1956&_f=md003606.

_____. "My Day, October 3, 1950." The Eleanor Roosevelt Papers Project, George Washington University, www2.gwu.edu/~erpapers/myday/displaydoc.cfm?_y=1950&_f=md001716.

_____. "My Day, October 12, 1960." The Eleanor Roosevelt Papers Project, George Washington University, www2.gwu.edu/~erpapers/myday/displaydoc.cfm?_y=1960&_f=md004862.

_____. "My Day, October 20, 1955." The Eleanor Roosevelt Papers Project, George Washington University, www2.gwu.edu/~erpapers/myday/displaydoc.cfm?_y=1955&_f=md003308.

_____. "My Day, October 24, 1960." The Eleanor Roosevelt Papers Project, George Washington University, www2.gwu.edu/~erpapers/myday/displaydoc.cfm?_y=1960&_f=md004867.

_____. "My Day, October 29, 1958." The Eleanor Roosevelt Papers Project, George Washington University, www2.gwu.edu/~erpapers/myday/displaydoc.cfm?_y=1958&_f=md004262.

_____. "My Day, October 29, 1947." The Eleanor Roosevelt Papers Project, George Washington University, www2.gwu.edu/~erpapers/myday/displaydoc.cfm?_y=1947&_f=md000796.

_____. "My Day, October 27, 1947." The Eleanor Roosevelt Papers Project, George Washington University, www2.gwu.edu/~erpapers/myday/displaydoc.cfm?_y=1947&_f=md000794.

_____. "My Day, September 18, 1959." The Eleanor Roosevelt Papers Project, George Washington University, www2.gwu.edu/~erpapers/myday/displaydoc.cfm?_y=1959&_f=md004540.

_____. "My Day, September 1, 1951." The Eleanor Roosevelt Papers Project, George Washington University, www2.gwu.edu/~erpapers/myday/displaydoc.cfm?_y=1951&_f=md002002.

_____. "My Day, September 4, 1941." The Eleanor Roosevelt Papers Project, George Washington University, www2.gwu.edu/~erpapers/myday/displaydoc.cfm?_y=1941&_f=md055982.

_____. "My Day, September 19, 1959." The Eleanor Roosevelt Papers Project, George Washington University, www2.gwu.edu/~erpapers/myday/displaydoc.cfm?_y=1959&_f=md004541.

_____. "My Day, September 12, 1950." The Eleanor Roosevelt Papers Project, George Washington University, www2.gwu.edu/~erpapers/myday/displaydoc.cfm?_y=1950&_f=md001698.

_____. "My Day, September 20, 1951." The Eleanor Roosevelt Papers Project, George Washington University, www2.gwu.edu/~erpapers/myday/displaydoc.cfm?_y=1951&_f=md002018.

_____. "My Day, September 28, 1960." The Eleanor Roosevelt Papers Project, George Washington University, www2.gwu.edu/~erpapers/myday/displaydoc.cfm?_y=1960&_f=md004856.

_____. "My Day, September 23, 1940." The Eleanor Roosevelt Papers Project, George Washington University, www2.gwu.edu/~erpapers/myday/displaydoc.cfm?_y=1940&_f=md055691.

_____. *On My Own*, Harper & Brothers, 1958.

_____. "*Stella Dallas* Inspires a Discussion of a Mother's Vital Problem." *True Story Magazine*, Sept. 1937, p. 17.

_____. "*Stella Dallas* Inspires a Discussion of a

Mother's Vital Problem." *Woman's Home Companion*, Sept. 1937, p. 69.

_____. Telegram to Harry Truman. 2 Dec. 1959. National Archives Catalog. catalog.archives.gov/id/4708628.

_____. "Television's Contribution to the Senior Citizen." *TV Guide*, 17 Oct. 1959, pp. 6–8.

_____. "What Are the Movies Doing to Us?" *Modern Screen*, Nov. 1932, pp. 26–27, 102.

_____. "Why We Roosevelts Are Movie Fans." *Photoplay*, Vol. 52, No. 7, July 1938, pp. 16–17, 84–85.

_____. "Why We Roosevelts Are Movie Fans" drafts. Franklin D. Roosevelt Presidential Library and Museum, Anna Eleanor Roosevelt Papers, Part 2, Series 50, Box 1406.

Roosevelt, Eleanor, and Lorena Hickok. *Ladies of Courage*, Putnam, 1954.

Roosevelt, Elliott. *Mother R.: Eleanor Roosevelt's Untold Story*, Putnam, 1977.

_____. "My Mother, Eleanor Roosevelt." *TV Screen*, Apr. 1951, pp. 16–19, 58.

_____. "Politics on TV." *Theatre Arts*, Feb. 1951, pp. 47–48.

Roosevelt, James. Letter to Walter Winchell. 20 July 1940. United States Holocaust Memorial Museum, accession number 2018.590.42, https://collections.ushmm.org/search/catalog/irn693033.

_____. *My Parents: A Differing View*, Playboy Press, 1976.

_____. Photostat of *Pastor Hall* letter to theaters. 20 Dec. 1940. United States Holocaust Memorial Museum, accession number 2018.590.43, https://collections.ushmm.org/search/catalog/irn693034.

Roosevelt, Patricia Peabody. *I Love a Roosevelt*, Doubleday, 1967.

"Roosevelt Calls Cuff Links Club." *Evening Star* (Washington, D.C.), 27 Jan. 1938, p. A-3.

"Roosevelt Releases." *Motion Picture Herald*, 20 July 1940, p. 8.

"Roosevelt Series Discussed for TV." *Broadcasting Telecasting*, 30 Aug. 1948, p. 27.

"*Roosevelt Story* Dramatic; *Pretender* Good Budgeter." *Hollywood Reporter*, 22 Aug. 1947, p. 3.

"Roosevelts Hosts to Sixty Children." *New York Times*, 27 Dec. 1933, p. 20.

Rose. "*Today with Mrs. Roosevelt*." *Variety*, 15 Feb. 1950, p. 34.

Ross, Gordon. *Television Jubilee: The Story of 25 Years of BBC Television*, W.H. Allen, 1961.

Ross, Wallace. "Easter Programming." *Ross Reports on Television Programming*, Vol. 3. No. 14, April 13–19, 1952, p. 2.

_____. "Local Station Activity." *Ross Reports on Television*, Vol. 6, No. 13, 28 Mar. 1954, p. 51.

_____. "Multiple and Across-the-Board Shows Friday June 24 thru Friday July 1." *Ross Reports on Television*, June 27–July 3, 1955, p. C.

_____. "Multiple and Across-the-Board Shows June 27-July 1." *Ross Reports on Television*, 27 June 1960, p. 26B.

_____. "Multiple and Across-the-Board Shows October 21-October 25." *Ross Reports on Television*, 21 Oct. 1957, p. D.

_____. "News Briefs." *Ross Reports on Television*, April 26–May 2, 1953, p. 5.

_____. "This Week: Debuts, Highlights, Changes." *Ross Reports on Television Programming*, July 22–28, 1951, p. 2.

Rosten, Leo C. *Hollywood: The Movie Colony, The Movie Makers*, Harcourt, Brace, 1941.

Rowan, Carl T. "As Saleswoman for New Deal, Mrs. Roosevelt Led All the Rest." *Minneapolis Tribune*, 12 Sept. 1957, p. 6.

Rowe, David E., and Robert Schulmann, eds. *Einstein on Politics: His Private Thoughts and Public Stands on Nationalism, Zionism, War, Peace, and the Bomb*, Princeton University Press, 2007.

Russell, Bertrand. *The Autobiography of Bertrand Russell*, Allen & Unwin, 1967.

Russell, Nell Dodson. "The Way I See It." *St. Paul Recorder*, 12 Dec. 1952, p. 7.

Russell, Rosalind. *Life Is a Banquet*, Random House, 1977.

"Russians Don't Want War, Mrs. F.D.R. Says." *Los Angeles Times*, 21 Oct. 1957, p. 14.

Sachar, Abram. *A Host at Last*, Little, Brown, 1976.

"The Saga of NBC Television." *Broadcasting Telecasting*, 26 Nov. 1951, p. 135.

Sanders, Marlene, and Marcia Rock. *Waiting for Prime Time: The Women of Television News*, University of Illinois Press, 1988.

Sanford, Herb. *Ladies and Gentlemen, The Garry Moore Show*, Stein and Day, 1976.

Schary, Dore. "Address delivered by Mr. Dore Schary." 30 May 1958. Franklin D. Roosevelt Presidential Library and Museum, Anna Eleanor Roosevelt Papers, Part 3, 1884–1964, Series 55: Correspondence, 1957–1962, Box 1882, Schary, Dore.

_____. *Heyday: An Autobiography*, Little, Brown, 1979.

_____. Letter to ER. 27 Mar. 1958. Wisconsin Historical Society, Dore Schary Papers, Box 20, Folder 5, Roosevelt collection, 1957–1958.

_____. Letter to Greer Garson. 3 Nov. 1960. Wisconsin Historical Society, Dore Schary Papers, G, General, 1941 October–1974 January, undated Box 98, folders 7–9, Garson, Greer.

Schlesinger, Arthur, Jr. *Journals 1952–2000*, Penguin Books, 2007.

Schmidt, Dana Adams. "President Seeks Home-Front Role for Peace Corps." *New York Times*, 6 Mar. 1961, p. 1.

Schlup, Leonard C., and Donald W. Whisenhunt, eds. *It Seems to Me: Selected Letters of Eleanor Roosevelt*, University Press of Kentucky, 2001.

Schroeder, Alan. *Celebrity-in-Chief: How Show Business Took Over the White House*, Westview Press, 2004.

Schumach, Murray. "Many Stars Join TV Cancer Show." *New York Times*, 30 Mar. 1962, p. 26.

_____. "Money No Object in Sinatra Show." *New York Times*, 13 May 1960, p. 63.

"The Screen in Review." *New York Times*, 25 July 1949, p. 11.

Seaton, Matt. "When Is a Nazi Salute Not a Nazi Salute?" *New York Review*, 25 July 2020, nybooks.com/daily/2020/07/25/when-is-a-nazi-salute-not-a-nazi-salute.

"Secretary Rusk Interviewed on *Prospects of Mankind*." *Department of State Bulletin*, 30 Oct. 1961, pp. 708–09.

"Segregation in the North." *Daily Defender* (Chicago, IL), 19 Sept. 1956, p. 9.

Shalit, Sid. "Televiewing and Listening In." *New York Daily News*, 15 Oct. 1952, p. 83.

Shanley, Jack. "TV: Documentary on Bias." *New York Times*, 17 June 1956, p. 47.

Shanley, John P. "TV: Backstage with *Sunrise at Campobello*." *New York Times*, 6 Apr. 1959, p. 55.

Shannon, Betty. "First Lady in Movie Debut!" *Screenland*, Vol. 42, No. 1, November 1940, pp. 26–27, 97–98.

———. "Mrs. Franklin D. Roosevelt Talks About the Movies." *Screenland*, Vol. 25, No. 6, Oct. 1932, pp. 18–21, 86.

Shelton, Isabelle. "Women Can Be Proud as Campaign Ends." *Evening Star* (Washington, D.C.), 6 Nov. 1956, pp. B-5, B-7.

Shepard, Richard F. "Adlai Stevenson to be Guest on TV." *New York Times*, 30 Dec. 1961, p. 37.

———. "TV Role is Barred by Mrs. Roosevelt." *New York Times*, 31 Aug. 1959, p. 43.

———. "U.S. and Russia to Begin TV Visits." *New York Times*, 7 June 1958, p. 39.

"Shirley Temple Visits Hyde Park." *New York Times*, 10 July 1938, p. 5.

"Show *Daily Bread* at White House." *Film Daily*, 2 Oct. 1934, p. 8.

Silverman, Syd. "Television Followup Comment." *Variety*, 27 Nov. 1957, pp. 50, 56.

"Sinatra and Mrs. FDR." *Newsday* (Long Island, NY), 16 Feb. 1960, p. 3C.

"Singing Roosevelt?" *Evening Star* (Washington, D.C.), 15 Feb. 1960, p. A-12.

Skolsky, Sidney. "Hollywood." *Pittsburgh Sun-Telegraph*, 21 Mar. 1938, p. 9.

Slater, Robert. *This ... Is CBS: A Chronicle of 60 Years*, Prentice Hall Direct, 1988.

Smith, C. Mark. *Raising Cain: The Life and Politics of Senator Harry P. Cain*, Book Publishers Network, 2011.

Smith, Margaret Chase. *Declaration of Conscience*, Doubleday, 1972.

"So Right." *New York Amsterdam News*, 29 Nov. 1958, p. 8.

Sokolsky, George. "These Days ...." *Rockland County Journal News* (Nyack, NY), 18 Oct. 1956, p. 4.

———. "These Days ...." *Washington Post and Time Herald*, 12 Nov. 1958, p. A15.

"Some Industry Parties Are Tossed, and the Cameraman Is Present." *The Exhibitor*, 2 Aug. 1939, p. 13.

"*Sons and Lovers* Tops National Board Poll." *Motion Picture Exhibitor*, 28 Dec. 1960, p. 12.

"The Soul-Searchers Find No Answer." *Life Magazine*, 27 Feb. 1950, pp. 37–40.

"Soviet Sends Color Film of Khrushchev's Tour." *Evening Star* (Washington, D.C.), 19 Nov. 1959, p. F-2.

Spear, Ivan. "Spearheads." *Box Office*, 3 Aug. 1940, p. 25.

Spiegel, Irving. "Kings Leaders Ask a 'Watchdog' Board Over All City Units." *New York Times*, 23 Oct. 1950, p. 1.

Spivak, Lawrence, correspondence. Franklin D. Roosevelt Presidential Library and Museum, Anna Eleanor Roosevelt Papers, Part 3, 1884–1964, Series 53: Correspondence, 1945–1952, Box 1641, Spivak, Lawrence.

Stal. "*Inside Israel*." *Variety*, 22 Oct. 1952, p. 26.

———. "*Mrs. Roosevelt Meets the Public*." *Variety*, 4 Oct. 1950, p. 29.

"Stanley Kramer to Film Life of F.D. Roosevelt." *Motion Picture Daily*, 5 Oct. 1951, p. 1.

"Statue of Liberty Faces Inland, Say Boultings." *Variety*, 5 Nov. 1947, p. 4.

Stein, Herb. "Rambling Reporter." *Hollywood Reporter*, 29 June 1950, p. 2.

Stein, Robert. "Life of JFK3: FDR's Widow Lends a Hand." *Connecting.the.Dots*, 12 Nov 2013, ajliebling.blogspot.com/2013/11/life-of-jfk3-fdrs-widow-lends-a-hand.html.

"Steinbeck *Village* Gets Past Censors." *Daily Variety*, 17 Nov. 1941, p. 5.

"Stevenson Weighs Soviet Shift." *New York Times*, 6 June 1960, p. 5.

Stewart, Alice G. "Daily Dialings." *Latrobe* (PA) *Bulletin*, 11 Oct. 1950, p. 6.

Stewart, Gilbert. Letter to ER. 22 Sept. 1952. Franklin D. Roosevelt Presidential Library and Museum, Anna Eleanor Roosevelt Papers, Part 3, 1884–1964, Series 53: Correspondence, 1945–1952, Box 1641, Spivak, Lawrence.

Stix, Thomas, correspondence. Franklin D. Roosevelt Presidential Library and Museum, Anna Eleanor Roosevelt Papers, Part 3, 1884–1964, Series 54: Correspondence, 1953–1956, Box 1750, Stix, Thomas L.

Stix, Thomas, correspondence II. Franklin D. Roosevelt Presidential Library and Museum, Anna Eleanor Roosevelt Papers, Part 3, 1884–1964, Series 55: Correspondence, 1957–1962, Box 1893, Stix, Thomas L.

Stix, Thomas. "Mrs. Roosevelt Does a TV Commercial." *Harper's Magazine* archive, Nov. 1963, harpers.org/archive/1963/11/mrs-roosevelt-does-a-tv-commercial.

Storm, Irene. "Jacqueline Kennedy: The Women Who Like Her ... the Women Who Don't!" *TV and Radio Mirror*, Vol. 59, No. 3, Feb. 1963, p. 99.

Streitmatter, Roger, ed. *Empty Without You: The Intimate Letters of Eleanor Roosevelt and Lorena Hickok*, Da Capo Press, 1998.

"Strictly Routine Says Mrs. FDR." *Daily Variety*, 25 Sept. 1947, p. 10.

Stringer, William H. "Campaign Ends as TV

Spectacle." *Christian Science Monitor*, 6 Nov. 1956, p. 1.

"Strong Letter of Protest Directed to the Mayor." *Box Office*, 21 Sept. 1940, p. 27.

"Studio Size-Ups." *Film Bulletin*, 8 July 1946, p. 18.

"Suggests Oscar for Pettijohn." *Film Daily*, 9 Dec. 1941, p. 9.

Sullivan, Ed. "Looking at Hollywood." *Chicago Daily Tribune*, 5 Oct. 1939, p. 27.

_____. "Looking at Hollywood." *Chicago Daily Tribune*, 31 Oct. 1939, p. 17.

"Sunday." *Quad-City Tele-Views*, Vol. 1, No. 22, 2–8 June 1951, p. 7.

"Sunday Television Programs." *Pittsburgh Press*, 19 April 1958, p. 18.

"*Sunrise at Campobello*." *Film Quarterly*, Vol. 14, No. 2, 1960, p. 62.

"*Sunrise at Campobello*." *Photoplay*, Dec. 1960, p. 6.

Svensrud, Lois. "Reviews." *Modern Screen*, Jan. 1940, p. 56.

"Swap Group to Ignore Castro Bid." *Courier-Post* (Camden, NJ), 8 June 1961, p. 2.

Sweeney, Emma Claire. "Nancy Hamilton and Helen Keller." *Something Rhymed*, 2 Feb. 2015, somethingrhymed.com/2015/02/02/nancy-hamilton-and-helen-keller.

Swisher, Viola. "Just for Variety." *Daily Variety*, 22 Feb. 1952, p. 2.

"Talent Fees and Philanthropy." *Broadcasting Telecasting*, 15 Oct. 1956, p. 170.

Tax Court of the United States, 15 Oct. 1963. Wisconsin Historical Society, Dore Schary Papers, Box 112, Folder 7, Roosevelt, Eleanor, 1959–1964.

Taylor, Fred, ed. and trans. *The Goebbels Diaries, 1939–1941*, Hamish Hamilton, 1982.

"Tele Chatter." *Variety*, 8 Feb. 1950, p. 32.

"Tele Follow-Up Comment." *Variety*, 27 Dec. 1950, p. 23.

"Tele Follow-Up Comment." *Variety*, 14 Dec. 1960, p. 27.

"Tele Followups." *Variety*, 15 Feb. 1950, pp. 34, 36.

"Telecasting Notes." *Television Digest*, 3 Oct. 1953, p. 8.

"Television." *New York Times*, 13 Nov. 1959, p. 59.

"Television." *New York Times*, 20 Nov. 1959, p. 63.

"Television." *New York Times*, 30 Aug. 1961, p. 67.

"Television Covers V-E Day." *Television*, June 1945, p. 21.

"Television Highlights of the Week." *New York Times*, 16 June 1955, p. X13.

"Television Log." *San Francisco Examiner*, 8 Mar. 1960, p. N7.

"Television Programs." *New York Times*, 19 Oct. 1958, p. X16.

"Television Programs." *New York Times*, 26 June 1960, p. X12.

"Television Programs." *New York Times*, 6 Nov. 1960, p. 20X.

"Television to Remember ... for March." *New York Times*, 1 Mar. 1959, p. X12.

"Television Today." *Evening Star* (Washington, D.C.), 16 June 1949, p. D-13.

Teltsch, Kathleen. "Lie Proposes Immediate Truce Talks." *New York Times*, 25 June 1951, p. 1.

Temple Black, Shirley. *Child Star: An Autobiography*, McGraw-Hill, 1988.

_____. As told to Joseph N. Bell. "Will Young People Ever Have Heroes Again?" *Seventeen*, Sept. 1977, pp. 136–37, 170–71.

"10G CBS-TV Tab on UN Rights Day." *Variety*, 11 Oct. 1950, p. 28.

"Theatre and Film Unit to Hold Roosevelt Rally." *Motion Picture Herald*, 28 Oct. 1944, p. 16.

"Theatres in Greek Aid Drive." *Showmen's Trade Review*, 22 Feb. 1941, p. 6.

"Theatrical Rally for Roosevelt." *Motion Picture Daily*, 24 Oct. 1944, p. 2.

"They Made the News." *Film Bulletin*, 2 Apr. 1956, p. 50.

"33D Acad Awards Sparkling Show." *Daily Variety*, 18 Apr. 1961, p. 3.

"This Hamster Can't Get Cancer." *Broadcasting Telecasting*, 28 Mar. 1955, p. 87.

Thomas, Helen. "Mrs. R. Confers with Caroline." *Washington Post*, 4 Mar. 1961, p. R1.

"$3,850,000 Credit Is Set by Monogram." *Film Daily*, 26 Jan. 1948, p. 6.

"3 Steps Suggested to Solve U.S. Ills." *New York Times*, 2 Apr. 1951, p. 18.

"Thrillers Upheld." *Broadcasting Telecasting*, 1 May 1940, p. 86.

"The Times of their Lives." *Screenland*, Sept. 1948, p. 29.

Tinee, Mae. "Film Story of F.D.R. Like Play." *Chicago Daily Tribune*, 9 Nov. 1960, p. B14.

"To Present Award." *Motion Picture Daily*, 18 Aug. 1958, p. 3.

"Today on ABC-TV." *New York Daily News*, 2 Apr. 1955, p. 22.

Today with Mrs. Roosevelt program notes. Franklin D. Roosevelt Presidential Library and Museum, Anna Eleanor Roosevelt Papers, Part 2, Series 50, Box 1419.

"Today's Best TV Programs Previewed." *Hammond* (IN) *Times*, 19 June 1955, p. B-8.

"Today's Programs." *Pittsburgh Press*, 27 Apr. 1958, p. TV-4.

"Today's Programs." *Pittsburgh Press*, 4 May 1958, p. 4.

"Today's Radio and Television Highlights." *New York Herald Tribune*, 22 Oct. 1950, p. D8.

"Today's TV Highlights." *Evening Star* (Washington, D.C.), 20 June 1954, p. E-7.

"Today's TV Tops." *Philadelphia Inquirer*, 19 Oct. 1958, p. D9.

"Tonight on TV." *Evening Star* (Washington, D.C.), 2 Dec. 1952, p. A-17.

Torre, Marie. "Best Space Program Spurned by Networks." *Democrat and Chronicle* (Rochester, NY), 23 Feb. 1960, p. 28.

_____. "Frank Sinatra Show." *New York Herald Tribune*, 16 Feb. 1960, p. 27.

_____. "Mrs. FDR Plans Spot on Sinatra TV Show." *Democrat and Chronicle* (Rochester, NY), 1 Feb. 1960, p. 23.

_____. "TV-Radio Today." *New York Herald Tribune*, 14 Dec. 1960, p. 39.

Traube, Leonard. "Local Live Television Programming." *Variety*, 5 Mar. 1958, p. 38.

Troyan, Michael. *A Rose for Mrs. Miniver: The Life of Greer Garson*, University Press of Kentucky, 1999.

"TV Ad Deplored by Mrs. Roosevelt." *New York Times*, 20 Nov. 1950, p. 32.

"TV and Radio Today." *Atlanta Constitution*, 21 Jan. 1954, p. 22.

"TV Ban on UNESCO?" *Broadcasting Telecasting*, 28 Mar. 1949, p. 50.

"TV Network Premieres." *Variety*, 21 Oct. 1959, p. 28.

"TV Program May Feature Mrs. Roosevelt." *Washington Post*, 8 Jan. 1950, p. L4.

"TV Programs." *New York Times*, 21 Jan. 1962, p. 112.

"TV Programs." *New York Times*, 26 Aug. 1962, p. 114.

"TV Programs." *TV Guide*, 2 Oct. 1954, p. A-22.

"TV Programs." *TV Guide*, 23 Oct. 1954, p. A-13.

"TV Programs." *TV Guide*, 19 Feb. 1955, p. A-21.

"TV Tea Party." *Newsweek*, 27 Feb. 1950, p. 48.

"TV Time Previews." *Sunday Press* (Binghamton, NY), 5 Nov. 1961, p. 12C.

"TV Topics." *Asbury Park* (NJ) *Sunday Press*, 20 June 1954, p. 11.

"TV Viewers Hear 15 Famous Americans Tell Why They're Helping WBC Further the Custom of Family Reading." *Broadcasting Telecasting*, 14 Mar. 1960, p. 49.

"TV-Radio Production Centres." *Variety*, 21 May 1958, p. 34.

"TV-Radio Production Centres." *Variety*, 7 Dec. 1960, p. 30.

"2 Pix Nixed by Split in Ideology." *Daily Variety*, 4 Dec. 1946, pp. 1, 14.

"Two TV Awards Made at Venice Film Festival." *Broadcasting Telecasting*, 12 Sept. 1955, p. 104.

"U.N. Celebrates Human Rights Day." *New York Times*, 11 Dec. 1950, p. 31.

The Unconquered Advertisement. *New York Times*, 13 June 1954, p. 4X.

Underhill, Charles. Letter to Henry Morgenthau III. 14 Apr. 1952. Franklin D. Roosevelt Presidential Library and Museum, Anna Eleanor Roosevelt Papers, Part 3, 1884–1952, Series 53: Correspondence, 1945–1952, Box 1606, Morgenthau, Henry, III.

"UNESCO on TV." *Broadcasting Telecasting*, 4 Apr. 1949, p. 38.

"United Nations." *Television*, Jan. 1960, p. 84.

Valentine, Ross. "A Truly Formidable Lady!" *Richmond* (VA) *Times-Dispatch*, 23 Oct. 1957, p. 16.

Vernon, Terry. "Tele-Vues." *The Independent* (Long Beach, CA), 26 Feb. 1950, p. 12A.

"Vice President Wallace to Appear in Film Short." *New York Times*, 15 Sept. 1942, p. 18.

Vidal, Gore. *Palimpsest: A Memoir*, Penguin Books, 1996.

_____. *Snapshots in History's Glare*, Abrams, 2009.

"Virgilia Peterson Is Dead at 62." *New York Times*, 27 Dec. 1966, p. 32.

Waldman, Walter. "Paris, Second Postwar New York Theatre, Opens in Swank Midtown Section." *Box Office*, 18 Sept. 1948, p. 53.

Walker, Danton. "Broadway." *New York Daily News*, 6 Nov. 1940, p. 62.

Wallace, Mike. *Between You and Me: A Memoir*, Hyperion, 2005.

_____. "Introduction." *Grandmère: A Personal History of Eleanor Roosevelt*, David Roosevelt, Warner Books, 2002, pp. vii–x.

Walt. "*Pastor Hall*." *Variety*, 31 July 1940, p. 104.

Wamboldt, Helen Jane. *A Descriptive and Analytical Study of the Speaking Career of Anna Eleanor Roosevelt*. PhD dissertation, University of Southern California, 1952.

"Want Mrs. Roosevelt in Nation's Councils." *Film Daily*, 18 Apr. 1945, p. 12.

Ward, Geoffrey. *A First-Class Temperament: The Emergence of Franklin Roosevelt*, Harper & Row, 1989.

Ware, Susan. *Holding Their Own: American Women in the 1930s*, Twayne, 1982.

Washington Area Spark. "DC Jim Crow Theaters: 1922–54." Flickr, flickr.com/photos/washington_area_spark/albums/72157632991166161/with/8557519734. Accessed 11 Nov 2022.

"Week's TV." *St. Louis Globe-Democrat*, 3 Dec. 1950, p. 6F.

Welky, David. *The Moguls and the Dictators: Hollywood and the Coming of World War II*, Johns Hopkins University Press, 2009.

Wellman, William. Telegram to Hedda Hopper. 11 Apr. 1957. Motion Picture Association of America, Hedda Hopper Papers, Margaret Herrick Library, Academy of Motion Picture Arts and Sciences.

Wexler, Jerry. "TV Toons." *The Billboard*, 20 Oct. 1951, p. 11.

What Shocked the Censors! National Council on Freedom from Censorship, Sept. 1933, pp. 53–55.

"What's Doing." *News and Observer* (Raleigh, NC), 27 Apr. 1950, p. 18.

"What's On TV?" *It's About TV!*, itsabouttv.com/2020/10/whats-on-tv-sunday-october-18-1953.html. Accessed 4 Nov. 2022.

Whedon, Peggy. *Always on Sunday: 1,000 Sundays with "Issues and Answers."* Norton, 1980.

Whitbeck, Doris. "Daring *Maedchen* Importer Pioneered for Half Century." *Hartford* (CT) *Courant*, 26 Aug. 1979, pp. G1, G5.

White, John F. Letter to ER. 29 Sept. 1960. Franklin D. Roosevelt Presidential Library and Museum, Anna Eleanor Roosevelt Papers, Part 3, 1884–1964, Series 55: Correspondence, 1957–1962, Box 1858, National Education Television.

White, Theodore H. *The Making of the President 1960*, Harper Perennial Political Classics, 2009.

White, Walter. "People, Politics and Places." *Daily Defender* (Chicago, IL), 13 Sept. 1947, p. 15.

Whitman, Alden. "Free-Swinging Critic." *New York Times*, 25 June 1969, p. 43.

Wilkinson, W.R. "Trade Views." *Hollywood Reporter*, 21 July 1937, p. 1.

Williams, Wendell. "*Youth and the United Nations.*" *Educational Screen*, Apr. 1955, p. 180.

Wilson, Earl. "It Happened Last Night." *Courier-Post* (Camden, NJ), 16 Feb. 1950, p. 18.

"Wiltwyck to Gain by Film Premiere." *New York Times*, 21 May 1948, p. 18.

Winchell, Walter. "New Yorkers Are Talking About …." *Cincinnati Enquirer*, 18 Apr. 1949, p. 14.

Wisdom Editors. *The Wisdom of Sarnoff and the World of RCA*, Wisdom Society for the Advancement of Knowledge, Learning and Research in Education, 1968.

Wolters, Larry. "Eleanor to Get TV Roles through Roosevelt, Inc." *Chicago Daily Tribune*, 26 June 1951, p. 16.

"Woman of the Year." *The Exhibitor*, 28 Jan. 1942, p. 936.

"Woman's Story on *Wide Wide World.*" *Las Vegas Evening Review-Journal*, 6 Jan. 1957, p. 23.

"*Women in Defense.*" *New York Times Magazine*, 7 Dec. 1941, pp. 6–7.

"*Women in Defense* Timely, Informative." *Hollywood Reporter*, 10 Dec. 1941, p. 6.

Woodstone, Art. "Truman Diamond Jubilee Closed-TV Fiesta Proves Show Biz Humdinger." *Variety*, 13 May 1959, pp. 51–52.

"World Affairs." *Television*, June 1960, pp. 112–13.

Worth, Sheila. "Movies in the White House." *Movie Mirror*, July 1935, pp. 36–37, 84–85.

"Would Curb Chicago Police Film Board." *Box Office*, 21 Sept. 1940, p. 7.

W.S. "Voice of the People." *New York Daily News*, 30 Nov. 1956, p. C11.

Wuthering Heights advertisement. *Democrat and Chronicle* (Rochester, NY), 12 Apr. 1939, p. 11.

"You and Human Rights" script. Franklin D. Roosevelt Presidential Library and Museum, Anna Eleanor Roosevelt Papers, Part 2, Series 50, Box 1419.

"*Youth and the United Nations.*" *Educational Film Guide*, 11th edition, 1953, p. 365.

Zeitlin, Arnold. "Television and Radio News." *Pittsburgh Post-Gazette*, 13 June 1961, p. 35.

Index

Numbers in **_bold italics_** indicate pages with illustrations.

Puerto Rico 203
The Pursuit of Happiness 88
Pygmalion 86

Queen Elizabeth II 76
Queen Elizabeth The Queen Mother 43, 55, 59, 65, 75–76, 218
The Quiet One 87

race 1, 4, 15, 30–31, 62, 64, 67–68, 77, 87–88, 103–104, 107, 126, 128, 135–141, 154–155, 159–163, 167, 169, 179, 186, 192, 197–198, 218–219, 221–222
Radio Corporation of America (RCA) 105
Raft, George 39, 57
Rainer, Luise 38
Rama Rau, Dhanvanthi 171
Rama Rau, Santha 171, 204
Rand, Ayn 197
Randall, Tony 197
Rappleye, Willard 115
Rayburn, Sam 127–128, 191
Read, Elizabeth 13
Reading Out Loud 195
Reap the Wild Wind 87
Reasoner, Harry 155–156
Rebecca 87
Redbook 44, 145
Reed, Philip 92, 107
Reichert, Philip 102
Renoir, Jean 3, 69
A Report from Miss Greer Garson 87
Republic Pictures 59
Republican National Committee 8, 67
Reston, James 211
Reuther, Victor 211
Reuther, Walter 157, 222
Reynaud, Paul 104
Reynolds, Quentin 44, 196
Rhodes, C.P. 125
The River (1938) 51, 86
The River (1951) 3, 69, 88
Rivers, Lucille 183
RKO Radio Pictures 30–31, 58, 60, 70
Robeson, Paul 1, 4, 103–104, 159–161
Robins, Tony 185
Robinson, Earl 75
Robinson, Edward G. 29, 38–41, 44, 90, 197
Robinson, Jackie 64, 179
Roche, Jack 194
Roche, Jean 194
Rockefeller, Nelson 110, 120, 142, 197, 200, 203, 222
Rodgers, Richard 179, 195, 197
Rogers, Ginger 38–39
Rogers, Roy 39
Rogers, Will 38
Romulo, Carlos P. 74, 114, 167, 206
Rooney, Mickey 39–40, 48–*50*
Roosevelt, Anna (daughter) 6, 21, 46, 65–66, 81, 90, 95, 101, 125, 145, 194
Roosevelt, Anna Hall (mother) 12
Roosevelt, Elliott (father) 12
Roosevelt, Elliott (son) 2, 6–7, 46, 53, 59, 74, 79, 81, 93–96, 101, *107*, 109–115, 120–121, 123, 125, 184, 190, 219
Roosevelt, Franklin Delano 1–3, 5, 7, *8*, 9, 11–13, 19, 21–22, *25*–26, 29, 35–42, 46–*50*, 54–56, 58–60, 62, 64–65, 68, 72–*76*, 77–*79*, 80–85, 87, 90–94, 96, 98–99, 130–131, 134, 136–137, 140, 142, 144–145, 147–148, 150–*155*, 156, 161, 166, 168, 170, 173, 177–178, 181, 183–186, 191–192, 196–197, 201, 208, 216–218, 222–224

Roosevelt, Franklin Delano, Jr. 29, 46, 80–81, 85, 132, 137, 183–184
Roosevelt, James 3, 6, 14, 20–21, 26–30, 41, 43–47, 49, 55–56, 72–74, 79–81, 84, 90, 101, 132, 184, 189
Roosevelt, John 46, 81, 184
Roosevelt, Patricia Peabody 101
Roosevelt, Sara Delano 12, 14, 29, 59, *76*, 78–79, 81, 218
Roosevelt, Theodore 12, 47, 49, 55, 151, 217
Roosevelt Enterprises 96, 109, 125, 179
The Roosevelt Story 3, 74–*76*, 87
Rootie Tootie Club Thanksgiving Day Party 177
Roper, Elmo 105
Rosenman, Samuel I. 93–94
Rosenstein-Rodan, Paul 203
Ross, Paul L. 115
Rossel, Agda 215
Rostow, Elspeth 174
Rostow, Walt 174
Rountree, Martha 170
Rubinstein, Max 124–125
Ruble, Lawrence S. 121
Rusk, Dean 211–212, 222
Russell, Bertrand 7, 200–201, 205–206
Russell, Ned 123
Russell, Rosalind 39–40, 70, 197

Sachar, Abram 199, 218
Salim Bey, Hussein Kamel 123
Salinger, Pierre 144, 147
Salisbury, Harrison 202
The Sam Levenson Show 232
Samuelson, Paul 211
Sandburg, Carl 182
The Sarah Churchill Show 6, 176–177
Sarkar, Chancal 210
Sarnoff, David 105
Schary, Dore 7, 78–85, 90, 168, 199, 223
Scheftel, Stuart 169
Schenck, Joseph 38
Schenk, Nicholas 72
Schlesinger, Arthur, Jr. 15, 84, 128, 169, 200, 210, 222
Schneider, Dick 197
Schorer, Mark 219
Schuman, Robert 122
Schumann, Maurice 206, 213, 219
Schwarzwalder, John 156, 174
Scourby, Alexander 147–148, 191
Screenland 5, 27, 46, 131
Search for America 174
Seattle, Washington 21, 46, 57
See It Now 88, 162
segregation 3, 30–31, 107, 135, 159, 161–162, 179, 221
Selective Service 115–116
Selznick, David O. 43
Senate Subcommittee on War Propaganda 3, 25–26, 30
Senz, Ed *27*
Sergeant York 30
Sevareid, Eric 172, 224
Seven Samurai 88
Seydoux, Roger 123
Shapiro, Harry L. 182
Shawcross, Hartley 121–122
Shearer, Norma 43
Sheil, Bernard J. 150
Shelton, Willard 179
Sherrill, Henry Knox 116
Sherwood, Robert E. 8, 27–28, 30, 40, 77